Dummies 101®: The Internet For Windows® 98

CHEAT SHEET

Accessing the CD's Files

Follow the instructions in Appendix B of this book to install and access the files on this book's CD.

Cruising the World Wide Web

To See . . .	*Click . . .*
The preceding page	The Back button
The next page	The Forward button
Your starting page	The Home button
A link's Web page	The link (underlined text)
A page at a Web address (URL)	The Address bar; then type the URL and press Enter
A list of pages you've visited	The File menu or History button
A list of favorites	The Favorites menu or Favorites button
A Web search program	The Search button
This book's home page	The Address bar; then type **net.gurus.com/net101** and press Enter

Refer to Units 1, 2, 3, and 4 to learn how to use the Internet Explorer browser to cruise the Web.

Reading Usenet Newsgroups

To Do This . . .	*Click . . .*
Open the Newsgroups dialog box	The News groups button
Subscribe to a newsgroup	The newsgroup name and then the Subscribe button
Quit a newsgroup	The newsgroup name and then the Unsubscribe button
List the articles in a newsgroup	The newsgroup name from the folder list
Read the contents of an article	The article heading from the message list
Reply to an article by e-mailing its author	The article and then the Reply to Author button
Reply to an article by posting a response to the newsgroup	The article and then the Reply to Group button
Find newsgroups and newsgroup articles	Internet Explorer's Address bar; then type **dejanews** and press Enter

Refer to Unit 7 to learn how to use Outlook Express to participate in Usenet newsgroups.

☑ Progress Check

Unit 1: Getting Started with Internet Explorer

- ❑ Lesson 1-1: Preparing to Go Online with Internet Explorer
- ❑ Lesson 1-2: Jumping onto the Web
- ❑ Lesson 1-3: Cruising the Web by Using Links

Unit 2: Searching for Information on the Web

- ❑ Lesson 2-1: Cruising the Web by Using Favorites
- ❑ Lesson 2-2: Creating and Organizing Favorites
- ❑ Lesson 2-3: Entering URLs
- ❑ Lesson 2-4: Searching a Web Page for Information
- ❑ Lesson 2-5: Searching the Entire Web for Information

Unit 3: Saving Information and Downloading Files

- ❑ Lesson 3-1: Printing and Saving Web Information
- ❑ Lesson 3-2: Downloading Files from the Web

Unit 4: Customizing the Browser

- ❑ Lesson 4-1: Enhancing Internet Explorer's Performance
- ❑ Lesson 4-2: Adjusting Internet Explorer's Settings

Unit 5: Getting Started with E-Mail

- ❑ Lesson 5-1: Telling Outlook Express How to Get Your Mail
- ❑ Lesson 5-2: Sending a Message
- ❑ Lesson 5-3: Reading E-Mail Messages
- ❑ Lesson 5-4: Replying to, Forwarding, Printing, and Deleting Messages
- ❑ Lesson 5-5: E-Mail E-tiquette

Unit 6: More Mail Maneuvers

- ❑ Lesson 6-1: Using Your Address Book

ur

to Read Newsgroups

- ❑ Lesson 7-2: Listing and Subscribing to Newsgroups
- ❑ Lesson 7-3: Reading Newsgroup Articles
- ❑ Lesson 7-4: Searching for Newsgroups of Interest
- ❑ Lesson 7-5: Replying to Newsgroup Articles

Unit 8: Tuning into Channels

- ❑ Lesson 8-1: Viewing Channels
- ❑ Lesson 8-2: Adding and Managing Channels

Dummies 101®: The Internet For Windows® 98

CHEAT SHEET

Setting Up Outlook Express to Receive and Send Your E-Mail

See Lesson 5-1 to learn how to get this information. ISP is short for Internet Service Provider.

Your ISP's POP Server (for storing your incoming mail): ______________________

Your ISP's SMTP Server (for sending your outgoing mail over the Internet): ______________________

Your ISP's NNTP Server (for getting Usenet newsgroup articles): ______________________

Your e-mail user name: ______________________

Your e-mail password (write on a separate piece of paper and store in a safe place)

Managing Your E-Mail

To Do This . . .	*Click . . .*
Run Outlook Express	The Start button and then choose Programs⇨Internet Explorer⇨Outlook Express
Get your new messages	The Send and Receive button
Read a message	The message heading from the message list
Reply to a message	The message, and then either the Reply to Author or the Reply to All button
Create a new message	The Compose Message button
Attach a file to a message	The Insert File button
Send a message	The message and then the Send button
Print a message	The message; then press Ctrl+P and Enter
Delete a message	The message and then the Delete button
Open the Address Book	The Address Book button
Add an Address Book entry	The New Contact button
Change an Address Book entry	The entry and then the Properties button
Delete an Address Book entry	The entry and then the Delete button
Close a window	The Close button in the upper-right corner

Refer to Units 5 and 6 to learn how to use Outlook Express to manage your e-mail.

Cheat Sheet $2.95 value. Item 0207-7
For more information about IDG Books, call 1-800-762-2974.

DUMMIES 101®: THE INTERNET FOR WINDOWS® 98

DUMMIES 101®: THE INTERNET FOR WINDOWS® 98

by Hy Bender & Margaret Levine Young

IDG Books Worldwide, Inc.
An International Data Group Company

Foster City, CA ✦ Chicago, IL ✦ Indianapolis, IN ✦ New York, NY

Dummies 101®: The Internet For Windows® 98

Published by
IDG Books Worldwide, Inc.
An International Data Group Company
919 E. Hillsdale Blvd.
Suite 400
Foster City, CA 94404
www.idgbooks.com (IDG Books Worldwide Web site)
www.dummies.com (Dummies Press Web site)

Library of Congress Catalog Card No.: 98-85436

ISBN: 0-7645-0207-7

Printed in the United States of America

10 9 8 7 6 5 4 3 2 1

1B/SS/QV/ZY/IN

Distributed in the United States by IDG Books Worldwide, Inc.

Distributed by Macmillan Canada for Canada; by Transworld Publishers Limited in the United Kingdom; by IDG Norge Books for Norway; by IDG Sweden Books for Sweden; by Woodslane Pty. Ltd. for Australia; by Woodslane Enterprises Ltd. for New Zealand; by Longman Singapore Publishers Ltd. for Singapore, Malaysia, Thailand, and Indonesia; by Simron Pty. Ltd. for South Africa; by Toppan Company Ltd. for Japan; by Distribuidora Cuspide for Argentina; by Livraria Cultura for Brazil; by Ediciencia S.A. for Ecuador; by Addison-Wesley Publishing Company for Korea; by Ediciones ZETA S.C.R. Ltda. for Peru; by WS Computer Publishing Corporation, Inc., for the Philippines; by Unalis Corporation for Taiwan; by Contemporanea de Ediciones for Venezuela; by Computer Book & Magazine Store for Puerto Rico; by Express Computer Distributors for the Caribbean and West Indies. Authorized Sales Agent: Anthony Rudkin Associates for the Middle East and North Africa.

For general information on IDG Books Worldwide's books in the U.S., please call our Consumer Customer Service department at 800-762-2974. For reseller information, including discounts and premium sales, please call our Reseller Customer Service department at 800-434-3422.

For information on where to purchase IDG Books Worldwide's books outside the U.S., please contact our International Sales department at 650-655-3200 or fax 650-655-3295.

For information on foreign language translations, please contact our Foreign & Subsidiary Rights department at 650-655-3021 or fax 650-655-3281.

For sales inquiries and special prices for bulk quantities, please contact our Sales department at 650-655-3200 or write to the address above.

For information on using IDG Books Worldwide's books in the classroom or for ordering examination copies, please contact our Educational Sales department at 800-434-2086 or fax 817-251-8174.

For press review copies, author interviews, or other publicity information, please contact our Public Relations department at 650-655-3000 or fax 650-655-3299.

About the Authors

Hy Bender: Hy Bender is the author or coauthor of ten computer books to date. Among his solo titles are *PC Tools: The Complete Reference* (Osborne/McGraw-Hill), which was selected as one of the dozen "Best Books of the Year" by *Computer Currents* magazine; and *Essential Software for Writers* (Writer's Digest Books), which was designated "Byte's Book of the Month" by Jerry Pournelle at *Byte Magazine*, praised as "exhaustive" and "lots of fun" by L. R. Shannon at *The New York Times*, and proclaimed "the best of its kind" by mega-selling author Peter McWilliams in his syndicated Personal Computers column.

Hy is also coauthor — with his writing partner Margy Levine Young — of *Dummies 101: The Internet for Windows 95*, *Dummies 101: Netscape Navigator*, and *Dummies 101: Netscape Communicator 4* — which was lauded by book superstore Amazon.com as "possibly the single best book to hand someone who is a relative beginner on the Web and new to Netscape." In addition, Hy is a coauthor of *The Internet for Dummies, Starter Kit Edition* (which, like his *Dummies 101* books, is from IDG Books Worldwide).

When he's not busy with computers, Hy writes humor articles for such publications as *Mad Magazine*, *Spy*, *American Film*, and *Advertising Age*. Hy also runs a fiction reading group for New York writers, and he's currently writing a book for DC Comics about mythic storytelling.

Margaret Levine Young: Unlike her peers in that 30-something bracket, Margaret Levine Young was exposed to computers at an early age. In high school, she got into a computer club known as the R.E.S.I.S.T.O.R.S., a group of kids who spent Saturdays in a barn fooling around with three antiquated computers. She stayed in the field through college against her better judgment and despite her brother's presence as a graduate student in the Computer Science department. Margy graduated from Yale and went on to become one of the first microcomputer managers in the early 1980s at Columbia Pictures, where she rode the elevator with Paul Newman, Bill Murray, and Jeff Goldblum.

Since then, Margy has coauthored over two dozen computer books on such topics as the Internet, UNIX, WordPerfect, and Microsoft Access, including *Dummies 101: The Internet for Windows 95*, *The Internet For Dummies*, *More Internet For Dummies*, *Internet FAQs: Answers to Frequently Asked Questions*, and *UNIX For Dummies* (all from IDG Books Worldwide).

Margy met her husband Jordan in the R.E.S.I.S.T.O.R.S. Her other passion is her children, Meg and Zac. She loves gardening, chickens, reading, and anything to do with eating. Margy lives in Cornwall, Vermont.

ABOUT IDG BOOKS WORLDWIDE

Welcome to the world of IDG Books Worldwide.

IDG Books Worldwide, Inc., is a subsidiary of International Data Group, the world's largest publisher of computer-related information and the leading global provider of information services on information technology. IDG was founded more than 25 years ago and now employs more than 8,500 people worldwide. IDG publishes more than 275 computer publications in over 75 countries (see listing below). More than 60 million people read one or more IDG publications each month.

Launched in 1990, IDG Books Worldwide is today the #1 publisher of best-selling computer books in the United States. We are proud to have received eight awards from the Computer Press Association in recognition of editorial excellence and three from *Computer Currents*' First Annual Readers' Choice Awards. Our best-selling *...For Dummies*® series has more than 30 million copies in print with translations in 30 languages. IDG Books Worldwide, through a joint venture with IDG's Hi-Tech Beijing, became the first U.S. publisher to publish a computer book in the People's Republic of China. In record time, IDG Books Worldwide has become the first choice for millions of readers around the world who want to learn how to better manage their businesses.

Our mission is simple: Every one of our books is designed to bring extra value and skill-building instructions to the reader. Our books are written by experts who understand and care about our readers. The knowledge base of our editorial staff comes from years of experience in publishing, education, and journalism — experience we use to produce books for the '90s. In short, we care about books, so we attract the best people. We devote special attention to details such as audience, interior design, use of icons, and illustrations. And because we use an efficient process of authoring, editing, and desktop publishing our books electronically, we can spend more time ensuring superior content and spend less time on the technicalities of making books.

You can count on our commitment to deliver high-quality books at competitive prices on topics you want to read about. At IDG Books Worldwide, we continue in the IDG tradition of delivering quality for more than 25 years. You'll find no better book on a subject than one from IDG Books Worldwide.

John Kilcullen
CEO
IDG Books Worldwide, Inc.

Steven Berkowitz
President and Publisher
IDG Books Worldwide, Inc.

Eighth Annual Computer Press Awards 1992

Ninth Annual Computer Press Awards 1993

Tenth Annual Computer Press Awards 1994

Eleventh Annual Computer Press Awards 1995

IDG Books Worldwide, Inc., is a subsidiary of International Data Group, the world's largest publisher of computer-related information and the leading global provider of information services on information technology. International Data Group publishes over 275 computer publications in over 75 countries. Sixty million people read one or more International Data Group publications each month. International Data Group's publications include: **ARGENTINA:** Buyer's Guide, Computerworld Argentina, PC World Argentina; **AUSTRALIA:** Australian Macworld, Australian PC World, Australian Reseller News, Computerworld, IT Casebook, Network World, Publish, Webmaster; **AUSTRIA:** Computerwelt Osterreich, Networks Austria, PC Tip Austria; **BANGLADESH:** PC World Bangladesh; **BELARUS:** PC World Belarus; **BELGIUM:** Data News; **BRAZIL:** Annuário de Informática, Computerworld, Connections, Macworld, PC Player, PC World, Publish, Reseller News, Supergamepower; **BULGARIA:** Computerworld Bulgaria, Network World Bulgaria, PC & MacWorld Bulgaria; **CANADA:** CIO Canada, Client/Server World, ComputerWorld Canada, InfoWorld Canada, NetworkWorld Canada, WebWorld; **CHILE:** Computerworld Chile, PC World Chile; **COLOMBIA:** Computerworld Colombia, PC World Colombia; **COSTA RICA:** PC World Centro America; **THE CZECH AND SLOVAK REPUBLICS:** Computerworld Czechoslovakia, Macworld Czech Republic, PC World Czechoslovakia; **DENMARK:** Communications World Danmark, Computerworld Danmark, Macworld Danmark, PC World Danmark, Techworld Denmark; **DOMINICAN REPUBLIC:** PC World Republica Dominicana; **ECUADOR:** PC World Ecuador; **EGYPT:** Computerworld Middle East, PC World Middle East; **EL SALVADOR:** PC World Centro America; **FINLAND:** MikroPC, Tietoverkko, Tietoviikko; **FRANCE:** Distributique, Hebdo, Info PC, Le Monde Informatique, Macworld, Reseaux & Telecoms, WebMaster France; **GERMANY:** Computer Partner, Computerwoche, Computerwoche Extra, Computerwoche FOCUS, Global Online, Macwelt, PC Welt; **GREECE:** Amiga Computing, GamePro Greece, Multimedia World; **GUATEMALA:** PC World Centro America; **HONDURAS:** PC World Centro America; **HONG KONG:** Computerworld Hong Kong, PC World Hong Kong, Publish in Asia; **HUNGARY:** ABCD CD-ROM, Computerworld Szamitastechnika, Internetto online Magazine, PC World Hungary, PC-X Magazin Hungary; **ICELAND:** Tolvuheimur PC World Island; **INDIA:** Information Communications World, Information Systems Computerworld, PC World India, Publish in Asia; **INDONESIA:** InfoKomputer PC World, Komputek Computerworld, Publish in Asia; **IRELAND:** ComputerScope, PC Live!; **ISRAEL:** Macworld Israel, People & Computers/Computerworld; **ITALY:** Computerworld Italia, Macworld Italia, Networking Italia, PC World Italia; **JAPAN:** DTP World, Macworld Japan, Nikkei Personal Computing, OS/2 World Japan, SunWorld Japan, Windows NT World, Windows World Japan; **KENYA:** PC World East African; **KOREA:** Hi-Tech Information, Macworld Korea, PC World Korea; **MACEDONIA:** PC World Macedonia; **MALAYSIA:** Computerworld Malaysia, PC World Malaysia, Publish in Asia; **MALTA:** PC World Malta; **MEXICO:** Computerworld Mexico, PC World Mexico; **MYANMAR:** PC World Myanmar; **NETHERLANDS:** Computer! Totaal, LAN Internetworking Magazine, LAN World Buyers Guide, Macworld Netherlands, Net, WebWereld; **NEW ZEALAND:** Absolute Beginners Guide and Plain & Simple Series, Computer Buyer, Computer Industry Directory, Computerworld New Zealand, MTB, Network World, PC World New Zealand; **NICARAGUA:** PC World Centro America; **NORWAY:** Computerworld Norge, CW Rapport, Datamagasinet, Financial Rapport, Kursguide Norge, Macworld Norge, Multimediaworld Norge, PC World Ekspress Norge, PC World Nettverk, PC World Norge, PC World ProduktGuide Norge; **PAKISTAN:** Computerworld Pakistan; **PANAMA:** PC World Panama; **PEOPLE'S REPUBLIC OF CHINA:** China Computer Users, China Computerworld, China InfoWorld, China Telecom World Weekly, Computer & Communication, Electronic Design China, Electronics Today, Electronics Weekly, Game Software, PC World China, Popular Computer Week, Software Weekly, Software World, Telecom World; **PERU:** Computerworld Peru, PC World Profesional Peru, PC World SoHo Peru; **PHILIPPINES:** Click!, Computerworld Philippines, PC World Philippines, Publish in Asia; **POLAND:** Computerworld Poland, Computerworld Special Report Poland, Cyber, Macworld Poland, Networld Poland, PC World Komputer; **PORTUGAL:** Cerebro/PC World, Computerworld/Correio Informático, Dealer World Portugal, Mac*In/PC*In Portugal, Multimedia World; **PUERTO RICO:** PC World Puerto Rico; **ROMANIA:** Computerworld Romania, PC World Romania, Telecom Romania; **RUSSIA:** Computerworld Russia, Mir PK, Publish, Seti; **SINGAPORE:** Computerworld Singapore, PC World Singapore, Publish in Asia; **SLOVENIA:** Monitor; **SOUTH AFRICA:** Computing SA, Network World SA, Software World SA; **SPAIN:** Communicaciones World España, Computerworld España, Dealer World España, Macworld España, PC World España; **SRI LANKA:** Infolink PC World; **SWEDEN:** CAP&Design, Computer Sweden, Corporate Computing Sweden, Internetworld Sweden, it.branschen, Macworld Sweden, MaxiData Sweden, MikroDatorn, Nätverk & Kommunikation, PC World Sweden, PCaktiv, Windows World Sweden; **SWITZERLAND:** Computerworld Schweiz, Macworld Schweiz, PCtip; **TAIWAN:** Computerworld Taiwan, Macworld Taiwan, NEW ViSiON/Publish, PC World Taiwan, Windows World Taiwan; **THAILAND:** Publish in Asia, Thai Computerworld; **TURKEY:** Computerworld Turkiye, Macworld Turkiye, Network World Turkiye, PC World Turkiye; **UKRAINE:** Computerworld Kiev, Multimedia World Ukraine, PC World Ukraine; **UNITED KINGDOM:** Acorn User UK, Amiga Action UK, Amiga Computing UK, Apple Talk UK, Computing, Macworld, Parents and Computers UK, PC Advisor, PC Home, PSX Pro, The WEB; **UNITED STATES:** Cable in the Classroom, CIO Magazine, Computerworld, DOS World, Federal Computer Week, GamePro Magazine, InfoWorld, I-Way, Macworld, Network World, PC Games, PC World, Publish, Video Event, THE WEB Magazine, and WebMaster; online webzines: JavaWorld, NetscapeWorld, and SunWorld Online; **URUGUAY:** InfoWorld Uruguay; **VENEZUELA:** Computerworld Venezuela, PC World Venezuela; and **VIETNAM:** PC World Vietnam.

3/24/97

Dedication

Hy dedicates this book, with love, to cherished friend and ace programmer Tracey Michele Siesser.

Margy dedicates this book to the town of Cornwall, Vermont, and its inhabitants. We survived the ice storm of 1998!

Authors' Acknowledgments

First, we give our heartfelt thanks to Kelly Ewing for both her meticulous care and consistent kindness as she expertly shepherded this book through the editing and production process. We also thank all the folks mentioned in the Publisher's Acknowledgments section that appears on the back of this page.

Hy thanks his fiction reading group for three years (and running) of lively discussions about great novels. Hy also thanks all his old classmates — including Harvey Armel, Roberta Cohen-Bernstein, Jeff Farkas, Shira Kavon-Grossman, Richard Langer, Paul Neiger, Paul Ofman, Tammie Roodner-Nahum, Bennett Spiegel, and Andrea Thau — for their help in making the 25th anniversary S.A.R. Academy reunion a spectacular success.

Margy thanks Hy for working solo writing this book — which is a complete overhaul of Hy's and Margy's *Dummies 101: The Internet for Windows 95* book, updated for Windows 98 — while she was tied up with other projects. Margy also thanks Hy for his many excellent video recommendations for her kids.

Publisher's Acknowledgments

We're proud of this book; please register your comments through our IDG Books Worldwide Online Registration Form located at: http://my2cents.dummies.com.

Some of the people who helped bring this book to market include the following:

Acquisitions, Editorial, and Media Development

Senior Project Editor: Kelly Ewing

Acquisitions Editor: Michael Kelly

Copy Editor: Wendy Hatch

Technical Editor: Dennis Cox

Associate Technical Editor: Joell Smith

Editorial Manager: Colleen Rainsberger

Media Development Manager: Heather Heath Dismore

Editorial Assistant: Darren Meiss

Production

Project Coordinator: Karen York

Layout and Graphics: Steve Arany, Lou Boudreau, Linda M. Boyer, J. Tyler Connor, Angela F. Hunckler, Drew R. Moore, Brent Savage, Janet Seib, Deirdre Smith, Michael A. Sullivan

Proofreaders: Christine Berman, Kelli Botta, Jennifer K. Overmyer, Rebecca Senninger, Christine Snyder, Janet M. Withers

Indexer: Rebecca R. Plunkett

Special Help

Access Technology, Inc.

General and Administrative

IDG Books Worldwide, Inc.: John Kilcullen, CEO; Steven Berkowitz, President and Publisher

IDG Books Technology Publishing: Brenda McLaughlin, Senior Vice President and Group Publisher

Dummies Technology Press and Dummies Editorial: Diane Graves Steele, Vice President and Associate Publisher; Mary Bednarek, Director of Acquisitions and Product Development; Kristin A. Cocks, Editorial Director

Dummies Trade Press: Kathleen A. Welton, Vice President and Publisher; Kevin Thornton, Acquisitions Manager

IDG Books Production for Dummies Press: Michael R. Britton, Vice President of Production; Beth Jenkins Roberts, Production Director; Cindy L. Phipps, Manager of Project Coordination, Production Proofreading, and Indexing; Kathie S. Schutte, Supervisor of Page Layout; Shelley Lea, Supervisor of Graphics and Design; Debbie J. Gates, Production Systems Specialist; Robert Springer, Supervisor of Proofreading; Debbie Stailey, Special Projects Coordinator; Tony Augsburger, Supervisor of Reprints and Bluelines; Leslie Popplewell, Media Archive Coordinator

Dummies Packaging and Book Design: Robin Seaman, Creative Director; Jocelyn Kelaita, Product Packaging Coordinator; Kavish + Kavish, Cover Design

♦

The publisher would like to give special thanks to Patrick J. McGovern,
without whom this book would not have been possible.

♦

ABC 123

Files at a Glance

Here's a list of all the programs, exercise files, and document files that are stored on this book's CD, and where in the book you can find more information about them. For instructions on how to install this software, see Appendix B.

Part I

Unit	Topic	File
Unit 1	Signing up for an Internet account	MindSpring software signup kit
Unit 1	Browsing the Web	Internet Explorer program
Unit 2	Installing a favorites folder	+Hy's and Margy's Favorites+ exercise folder
Unit 3	Decompressing files to make them useable	WinZip program
Unit 3	Ensuring efficient file downloads	GetRight program
Unit 3	Detecting electronic viruses	ThunderBYTE Anti-Virus program

Part II

Unit	Topic	File
Unit 5	Sending, receiving, and managing Internet e-mail	Outlook Express program
Unit 6	Attaching a file to an e-mail message	Leo.jpg exercise file
Unit 6	Sending, receiving, and managing Internet e-mail	Eudora Light program
Unit 7	Reading and participating in Usenet newsgroups	Free Agent program
Unit 7	Chatting live over the Internet	mIRC program

Appendix B	Viewing and printing pdf document files	Acrobat Reader program
Appendix B	Joining mailing list discussion groups	MailList.pdf document file
Appendix B	Creating your own Web pages	WebPage.pdf document file
Appendix B	Browsing the Web, managing e-mail, and participating in newsgroups	Netscape Communicator program

On the CD

Unit WP	Composing, editing, and publishing Web pages	FrontPage Express program
Unit WP	Viewing and manipulating picture files	Paint Shop Pro program
Unit WP	Placing a picture on a Web page	Fern.gif, Mounts.gif, and Rainbow.gif exercise files
Unit WP	Uploading and downloading files	WS_FTP LE program

Note: Your *Dummies 101* CD contains two bonus units: Unit ML, "Joining Discussions by E-Mail," which is stored in document file MailList.pdf; and Unit WP, "Creating Your Own Web Pages," which is stored in document file WebPage.pdf. To learn how to view and print out these pdf document files, see Appendix B.

Contents at a Glance

Table of Contents

Introduction

Welcome to *Dummies 101: The Internet for Windows 98,* part of the acclaimed hands-on tutorial series from IDG Books Worldwide. Like our *...For Dummies* books, this book will give you lots of information in a form you can understand, without taking computers and software too seriously.

The Internet is a hot buzzword right now. All your friends are online, or plan to be. The business cards and letterhead that pass your way increasingly have e-mail addresses on them. And magazines and newspapers seem to be full of articles about the Net.

Unlike most fads, the Internet actually deserves all this attention. Electronic mail makes it easy to communicate with millions of people around the planet quickly and cheaply. The World Wide Web lets you find information on virtually any subject in minutes. Newsgroups allow you to conduct ongoing conversations about your favorite subjects with thousands of other like-minded people. And these are just some of the things the Internet has to offer!

If you're new to the Internet, the best way to learn about it is to take a course, with step-by-step instructions that build up your expertise as you go along. That's just what this book does. As opposed to a stuffy reference book with vague guidelines, this book provides a series of specific, detailed lessons that take you through signing up for an Internet account, browsing the World Wide Web, sending and receiving e-mail, joining mailing lists, participating in newsgroups, publishing your own material on the Internet, and more. The tutorials in this book take the place of a class, with lessons, exercises, quizzes, and tests.

This is the book for you if:

- You want to use the Internet, but are daunted by all the incomprehensible technical terms and all the different choices you need to make to get started.
- You've got to learn to use the Internet for a project.
- You want to take a class so that you can learn how to use e-mail, the World Wide Web, and the other stuff on the Internet, but you just don't have time or the inclination to spend weeks going out to sit-down classes.
- You want to learn all the basic tasks of using the Internet so that you don't have to run for help every time you need to get some work done.

Unlike most other computer books, this book does *not* assume that you already have the programs we describe. As long as you're running Windows 98 and have the right equipment (which we talk about later in this Introduction), you're set. All the other software you need is provided on this book's CD, which includes Internet Explorer (an enormously popular program that lets you interact with the World Wide Web), FrontPage Express (a composition program that lets you create and publish material on the World Wide Web), Outlook Express (a powerful message manager that lets you send and receive electronic mail, and also allows you to participate in any of 30,000 online discussions called *newsgroups*), and a bunch of other goodies. You'll learn about all of the programs on the CD over the course of this book's lessons and in Appendix B.

Assumptions about You, the Reader

This book is designed for the beginning or intermediate computer user who wants more than just technical geekspeak about the Internet. We have to make some assumptions about you in order to make the course work for you. We assume that:

- You have Windows 98 installed on your computer.
- You have a modem that communicates at 14,400 bps or faster (for example, 33,600 bps or 56,000 bps) connected to your computer.
- You have a phone line connected to your modem.
- You have a CD-ROM drive (so that you can use the CD that comes with this book).

How the Book Works

This book contains a course in using the Internet with Windows 98. The step-by-step approach leads you through each Internet feature by telling you exactly what to do and what your computer will do in response. Each unit has hands-on procedures to follow as you learn the basics, and then an additional exercise at the end of the unit that helps you review what you've learned.

Once you've covered the basics, you can skip to the units that discuss what you need to learn right away. Each unit indicates what you have to know before beginning the unit, in case you're skipping around, as well as what you'll learn in the unit. There's even a progress check at the end of each lesson so that you can gauge how you're doing.

Best of all, we don't take the Internet (or computers, for that matter) very seriously. After all, there's more to life than cruising the Net (or so we hear)!

Here's how to follow the lessons in this book:

- The course contains nine *units,* each starting with an introduction to the topic to be covered. Then you'll get to the *lessons* that delve into the topic with step-by-step instructions on what to do.

- Topics that are more complicated or less widely used are covered in *Extra Credit* sidebars. These topics aren't critical for your learning, but they may contain just the information you need to make your Internet use more productive or more fun.
- When we tell you something important to remember, we summarize the information in a note in the margin (like the one in this margin).
- A *Recess* section indicates a good place to stop and take a breather (perhaps a walk around the block, or your office's block of cubicles, to clear your head).
- At the end of each unit, a quiz provides a way for you to review what you've learned, and it also adds some comic relief. If a question stumps you, flip back through the unit to find the point that you missed. You'll also find an exercise that lets you practice what you've learned. At the end of each part of the book is a review of all the units in that part, along with a grueling test. (Well, maybe it's not so grueling, considering that the answers are in the back of the book.)

a note in the margin summarizes an important point

Notes:

In the text, stuff you need to type appears in **boldface**. When you have to press more than one key at a time, we show the names of the keys connected with a plus sign, like this: Ctrl+C. Hold down the first key (Ctrl, in this example), tap the second key (C), and then release both keys.

When we tell you to choose a command from the menu bar, a little arrow appears between the parts of the command, like this: File⇨Open. Click the first part of the command (File, in this example) on the menu bar, then click the second part of the command (Open) on the menu that appears.

A note about the Internet and moving targets: The Internet is in a perpetual state of flux. The ever-changing face of the Internet makes it an interesting place, but it also makes writing a book about it a little problematic. If you find that an electronic address in this book doesn't work, don't panic; the address may simply have changed. Luckily, we provide online updates to the book. See the section "Send Us E-mail" at the end of this introduction for how to get updated information.

How This Book Is Organized

This book is divided into three parts:

Part I: Swinging on the World Wide Web

The first part of this book guides you around the World Wide Web, the newest, zoomiest part of the Internet. You'll use the Microsoft Internet Explorer program, or *browser,* to browse through colorful Web pages, cruise links from one Web page to another, search the Web for any type of information, and download all kinds of nifty program, graphics, sound, and video files from the Web.

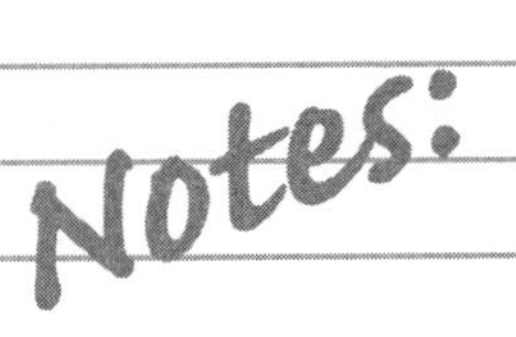

Part II: Reading E-Mail and Newsgroups

In the second part of this book, you'll learn how to use Microsoft Outlook Express to send and receive electronic mail, or *e-mail,* which allows you to communicate with friends and colleagues around the globe in seconds. You'll also find out how to use Outlook Express as a *newsgroup reader* that lets you participate in over 30,000 ongoing discussions devoted to virtually every subject under the sun via Usenet newsgroups. In addition, you'll discover how to tune into a Windows 98 feature called *channels* to display World Wide Web information — including regularly updated reports on stock prices, news, weather, sports, and almost anything else you can think of — directly on your desktop.

This part also offers two appendixes. Appendix A gives you the answers to the test questions that appear at the ends of Parts I and II. Appendix B tells you how to install and use the fabulous programs that are stored on this book's *Dummies 101* CD.

Icons Used in This Book

We put one of the following four icons in the margin when we want to point out important information:

This icon tells you when you need to use a file that comes on the *Dummies 101* CD.

Here's an item you're going to need to know when you get to the quiz at the end of the unit. If it's on the test, it must be important!

Descriptions of advanced topics appear in sidebars highlighted with this icon.

heads up

Heads up! Here's a piece of information that can make your life easier or may avert disaster.

About the *Dummies 101* CD

Windows 98 normally includes the Internet Explorer, Outlook Express, and FrontPage Express programs that you need to work through this book's lessons. If your copy of Windows 98 doesn't have these programs, however, you can install them from the *Dummies 101* CD that comes in the back of this book. The CD also contains all the exercise files you need to perform this book's exercises — including a collection of over 200 links we've put together that take you to the most useful and/or fun places on the World Wide Web!

In addition, the CD includes a MindSpring startup kit that you can use to sign up for an Internet account (see Unit 1). The CD also provides about a dozen powerful Internet programs that *aren't* bundled with Windows 98, including Eudora Light for managing e-mail, Free Agent for participating in Usenet newsgroups, mIRC for chatting live with others on the Net, WinZip for making compressed files useable again, Paint Shop Pro for viewing and revising picture files, and ThunderBYTE Anti-Virus for detecting computer viruses.

Finally, the CD comes with a handy Installer program that copies the programs you choose to use to your hard disk. For information about how to use the Installer, as well as more detailed descriptions of all the programs and files on the CD, see Appendix B.

If you have trouble with the CD (for example, if your computer can't read it, or it arrives in three pieces), call IDG Books Customer Support at 800-762-2974.

Send Us E-Mail

We love to hear from our readers. If you have questions or comments about the book, send us e-mail at `net101@gurus.com`. We can't answer all your questions about the Internet — after all, we are authors, not consultants — but we'd love to hear how the course worked for you.

If you want to know about other *Dummies 101* or *...For Dummies* books, call 800-762-2974, write to `info@idgbooks.com`, or look at this page on the World Wide Web:

```
www.dummies.com
```

For more information about the Internet and updates to this book, look at this Web page:

```
net.gurus.com/net101
```

If you can't send e-mail, you can always send plain old paper mail by using the address listed toward the end of this book. You'll receive a catalog of IDG Books in return. Don't worry — we authors will see your comments, too.

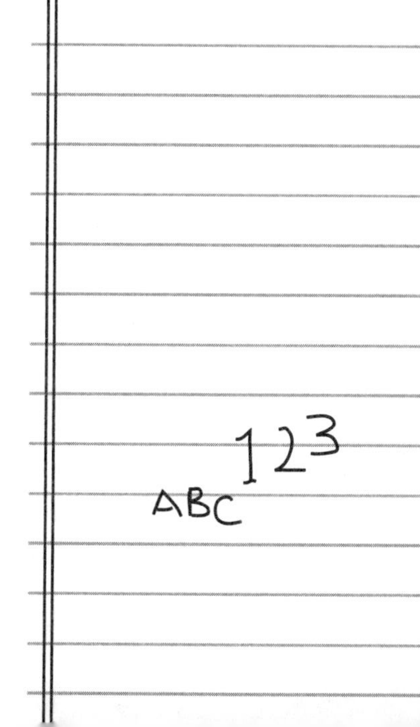

Part I

Swinging on the World Wide Web

In this part . . .

This part of the book tells you how to sign up for an Internet account and make sure that you have a recent copy of Internet Explorer installed. It then steps you through using Internet Explorer to take in the many colorful and fascinating sights on the World Wide Web, locate information on virtually any subject via the Web, and copy any of thousands of programs, electronic pictures, sound and video clips, and other fun files from the Web.

Unit 1

Getting Started with Internet Explorer

Objectives for This Unit

- ✓ Preparing to go online
- ✓ Jumping onto the World Wide Web using Internet Explorer
- ✓ Moving around a Web page and identifying its links
- ✓ Using links to move to Web pages
- ✓ Switching between Web pages

Prerequisites

- A PC running Windows 98
- A CD-ROM drive connected to your computer
- A 14,400 bps or faster modem connected to your computer

on the CD

- Internet Explorer
- Outlook Express
- FrontPage Express

The Internet seems to be everywhere lately. Hundreds of articles about it appear regularly in newspapers and magazines, dozens of TV specials and videotapes are devoted to it, major motion pictures such as *The Net* are based on it — coffee shops are even springing up that let you cruise the Internet while you sip an espresso!

Does the Internet deserve all this hoopla? In a word, *yes*. The Internet's most famous component, the visually striking World Wide Web, lets you find information about any subject with a few keystrokes or mouse clicks. The Internet also enables you to send electronic mail, or *e-mail,* messages to friends and colleagues around the globe in seconds; participate in ongoing discussions about virtually any topic via Internet talk groups, called *newsgroups*; chat with people live through your keyboard by using Internet Relay Chat, or *IRC*; and freely copy thousands of programs, picture files, and other goodies that are just waiting for you to come and get them.

Internet Explorer = program that lets you cruise the World Wide Web

Outlook Express = e-mail and newsgroup manager

FrontPage Express = World Wide Web composer/editor

To take advantage of such Internet features, you need programs that let you access and interact with the Net. That's why Microsoft Corporation, the company that publishes Windows 98, includes these three enormously popular Internet programs as part of Windows 98:

- **Internet Explorer:** A browser that lets you view and interact with the World Wide Web. This program is covered in Units 1, 2, 3, and 4.
- **Outlook Express:** A message manager that lets you send and receive e-mail, and that also lets you participate in newsgroups. The e-mail component of this program is covered in Units 5 and 6, and the newsgroup component is covered in Unit 7. In addition, how to use this program to join ongoing discussions by e-mail is covered in Unit ML, a bonus unit that's stored in electronic form on this book's CD (see Appendix B for details).
- **FrontPage Express:** A composer/editor that lets you create and publish your own material on the World Wide Web. This program is covered in Unit WP, which is a bonus unit stored on your *Dummies 101* CD (see Appendix B).

At the time we write this, Internet Explorer, Outlook Express, and FrontPage Express are all bundled in with Windows 98, and we'll help you verify that you have these programs later in this unit. If for some reason your version of Windows 98 doesn't include these programs, don't worry, because we've also provided them on the CD that came with this book — along with a bunch of other excellent Internet software. (For more information about the CD, see Appendix B.)

Note: *Don't* install Internet Explorer from this book's CD if the program is already on your hard disk, because installing an older version of Internet Explorer on top of a newer one can create software problems.

Internet Explorer is used by more than 40 percent of folks on the Net — that is, about 40 million people! In fact, Internet Explorer isn't simply one of the best-liked Internet programs around; it's one of the five most popular programs of *any* kind in the history of computers. Internet Explorer, Outlook Express, and FrontPage Express are packed with features that let you cruise the World Wide Web, send and receive e-mail, participate in ongoing discussions over the Net, and much more.

This book is designed to teach you how to use Internet Explorer, Outlook Express, and FrontPage Express to take advantage of all the wonderful things on the Internet. In addition, this book and the CD that comes with it are designed to supply you with the basics you need to try out and use other great Internet programs (such as Netscape Communicator, Eudora Light, and Free Agent — which are also included on your *Dummies 101* CD). By the time you finish this book, you'll have turned from a *newbie* (Internet newcomer) into a *nethead* (Internet expert)!

The version of Internet Explorer that we'll be covering is 4.0, which is the most current version at the time of this writing. Because Internet Explorer tends to keep its key features operating the same way across versions, however, much of the material in this book is likely to apply to future versions of Internet Explorer as well.

This first unit will tell you what you need to know to get started. It will then guide you through an initial look at the World Wide Web using Internet Explorer.

Preparing to Go Online with Internet Explorer

Lesson 1-1

Before you can cruise the Net with Internet Explorer, you have to prepare yourself for the journey. Specifically, you need to own the right equipment, set up an Internet account, have a copy of Internet Explorer, and know a few basic terms.

Understanding what equipment you need

You need several pieces of equipment to make full use of this book:

- A PC that runs Windows 98
- A CD-ROM so that you can transfer the terrific software on this book's CD to your hard disk
- A phone line that's available for use with your PC
- A device called a *modem* (see the next paragraph)

on the test

What a modem does requires some explanation. To *go online* means to get your computer to communicate with other computers over a phone line. (In fact, while on the Internet, you can access *millions* of other computers.) Talking over the phone isn't a capability built into your machine, however, so it needs help from your modem. The modem converts your computer's digital language into audio that can travel over phone wires, and it converts the audio signals from other computers back into digital data.

online = connected to other computers via a phone line

Not all modems are created equal. For example, if you have an internal modem, it's tucked away in a slot inside your computer, and you don't have to think about it much because it's always on and available. If you have an external modem, it resides outside your computer, has an on/off switch, and is connected to a socket in the back of your machine by a special cable. (If you ever encounter a problem getting online with an external modem, make sure that the modem's power switch is turned on and that its cable is still tightly attached to your computer.)

Modems also have different speed capabilities, which are measured in bits per second, or *bps*. As we write this book, the current standard speed is 33,600 bps, which can transmit and receive data at a good clip — for example, transferring the contents of a 1.44MB floppy disk at 33,600 bps takes about six minutes. A rapidly emerging standard is 56,000 bps, which is almost twice as

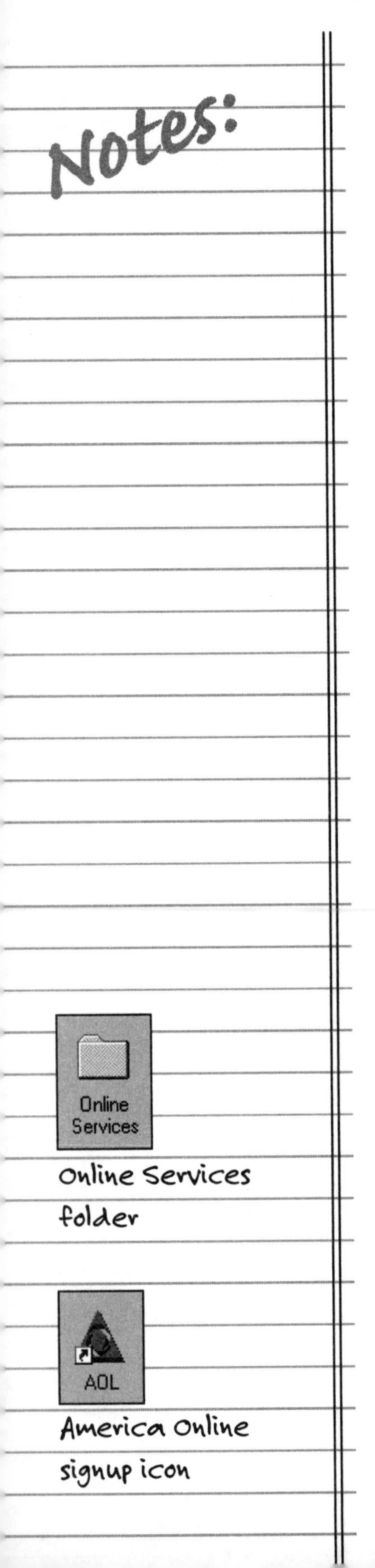

Online Services folder

America Online signup icon

fast as 33,600 bps — transferring 1.44MB at this speed takes about three minutes. The bare minimum speed you need to use the Internet effectively is 14,400 bps, which is less than half as fast as 33,600 bps (and which may cause you to tap your foot impatiently while waiting for data to appear on your screen).

To sum up, if you have a PC running Windows 98, a CD-ROM, a modem, and a phone line that you can plug into your modem, you're set as far as equipment goes. Your next step is to decide how to connect to the Internet.

Getting an Internet account

One of the wonderful things about the Internet is that no one owns it — it's a resource that millions of people and organizations around the world share. Before you can go online, however, you need to sign up with a company that has the proper hardware and software to provide you with access to the Internet. Such a company is called, appropriately enough, an *Internet Service Provider,* or *ISP,* and it typically charges a monthly fee for its service (such as $19.95 per month for unlimited Internet access). Thousands of ISPs exist, so you have lots of choices.

For example, you can join a small ISP located in your area to get a personal touch to your service; or you can join a large ISP that provides hundreds of phone numbers across the country that allow you to dial into the Net from almost anywhere for the price of a local call.

Most ISPs are devoted to connecting you to the Internet, and little else. You can alternatively join a special type of ISP called an *online service,* such as America Online or CompuServe. An online service gives you Internet access but also provides extra features, such as easy-to-use discussion sections and information-rich databases that aren't available to the general public. An online service may be more expensive than a vanilla ISP, however, or it may be more prone to problems such as excessive busy signals or slow Internet access.

Windows 98 includes signup programs for several of the most popular ISPs and online services. You can display these programs by locating a folder named Online Services on your Windows 98 desktop and double-clicking it — that is, clicking the folder twice in rapid succession. You can then join any ISP listed by double-clicking its signup icon (and, when you're prompted for it, supplying your credit card number).

At the time we write this, the following ISPs are represented in the Online Services folder:

- **America Online:** By far the largest online service in the world, America Online, or *AOL,* has more than 10 million members. Among this service's advantages are that it's easy to use, and — in addition to providing Internet access — it offers special discussion sections, news services, and databases that furnish information not available on the Net. Telephone technical support for AOL isn't always easy to reach,

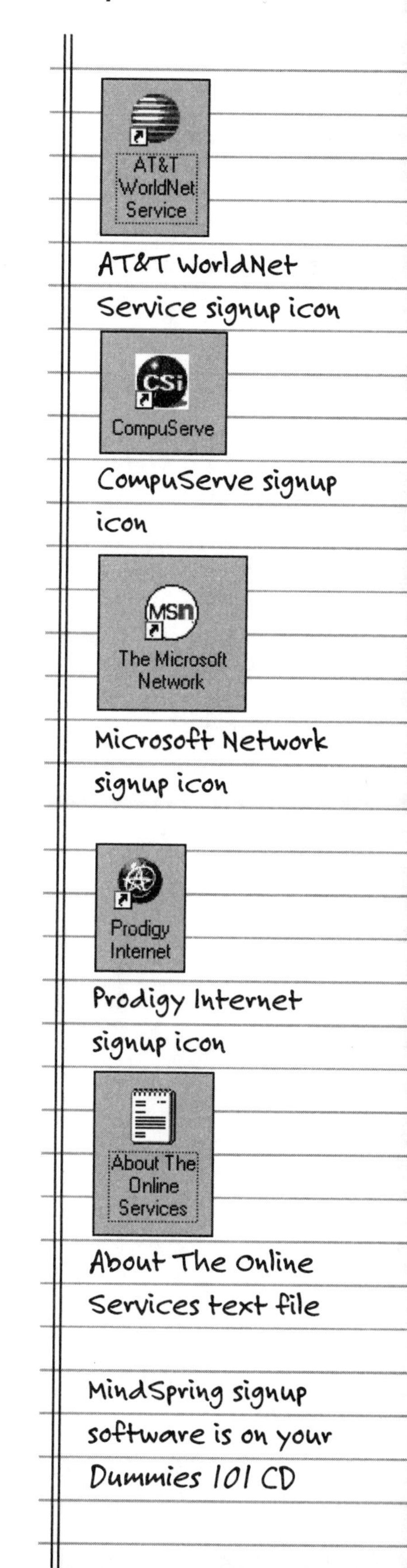

however, and its Internet connection may not always be as available or as fast as that of a "pure" ISP that does nothing but hook you into the Net. For more information about AOL, call 800-827-6364.

- **AT&T WorldNet Service:** An international ISP with about a million members, this Internet provider is a division of the AT&T telephone company and prides itself on customer service, which it offers via a toll-free number 24 hours a day, seven days a week. AT&T WorldNet can therefore be a good choice for people just starting out on the Net. For more information about AT&T WorldNet, call 800-967-5363.
- **CompuServe:** An international online service with about two million members, CompuServe offers numerous discussion sections and databases that furnish terrific information not available on the Net, as well as standard Internet access. CompuServe is targeted at business customers who need the extra data it offers, so this service is more expensive than a typical ISP. Also, CompuServe's telephone support isn't always easy to reach, so it may not be an ideal choice for beginners. To learn more about CompuServe, call 800-848-8990.
- **Microsoft Network:** An international ISP run by Microsoft Corporation (the publisher of Windows 98), with more than a million members. You can join this Internet provider by double-clicking either the Microsoft Network icon in the Online Services folder or the Setup The Microsoft Network icon that resides directly on your desktop. For more information about Microsoft Network, call 800-386-5550.
- **Prodigy Internet:** An international online service with about one million members. Like America Online, Prodigy Internet is designed to be easy to use. Unlike AOL, however, all Prodigy Internet features are provided directly through the World Wide Web, a unique approach for an online service that many find appealing. For more information about Prodigy Internet, call 800-213-0992.

In addition to signup programs, the Online Services folder contains an About The Online Services information file. Double-click this text file to bring up a window with more facts about the services, as well as international telephone numbers for customer service and technical support.

If you decide to join one of the Internet service providers represented in the Online Services folder, grab your credit card and then double-click the signup icon of the service you've selected. After you do so, follow the prompts that appear on your screen to join the service and to install any software required by the service.

Of course, you're not restricted to just the ISPs represented in the Online Services folder. For example, another top-rated ISP you might consider is MindSpring, which is a U.S. provider that's gotten high marks for its reliable and fast Internet connections. The signup software for MindSpring is on this book's CD; for information on how to install the software, see Appendix B.

Two other well-regarded services are Concentric, which is another U.S. Internet provider, and IBM Internet Connection, which is an ISP that offers a tremendous selection of local telephone numbers around the world and is a great choice for international travelers.

you can search for ISPs at World Wide Web site thelist.iworld.com

Then again, you might consider hooking up with a small local service. Although such companies aren't able to provide local telephone numbers for connecting to the Net outside your area, you don't need such numbers unless you travel frequently. In addition, local companies can often provide a more personal touch (for example, by offering beginner classes, or organizing subscriber get-togethers, or connecting you to the president of the firm to solve a business-related Internet crisis) than their national and international competitors. You can locate ISPs in your area by checking the Internet or Computer Services sections in your phone book's Yellow Pages, leafing through ads in your newspaper's Science or Technology section, or asking your friends and colleagues which providers they recommend. Alternatively, if you know someone who's already on the Net and is willing to spare a few minutes, ask your friend to go to the World Wide Web location `thelist.iworld.com`. This location is the home of a search program named The List that contains information on over 4,000 ISPs and displays them based on the criteria you specify (such as your country, state, or area code).

Finally, if you have trouble choosing among ISPs, keep in mind that you can always sign up with more than one provider — which is especially reasonable if you'll be using your online resources as serious business tools. For example, we belong to both America Online and CompuServe so that we can access their special discussion sections and databases, but we do all our Internet work through a dedicated ISP for its speed and reliability. (America Online makes going this route especially appealing, because AOL drastically reduces its charges if you access it through your ISP instead of dialing in directly.)

If you'd like to contact any of the companies we just mentioned, see Table 1-1. Whether you select a large international ISP, a small local ISP, or an online service, the important thing is that you have an account with a company that can serve as your connection to the Internet.

Table 1-1 Some Popular Internet Service Providers

Company	*Telephone Number*	*Comments*
America Online	800-827-6364 or 703-448-8700	International online service that includes Internet access among its many features
AT&T WorldNet Service	800-967-5363 or 201-967-5363	International ISP
CompuServe	800-848-8990 or 614-457-8600	International online service that includes Internet access among its many features
Concentric	800-939-4262 or 408-342-2800	U.S. ISP
IBM Internet Connection	800-455-5056 or 770-863-1234	International ISP
The Microsoft Network	800-386-5550 or 425-882-8080	International ISP

Company	Telephone Number	Comments
MindSpring	800-719-4332 or 404-815-0082	U.S. ISP; we provide its sign-up software on this book's CD
Prodigy Internet	800-213-0992 or 914-448-8000	International online service that centers on Internet access but also provides other features

Making sure you have Internet Explorer

Before you can tackle the exercises in this book that teach you how to use Internet Explorer, you need to *have* Internet Explorer.

At the time we write this, Internet Explorer (along with its companion programs, Outlook Express and FrontPage Express) is included free as part of Windows 98. You can verify whether your particular copy of Windows 98 has Internet Explorer in several ways:

- **Check your desktop:** If you have Internet Explorer, one of the icons appearing on your Windows 98 desktop will normally be an Internet Explorer icon, which looks like the letter "e" with a moon revolving around it and has the text *Internet Explorer* underneath it. You can run Internet Explorer by double-clicking this icon (that is, by clicking it twice in rapid succession).
- **Check the taskbar:** One of the key components of Windows 98 is the *taskbar,* which is the gray bar that runs across the bottom of your screen and houses buttons you can click to perform various program tasks. For example, the taskbar has a *Start button* in its left corner that lets you list and run your PC's programs; a *system tray* in its right corner that displays the time and lets you access special programs affecting your entire system (such as sound volume, printing, and modem controls); and a middle section that displays a button for each program you're currently running and that lets you switch between the programs by clicking their buttons.

  In addition, the taskbar can house several toolbars that provide extra buttons. Specifically, the taskbar is initially set to display a Quick Launch toolbar that has three buttons named Launch Internet Explorer Browser, Show Desktop, and View Channels. Clicking the Show Desktop button shrinks all your open windows so that you can instantly access your desktop, and clicking the View Channels button lets you work with electronic channels (which are covered in Unit 8). The Launch Internet Explorer Browser button looks like an "e" with a moon revolving around it, and, as the button's name indicates, clicking it immediately launches Internet Explorer. (***Tip:*** You can adjust which toolbars appear by clicking any blank spot on the taskbar with your *right* (not left) mouse button, clicking the Toolbars option from the menu that appears, and then clicking the toolbar you want to turn on or off from the second menu that appears.)

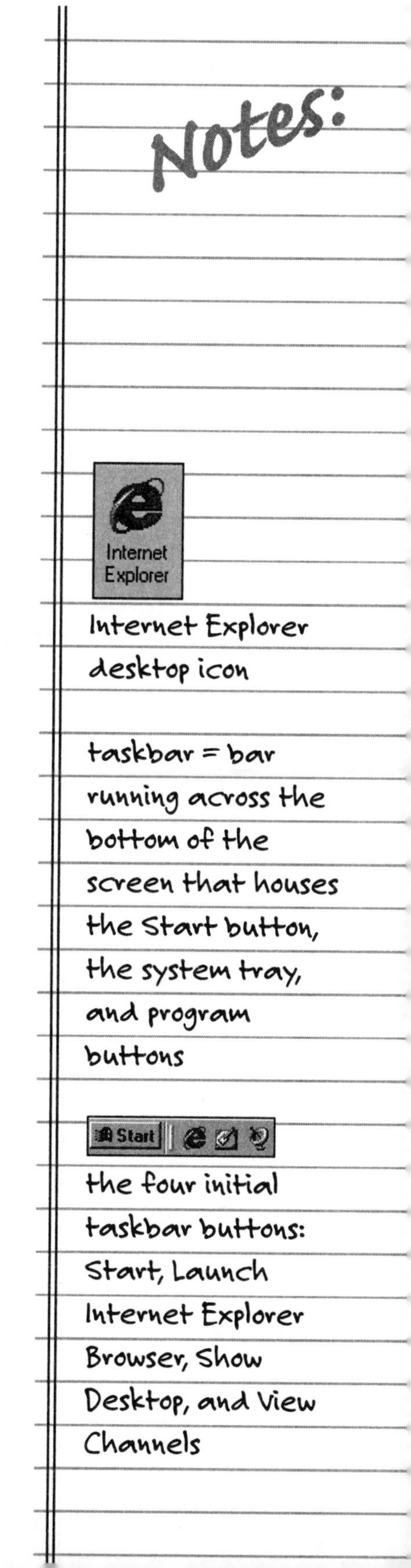

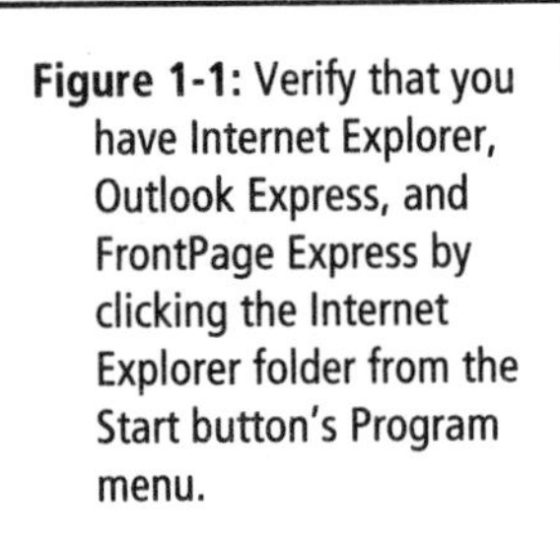

Figure 1-1: Verify that you have Internet Explorer, Outlook Express, and FrontPage Express by clicking the Internet Explorer folder from the Start button's Program menu.

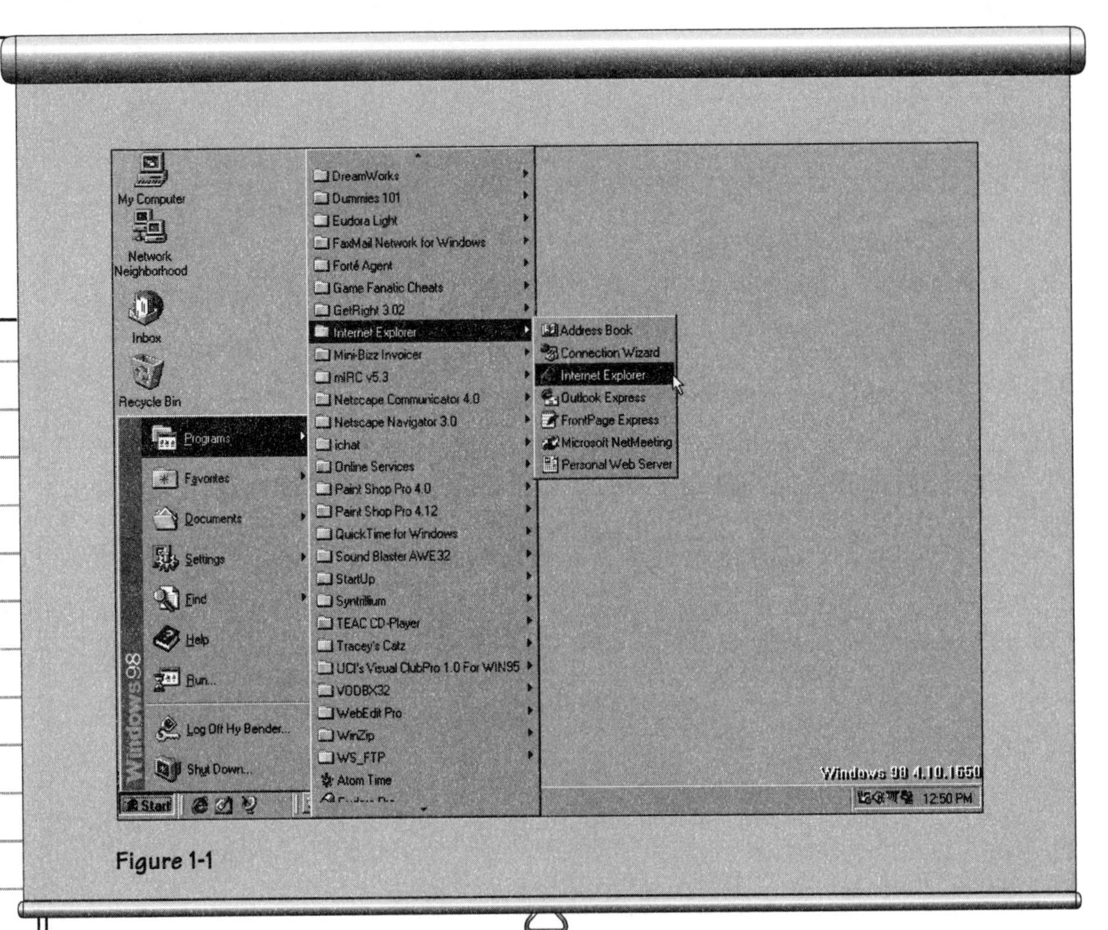

Figure 1-1

- **Check the Programs menu:** As we just mentioned, the Start button in the lower-left corner of your screen lets you list and run the programs on your hard disk. To run Internet Explorer, first click the Start button to display an initial menu. Next, click the Programs option to display a second menu that lists program folders and individual programs. Locate and click the Internet Explorer option; you should see the contents of the Internet Explorer folder, which includes the programs Internet Explorer, Outlook Express, and FrontPage Express (as shown in Figure 1-1). Finally, launch Internet Explorer by clicking the Internet Explorer option on this third menu.
- **Check the Add/Remove list:** As a final check, you can click the Start button, click Settings, click Control Panel to open a folder, and double-click the Add/Remove Programs icon to display a list of programs installed on your hard disk. Click anywhere in the alphabetical list, and then scroll through it using either your Down Arrow key or your mouse. If one of the entries is Microsoft Internet Explorer (with a version number of 4.0 or higher), then you have the browser program. After you're done examining the program list, click the Cancel button to exit the list, and click the Close button in the folder's upper-right corner to exit the folder.

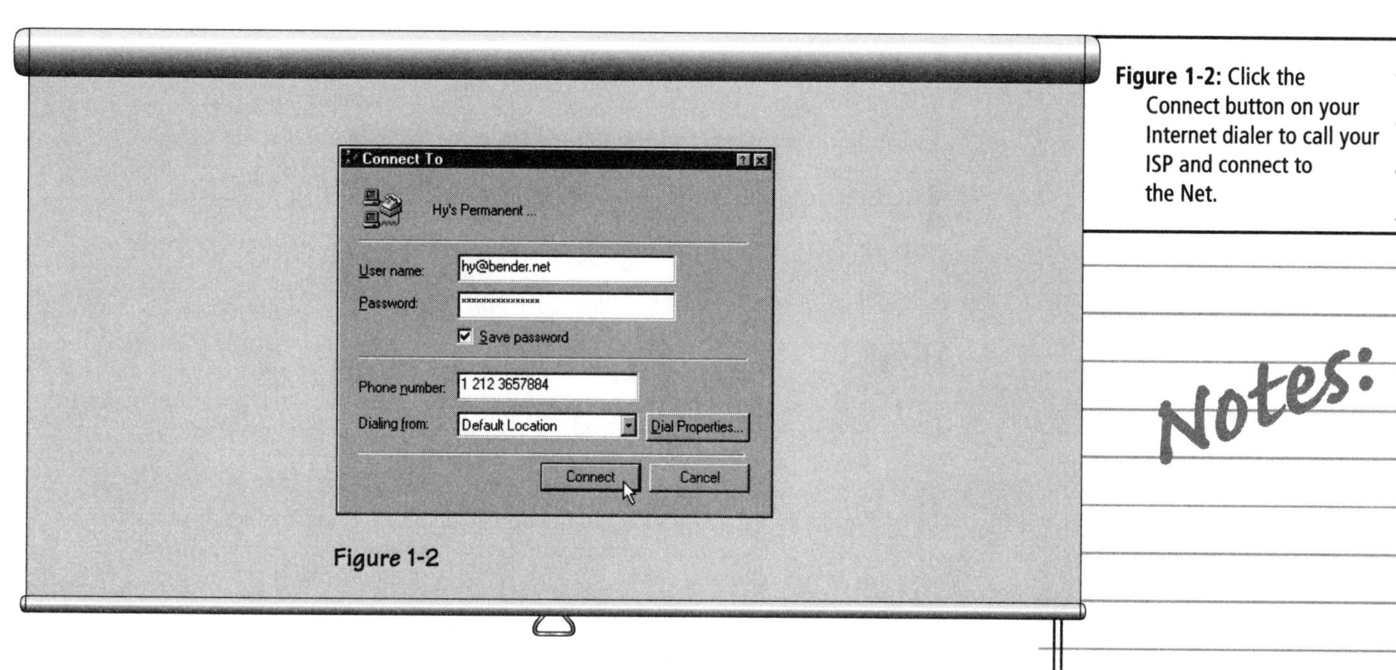

Figure 1-2

Figure 1-2: Click the Connect button on your Internet dialer to call your ISP and connect to the Net.

heads up

If you don't see any sign of Internet Explorer on your system, then your version of Windows 98 doesn't include the program. In this case, install Internet Explorer from the *Dummies 101* CD that came with this book, following the instructions that appear in Appendix B. When the Internet Explorer installation program asks whether you want to perform a Minimal, Standard, or Full installation, be sure to select the Full option, since this is the only option that installs the Outlook Express and FrontPage Express programs along with Internet Explorer.

After you've either verified that you have Internet Explorer or have installed Internet Explorer, you're all set to use the program as your window on the Net.

Using an Internet dialer

In addition to the programs you use to communicate with the Net, you need a program that can *connect* you to the Net — that is, that can dial one of your ISP's phone numbers and hook you up to the Internet via your ISP's computers. Such a program is called a *dialer,* and it's typically popped up automatically by programs that require it (such as Internet Explorer and Outlook Express). A dialer operates independently of other software you're using, however, which means that you're always free to open or close any combination of Internet programs while keeping your dialer running to stay connected to the Net.

Specifically, after your dialer's initial dialog box appears on your screen, click a button on it that says something like *Connect* (as shown in Figure 1-2). This makes your dialer call up your ISP and log you on to the Net. As long as you're connected, any Internet program that you run automatically takes advantage of the connection to allow you to interact with the Internet.

After you log on to the Net, the dialer's dialog box transforms into a small modem icon that resides in your system tray (that is, the area in the lower-right corner of your screen that displays the current time). When you double-click this modem icon, a dialog box appears that tells you how long you've

Notes:

PC = Windows-based personal computer

Net = the Internet

been connected and the speed of your connection. This box also contains a button that says something like *Disconnect;* when you click the Disconnect button, the dialer severs your Internet connection. The dialer then exits, and both its status dialog box and modem icon disappear.

You don't have to do anything to obtain a dialer program because one is included with Windows 98. In addition, some Internet programs bundle in a dialer, and some ISPs provide you with dialers as part of their services. It doesn't matter which dialer program you use; what's important is that your dialer successfully connects you to the Internet. If you have problems making your dialer perform this critical task, call your ISP's technical support staff for information on how to adjust the dialer's settings so that it can properly connect your computer to the ISP's computers.

You have just one more thing to do before jumping on the World Wide Web, and that's to become familiar with some key words and phrases related to using your PC and the Net.

Understanding a few basic terms

We try to avoid jargon as much as possible, but writing a computer book requires throwing in some technical words. We introduce most new terms as they're needed over the course of the book (and, we hope, always clearly define them when they pop up!). You should know a few words and phrases right away, though, so here's a quick list:

- **PC:** Short for personal computer and, in the context of this book, a computer that's designed to run Microsoft Windows.
- **The Net:** Short for the Internet.
- **Click:** Press your left mouse button.
- **Click the OK button:** Position your mouse pointer over the OK button and then press your left mouse button.
- **Double-click:** Press your left mouse button twice in rapid succession.
- **Right-click:** Press your right mouse button.
- **Click and drag:** Click an object that you want to move and, while keeping your mouse button held down, move your mouse to another location; the object will be dragged along by your mouse.
- **Dialog box:** A box that displays a message and/or various options.
- **Run, launch, or fire up a program:** Get a program going.
- **Dial in or log on:** Use your modem and phone line to call an ISP and get connected to the Internet.
- **Go online:** Take steps to connect with other computers by using your modem and a phone line.
- **Go offline:** Disconnect from your online session.
- **Web page:** A collection of text, pictures, and other multimedia elements (such as sound or video) on the World Wide Web.

- **Web site:** A collection of related Web pages created by a particular person or organization.

heads up

- **Web style:** You normally open folders and activate icons by double-clicking them. However, Windows 98 can also operate in *Web style,* which opens folders and activates icons in response to a single mouse click. If your system is set to Web style, click only once when we tell you to double-click. (***Tip:*** To turn Web style on or off, click the Start button in the lower-left corner of your screen; click the Settings option from the menu that appears; click Folder Options to open a dialog box; click Web Style for single-clicking or Classic Style for standard clicking (or click Custom and use the Settings button to create customized settings); and click OK to save your changes.)
- **Default option:** The option that's selected before you make any adjustments (sort of like the factory setting).
- **Character:** A single letter, number, punctuation mark, or other symbol that you can type on your keyboard. (For example, the word *cat* has three characters, as does the date *5/9.*)
- **Filename:** The name of an electronic file. A Windows 98 filename can be up to 255 characters, and can include spaces and punctuation.
- **Extension:** The one to three characters following the final period in a filename. (For example, the filename *Letter.txt* has the extension *txt,* the filename *Program.exe* has the extension *exe,* and the Web page file *My Home Page.htm* has the extension *htm.*)
- **Folder:** An area on your hard disk that stores files. Folders help keep your files organized in logical groups, just as physical folders help organize your papers in a filing cabinet.
- **Directory:** An older term for *folder* that you may sometimes encounter. *Directory* and *folder* mean the same thing, and this book simply uses the term *folder.*
- **Desktop:** The foundation of Windows 98, the desktop houses such critical elements as program windows and icons (similar to the way a physical desktop holds your papers, pens, and other work tools).

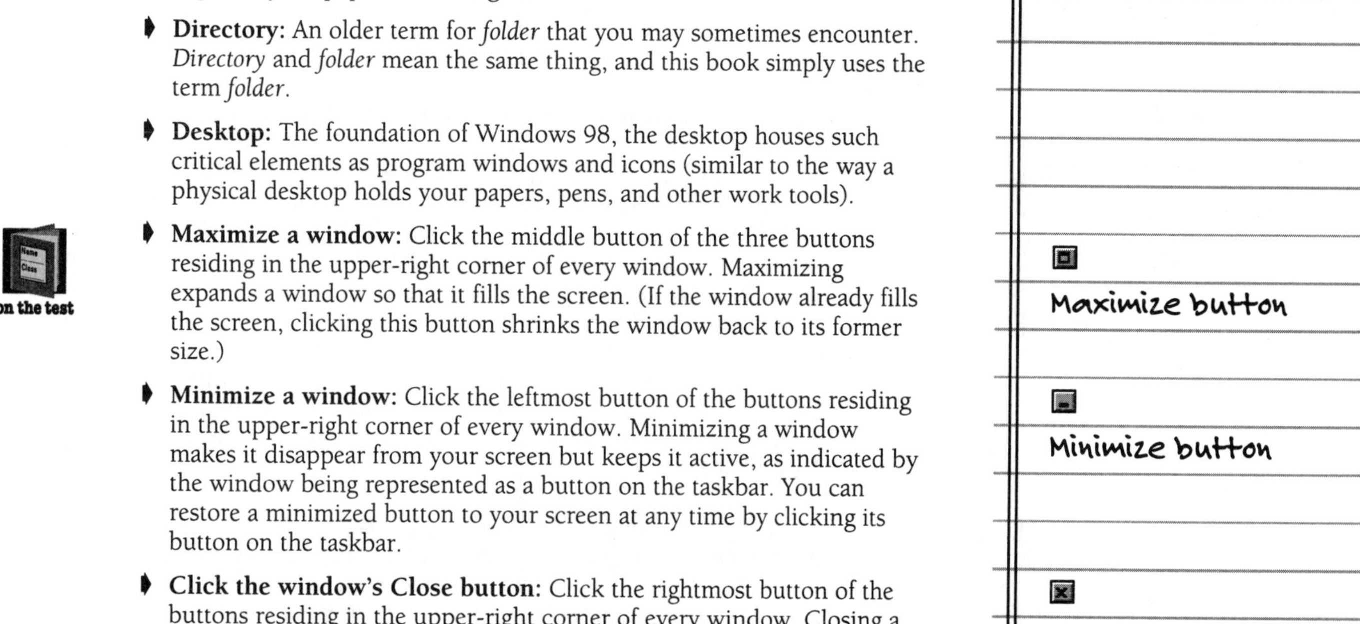

- **Maximize a window:** Click the middle button of the three buttons residing in the upper-right corner of every window. Maximizing expands a window so that it fills the screen. (If the window already fills the screen, clicking this button shrinks the window back to its former size.)
- **Minimize a window:** Click the leftmost button of the buttons residing in the upper-right corner of every window. Minimizing a window makes it disappear from your screen but keeps it active, as indicated by the window being represented as a button on the taskbar. You can restore a minimized button to your screen at any time by clicking its button on the taskbar.
- **Click the window's Close button:** Click the rightmost button of the buttons residing in the upper-right corner of every window. Closing a window makes it disappear from your screen, deactivate, and free up space in your computer's memory for new windows.

☑ **Progress Check**

If you can do the following, you've mastered this lesson:

- ❑ Identify the hardware that you need to jump on the Internet.
- ❑ Know how to sign up with an Internet Service Provider (ISP).
- ❑ Verify that your PC has Internet Explorer installed.
- ❑ Understand fundamental computer terms.

- **Title bar:** The bar running across the top of every window that contains the window's name on its left side and the window's Minimize, Maximize, and Close buttons on its right side.
- **Menu bar:** The bar directly below the title bar that contains the names of menus you can click to access program options. A menu bar typically starts with File and Edit menus and typically ends with a Help menu.
- **Press Ctrl+D:** Hold down the Ctrl key and, while keeping it pressed, tap the D key.
- **Choose File⇨Save:** Click File from your window's menu bar to display a list of options and then click the Save option. Alternatively, hold down the Alt key and press F followed by S.

If you don't memorize all these terms on the spot, don't worry; we'll go over their definitions again as needed. If most of these terms are entirely new to you, however, you may find doing some additional reading about Windows helpful. One (of many) fine books on this subject is *Dummies 101: Windows 98* by Andy Rathbone from IDG Books Worldwide.

Lesson 1-2 Jumping onto the Web

Web = World Wide Web section of the Internet

It's time for all the preparation work you did in Lesson 1-1 to pay off. You're about to crawl onto the World Wide Web!

World Wide Web may sound like the title of a 1950s conspiracy movie involving radioactive Communist spiders. However, the WWW, or *Web* (as savvy Net users refer to it), is much cooler than that. Though it didn't even exist until 1990, the Web is rapidly becoming the most popular feature of the Internet.

The Web consists of electronic pages that display text and pictures, similar to the pages of a paper book or magazine (though some jazzier Web pages also can play sound and video clips). Well-designed Web pages are a visual treat, and they cover virtually every topic that you can think of — from the stock market to stock racing, from bass to baseball, and from Picasso to Prozac. The neatest thing about the Web, however, is that each page typically contains *links* to other pages, allowing you to jump from one page to another with a single mouse click.

For example, you might be reading a Web page about the life of William Shakespeare and notice that various phrases and pictures in the biography are underlined, are a different color, or are marked in some other special way. This special marking usually means that clicking the phrase or picture (called a *link*) with your mouse takes you to another page covering that topic in more depth. At the William Shakespeare page, clicking the phrase *Romeo and Juliet* might take you to a page with the full text of that play, and clicking an image of the Globe Theatre could take you to a page with a series of detailed drawings of that famous Elizabethan playhouse.

Your voyage wouldn't have to end there, either. For example, the Globe Theatre page might contain a link to *modern theatre.* Clicking that phrase could offer you additional links to such disparate topics as Arthur Miller, movie adaptations, and Andrew Lloyd Webber's *Cats.* Clicking the latter might furnish — in addition to information about other Lloyd Webber hits, such as *Evita* and *The Phantom of the Opera* — links to Web pages about *real* cats. And any feline Web page worth its fur inevitably offers a link to pictures of Socks, the First Cat of the Clinton White House.

This hypothetical journey from Shakespeare to Socks shows you what jumping around the Web, also known as *cruising* or *surfing,* is all about. Because these electronic pages — which are created independently by thousands of individuals and organizations around the planet — are all linked together in various intricate ways, they truly form a World Wide Web of information.

In this unit, you'll get on the Web by using the Internet Explorer *browser,* which lets you browse through electronic pages. You'll first learn how to examine a Web page and use its links to move to other pages. You'll then learn how to use Internet Explorer buttons to switch among a few pages, and how to use Internet Explorer's File menu and History bar to switch among many pages.

Notes:

browser = program that lets you cruise the Web

Opening Internet Explorer and connecting to the Net

In Lesson 1-1, you signed up with an ISP and verified that you have Internet Explorer installed on your hard disk. Now follow these steps to actually run Internet Explorer and use it to browse the Web:

1. **Make sure that your modem is turned on, that you have a phone line connected to your modem, and that you don't have another telecommunications program running.**

2. **Click the taskbar's Internet Explorer button (the "e" icon next to the Start button in the lower-left corner of your screen).**

   Alternatively, double-click the Internet Explorer icon on your desktop; or click the taskbar's Start button, click Programs, click the Internet Explorer folder icon from the second menu that appears, and click the Internet Explorer program icon from the third menu that appears.

   The Internet Explorer window opens, and whatever Internet dialer program you're using appears. For example, if you're using the Windows 98 Dialer, a Dial-up Connection dialog box appears in front of the Internet Explorer window, as shown in Figure 1-3.

   Note: Some dialer programs don't pop up automatically when you run Internet Explorer. If that's true of your dialer, simply run it manually by double-clicking the dialer's icon.

Internet Explorer

click the Internet Explorer button on the taskbar to launch the browser

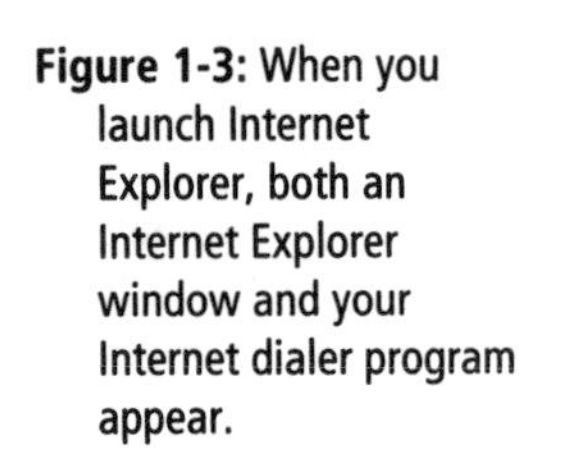

Figure 1-3: When you launch Internet Explorer, both an Internet Explorer window and your Internet dialer program appear.

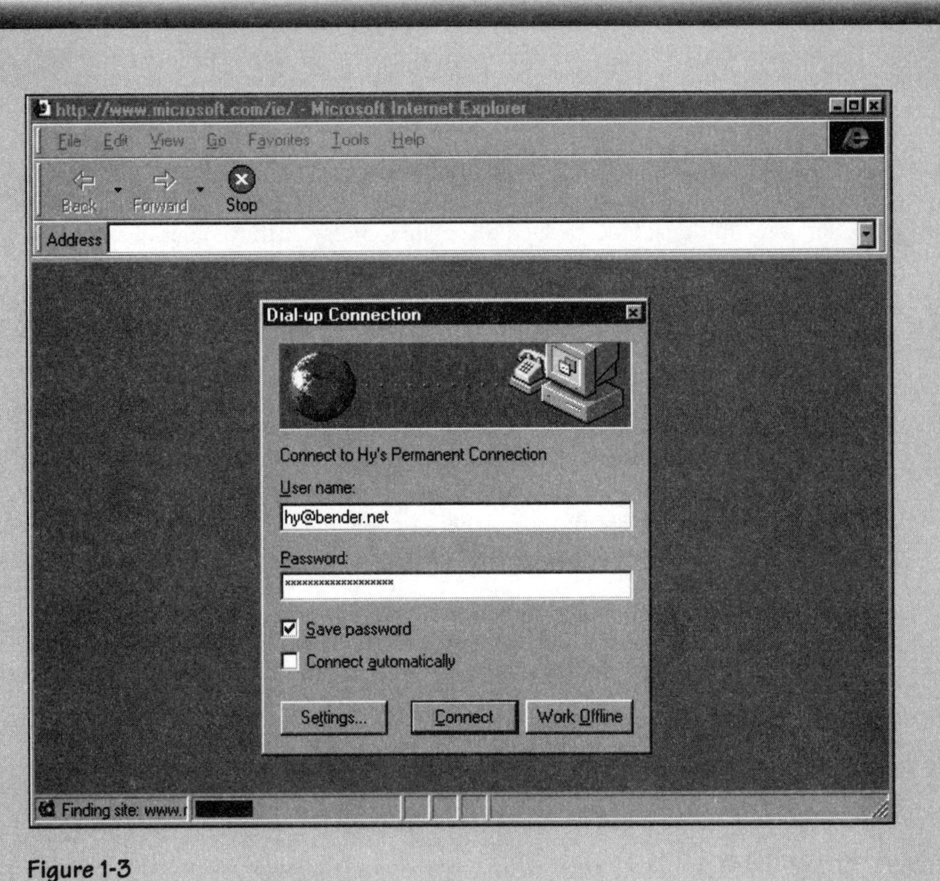

Figure 1-3

3 Click the appropriate button on your dialer program to connect to the Internet.

For example, if you're using the Windows 98 Dialer, click the Connect button. After a few moments, your dialer program calls the local phone number that you're using to access your ISP, gets your modem talking to your provider's modem, and transmits the user name and password that identify you to your ISP. If all goes well, you're connected to the Internet. Your dialer program then becomes minimized — that is, it disappears from your screen but stays active — and is represented as a cute modem icon in the taskbar's system tray (in the lower-right corner of your screen).

heads up

If your connection isn't successful, make sure that your computer, modem, and phone line are all securely attached. Also, make sure that you entered the phone number, user name, and password information correctly in your dialer program. If none of that helps, try again a little later; your ISP's computers may be temporarily overloaded or experiencing a technical problem. If after several tries you're still having trouble, call your ISP for help identifying the difficulty.

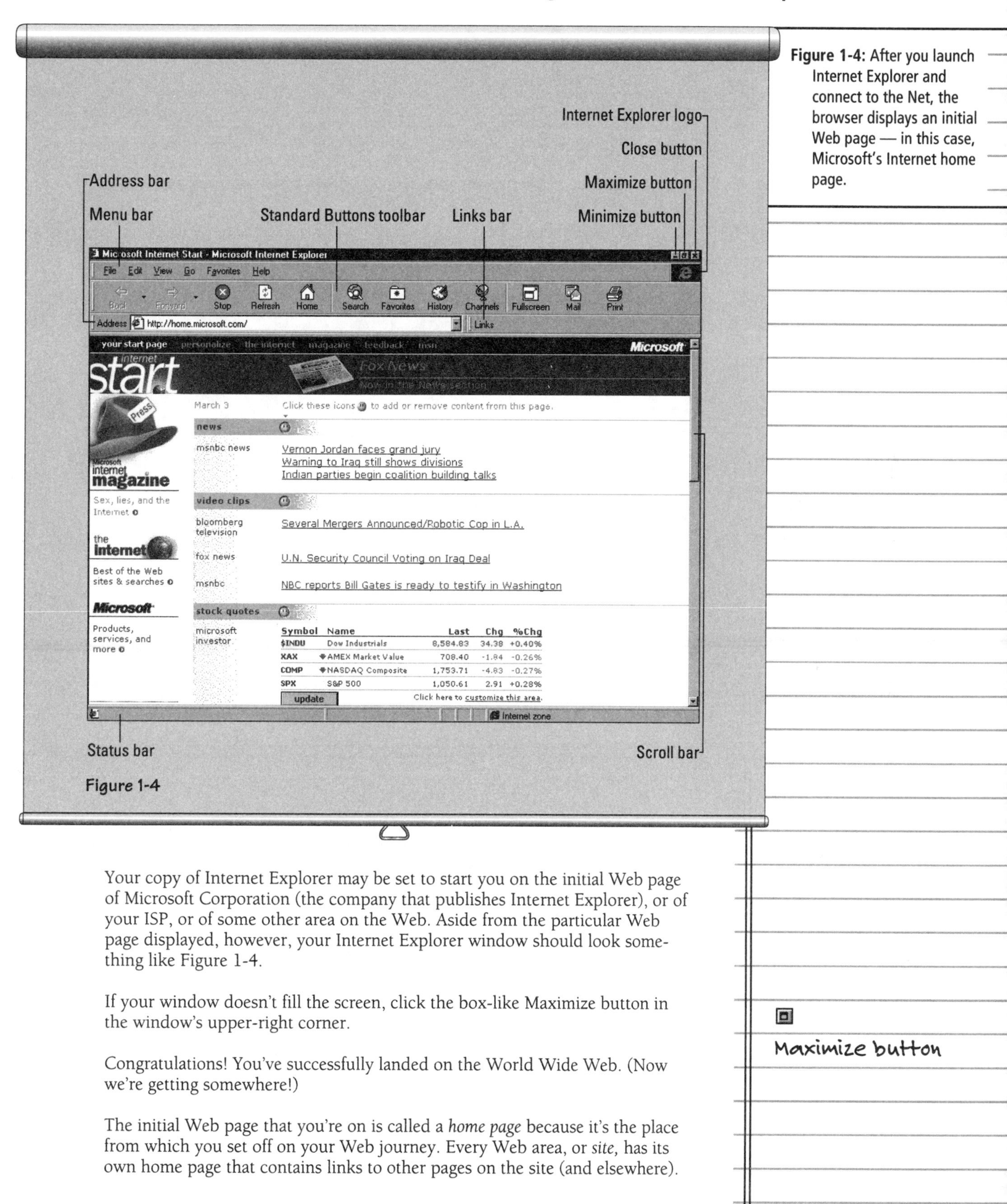

Figure 1-4

Figure 1-4: After you launch Internet Explorer and connect to the Net, the browser displays an initial Web page — in this case, Microsoft's Internet home page.

Your copy of Internet Explorer may be set to start you on the initial Web page of Microsoft Corporation (the company that publishes Internet Explorer), or of your ISP, or of some other area on the Web. Aside from the particular Web page displayed, however, your Internet Explorer window should look something like Figure 1-4.

If your window doesn't fill the screen, click the box-like Maximize button in the window's upper-right corner.

Maximize button

Congratulations! You've successfully landed on the World Wide Web. (Now we're getting somewhere!)

The initial Web page that you're on is called a *home page* because it's the place from which you set off on your Web journey. Every Web area, or *site*, has its own home page that contains links to other pages on the site (and elsewhere).

Figure 1-5: Click Internet Explorer's vertical scroll bar to see more of a Web page.

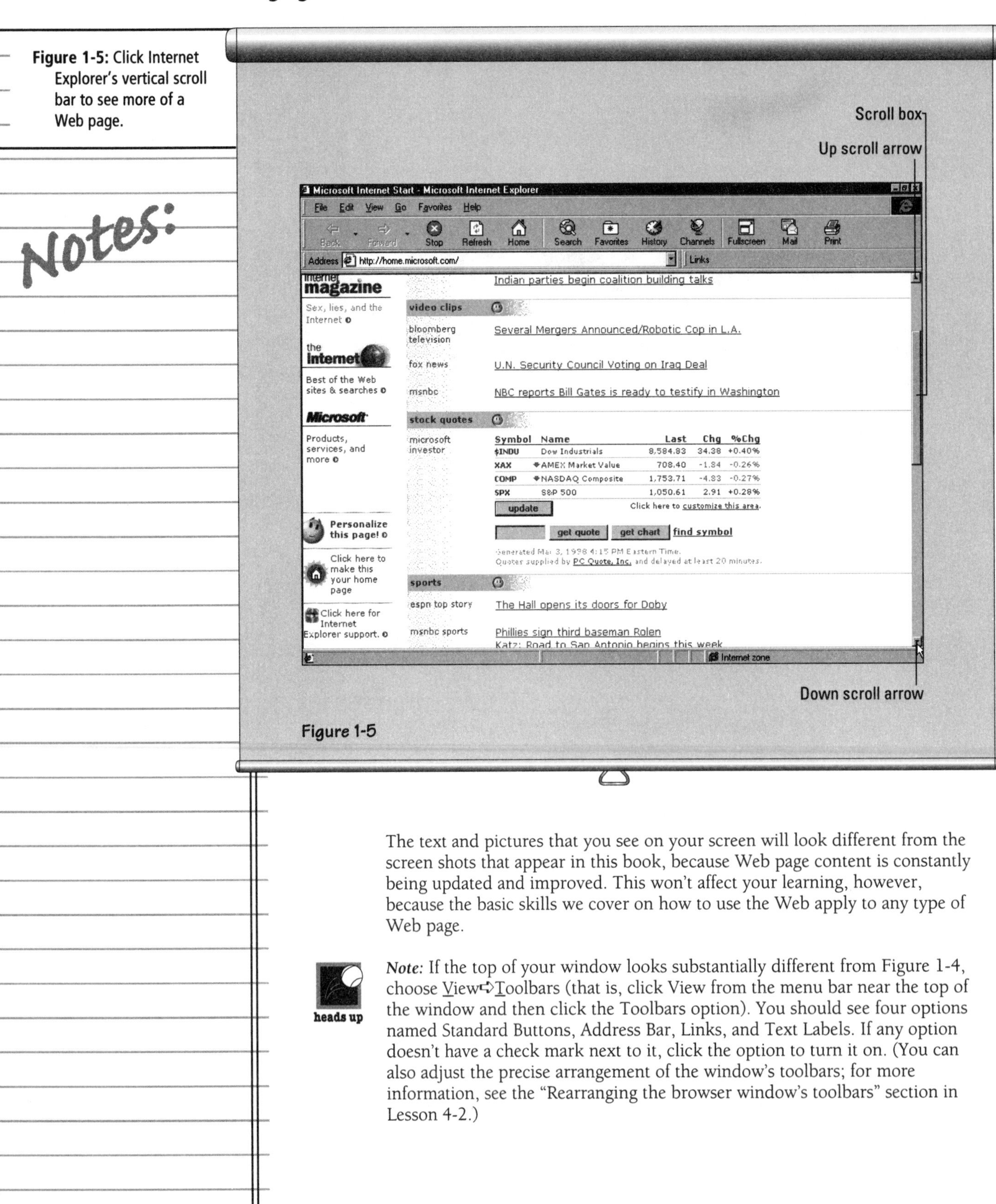

Figure 1-5

The text and pictures that you see on your screen will look different from the screen shots that appear in this book, because Web page content is constantly being updated and improved. This won't affect your learning, however, because the basic skills we cover on how to use the Web apply to any type of Web page.

heads up

Note: If the top of your window looks substantially different from Figure 1-4, choose View➪Toolbars (that is, click View from the menu bar near the top of the window and then click the Toolbars option). You should see four options named Standard Buttons, Address Bar, Links, and Text Labels. If any option doesn't have a check mark next to it, click the option to turn it on. (You can also adjust the precise arrangement of the window's toolbars; for more information, see the "Rearranging the browser window's toolbars" section in Lesson 4-2.)

Moving up and down a Web page

If you take a close look at the page displayed in your Internet Explorer window, you see that only part of the page is visible. Web pages are almost always longer than a browser's window, so you typically must view them a section at a time. One way to view different sections of a page is to use the vertical scroll bar — that is, the gray stripe along the right edge of your Internet Explorer window.

The vertical scroll bar has three main elements: the down and up scroll arrows on its ends and the scroll box between them, which indicates by its position in the bar just how far down you are on the page (see Figure 1-5). Clicking the down or up arrow moves the page about a line at a time, and clicking and dragging the scroll box, as described in the next exercise, moves you around the page more rapidly.

1. **Click the down arrow of your window's vertical scroll bar.**

   The page scrolls down a bit in your window, allowing you to see more of the page's content.

2. **Click the down arrow repeatedly until the scroll box is at the bottom of the bar.**

   The page continues to scroll down until the end of its content appears in the window.

3. **Click the up arrow of the vertical scroll bar.**

   The page scrolls up a bit in the window.

4. **Click the scroll box in the vertical scroll bar and, while keeping your mouse button pressed, drag the box to the top of the bar.**

   This procedure is called *clicking and dragging.* After you move the scroll box, the page jumps back up in the window to its top section.

clicking and dragging = clicking an object and, while keeping your mouse button held down, moving your mouse

Of course, if you get tired of using the scroll bar, you can press your keyboard's PgDn and PgUp keys instead.

1. **Press PgDn.**

   The page zips down, displaying its lower section in your window.

2. **Press PgUp.**

   The page swooshes up to its top section again.

to examine a Web page, click the vertical scroll bar arrows or press the PgDn and PgUp keys

That's all there is to moving up and down in a Web page!

To sum up: Your browser window is almost always shorter than the Web page you're looking at. To see the whole page, simply use the vertical scroll bar or the PgDn and PgUp keys.

Figure 1-6: When you point to regular text on a Web page, your mouse pointer retains its arrowhead shape.

Figure 1-7: When you point to a Web page link, your mouse pointer changes to the shape of a pointing hand.

PC Magazine: Internet Explorer 4.0 "Best Web Browser of 1997"
We can't say it any better than PC Magazine: "The browser that provides the best Web experience today and promises the best for tomorrow is Microsoft Internet Explorer 4.0. Whether you want a state-of-the-art browser, a very capable mail client, or best-of-breed conferencing tools, you'll find what you need with the free IE4 and its added components, Outlook Express, and NetMeeting." Download Internet Explorer today!

Figure 1-6

PC Magazine: Internet Explorer 4.0 "Best Web Browser of 1997"
We can't say it any better than PC Magazine: "The browser that provides the best Web experience today and promises the best for tomorrow is Microsoft Internet Explorer 4.0. Whether you want a state-of-the-art browser, a very capable mail client, or best-of-breed conferencing tools, you'll find what you need with the free IE4 and its added components, Outlook Express, and NetMeeting." Download Internet Explorer today!

Figure 1-7

Finding links on a Web page

Notice that certain phrases and images on the Web page that you're viewing are distinguished from the other text and pictures by underlines, different colors, or other effects. Such markings indicate that these areas are links that you can use to jump to other Web pages.

Finding out whether a highlighted phrase or image is really a link is easy. All you have to do is move your mouse.

1. **Move your mouse pointer over a word, phrase, or picture that you suspect is a link.**

   If the area that you choose is a link, your mouse pointer changes from its usual arrowhead shape to a hand with a pointing finger (see Figures 1-6 and 1-7).

2. **Move your mouse pointer slowly over every area of the Web page in your window.**

   Your mouse pointer turns into a hand when it's over areas that are links, and the pointer reverts to its usual arrowhead shape when it's over areas that contain only normal text and pictures.

Identifying a link's electronic address

URL = electronic address of a Web page or other information area on the Net

Another way to prove that you found a link is to keep an eye on the gray status bar at the bottom of your window (see Figure 1-8). When your mouse is pointing to a link, the status bar displays the Internet location, or electronic *address,* of the page to which the link takes you. This location is called a *URL.* (Actually, the official techie term is *Uniform Resource Locator,* but, understandably, almost everybody just calls 'em URLs.) For example, the URL of the page in Figure 1-8 is `http://www.rubberflex.com`. That's why (in case you were wondering) the address `http://www.rubberflex.com/` appears in the Address bar in the upper portion of that window. Similarly, you can tell the URL of the page that *you're* on right now by looking at the contents of your window's Address bar — that is, the bar that starts with the word `Address` and an "e" (for Explorer) icon, followed by a long text box that displays the URL of whatever Internet area you're currently visiting.

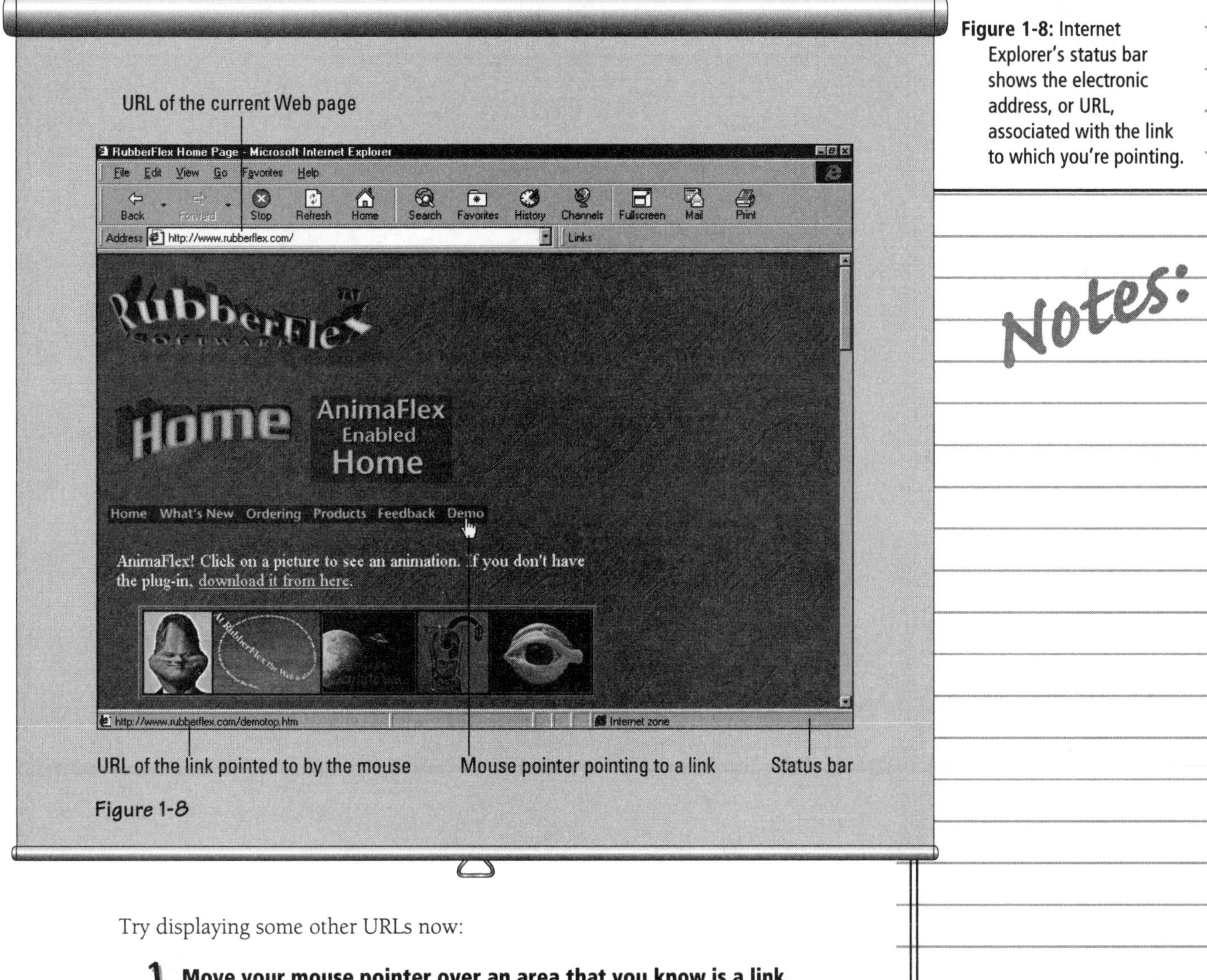

Figure 1-8

Figure 1-8: Internet Explorer's status bar shows the electronic address, or URL, associated with the link to which you're pointing.

Notes:

Try displaying some other URLs now:

1. **Move your mouse pointer over an area that you know is a link.**

   Your mouse pointer turns into a hand, and the address of the Web page associated with the link — that is, the page's URL — is displayed in the status bar at the bottom of the window.

2. **Move your mouse pointer over a different area that you know is a link.**

   Your mouse pointer remains a hand, but the Web address in the status bar changes to reflect the URL of the new link that you're on.

3. **Move your mouse pointer over an area that you know is *not* a link.**

   Your mouse pointer reverts to its arrowhead shape, and the status bar either goes blank or displays a previous message (such as `Done`) because you're no longer pointing to an area associated with a URL.

☑ **Progress Check**

If you can do the following, you've mastered this lesson:

❑ Connect to a Web page.

❑ Move up and down a Web page.

❑ Locate links on a Web page.

❑ Identify the URL associated with a link.

extra credit

The wacky world of URLs

Some fun facts about Web page URLs:

- Web URLs usually have the format `http://www.name.com`.
- Web URLs usually begin with *http://*, which stands for *HyperText Transfer Protocol*. *HyperText* refers to the art of linking disparate sections of text together; *transfer* refers to the transmission of data; and *protocol* refers to the rules and standards that allow computers to communicate with each other.
- Following the double slash *(//)*, Web URLs usually sport a *www* — which stands for World Wide Web— and a period (also referred to as a *dot*).
- Following *www.*, URLs usually contain a name representing the organization affiliated with the Web site, plus another period; for example, *att.* for AT&T or *microsoft.* for — well, you know.
- U.S. Web sites have URLs that usually end with a three-letter code, such as *com* for a commercial organization, *gov* for a government department, *mil* for a military site, *edu* for an educational institution, *net* for groups running a network (that is, a bunch of connected computers), and *org* for miscellaneous others (such as nonprofit organizations).
- Non-U.S. Web sites have URLs that usually end in a two-letter country code, such as *au* for Australia, *ca* for Canada, *fr* for France, *jp* for Japan, and *se* for Sweden.
- URLs can also refer to other areas of the Internet. Non-Web codes include *ftp://* for FTP file transfers (see Lesson 9-4) and *news://* for newsgroups (see Unit 7).

You don't really need to remember any of this stuff. Then again, the info may prove handy for impressing people at parties.

Lesson 1-3 Cruising the Web by Using Links

Now that you know how to move around a Web page and identify its links, you're ready for the big step — jumping to another Web page.

to use a link, click it

To perform this incredible technical feat, you need to do two things: Point to a link, and click. It's that simple!

After you click, Internet Explorer uses the Web address associated with the link to connect you to the page to which you want to jump. If the page is available (for example, if it isn't tied up by too many other people trying to access it simultaneously), Internet Explorer connects to the page and copies its text, pictures, and other data to your browser window. When that process is complete, you're all set to explore the new page.

Sound good? Then go for it!

1. **If you aren't still online, repeat the steps at the beginning of Lesson 1-2 to run Internet Explorer and connect to the Internet.**

   Your browser window should be maximized and displaying a Web page.

2. **Point to a link that interests you on the current Web page.**

   Your mouse pointer turns into a hand, and the URL of the link — that is, the address of the Web page the link is associated with — appears in the status bar.

3. **Click (that is, press your left mouse button).**

   The Internet Explorer logo in your window's upper-right section starts rotating like a planet with a moon revolving around it. This eye-catching activity is a cool way of letting you know that Internet Explorer is operating to fulfill your request for new data.

   At the same time, several notices appear in the status bar, although some may flash by too quickly for you to read. First, you see `Connecting to site`, which indicates that Internet Explorer is trying to connect to the URL you selected. Next — if you connect to the page successfully — you see `Web site found.`, `Waiting for reply`, and `Opening page` messages, which mean that Internet Explorer is transmitting the text and graphics of the new Web page to your computer. As bits of the new page appear, Internet Explorer continuously indicates how much data still needs to be transferred to complete the process. Finally, you see the message `Done`, which means that Internet Explorer successfully copied all of the new Web page's contents to your computer. Also, the "e" logo stops rotating to show that the data transfer has been completed. (If the transfer was *not* successful for some reason, simply try again by clicking a different link.)

4. **Read the new page.**

   Skim through the page. When you're done, pick out a link on this page that interests you.

5. **Point to a link for a page that you want to explore and then click the link.**

   Once again, the status bar displays `Connecting to site` and `Opening page` notices. A short time after that, the page you selected appears on your screen.

6. **Read the new page.**

   Notice that this page contains links leading to additional Web pages.

7. **Point to a link for a page that you want to explore and then click the link.**

   Again, the status bar displays `Connecting to site` and `Opening page` notices. A short time after that, the page you selected appears on your screen.

Clearly, you could go on and on like this, jumping from Web page to Web page. (Indeed, we've lost more people that way. . . .) However, for now, you should push on to the next exercise.

Notes:

Figure 1-9: Internet Explorer's Back, Forward, and Home buttons make jumping back and forth between Web pages that you visit in the same session a snap.

Notes:

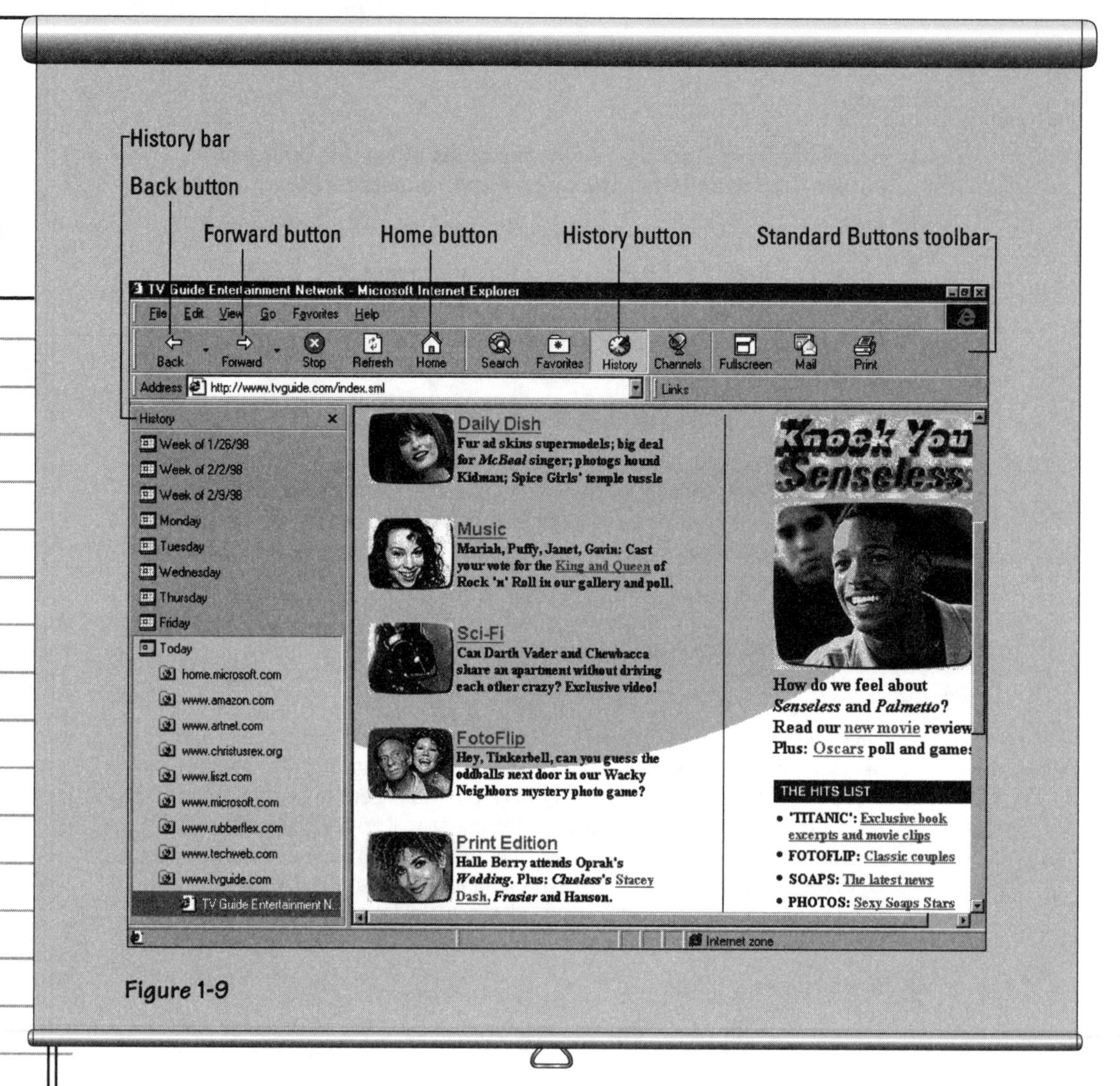

Figure 1-9

click the Stop button to quit transferring a Web page to your browser

Typically, you receive all of a Web page's data within a minute or two. Occasionally, however, a page requires more time. In such a case, the page may have lots of pictures (which take much longer to transmit than text), numerous other people may be trying to access the page simultaneously, or the Web site may be experiencing technical problems. If you become impatient, you can abort a transfer by clicking the Stop button, which is on the Standard Buttons toolbar near the top of the browser window. You can then read whatever information and use whatever links on the page were transmitted before you clicked Stop.

Another way to avoid long waits is to prevent Internet Explorer from automatically transferring pictures at all. For more information about this option, see the "Cruising without pictures" section in Lesson 4-1.

Moving back and forth on the Web

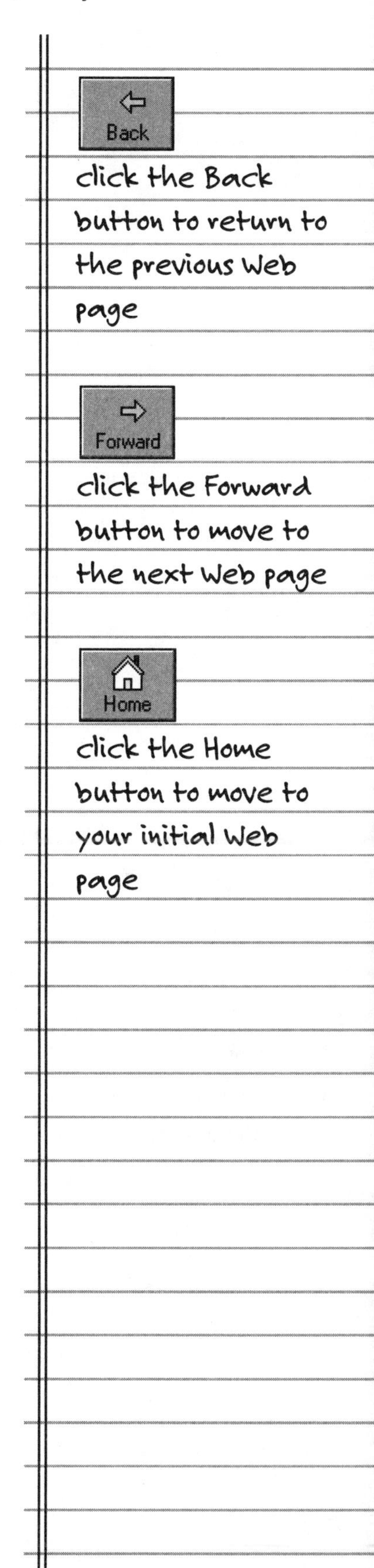

Constantly leaping to new Web pages is all well and good, but what if you want to go back to a previous page? No problem! All you've gotta do is click Internet Explorer's cleverly named Back button, which is the first button on the Standard Buttons toolbar (see Figure 1-9).

Similarly, if you want to move forward again, you can click — you guessed it! — Internet Explorer's Forward button. (Who says that computers are complicated?)

Finally, if you want to jump directly to your starting point, you can click Internet Explorer's Home button. This button instantly returns you to the place where you began your session (in this case, the Internet Explorer Communications home page).

But don't take our word for it; check it out for yourself. (You should still be connected to the Internet from the preceding exercise.)

1. **Click the Back button (the first button on the Standard Buttons toolbar).**

   The current Web page is quickly replaced in your window by the preceding page you viewed.

2. **Click the Back button again.**

   Again, the current page is replaced by the preceding page.

3. **Click the Back button again.**

   The current page is replaced by the preceding page. If you scrupulously followed the steps in the preceding exercise, this page is the page that you started on. (And if you didn't, simply click the Back button a few more times until you return to the page where you started.) The Back button is now dim, or *grayed out,* indicating that you can't move back any farther.

4. **Click the Back button again.**

   Nothing happens because you returned to your starting point.

5. **Click the Forward button, which is to the right of the Back button.**

   Your initial Web page is quickly replaced by the second page that you visited during this session.

6. **Click the Forward button again.**

   Your current page is replaced by the third page that you moved to during this session.

7. **Click the Forward button again.**

   Again, your current page is replaced by the next page that you visited during this session. If you scrupulously followed the steps in the preceding exercise, this page is the last page that you visited. (And if you didn't, simply click the button a few more times until you arrive at your last page.) The Forward button dims to indicate that you can't move forward any farther.

Notes:

8. **Click the Forward button again.**

   Nothing happens because you reached the end of the sequence of Web page links that you selected.

9. **Click the Home button (the button on the toolbar that looks like a house).**

   You immediately jump back to your starting point, the Internet Explorer Communications home page.

We're tempted to note the last step of this exercise proves that, through the wonders of technology, you *can* go home again. However, we're worried that you'd want to hit us if we did, so we won't.

Remember, click the Back button to move to the preceding Web page, click the Forward button to move to the next Web page, and click Home to return immediately to your initial Web page.

The Back, Forward, and Home buttons keep track of only the Web pages that you select during your *current* Internet session. When you disconnect by closing Internet Explorer, these buttons "forget" the Web pages that you just visited; and when you reopen Internet Explorer for a new session, the buttons start from a clean slate, paying attention only to the Web pages that you visit during your new session.

Using the File menu and History bar

The Back and Forward buttons are all you need for moving among a few Web pages. If you're using ten or more Web pages during a session, however, you may find it a nuisance to click through lots of intermediate pages to reach the one you want. In such cases, you can use Internet Explorer's File menu, which lists the URL of each page that you've visited and lets you move directly to whichever URL you choose. For a demonstration, follow these steps:

to return directly to a Web page, use the File menu

1. **Choose File (that is, click the File heading on the menu bar).**

   A menu pops down that, in its lower section, lists the URL of each Web page you've visited during this session. Also, a check mark appears next to the URL of the page you're currently on.

2. **Click a URL without a check mark next to it.**

   You move to the Web page located at the URL that you selected.

3. **Choose File again.**

   The menu pops down, and the check mark now appears next to the URL that you selected.

4. **Click a URL without a check mark next to it.**

   You move to the Web page located at the new URL that you selected. (And so on.)

That's all there is to returning to a Web page via the File menu!

Tip: You can also display mini-lists of Web pages by using the thin buttons to the right of the Back and Forward buttons, or by right-clicking. Specifically, if you click the thin button directly to the right of the Back button, or right-click the Back button, a list of the Web pages you can move back to appears. Similarly, if you click the thin button directly to the right of the Forward button, or right-click the Forward button, a list of the Web pages you can move Forward to appears. You can then move to any listed page by clicking the page's name.

The File menu has a limited amount of space and so can list only a small number of Web pages. Also, like the Back and Forward buttons, the File menu keeps track of the Web pages that you select during your current Internet session exclusively; every time you restart Internet Explorer for a new session, the File menu begins with a clean slate, paying attention just to the Web pages that you visit during your new session.

So, what if you visit too many pages during a session to be listed on the File menu, or if you want to access pages that you visited in previous sessions? Simple; click the History button on the window's toolbar. Doing so opens a History bar that runs down the left edge of your window and can display a virtually unlimited number of URLs. In addition, the History bar remembers not only the pages you've visited during your current session, but pages that you visited days ago, or even *weeks* ago. Try it!

1. **Click the History button from the Standard Buttons toolbar.**

   After a few moments, a History bar appears in the left side of your window (see Figure 1-9). This bar displays a folder for each Web site you've visited and the name of each Web page you've visited within the site. To move to a Web page, first click the URL of the site that contains the page (if the site's folder isn't already open) and then click the name of the page.

   If this isn't the first time you've used Internet Explorer, the History bar also includes folders for pages you've visited in previous days, and even previous weeks. You can list the pages you visited in any available time period by simply clicking the name of the day or week.

History

to switch between lots of Web pages, click the History button

2. **If the contents of the History bar are longer than your window, click the arrowhead at the bottom of the bar until you've scrolled through its list of Web sites.**

   You can scroll back up by clicking the arrowhead at the top of the History bar.

3. **Click a Web site with a closed folder (that is, a URL with a folder icon to its right but no Web pages indented under it).**

   The site's folder expands to display the Web pages you've visited from that site.

4. **Click a Web page from the site you've just opened.**

   After a few moments, the Web page appears in your browser window.

5. **Click a different Web page.**

   Again, the Web page you just chose appears in your browser window.

☑ Progress Check

If you can do the following, you've mastered this lesson:

- ❑ Move to a new Web page by using a link.
- ❑ Move to the preceding page, the next page, or your home page by using Internet Explorer's toolbar buttons.
- ❑ Move directly to a page by using the File menu.
- ❑ Move directly to a page by using the History bar.

6. **Click a Web site with an open folder (that is, a URL with Web pages indented under it).**

   The site's folder collapses to hide the pages you've visited from that site, providing more room on the bar for displaying other Web sites.

7. **Click the History button on the toolbar again.**

   The History bar disappears, returning your browser window to a full Web page display.

As you've just seen, the History bar stays open until you explicitly close it. When you need to switch among many Web pages frequently, you may find it convenient to leave the History bar displayed and move to each page you want by clicking it from the bar.

Tip: The History bar is normally set to remember the Web pages you've visited during the past 20 days. However, you can extend this period if you want a fuller record of your Web visits; or you can shorten it to save disk space, and to make the History bar less cluttered and easier to navigate. To learn how to set the number of days the History bar tracks, see the "Changing Internet Explorer settings" section in Lesson 4-2.

Recess

You have much more to learn about cruising the Web, but you've just mastered the basics. (And performed brilliantly!) Give yourself a reward (we favor chocolate) and then tackle the following tricky quiz questions.

Unit 1 Quiz

For each of the following questions, circle the letter of the correct answer or answers. Remember, each question can have more than one right answer.

1. **Before you can start using Internet Explorer, you need**

   A. Nerves of steel.

   B. A 14,400 bps, 33,600 bps, or 56,000 bps modem.

   C. An account with an Internet Service Provider (ISP).

   D. A copy of Internet Explorer version 4.0 or higher.

   E. Happy feet.

2. **Examples of popular ISPs include**

   A. AT&T WorldNet Service and Microsoft Network.

   B. McDonald's and Burger King.

C. America Online and CompuServe.

D. Coke and Pepsi.

E. MindSpring and IBM Internet Connection.

3. The World Wide Web:

A. Was created by the U.S. military during the height of the Cold War in the 1950s.

B. Is currently funded by evil alien spiders.

C. Consists of electronic pages created by thousands of independent individuals and organizations from all over the globe.

D. Is often referred to as *the Wide W*.

E. Is typically accessed with a special program called a *WoWWzer*.

4. To determine whether a word, phrase, or image on a Web page is a link:

A. Ask it politely.

B. Look for a chain icon to its left.

C. Check whether it's surrounded by the colors of the rainbow.

D. Move your mouse pointer over it and see whether the pointer changes to a hand.

E. Move your hand over it and see whether your fingers change to mouse pointers.

5. A URL is

A. An address indicating the electronic location of something on the Internet, such as a Web page.

B. The name of a hot Irish rock band.

C. Internet shorthand for *URban Legend*, meaning a story that may sound plausible but isn't true.

D. The title of episode 68 of *The X-Files*.

E. What appears in Internet Explorer's status bar when you point to a link.

6. To return to a Web page you've visited during your current session, you can

A. Click the Back button until you return to the page.

B. Right-click the Back button to display a list of Web pages and then click the page you want.

C. Click the page's name from the File menu or the History bar.

D. Click a link that points to the page.

E. Click the Lost & Found button and then follow the prompts.

Notes:

Unit 1 Exercise

Notes:

If your setup is typical, you can run Internet Explorer and your dialer program independently of each other. Try it!

1. Launch Internet Explorer to both run the program and pop up your Internet dialer program.
2. Connect to the Internet.
3. Disconnect from the Internet without closing Internet Explorer. (*Hint:* Double-click the dialer's modem icon from the right side of the taskbar to pop up a dialog box with a disconnect option.)
4. Because you're not being charged for online time now, spend a few leisurely minutes examining the Internet Explorer browser window, including its various menus and buttons.
5. Fire up the dialer by itself. (***Hint:*** Look for a dialer icon that you can double-click.)
6. Reconnect to the Internet. After you connect, Internet Explorer automatically becomes your window on the Net again.
7. Click the browser window's Close button. This action should exit Internet Explorer but maintain your Internet connection (indicated by your dialer's modem icon appearing unchanged in the taskbar's system tray). You can now run Internet programs other than Internet Explorer. You'll learn how to get such programs directly from the Web in Lesson 3-2. You can also find Internet programs on the CD that came with this book; for more information, see Appendix B.
8. Log off from the Internet using your dialer program.

Unit 2

Searching for Information on the Web

Objectives for This Unit

- ✓ Using favorites to move to Web pages
- ✓ Creating favorites
- ✓ Organizing favorites
- ✓ Typing in a URL
- ✓ Searching a Web page for information
- ✓ Searching the entire Web for information

The World Wide Web encompasses tens of millions of Web pages — a mind-boggling amount of information. To help you navigate your way through this sea of data, Internet Explorer provides you with several invaluable tools. These include *favorites,* which let you create pointers to your favorite Web pages; an *Address bar* that allows you to type in Web addresses; a search command that helps you quickly locate information on a Web page; and access to powerful search programs that help you locate information *anywhere* on the Web. This unit will teach you how to use these tools to cruise the Web like a pro.

Prerequisites

- Cruising the Web with Internet Explorer (Lessons 1-2 and 1-3)

on the CD

- Exercise folder +Hy's and Margy's Favorites+

Lesson 2-1

Cruising the Web by Using Favorites

As you saw in Unit 1, links on Web pages give you an intuitive, rambling way to explore the Web and discover information you didn't even know you wanted. When you find a Web page that you consider especially useful, however, you may want some way of returning to it easily and repeatedly. The navigation tools you've learned about so far — such as Internet Explorer's Back and Forward buttons and its File menu — let you return to pages that you've visited during your current session, but they don't maintain a permanent record of those pages for future sessions.

Fortunately, Internet Explorer also provides a nifty feature called *favorites.* Just as a bookmark helps you quickly go to a particular page in a book, a favorite lets you jump to a particular page on the Web.

A favorite is a type of link; after you click it, you go to the Web page it represents. What distinguishes a favorite is that it's permanently stored on your hard disk (until you explicitly delete it), and it's always readily available from Internet Explorer via a Favorites menu. Therefore, you can use a favorite at any time to move to a specific Web page.

This lesson will show you how to use predefined favorites, create your own favorites, and delete favorites. By the time you're done, you'll be able to create a Web page library that's tailored to your personal tastes and needs.

Installing Hy's and Margy's Favorites

Favorites are stored on your hard disk in a folder named, appropriately, *Favorites* (which itself is stored within your Windows folder). Your Favorites folder is typically almost empty until you add favorites to it yourself. To jump-start your ability to get around the Web, however, we've created a folder crammed with favorites for what we consider to be many of the best sites on the Internet. To take advantage of this predefined collection of favorites, which is stored on your *Dummies 101* CD, follow these steps:

on the CD

1. **If Internet Explorer is currently running, choose File⇨Exit to close it.**

2. **Insert the CD that came with this book into your computer's CD-ROM drive.**

   Be careful to touch only the sides of the CD and to insert the CD with its printed side up.

3. **Click the Windows 98 Start button (located in the lower-left corner of your screen) and locate the Run option.**

   If you don't see the Run option, place your mouse pointer on the small arrowhead at the bottom of the menu until the menu scrolls up sufficiently to display the Run command.

Notes:

4 Click Run.

A Run dialog box appears that lets you type the name of a program you want to launch. If a program name already appears highlighted in the box, ignore it; the text will be replaced as soon as you begin typing.

5 Type d:\setup **— that is, the letter d, a colon (:), a backslash (\), and the program name** setup.

If your CD-ROM player isn't at D:, type the letter appropriate for your drive.

6 Press Enter or click OK.

The Run dialog box closes, and the CD's Installer program launches.

If this is the first time you're running the Installer, an IDG Books Worldwide license agreement is displayed. This is the only time you'll see this document.

7 Read (or at least skim) the license agreement to make sure you're comfortable with its terms. When you're ready, click the Accept button.

If you don't click Accept, you can't use the Installer program. After you click, a message tells you that the CD program is about to be launched.

8 Click OK.

After about a minute, an opening screen appears. Notice that the top option on this screen is named Install Favorites Folder.

9 Click the Install Favorites Folder option, and follow the prompts that appear on your screen to complete the installation.

When the installation is finished, you return to the opening screen.

10 Click the Exit button in the lower-right corner of the Installer window, and click the button on the left to confirm that you're done.

The Installer program closes.

11 Eject your *Dummies 101* CD and store it in a safe place.

Don't store it very far away, though; you'll need it again in subsequent units.

heads up

Note: If for some reason the preceding exercise doesn't work properly for you, you can install our favorites collection manually. To do so, first open a Windows Explorer window; switch to the *Dummies 101* CD in your CD-ROM drive; and locate and double-click a folder named HMFaves in the root (that is, the first level) of the CD to display a folder named +Hy's and Margy's Favorites+. Next, right-click the +Hy's and Margy's Favorites+ folder (that is, click it with your *right* mouse button), and click the Copy option from the menu that appears. Finally, use your Windows Explorer window to switch to your Windows folder and then to a subfolder named Favorites (in other words, move to the folder \Windows\Favorites); right-click a blank spot in the Favorites folder's list of files; and click the Paste option from the menu that appears. After a minute or two, the +Hy's and Margy's Favorites+ folder is copied to your Favorites folder, which completes the installation.

You now have a bunch of interesting Web page links. Proceed to the next section to check 'em out.

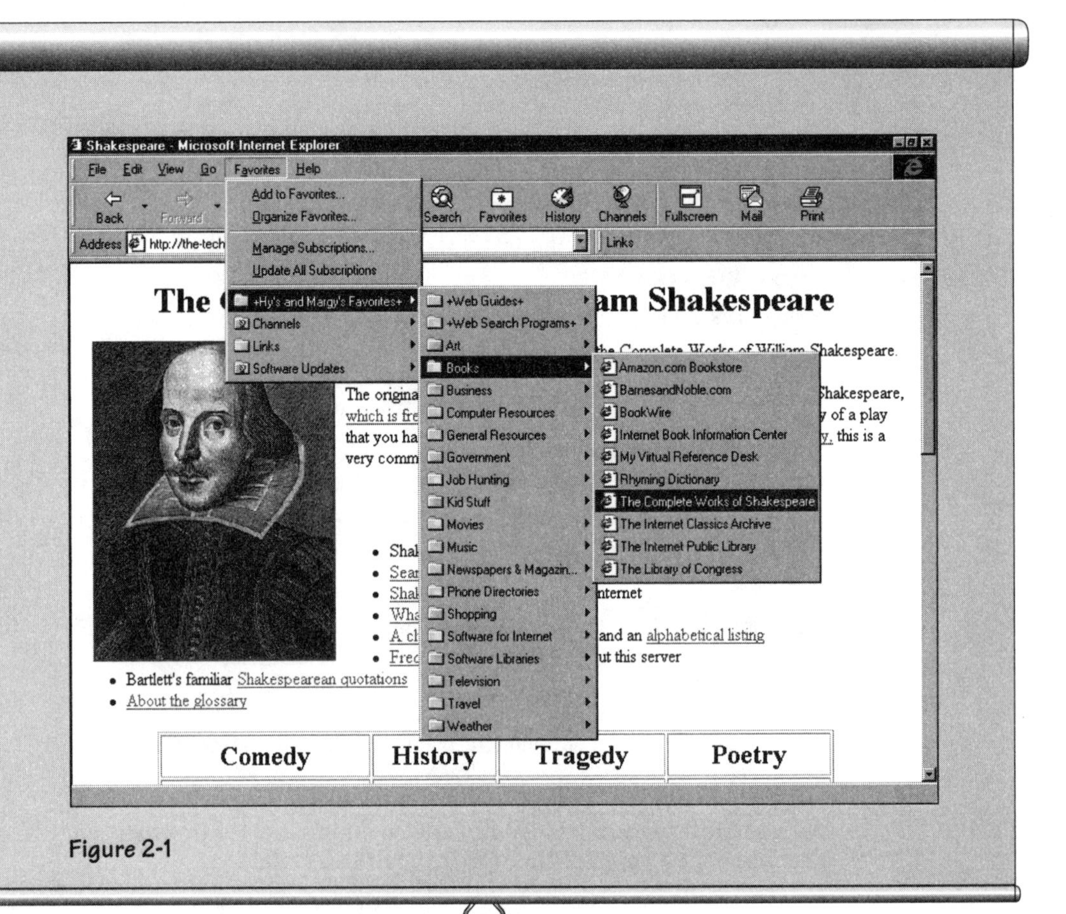

Figure 2-1: The folder you installed from your *Dummies 101* CD contains over 200 favorites, divided into 20 categories, that point to the best sites on the Web.

Leafing through your favorites

To examine the collection of favorites you just installed, follow these steps:

1 **Launch Internet Explorer and connect to the Net.**

Your browser window should be maximized and displaying a Web page. Notice that one of the window's menus is named Favorites.

2 **Click the Favorites menu.**

You see four options named Add to Favorites, Organize Favorites, Manage Subscriptions, and Update All Subscriptions. Below these options is a list of your available folders and favorites, including the +Hy's and Margy's Favorites+ folder that you installed in the preceding exercise.

3 **Click the +Hy's and Margy's Favorites+ folder.**

A list of subfolders representing Web page categories is displayed, as shown in Figure 2-1. You can move your mouse pointer over any category to view the favorites in that category.

4 Move your mouse pointer over the Books category folder.

You see the names of book-related Web sites, including The Internet Classics Archive (offers full-text translations of nearly 400 classic Greek, Roman, and Italian works, such as the *Iliad* and *Odyssey*), The Complete Works of Shakespeare (provides all the plays and sonnets of William Shakespeare), BookWire (supplies book news, reviews, and handy guides to book resources on the Net), and Amazon.com (an online bookstore with more than two million titles in its searchable electronic catalog).

5 Move your mouse pointer over Newspapers and Magazines.

You see the names of more Web sites, including *The New York Times* on the Web (a searchable version of the daily "newspaper of record"), *USA Today* (a searchable version of the visually splashy daily newspaper), *The Wall Street Journal* Interactive Edition (a source for up-to-date stock prices, business news, and other timely financial information), and Time Warner's Pathfinder (which lets you search for and read articles from a variety of Time-Warner publications, including *Entertainment Weekly, Fortune, Money, People, Sports Illustrated,* and *Time* magazine).

6 Move your mouse pointer over Job Hunting.

You see the names of additional Web sites, including America's Job Bank (lists over 250,000 jobs from 1,800 state Employment Service offices), CareerPath.com (lets you search through the employment ads of dozens of major newspapers, including *The New York Times, The Washington Post,* and the *Los Angeles Times*), and Online Career Center (lets you search for work by job category and region, and lets you post your resume online).

7 Move your mouse pointer over Travel.

You see the names of yet more Web pages, including City.Net (provides extensive information on virtually any city or region in the world), Microsoft Expedia (makes it easy to find and book the best airline ticket, hotel, and car rental for virtually any destination), and Epicurious Travel (helps you locate great vacation spots and gives you tips on how to best enjoy them).

8 Move your mouse pointer over the Epicurious Travel favorite (in the third menu).

After a few moments, a box pops down that shows you the URL of the Web page represented by the favorite — in this case, `http://travel.epicurious.com`. This is the URL you would move to if you clicked Epicurious Travel.

9 Return to the second menu, and move your mouse pointer over each of the other categories.

The 20 categories on the menu contain over 200 favorites that represent the very best sites on the Web.

10 Move your mouse pointer away from the menus and click on a blank spot anywhere in the window.

The menus close.

Notes:

Intrigued? Good! Because your next step is to use the favorites you just viewed to actually visit some of the coolest places the Net has to offer.

Using favorites to sample the best of the Web

As we mentioned previously, using a favorite to visit a Web page is just as easy as using a link — you simply point to it and click. The only caveat is that everything on the Internet changes rapidly, including Web addresses, so a favorite in the following exercise may no longer work by the time you try it. If you find that a favorite has expired, just select a different one.

1. **Choose Favorites⇨+Hy's and Margy's Favorites+⇨Books⇨The Complete Works of Shakespeare.**

   You're greeted with information about the bard and his works. If you're so inclined, delve deeper into this Web site by choosing to read scenes from a particular play. You don't have to rush; we'll wait for you. (After all, his work *is* timeless. . . .)

2. **Choose Favorites⇨+Hy's and Margy's Favorites+⇨Newspapers and Magazines⇨USA Today.**

   You see the latest headline news from *USA Today* (complete with full-color photographs!).

3. **Choose Favorites⇨+Hy's and Margy's Favorites+⇨Travel⇨City.Net.**

   You're met by a map of the world and an invitation to click the name of the area in which you're interested. Follow the prompts and click progressively more detailed maps until you zero in on information about the country, state, or city you're seeking.

Pretty nifty, huh?

If you enjoyed visiting those Web sites, you may want to take some time to explore a few of the other Web pages represented in your Favorites folder. In each case, move to the site that you want by clicking the Favorites menu, clicking the +Hy's and Margy's Favorites+ folder, moving your mouse pointer over the appropriate category, and finally clicking the favorite you're after.

Tip: Another way to navigate your collection of favorites is to click the Favorites button on the Standard Buttons toolbar. This opens a Favorites bar that runs down the left side of your window and that can be more convenient to use because, unlike the Favorites menu, it stays open until you explicitly close it. On the other hand, the Favorites bar takes up a substantial portion of your window, which leaves less room for the display of the Web pages you want to view. When you're finished using the Favorites bar, close it by clicking the Favorites button again.

After you're done exploring, go on to the next lesson, which explains how to create and organize favorites.

☑ Progress Check

If you can do the following, you've mastered this lesson:

- ❑ Install a file containing predefined favorites.
- ❑ Display favorites from the Favorites menu.
- ❑ Use favorites to move to Web pages.

Favorites

Favorites button

Creating and Organizing Favorites

Lesson 2-2

Using predefined favorites is a fun and easy way to get acquainted with what's available on the Web. Nobody else can judge which Web pages are of the most interest to *you*, however, so we recommend that you get in the habit of creating and organizing your *own* favorites. If you do so regularly and thoughtfully, you'll soon build up an extremely useful Web page library tailored to your particular needs.

Creating favorites

Creating a favorite is easy, and you can do it in several ways. First, move to the Web page for which you want to create a permanent link. You can then perform any of the following actions:

on the test

- **Press Ctrl+D:** Hold down the Ctrl key and tap the "D" key to add the current Web page to the bottom of your Favorites list. This method is the fastest way to create a favorite.
- **Drag the page icon to the Favorites menu:** Between the word "Address" and the URL in the Address bar is an icon that looks like the letter "e" in front of a paper page. Click this *page icon* (which represents the Web page being displayed) and drag it over to the Favorites menu to open the menu; continue dragging the icon down and across menus until you open a category folder that's appropriate for the page; drag the icon into the folder and position it where you want it; and release your mouse button to store the new favorite in the folder. This slick method lets you both create and file a favorite in one step, which helps keep your favorites organized and easy to find.
- **Choose Favorites⇨Add to Favorites:** Click the top option on the Favorites menu to pop up an Add Favorite dialog box. Like the preceding method, the dialog box lets you select a category folder for storing your favorite. In addition, however, it allows you to rename the favorite and to set Internet Explorer to periodically check the favorite's Web page for updated information. This method is the slowest, but it provides you with the most choices.

After you've created a favorite, you can use it in exactly the same way you use a predefined favorite — that is, by displaying it via the Favorites menu and clicking it.

Try out the various ways of making a favorite by working through the next three exercises.

Notes:

to create a favorite, press Ctrl+D, or drag the page icon to the Favorites menu, or choose Favorites→Add to Favorites

Creating a favorite with a keystroke

To create a favorite quickly, follow these steps:

1. **If you aren't still connected to the Internet, log on again now.**

   Your browser window should be maximized and displaying a Web page.

2. **Examine the current Web page and locate a link that interests you.**

   When you point to the link, your mouse pointer turns into a hand, and the link's URL appears in the status bar.

3. **Click the link.**

   You move to the Web page associated with the link.

4. **Repeat Steps 2 and 3 until you reach a page that you'd enjoy visiting repeatedly in the future.**

   You're on a Web page that you've reached through a series of links.

5. **Press Ctrl+D.**

   A favorite pointing to the page is added to the bottom of your favorites list. To verify this, display the Favorites menu.

6. **Click Favorites from the menu bar.**

   You see a favorite for the current Web page at the bottom of the menu, proving that you successfully created a permanent link to the page.

7. **Click the Home button on the Standard Buttons toolbar.**

   You move to your initial Web page.

8. **Click the Favorites menu and then click the favorite you just created.**

   You move to the Web page represented by the favorite, proving that your new favorite works.

Creating a favorite using the page icon

Pressing Ctrl+D is the fastest way to create a favorite, but it doesn't give you the opportunity to file the favorite in an appropriate category folder. You can always move the favorite into a folder later on (as you'll see shortly in this lesson's "Organizing Favorites" section), but you can spare yourself some extra work by creating and filing the favorite at the same time. Try doing so now by using the Address bar's page icon:

page icon

1. **Browse the Web until you reach a page that you'd enjoy visiting repeatedly in the future.**

   You're on a Web page that interests you.

2. **Click the page icon (the "e" icon directly in front of the page's URL in the Address bar) and, while keeping your mouse button held down, drag the icon to the Favorites menu.**

   The Favorites menu opens.

Notes:

3. **Drag the page icon down and across Favorites menus until you open a folder whose category matches the subject covered by the Web page; drag the icon into the folder until it's positioned where you want it; and then release your mouse button.**

   Your favorite is both created and filed in the folder that you selected.

4. **Move to a different page by clicking the Internet Explorer logo in the upper-right section of the window.**

   You move to the Microsoft Internet home page at `home.microsoft.com`! That's because, in addition to its function as an activity indicator, the logo acts as a favorite that always points to this Microsoft page.

5. **Click the Favorites menu and then move your mouse pointer over the folder you selected in Step 3.**

   You see the favorite that you just created stored inside the folder.

6. **Click your new favorite.**

   You move to the Web page associated with the favorite, proving that this second favorite you made works perfectly, too.

Creating a favorite using the Add Favorite dialog box

As you've just seen, using the page icon lets you file a favorite at the same time that you create it. However, there are also other actions you can take when creating a favorite. For example, you can edit the favorite's name, which we recommend doing because the default name (copied from the Web page's title bar) is likely to either be too wordy or provide too little information.

on the test

In addition, you can *subscribe* to the favorite's Web page. Subscribing to a page has nothing to do with signing up with the page's creators or paying a fee. Instead, it simply means setting Internet Explorer to automatically check the page on a regular basis for changes. Whenever Internet Explorer finds that the page's contents have been updated, it can do three things to notify you:

- Add a red tinge to the page's favorite to visually notify you that new information is available.
- Send you an e-mail message telling you that the page has been updated (which is a very cool option, though probably overkill for anything but the most timely and important Web pages).
- Actually copy the updated page to your hard disk during a period when your PC isn't busy — for example, at night or during your lunch hour. You can then examine the page at your leisure, even when you aren't connected to the Net.

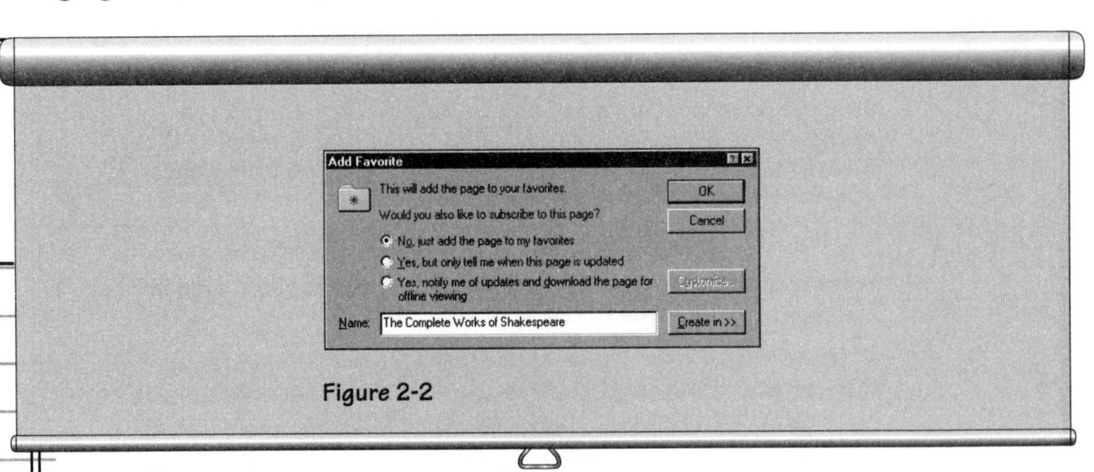

Figure 2-2: Use the Add Favorite dialog box to set the name, folder location, and subscription status of a new favorite.

You can always file, rename, and/or subscribe to a favorite *after* you create it (as you'll see in the next section), but you may find it more convenient to tackle those housekeeping chores up front. To be offered the maximum number of options when making a favorite, follow these steps:

1. **Browse the Web until you reach a page that you'd enjoy visiting repeatedly in the future.**

   You're on a Web page that interests you.

2. **Click the Favorites menu.**

   Notice that the top option on the menu is named Add to Favorites.

3. **Choose the Add to Favorites option.**

   An Add Favorite dialog box like the one in Figure 2-2 appears. At its bottom is a Name box that lets you edit the name of your favorite. Take advantage of this option, because the default text (which is the name that appears in the page's title bar) is unlikely to be as helpful as a label that you supply.

4. **Click in the Name box, and revise the existing text to create an appropriate name for your favorite.**

   You can edit the text using standard word processing keystrokes, such as Backspace and Del to delete a character at a time, Ctrl+Right Arrow and Ctrl+Left Arrow to move forward or backward by a word at a time, and End and Home to jump to the end or start of the line.

   After you're done, notice that the dialog box also includes a Create In button, which allows you to select a folder for storing your new favorite. Take advantage of this option as well, because filing your favorite properly will make it easy to find when you need it.

5. **Click the Create In button.**

   A tree-like list of your primary favorites folders pops down from the bottom of the dialog box. You can open any folder by double-clicking it or by clicking the plus (+) sign to its left. After you do so, the folder expands to display its subfolders (if any). Similarly, you can close the folder again by double-clicking it or by clicking the minus (-) sign to its left, which hides the folder's contents and prevents the display from getting cluttered. Alternatively, if a folder doesn't already exist that's appropriate for your favorite, you can create one by clicking the New Folder button.

6. **Use your mouse to choose an appropriate folder for storing your new favorite (or optionally create a new folder).**

   After you've chosen a folder, it shows that it's been selected by displaying an open folder icon to the left of its name.

   Finally, notice that the second and third options in the dialog box allow you to subscribe to the current Web page, which sets Internet Explorer to automatically check the page once a day for changes. If you select the Yes, But Only Tell Me When This Page is Updated option, Internet Explorer will add a red tinge to the page's icon in your favorites list whenever it finds that the page has been revised. If you select the Yes, Notify Me of Updates and Download the Page for Offline Viewing option, Internet Explorer will both mark the page's icon red and actually copy the new page to your hard disk during a period when your PC isn't busy, allowing you to examine the new page at your leisure. You can also fine-tune your subscription options by clicking the dialog box's Customize button, which lets you do such things as adjust how frequently Internet Explorer checks the Web page and instruct Internet Explorer to send you an e-mail notification every time the page changes.

   You may occasionally want to subscribe to a page that contains timely and important information such as financial data. Most of the time, however, simply accept the No, Just Add the Page to My Favorites option, which is the default.

7. **Make sure that the No, Just Add the Page to My Favorites option is selected and then click the OK button (in the upper-right of the dialog box).**

   Your favorite is saved.

8. **Click the Home button on the toolbar.**

   You move to your initial Web page.

9. **Click the Favorites menu and move your mouse pointer over the folder you chose to store your new favorite.**

   You see the favorite, with the name you assigned it, among the contents of the folder.

10. **Click the favorite.**

    You move to the Web page represented by the favorite, proving that this third favorite you created performs as flawlessly as your two previous ones.

Nice work! The favorites you've just created will remain on your favorites list until you explicitly delete them. You learn how to remove favorites that are redundant or have outlived their usefulness in the next section.

Creating favorites is quick, easy, and even fun. Therefore, as you continue to cruise the Internet and discover interesting Web pages, don't hesitate to take advantage of this great feature.

Notes:

Creating Web page shortcuts

Creating a favorite isn't the only way for you to make a pointer to a Web page. You can also create a *shortcut,* which is a file that you can keep directly on your desktop. To do so, simply move to a Web page that you want to access frequently, click the page icon from the Address bar, and, while keeping your mouse button held down, drag the icon to your desktop. Lastly, release your mouse button. The shortcut to the Web page appears as an icon on your desktop!

If you double-click the shortcut when Internet Explorer is running, Internet Explorer responds by moving to the page. More importantly, if you double-click the shortcut when Internet Explorer *isn't* running, Internet Explorer and your dialer program automatically open, and, after you connect to the Net, Internet Explorer moves to the appropriate Web page. The latter is more efficient than clicking the Internet Explorer icon on the taskbar, clicking the Favorites menu, and then locating and clicking the favorite. It's best to avoid cluttering your desktop with a lot of icons, however, so we suggest that you create shortcuts for no more than two or three Web pages that you access constantly.

Organizing favorites

Just as you should keep your hard disk organized by grouping your files into folders, you should keep your favorites organized by grouping *them* into folders. Doing so helps to ensure that you can always find the favorite you need quickly and easily.

To put your favorites in order, first choose Favorites⇨Organize Favorites. This command opens an Organize Favorites dialog box that lets you create favorites folders and move or copy favorites between folders. In addition, the dialog box allows you to rename favorites, subscribe to favorites, and delete obsolete favorites.

To learn how to arrange and adjust existing favorites, follow these steps:

1. **Click the Favorites menu.**

   Notice that the second option on the menu is named Organize Favorites.

2. **Choose the Organize Favorites option.**

   An Organize Favorites dialog box appears that displays your primary folders and that has five unlabeled buttons in its upper-right section (as shown in Figure 2-3). The first button is named Up One Level, because it lets you move from a subfolder to its parent folder; and the middle button is named Create New Folder, because it lets you make additional folders for organizing favorites.

3. **Click the Create New Folder button (the third button in the upper-right section of the dialog box).**

   A new folder instantly appears, with the temporary name *New Folder* highlighted.

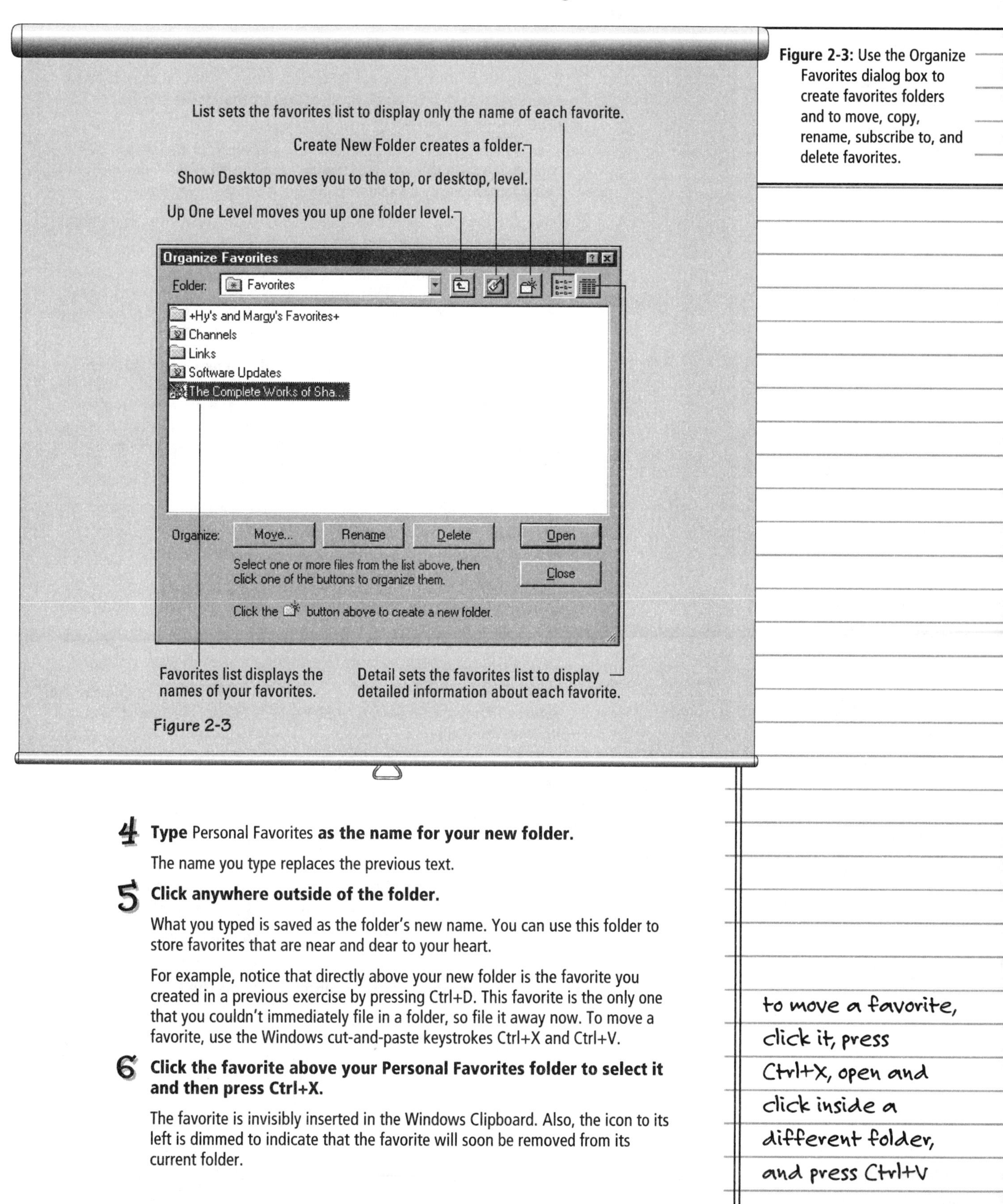

Figure 2-3

Figure 2-3: Use the Organize Favorites dialog box to create favorites folders and to move, copy, rename, subscribe to, and delete favorites.

4. **Type** Personal Favorites **as the name for your new folder.**

   The name you type replaces the previous text.

5. **Click anywhere outside of the folder.**

   What you typed is saved as the folder's new name. You can use this folder to store favorites that are near and dear to your heart.

   For example, notice that directly above your new folder is the favorite you created in a previous exercise by pressing Ctrl+D. This favorite is the only one that you couldn't immediately file in a folder, so file it away now. To move a favorite, use the Windows cut-and-paste keystrokes Ctrl+X and Ctrl+V.

6. **Click the favorite above your Personal Favorites folder to select it and then press Ctrl+X.**

   The favorite is invisibly inserted in the Windows Clipboard. Also, the icon to its left is dimmed to indicate that the favorite will soon be removed from its current folder.

to move a favorite, click it, press Ctrl+X, open and click inside a different folder, and press Ctrl+V to open a folder, double-click it

to return to the previous folder, click the Up One Level button

to copy a favorite, click it, press Ctrl+C, select a different folder, and press Ctrl+V

to rename a favorite, click it and click the Rename button

to subscribe to a Web page, right-click the page's favorite and choose Subscribe

to delete a favorite, click it and press the Del key

7. **Double-click your Personal Favorites folder (that is, click it twice in rapid succession) to open it; click anywhere inside the folder to select it; and press Ctrl+V.**

   Your favorite is inserted, or *pasted,* into the folder. Also, though you don't see it happen, the favorite is removed from its previous folder. To verify the deletion, return to your previous folder by clicking the Up One Level button.

8. **Click the Up One Level button (the first button in the upper-right section of the dialog box).**

   You return to your first-level folders. Double-clicking to move down a folder level and clicking the Up One Level button to move up a folder level is how you'll typically navigate your hard disk from a Windows 98 dialog box. You can now see that your favorite has been removed from its original location.

   Tip: If instead of moving a favorite, you want to *copy* it — for example, because you want it available in multiple folders for easy access — click the favorite and then press Ctrt+C instead of Ctrl+X. This places a copy of the favorite into the Clipboard but doesn't affect the original. You can then open and click inside a different folder, and press Ctrl+V to insert the copy.

9. **Double-click your Personal Favorites folder to open it again.**

   You see your favorite again. Next, improve your favorite's label by using the Rename button near the bottom of the dialog box.

10. **Click the favorite to select it and then click the Rename button (in the lower section of the dialog box).**

    The favorite's name is highlighted, allowing you to edit or replace the text.

11. **Type a name that best represents your favorite's Web page and then click anywhere outside the favorite to save your change.**

    The name you typed replaces the previous name. Since renaming is quick and easy, be sure to take advantage of this feature to clarify what each of your favorites represents.

    Now assume that you want to subscribe to your favorite's Web page. You can do so quickly by right-clicking.

12. **Click the favorite with your *right* (not left) mouse button and then choose Subscribe from the menu that appears.**

    A dialog box pops up that offers the same subscription options you saw previously after choosing Favorites⇨Add to Favorites. Optionally use the box to subscribe to the Web page, or simply click the Cancel button to exit the box.

    Finally, pretend that your favorite has become obsolete. You can eliminate a favorite by selecting it and pressing the Del key.

13. **Click the favorite to select it and then press the Del key.**

    The favorite disappears. It's not permanently gone yet, though; if you press Ctrl+Z right away, you can get it back, or *undelete* it.

14 Press Ctrl+Z.

The favorite reappears. This trick works only if you press Ctrl+Z immediately after pressing Del, however, so always think twice before deleting.

You've now finished running this favorite through its paces, so finish up by closing the dialog box.

15 Click the Close button (in the lower-right section of the dialog box).

The dialog box exits.

Tip: In addition to organizing favorites, you can organize your subscriptions to Web pages by choosing Favorites⇨Manage Subscriptions. You can also force Internet Explorer to immediately check all your subscription Web pages for changes by choosing Favorites⇨Update All Subscriptions. For more information about these commands, see Unit 8, "Tuning into Channels."

to restore a favorite you've accidentally deleted, immediately press Ctrl+Z

Notes:

Adding and revising favorites on the Links bar

If you expect to use a certain favorite constantly, you may prefer to access it directly from the browser window rather than always hunt around for it on the Favorites menu. For this reason, Internet Explorer allows you to create buttons that behave like favorites but are displayed on the *Links bar*, which is a gray bar near the top of the browser window.

heads up

Note: All Internet Explorer toolbars are moveable, but the Links bar is typically located either to the right of the Address bar or underneath the Address bar. If you can't find the Links bar, choose View⇨Toolbars⇨Links to turn on a check mark to the option's left.

Adding a button favorite to the Links bar is as easy as creating a conventional favorite. Simply move to a Web page that you expect to visit frequently, click and drag the page icon from the Address bar to the Links bar (as opposed to the Favorites menu), and release your mouse button. A button with the name of the Web page is created on the toolbar. You can then move to the Web page at any time by just clicking the button!

To take advantage of this nifty feature, follow these steps:

1 If you aren't still connected to the Internet, log on again now.

Your browser window should be maximized and displaying a Web page.

2 Move to a Web page that you expect to visit often (by using an existing favorite and/or by clicking links).

Notes:

3. **Click the page icon (the icon in front of the current page's URL in the Address bar) and, while keeping your mouse button held down, drag the icon to the Links bar; then release your mouse button.**

   A button is automatically created on your Links bar with the name of the Web page. (Only the first word or two of the name may fit on the bar, but if you hold your mouse pointer over the button for a second, the entire name is displayed — as well as the page's URL.)

4. **Click the Home button on the toolbar to move to a different page.**

   You move to your default home page.

5. **Click the button favorite you created on the Links bar.**

   You move to the Web page associated with the button, proving that your new button favorite works.

That's all it takes to add a button to the Links bar! To keep your Links bar useful, however, you should treat it like prime real estate — that is, a space to be kept well-ordered and free of clutter. You can delete obsolete buttons and reorganize buttons using the Organize Favorites dialog box. Give it a try:

1. **Choose Favorites⇨Organize Favorites.**

   The Organize Favorites dialog box appears.

2. **Double-click a folder named Links.**

   If you don't see the folder right away, scroll through the window until you find it. After you double-click, you should see your new favorite inside the Links folder.

3. **Click the favorite to select it and then press the Del key.**

   The favorite disappears. At the same time, its button disappears from the Links bar! (If you can't see the Links bar, click the title bar at the top of the dialog box and drag the box down until the Links bar is visible.)

4. **Press Ctrl+Z to restore the favorite.**

   The favorite reappears — and its button returns to the Links bar.

5. **Click the favorite again, press Del again, and click the dialog box's Close button.**

   The window exits — and the Links bar no longer displays the button that you created.

In other words, what's displayed on the Links bar is controlled by the favorites that you move, copy, rename, and delete in the Links folder. Therefore, any time that you want to revise the buttons on your Links bar, simply edit the contents of the bar's folder from the Organize Favorites dialog box.

As you've seen in this lesson, you have a lot of freedom in choosing how to create and organize your favorites. Play around with different options until you find the methods that work best for you.

☑ Progress Check

If you can do the following, you've mastered this lesson:

- ❑ Create favorites using Ctrl+D, the page icon, and the Favorites menu.
- ❑ Open and navigate the Organize Favorites dialog box.
- ❑ Create favorites folders.
- ❑ Move and copy favorites.
- ❑ Rename favorites.
- ❑ Subscribe to the Web pages of favorites.
- ❑ Delete and restore favorites.
- ❑ Add and delete buttons on the Links bar.

Recess

You've done a *fabulous* job of learning how to use cruise the Web with favorites, so take some time to brag to your friends about the new skills you've mastered. When you're refreshed, forge ahead to the next lesson, which teaches you how to jump directly to *any* Web page.

Entering URLs

Lesson 2-3

Cruising the Web using links is fast and fun, but it can take you only so far. For example, if a friend tells you the addresses of some hot new Web pages, or if a favorite magazine prints a list of great Web sites that you'd probably enjoy, how can you get to the Web pages unless you happen to have access to links that point to them? To take advantage of such recommendations, you need to know how to jump directly to a Web page by entering its URL (which, as we explained in Unit 1, is an electronic address that tells browsers such as Internet Explorer precisely where on the Net a particular Web page is located). By typing a page's URL, you can move straight to the page without passing Go!

on the test

Fortunately, typing a URL isn't very hard. To begin, click anywhere inside Internet Explorer's Address bar near the top of the browser window (see Figure 2-4). Your click highlights the text in the box, which is typically the URL of your current Web page. Start typing the URL of the new Web page that you're after; the first letter that you type automatically replaces the entire old URL. Finally, press Enter to activate your new URL. If you typed the URL correctly, Internet Explorer jumps to the Web page you want.

to enter a page's URL, click in the Address bar and then type the page's Web address

heads up

The only tricky part is that URLs are about as easy to remember and type correctly as social security numbers. You must remember to type a URL *carefully*. If you get even one number, letter, or punctuation mark wrong, the URL won't work, and you'll end up with an error message rather than a new Web page.

Note: Whether you type the characters in a URL in lowercase or uppercase usually doesn't matter, but using the capitalization that you're provided is the safest way to go.

On the up side, though, you seldom need to type a particular URL more than once. After the URL takes you to the Web page that it's associated with, you can click and drag the Address bar's page icon to create a favorite for the page, and then simply click your favorite to subsequently return to the page.

Maybe we're a tad biased, but the first URL that we want you to type goes to the *Dummies 101: The Internet for Windows 98* home page, which has the URL `http://net.gurus.com/net101`.

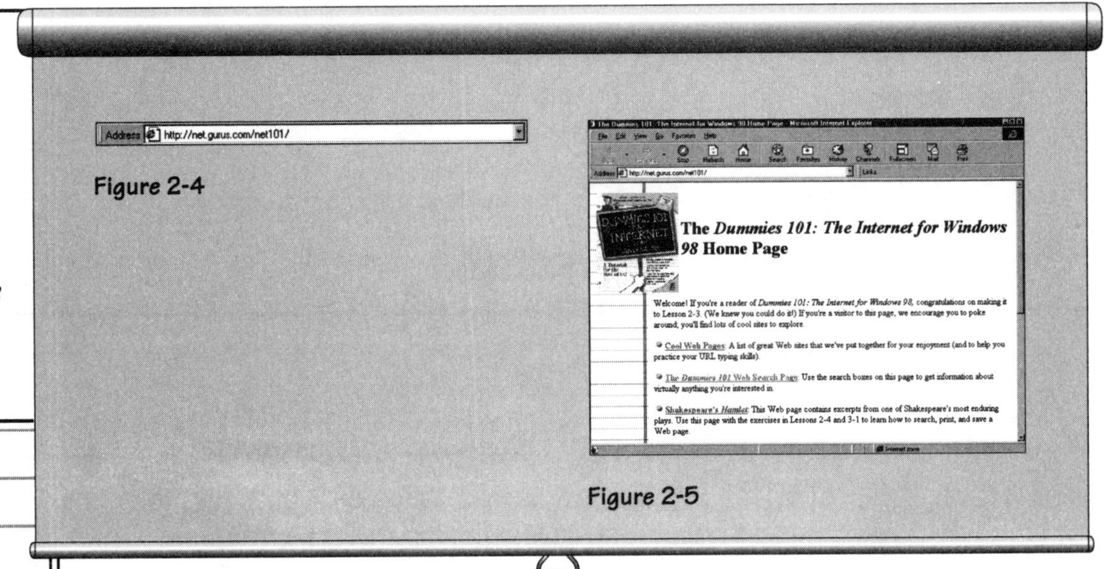

Figure 2-4

Figure 2-5

Figure 2-4: When you learn about a hot new Web page, check it out by typing its URL in Internet Explorer's Address bar.

Figure 2-5: You can find the *Dummies 101: The Internet for Windows 98* home page at `http://net.gurus.com/net101/`.

Tip: The first part of the *Dummies 101* Web page URL, *http://*, is the prefix for *all* Web page URLs, so you can skip typing it; when you press Enter, Internet Explorer fills in the http:// prefix for you automatically.

1. **Run Internet Explorer and connect to the Net.**

   Your browser window should be maximized and displaying a Web page.

2. **Click anywhere inside the Address bar (the long text box near the top of the window).**

   The text inside the box — which is the URL of your current page — is highlighted.

3. **Type** n.

   The first letter that you type (n) immediately replaces the highlighted text.

4. **Type** et **and a period.**

   The box contains `net.`, which stands for *Internet* and is the beginning of the *Dummies 101: The Internet for Windows 98* URL (following the standard http:// prefix, which you don't have to type). A URL can begin with anything, although many start with www (which, of course, stands for World Wide Web).

5. **Type** gurus **and a period.**

   The box contains `net.gurus.` The word *guru* means "guide," and it's part of the URL because this site plays host to several authors who act as Internet guides to readers of *Dummies 101* and *...For Dummies* books.

6 **Type** com **and a forward slash — that is, the / on the ? key.**

Note: Be sure to not confuse / with the backslash (\ ), which you use to specify file locations on your hard disk.

The box contains `net.gurus.com/`. The *com* text is a three-letter code that tells you the page is published by a commercial organization (as opposed to, say, a government agency or nonprofit organization). For a list of other common Internet three-letter codes, see "The wacky world of URLs" sidebar in Lesson 1-2.

You've now typed enough to specify the Internet For Dummies Central home page, which provides information about various *Dummies* books and their authors. Internet For Dummies Central is a perfectly nice page, and you should be sure to visit it later, but at the moment you want a different page, so you have one more piece of text to type.

7 **Type** net101 **to finish up.**

The box now contains `net.gurus.com/net101`. The *net101* text tells Internet Explorer that you want the *Dummies 101: The Internet for Windows 98* home page, so you've completed typing the URL.

8 **Press Enter.**

After a few moments, you move to this book's home page, which looks similar to Figure 2-5. If you examine the Address bar, you see that Internet Explorer has automatically filled in the prefix and added a final slash so that the URL now reads `http://net.gurus.com/net101/`.

Note: If you didn't connect properly, double-check your URL to make sure that you typed it correctly. If you did type the URL exactly as you see it in this book and you still don't reach the page, technical problems with the *Dummies* site may be blocking your progress — for example, the page may be too busy at the moment to accept your connection request — so just try again a little later until you access the page.

9 **Create a Links bar button to access the page easily.**

Click the page icon from the Address bar and, while keeping your mouse button held down, drag the icon to the Links bar. Finally, release your mouse button. A button favorite pointing to the *Dummies 101: The Internet for Windows 98* page magically appears on your Links bar.

Congratulations; you successfully typed a URL! You can now take advantage of any recommendation that you receive about the latest and greatest Web pages.

While you're on the *Dummies 101: The Internet for Windows 98* home page, take a few moments to look it over. We use this page quite a bit in subsequent exercises, so you may want to take some time to get to know it.

Notes:

Notes:

extra credit

URL typing tips

If you'd like to practice your newfound URL typing skills, try them on some of the hot Web sites listed on the *Dummies 101: The Internet for Windows 98* page. The list includes most of the Web sites you installed in Lesson 2-1 (with up-to-date links), as well as exciting new Web sites that have popped up since we created our favorites folder. Flex your fingers and get typing!

Tip #1: If a Web URL begins with `www` and ends with `com`, you can simply type the middle portion of the URL to get to the appropriate page; Internet Explorer fills in the rest of the URL for you automatically! For example, to jump to the first site on this list, `www.amazon.com`, you can just click in the Address bar, type *amazon* and press Enter. Try it!

Tip #2: Internet Explorer normally remembers all the Web pages you've visited for the past 20 days. As a result, if you click the Address bar and begin to type the URL of a page you've already been to, the browser will eventually recognize the initial letters of the address and type out the rest of the URL for you! If Internet Explorer guesses incorrectly about the URL you want, just keep typing; the program will automatically withdraw its suggestion in favor of your new Web page address.

extra credit

Copying URLs into the Address bar

If a URL is printed on paper, you've gotta type it to use it. If a URL appears on your screen, though — for example, as a result of a friend e-mailing it to you or the URL appearing in an article that you're reading online — you can simply copy the URL to the Windows Clipboard and then paste it into the Address bar. Here's how:

1. Click in front of the first character of the URL that you want to copy.
2. While holding down your mouse button, drag the mouse's cursor over the URL until the entire electronic address is highlighted and then release your mouse button.
3. Press Ctrl+C to copy the highlighted text to the (invisible) Clipboard.
4. Click anywhere inside the Address bar to highlight the bar's current text.
5. Press Ctrl+V to paste in your URL.
6. Press Enter to activate the URL and jump to its Web page.

Copying URLs saves your fingers a lot of energy that they can use to do more exploring on the Web.

☑ Progress Check

If you can do the following, you've mastered this lesson:

- ❑ Enter a URL into the Address bar.
- ❑ Use the URL that you typed to move to a Web page.

Searching a Web Page for Information

Lesson 2-4

When a Web page consists of only a few paragraphs, you can pick out the facts that you want from it pretty easily. If a page is long and contains lots of text, though, you may appreciate some help locating the information you seek.

on the test

That's why Internet Explorer provides a Find command. Like the Find option in a word processor, it lets you search for a word or phrase in an electronic document. To invoke the Find command, choose Edit⇨Find or press the keystroke shortcut Ctrl+F. Either of these actions pops up a Find dialog box. After you type your search text in the dialog box and press Enter, Internet Explorer looks for occurrences of your text on the current Web page.

to search for a word or phrase, choose Edit→Find or press Ctrl+F

To try out the Find command, follow these steps to access and search through excerpts from William Shakespeare's classic play *Hamlet:*

1. **If you aren't still connected to the Internet, dial in again now.**

   Your browser window should be maximized and displaying a Web page.

2. **Click the Links bar button that you created in Lesson 2-3 to move to the *Dummies 101: The Internet for Windows 98* home page.**

   You can also jump to the page by clicking in the Address bar, typing the URL `net.gurus.com/net101`, and pressing Enter.

3. **Locate and click a link on the page named *Shakespeare's Hamlet.***

   The link is activated, and you move to a page containing excerpts from the bard's immortal drama.

4. **Choose Edit⇨Find or press Ctrl+F.**

   A Find dialog box like the one in Figure 2-6 appears. The dialog box contains the following elements:

   - A Find What text box that lets you type the word or phrase you're looking for.
   - A Match Whole Word Only option that locates only full words, as opposed to parts of words, to match your text.
   - A Match Case option that locates exact uppercase and lowercase matches of your search text.
   - Direction buttons to specify whether to search Up or Down from your current position on the Web page.
   - A Find Next button to execute your search.

   For this exercise, leave the Match Case and Match Whole Word Only boxes unchecked, and the Down button selected.

Figure 2-6: Use the Find dialog box to search for a word or phrase on a Web page.

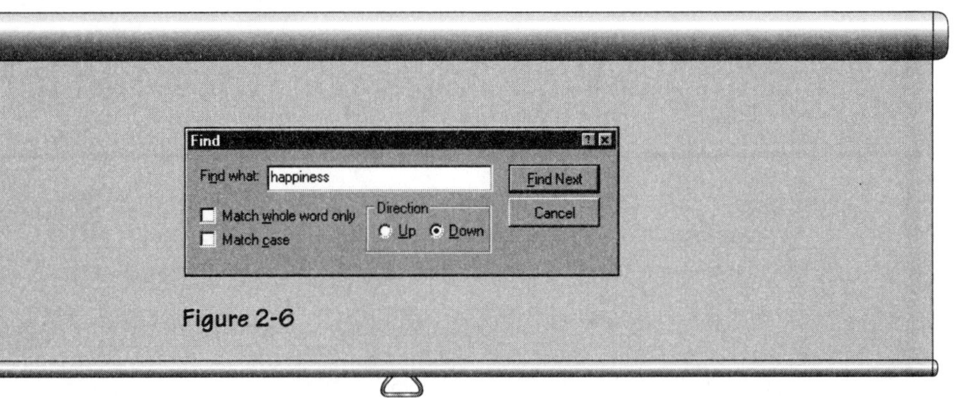

Figure 2-6

Notes:

5 Drag the Find dialog box to the bottom of the screen so that it doesn't block your view of the page.

The Find What box and Find Next button should still be visible, but the rest of the dialog box can be hidden behind your Windows taskbar.

6 Type life **in the Find What box to search for the various ways Shakespeare used this word to weave poetic phrases in *Hamlet.***

The previous text in the box (if any) is replaced by the word *life*.

7 Press Enter to execute the search.

Internet Explorer highlights the first occurrence of *life*, which is in Hamlet's bold proclamation concerning his pursuing a ghost: "I do not set my life at a pin's fee;/And for my soul, what can it do to that,/Being a thing immortal as itself?"

8 Click Find Next to continue searching.

The page jumps to the second occurrence of *life*, which is in this terrible revelation by the ghost of Hamlet's father: "But know, thou noble youth,/The serpent that did sting thy father's life/Now wears his crown."

9 Click Find Next to continue searching.

The page jumps to the third occurrence of *life*, which is in Hamlet's fearsome reply, "You cannot, sir, take from me anything that I will more willingly part withal — except my life, my life, my life."

10 Continue clicking Find Next to locate more matches.

You should find *life* in several more places, including this section from Hamlet's most famous soliloquy: "To sleep, perchance to dream. Ay, there's the rub,/For in that sleep of death what dreams may come/When we have shuffled off this mortal coil/Must give us pause. There's the respect/That makes calamity of so long life."

After you've found all the occurrences of *life*, a message box tells you that Internet Explorer has `Finished searching the document.`

11 **Click OK to close the message box, and click the Close button in the upper-right corner of the Find dialog box to quit searching.**

The message box and Find dialog box disappear.

12 **Click the Back button (the first button on the Standard Buttons toolbar).**

You return to the *Dummies 101: The Internet for Windows 98* home page.

That's all there is to searching for *any* type of text on a Web page. (We should probably add that you'll find most Web material to be considerably cheerier than *Hamlet* . . . though not nearly as well written.) The Find command can save you a lot of time, so make ample use of it when examining text-intensive Web pages.

☑ Progress Check

If you can do the following, you've mastered this lesson:

- ❑ Open the Find dialog box.
- ❑ Use the Find dialog box to locate a word or phrase on a Web page.

Searching the Entire Web for Information

Lesson 2-5

on the test

Just as you can use your browser's Find command to search a Web page for a word or phrase, you can use Internet search programs to scour the entire Web for pages dealing with a particular topic. Because literally *tens of millions* of Web pages exist — giving a whole new meaning to the phrase "information overload" — such search programs are indispensable for zeroing in on the data you need.

Happily, these *Web searchers* (also called *search engines*) are available on the Web itself and can be accessed with just a few mouse clicks. Further, most of them are free! (The publishers of Web searchers generate revenue by selling advertising space on their search sites or by selling related products.)

Because the Web is so enormous and ever-changing, no single search program can do a perfect job of finding the most appropriate pages dealing with your topic. A number of excellent Web searchers are available, though, so if you aren't satisfied with the results that you get from one, you can simply turn to another.

Two different kinds of search programs exist. The first relies on human editors who attempt to bring order to the Web's chaos by organizing Web pages into broad categories (for example, Government, Business, or Arts) and narrower subcategories (for example, Arts⇨Art History⇨Artists⇨da Vinci, Leonardo⇨ Leonardo da Vinci Drawings on Web page `http://banzai.msi.umn.edu/leonardo`). This type of category-based Web searcher (represented by such programs as *Yahoo!*) is best when you're researching a broad, popular topic that human editors are likely to have assigned a subcategory.

Notes:

The second type of search program is *open-ended* — that is, it doesn't rely on any kind of predefined structuring or categorizing of Web pages. Instead, programs such as *HotBot* and *AltaVista* try to match your search text to their enormous databases on the fly, and depend entirely on their own intelligence (or, to be more precise, on a number of sophisticated programming tricks) to come up with the most appropriate Web pages for your topic. Using an open-ended search program is best when you're researching a narrow or obscure topic. You'll learn more about the advantages and disadvantages of each approach shortly.

New Web searchers are constantly popping up on the Net. As we write this book, the following are some of the best search programs available:

on the test

- **AltaVista (`www.altavista.digital.com`):** Provides extremely fast, accurate searching of more than 40 million Web pages. AltaVista is one of the two most comprehensive Web search programs (the other being HotBot), and it's among our favorites.
- **Excite (`www.excite.com`):** Offers a variety of fine services, including a search program named Excite Search, and a set of links named Excite NewsTracker (`nt.excite.com`) that leads you to articles from more than 300 newspapers and magazines.
- **HotBot (`www.hotbot.com`):** Provides extremely fast, accurate searching of more than 40 million Web pages. HotBot is one of the two most comprehensive Web search programs (the other being AltaVista), and it's among our favorites.
- **InfoSeek (`guide.infoseek.com`):** Produces highly accurate results within the confines of its database. InfoSeek is excellent at matching your search topic with relatively new Web pages, but sometimes at the price of ignoring older Web sites.
- **Lycos (`www.lycos.com`):** Furnishes sophisticated search options (for example, letting you search for Web pages that mention Dean Martin but *don't* mention Jerry Lewis) and a huge Web page database. Lycos also offers a Web guide organized by category (`a2z.lycos.com`) and recommendations of top Web sites (`point.lycos.com/categories`).
- **Yahoo! (`www.yahoo.com`):** The oldest major category-based search program and a great place to start when researching broad topics. Yahoo! isn't as comprehensive as some of the programs in this list, but it's likely to produce the most targeted matches, which has led to it becoming one of the most popular sites on the Net. Yahoo! also offers great features such as Picks of the Week (`www.yahoo.com/picks`), a savvy list of the best of the Web (`www.yahoo.com/Entertainment/Cool_Links`), a weekly listing of new Web sites (`www.yahoo.com/weblaunch.html`), and a search program devoted to finding Web sites for kids (`www.yahooligans.com`).
- **Savvy Search (`www.cs.colostate.edu/~dreiling/smartform.html`):** A high-level or "meta-search" program that, instead of scouring the Web directly, plugs your search term into several popular Web searchers and then gives you all the initial matches together on the same page, organized by search program! Use this tool to avoid the time and effort of entering text into each search program separately.

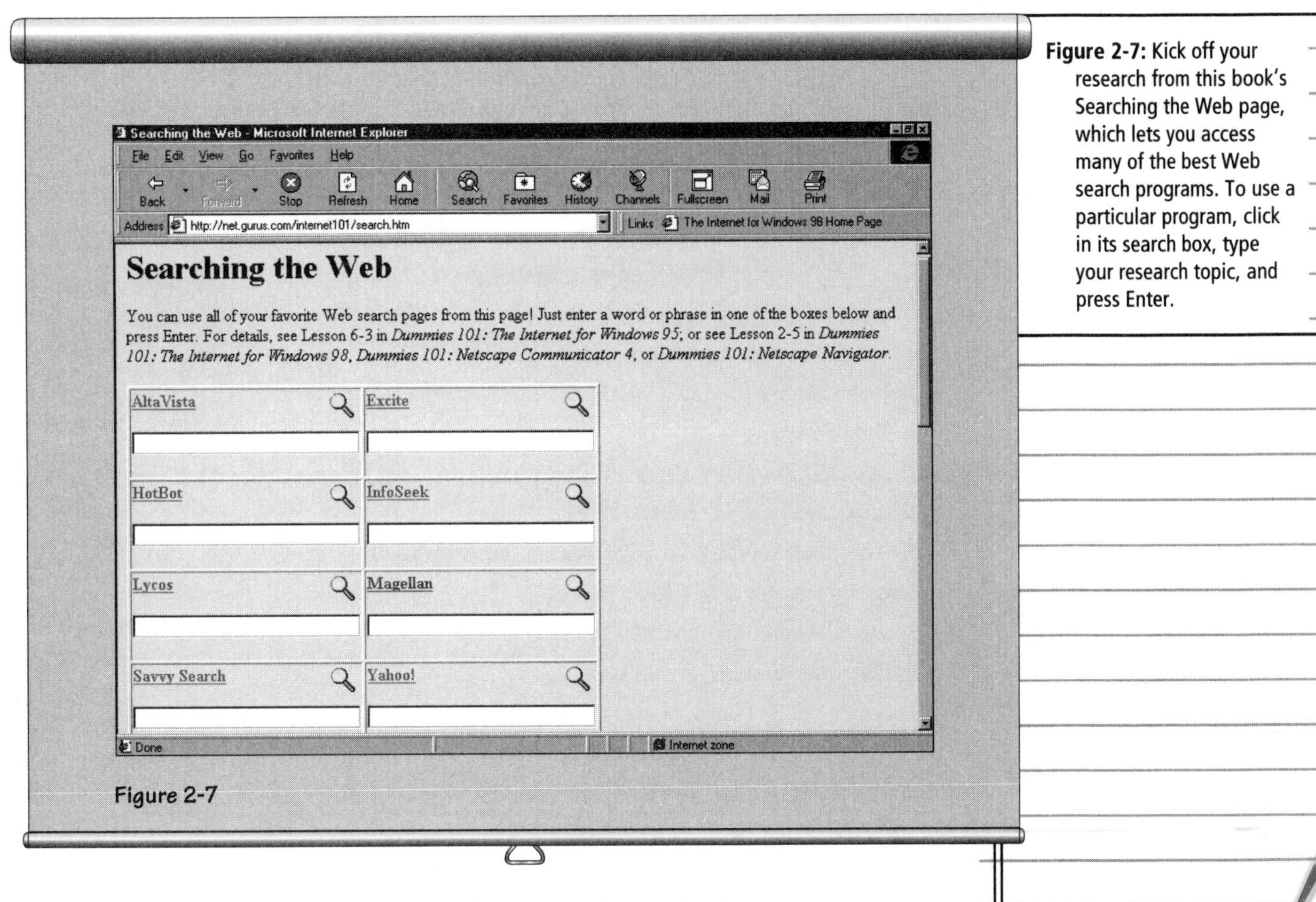

Figure 2-7

Figure 2-7: Kick off your research from this book's Searching the Web page, which lets you access many of the best Web search programs. To use a particular program, click in its search box, type your research topic, and press Enter.

At this point, you're probably thinking, "Sounds great, but how can I easily get to all these different search programs?" Well, by an amazing coincidence, you can access them with a mouse click from the *Dummies 101: The Internet for Windows 98* home page!

heads up

Because there's no way to predict what will change on the Web, a Web searcher that we discuss in this lesson may no longer be available (or available for free) when you try to access it. If a search program becomes unavailable, don't sweat it — simply use a different search program. At the same time, keep an eye on our *Dummies 101: The Internet for Windows 98* Web site for links to fabulous new search programs.

Using a category-based Web searcher

To hone your Web research skills, try using Yahoo! — a category-based Web searcher — to find Web sites dealing with movies.

1. **If you aren't still connected to the Internet, dial in again now.**

   Your browser window should be maximized and displaying a Web page.

Figure 2-8: Yahoo! generates a list of Web categories most relevant to your search topic. You can scan the list and select appropriate subcategories until you arrive at a list of Web pages covering your specific topic.

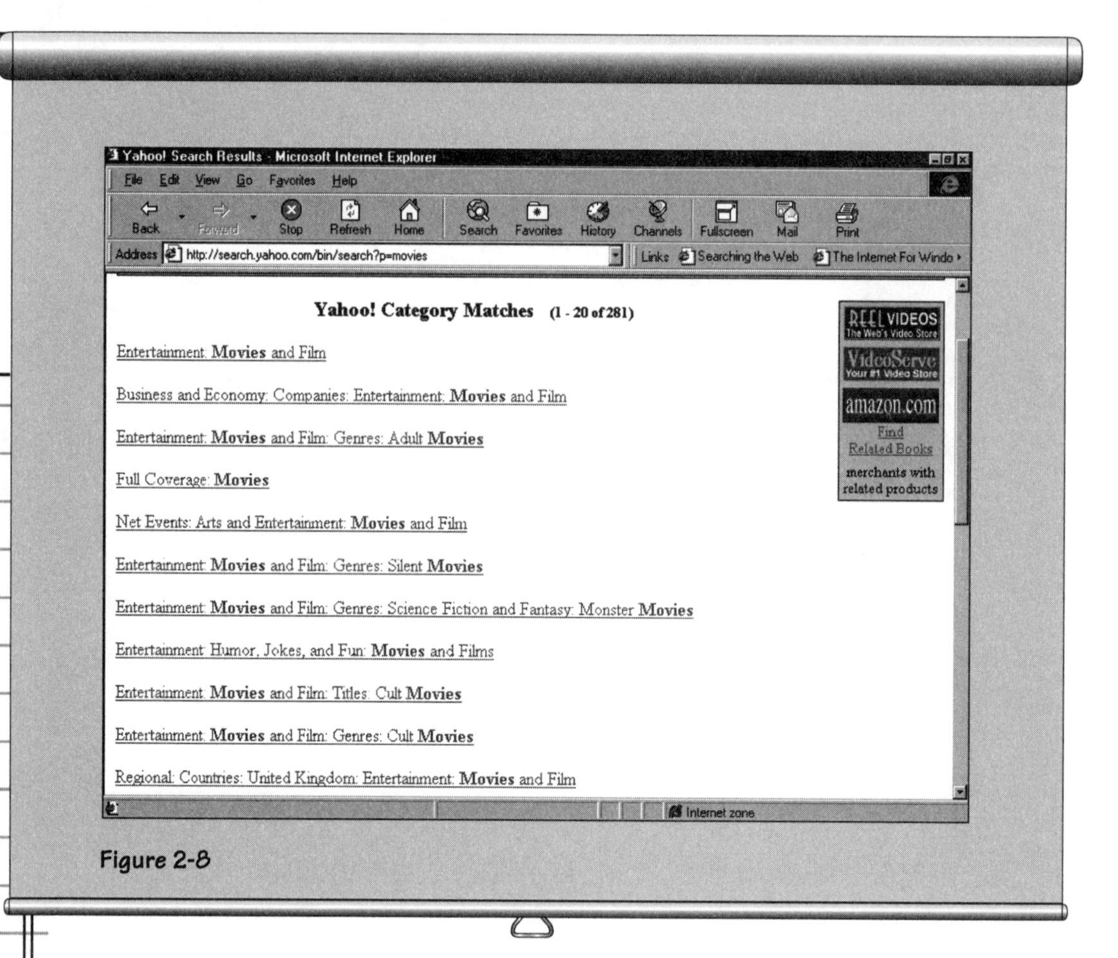

Figure 2-8

2. **If you aren't on the *Dummies 101: The Internet for Windows 98* home page, click the Links bar button that you created in Lesson 2-3.**

   You can also jump to the page by clicking in the Address bar, typing the URL `net.gurus.com/net101`, and pressing Enter.

3. **Locate and click the link named The *Dummies 101* Web Search Page.**

   You move to a page with text entry boxes linked to popular Web search programs (see Figure 2-7).

4. **Create a button favorite to access the page easily.**

   Click and drag the page icon from the Address bar to the Links bar, and then release your mouse button. A button favorite pointing to the Searching the Web page pops out of thin air and lands on your Links bar.

5. **Locate the Yahoo! search box and then click in the box.**

   A blinking cursor appears inside the Yahoo! box to indicate that you can now enter your search text.

6. **Type** movies **to research movie-related Web sites, and press Enter.**

   Your search request takes you to a Yahoo! page like the one in Figure 2-8. This page lists the first batch of categories in Yahoo!'s Web catalog that best matches your search phrase *movies.* (You can display additional categories by clicking a link near the bottom of the page that says something like *Next 20 Matches.*)

Notice that all the topics listed on the Yahoo! Category Matches page are links. To explore a topic, simply click it.

7 **Locate the *Entertainment: Movies and Films* category and then click it.**

If you don't see this topic, simply pick out and click a different broad movie category. You move to a subgroup of categories within your selected category. Press PgDn once or twice to view the entire list.

8 **Pick out a category that interests you — say, Actors and Actresses, Box Office Reports, Genres, or anything else you see listed — and then click it.**

You again move to a subgroup of categories within your selected category.

9 **Continue picking out and clicking categories that interest you until you work your way down to a list of specific Web sites.**

After you're done clicking through subcategories, you find yourself on a page listing the names and descriptions of Web sites that deal with the particular *movies* subtopic that you selected.

10 **Click a listed Web site name (which is a link).**

You arrive at a Web page. (All right!) Explore the page at your leisure and then click Internet Explorer's Back button to return to your Yahoo! list of sites. Continue by clicking any other Web site link that interests you, examining the page, and clicking the Back button to return to your Yahoo! list until you've visited all the Web pages that seemed relevant to what you were searching for.

As you just saw, a category-based guide to the Web such as Yahoo! is especially useful for kicking off research on a broad topic. That's because the categories let you quickly see what kinds of information are available. Also, human editors make sure that the Web pages listed under each category are directly relevant, thus sparing you from wasting time with false leads.

However, category-based search programs also have a few disadvantages:

- They force you to do some work before arriving at a list of Web pages.
- They're less likely to help you discover pages that aren't directly relevant, but that you may find interesting anyway.
- They're not as helpful for researching narrow or obscure topics, because they tend to include fewer Web pages and center on popular subjects.

Because of these shortcomings of category-based searchers, you should also get in the habit of using open-ended search programs — which we discuss in the next section.

Using an open-ended Web searcher

Open-ended Web searchers don't depend on human editors and don't list categories. Instead, these programs immediately present you with the names of Web sites related to your topic and ordered by relevance (based on a number of clever programming tricks, such as checking how often your search phrase

Notes:

Figure 2-9: Instead of using Web categories, AltaVista directly generates a list of the Web pages it considers the most relevant to your search topic.

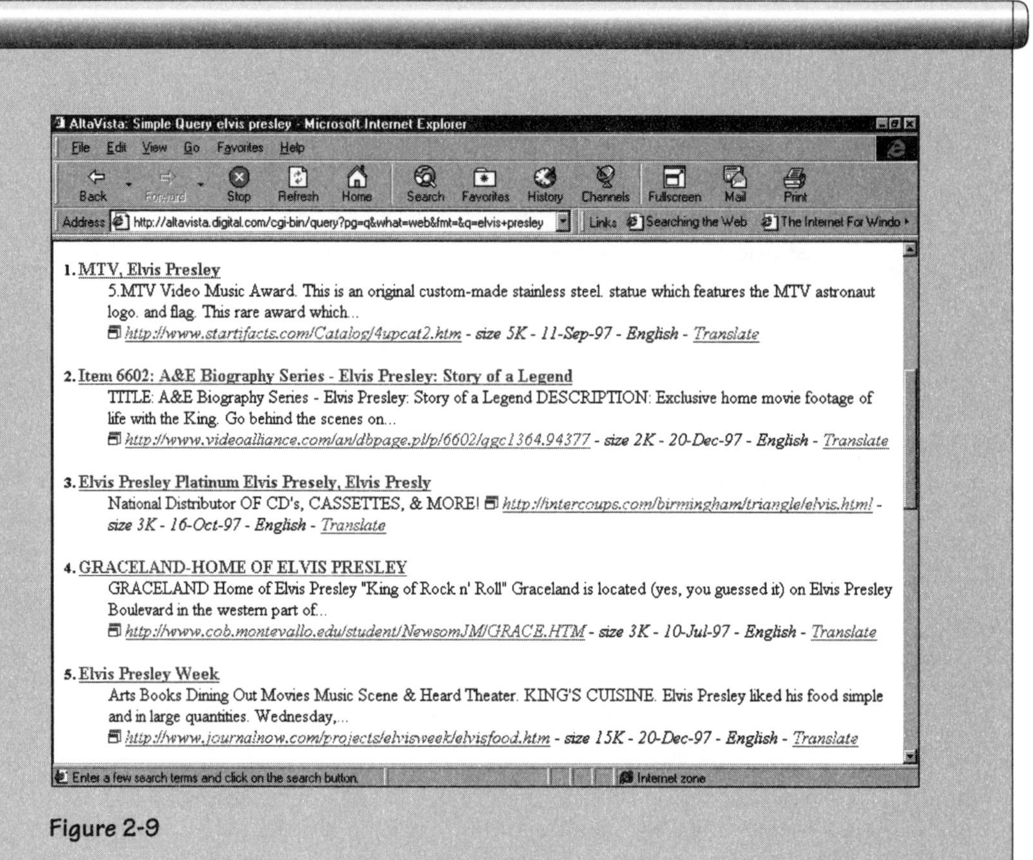

Figure 2-9

appears on a particular Web page). Because they don't require people to help them organize information, these programs are able to include a lot *more* information; in fact, popular open-ended searchers such as AltaVista and HotBot cover tens of millions of Web pages, making them powerful tools for turning up raw data.

On the other hand, search programs still aren't nearly as smart as humans are, and so they may sometimes give you useful and useless sites mixed together, leaving you with the job of sifting through the list and identifying the pages you really need. Open-ended searchers are therefore best when you're looking for a wide range of sites, need information about esoteric topics, or simply want a quick list of Web pages (as opposed to having to first wade through a bunch of categories and subcategories).

To get a feel for how open-ended searches work, use AltaVista to find Web sites devoted to Elvis Presley:

1. **Click the Links bar button you created in the preceding exercise to return to the Searching the Web page.**

   You move back to the page that you used to launch your Yahoo! search. (You can also reach this page by clicking in the Address bar, typing the URL `net.gurus.com/internet101/search.htm` and pressing Enter.)

2. **Locate the AltaVista search box and then click in the box.**

   A blinking cursor appears inside the AltaVista box to indicate that you can now enter your search text.

3. **Type** Elvis Presley **to locate Web sites about the King of rock 'n' roll and then press Enter.**

   You move to an AltaVista page that lists an initial batch of Web pages it considers most relevant to your topic (as in Figure 2-9). Notice that each entry in the list includes the Web page's name and URL (both of which are links that you can use to jump to the page), and the first two lines of text from the page, which give you a sense of the page's contents.

4. **Use the PgDn key to read through the first batch of matches. To see more matches, click the number *2* (for page 2) or the word *Next* near the bottom of the page.**

   You move to the second set of matches. Similarly, you can move to the third, fourth, and fifth batches of matches by clicking the numbers or *Next* at the bottom of the page. You can go on like this for some time because AltaVista has generated *thousands* of matches. Instead, try narrowing your search a bit by centering on Elvis's movie career.

5. **Click your Links bar button to return to the *Searching the Web* page, click in the AltaVista box, type** Elvis Presley movies**, and press Enter.**

   You move to a new AltaVista screen that identifies Web pages dealing with Elvis Presley movies. This list of pages is a little more focused than the preceding list because it concerns a narrower topic.

6. **Click Internet Explorer's Back button to return to the *Searching the Web* page, click toward the end of the AltaVista box, use the Backspace key to delete the word *movies,* type the word** stamps **instead, and press Enter.**

   You jump to a new AltaVista screen that lists Web pages dealing with Elvis stamps (such as the famous one issued by the U.S. Postal Service in 1993). The results of this search are much more focused because this time your topic is quite narrow.

Notes:

Using multiple Web searchers

Because an open-ended Web searcher has to *guess* at the relevance of a page to your interests, the quality of a program's matches can depend largely on luck. If you aren't entirely satisfied with the sites that one search program generates, though, don't give up; simply run your search through one or two other programs.

1. **Click your Links bar button to return to the Searching the Web page.**

   This time, pick a different search program to use, such as HotBot or Excite.

Notes:

2 Click in the search box of a different search program you'd like to try, type Elvis Presley **and press Enter.**

You move to an initial list of Elvis Web pages generated by the program that you selected. Notice that the list is different from AltaVista's initial list (though you may see some overlap).

3 Click Internet Explorer's Back button to return to the *Searching the Web* page.

Pick another search program to try out, such as InfoSeek or Lycos.

4 Click in the search box of another search program you'd like to try, type Elvis Presley **and press Enter.**

Again, you move to an initial list of Elvis Web pages that's different from any of the others you've generated. You always get unique results from each Web searcher because each has its own special methods of adding Web sites to its database, matching Web pages to a search phrase, and ranking the pages by relevance.

5 Click the Back button to return to the *Searching the Web* page, and this time use the meta-search program Savvy Search by clicking in its search box, typing Elvis Presley **and pressing Enter.**

You move to a list of initial matches from several different Web searchers (typically a mix of category-based and open-ended searchers), organized by program. If you want to delve further, you can click the link to the program that you feel produced the best matches. Doing a search in this way is more efficient than typing the search text yourself for each separate program.

Narrowing your search

Your search results can be affected by more than just which search program you pick; they can also vary depending on the syntax you use to specify your topic. For example, in most search programs, the phrase *Al Gore* matches Web pages that contain the name *Al* and/or the word *gore.* To narrow the results, you can enclose the phrase in quotation marks ("Al Gore"), which forces the search to match only Web pages that contain the entire phrase *Al Gore.*

Other ways to zero in on your topic by using syntax exist, but they vary from search program to search program. Therefore, to get the specifics, visit the page of a Web searcher you enjoy and then read about the particular options available for that program.

Using your browser's built-in search features

Internet Explorer has two of its own built-in aids for searching the Web: the Search button and the Address bar.

To activate the Search button, simply click it from the Standard Buttons toolbar. After you do so, a search program randomly selected from a pool of Web search sites appears in a bar running down the left side of your window. You can use this search program to find Web pages covering your topic. After you're done, close the bar by clicking the Search button again.

Alternatively, type your search phrase directly into the Address bar. To do so, click in the Address bar; type the word **find**, the word **go**, or a **?** (question mark), followed by a space; type your search phrase; and press Enter. Internet Explorer plugs your text into a search program randomly selected from a pool of Web search sites and then displays the results in your browser window.

The main problem with using the Search button or the Address bar for research is that you aren't able to control which Web search program is used, so you won't always get the best results possible. However, if you ever become impatient clicking favorites and waiting for specific search pages to appear, these built-in tools can't be beat for initiating a search quickly.

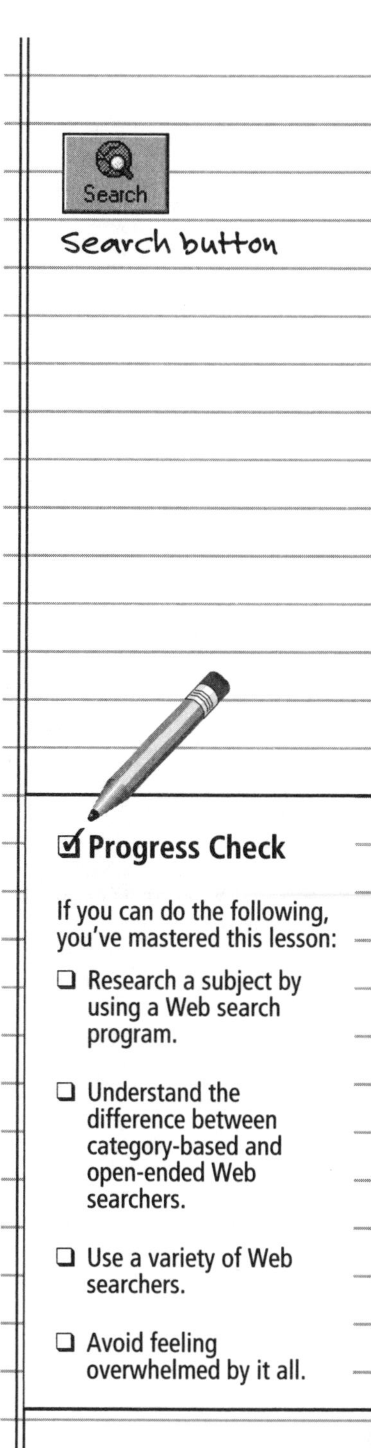

To sum up, there's no one right way to search the Web. The program that you use — and whether you should use one Web searcher or several, or a meta-searcher such as Savvy Search — depends on how general your search topic is, how comprehensive you need your research to be, how much work you want to do, and your personal tastes.

The main thing is that you don't feel overwhelmed by it all! Although the Web offers a staggering amount of information, so does a library, a museum, or a television set with 100 cable channels. In each case, don't hesitate to follow the advice of author Ken Kesey: "Take what you can use and let the rest go by."

☑ Progress Check

If you can do the following, you've mastered this lesson:

- ❑ Research a subject by using a Web search program.
- ❑ Understand the difference between category-based and open-ended Web searchers.
- ❑ Use a variety of Web searchers.
- ❑ Avoid feeling overwhelmed by it all.

Recess

You've opened a lot of doors for yourself in this unit. You can now use favorites to preserve Web page addresses, move to any URL by using the Address bar, and find information about virtually anything on the Web. Take a few minutes to contemplate your impressive new powers, and then challenge yourself with the following crafty quiz questions.

Unit 2 Quiz

For each of the following questions, circle the letter of the correct answer or answers. Remember, each question may have more than one right answer.

Notes:

1. **To create a favorite for a Web page, move to the page and:**
   A. Click the Internet Explorer logo.
   B. Press Ctrl+D.
   C. Choose Favorites➪Add to Favorites.
   D. Click and drag the page icon from the Address bar to the Favorites menu.
   E. Fasten the page and the Favorites menu together by choosing Favorites➪Glue.

2. **To remove a favorite:**
   A. Make it feel unwanted.
   B. Apply a dab of dry cleaning solution and wait an hour.
   C. Choose Favorites➪Organize Favorites, click the favorite, and press the Del key.
   D. Choose Favorites➪Organize Favorites, right-click the favorite, and choose Delete from the menu that appears. (Try it!)
   E. None of the above; favorites are permanent and can't be removed.

3. **To organize your favorites, you can**
   A. Hold up a sign that says *Union!* in front of your screen.
   B. Use the Create New Folder button to make folders for grouping related favorites..
   C. Use the cut-and-paste keystrokes Ctrl+X and Ctrl+V to move favorites to appropriate folders.
   D. Choose Favorites➪Fashion to automatically arrange favorites by color and pattern.
   E. Ride them until their wild ways are broken.

4. **If a newspaper article tells you about a great new Web page, you can check it out by:**
   A. Showing the article to Internet Explorer and typing **Go fetch**.
   B. Clicking in the Address bar, typing the Web page's URL, and pressing Enter.
   C. Closing your eyes, breathing deeply, and, like, letting your mind journey to the URL, man.
   D. Using a Web search program to locate the page and then clicking the page's link.
   E. Playing hard to get with the Web page until it eventually comes to you.

5. **To locate a word or phrase on a Web page:**
   A. Use the vertical scroll bar to examine the page carefully.
   B. Use the PgDn and PgUp keys to examine the page carefully.

C. Use the Web Psychic program to make the desired text float to the front of your screen.

D. Press Ctrl+F, type your search text, and press Enter.

E. Click inside the Address bar, type your search text, and press Enter.

6. **Some programs that you can use to search the Web are**

A. Yahoo!, HotBot, and Lycos.

B. Yippee, Sneezy, and Dopey.

C. AltaVista, Excite, and Savvy Search.

D. Huey, Dewey, and Louie.

E. Groucho, Chico, and Harpo.

Unit 2 Exercise

Apply what you've learned about using favorites and finding information on the Web by creating a mini-library of Web pages devoted to subjects that interest you.

1. Write down at least three topics that are dear to your heart.
2. Run Internet Explorer and connect to the Net.
3. Open the Organize Favorites dialog box, create an empty folder for each of your three topics, and close the dialog box.
4. Move to the HotBot home page at `www.hotbot.com`. (***Tip:*** Try typing just hotbot in the Address bar and letting Internet Explorer fill in the rest of the URL after you press Enter.)
5. Create a button on the Links bar for the HotBot page so that you can return to the site easily.
6. For each item on your list, search for Web pages devoted to the topic.
7. Whenever you locate a Web page that you feel is interesting, use the Address bar's page icon to simultaneously create a favorite for the page and file the favorite in the appropriate category folder.
8. Repeat Steps 6 and 7 using the Yahoo! site at `www.yahoo.com`. (***Tip:*** Try typing just yahoo instead of the full URL.)
9. After you're entirely done with your searching, open the Organize Favorites dialog box and rename each of your new favorites so that every name briefly but clearly describes the favorite's Web site.
10. Test out your favorites by using them to revisit some of the Web pages that you most enjoyed.
11. After you're finished, disconnect from the Net and exit Internet Explorer.

Notes:

Unit 3

Saving Information and Downloading Files

Objectives for This Unit

- ✓ Printing Web pages
- ✓ Saving Web pages as text files
- ✓ Saving Web pages as HTML files
- ✓ Copying files from the Web

Prerequisites

- Cruising the Web with Internet Explorer (Lesson 1-2)
- Creating favorites (Lesson 2-2)
- Entering URLs (Lesson 2-3)
- Searching for information on the Web (Lesson 2-5)

You've spent a lot of time on the Web by now, but you've interacted with it in only one way — by viewing Web pages online through your Internet Explorer window. In this unit, you'll learn how to read Web pages offline and at your leisure by printing them to paper or saving them to disk. You'll also discover how to access the tens of thousands of programs, electronic images, digital sounds, and other wonderful goodies that are just waiting for you to reach out and pluck from the Web.

Printing and Saving Web Information — Lesson 3-1

In Unit 2, you learned how to use Internet Explorer to locate information. If the information is complicated or important, though, you may not want to simply read it on your screen but also preserve it in some way for further study offline.

Notes:

Saving Web data allows you to examine the information that you found at your leisure and to organize it, edit it, and reuse it. In addition, perusing text-heavy Web information from paper pages or your favorite word processor gives you the opportunity to mark up the text as you go along and saves you from racking up phone charges while you read.

You can preserve Web data in two ways: by printing it to paper and by saving it to disk. Both methods are quick and easy.

on the test

You can print the contents of your current Web page immediately by clicking the Print button on the Standard Buttons toolbar. Alternatively, you can choose File➪Print or press Ctrl+P to pop up a Print dialog box, adjust whatever options you want to change in the dialog box, and then print by clicking OK.

Similarly, you can save the contents of your current Web page to disk by choosing File➪Save As or pressing Ctrl+S, which pops up a Save HTML Document dialog box. After you type a filename (for example, C:\WebData\NewFile) and press Enter, the file is saved to the hard disk location that you specified.

To try out these convenience features — and also learn about various printing and saving options — work through the next two exercises.

Printing the contents of a Web page

Although Internet e-mail and Web pages may ultimately save a lot of trees, paper still has its uses. For example, paper pages are light, portable, and easy to read and mark up. They also can serve as permanent records, as opposed to Web pages that can disappear overnight or even computer file formats that can become obsolete after a number of years. Finally, printing on paper lets you preserve the whole "look" of a Web page, including its graphics, whereas saving to disk preserves a Web page's text but not its graphics.

In Lesson 2-4, you searched through excerpts from Shakespeare's *Hamlet.* Now follow these steps to print the text on the *Hamlet* Web page:

1. **Launch Internet Explorer and connect to the Net.**

   Your browser window should be maximized and displaying a Web page.

2. **Click the Links bar button that you created in Lesson 2-3 to move to the *Dummies 101: The Internet for Windows 98* home page.**

   You can also move to the page by clicking in the Address bar, typing the URL `net.gurus.com/net101` and pressing Enter.

3. **Locate and click the *Hamlet* link that you used in Lesson 2-4.**

   You move to the page containing the excerpts from *Hamlet.*

4. **Make sure that your printer is on.**

   Also check that your printer is connected to your computer, that its on-line light is on, and that it has at least ten sheets of paper in its paper tray. After you do so, you're ready to print the contents of the Web page.

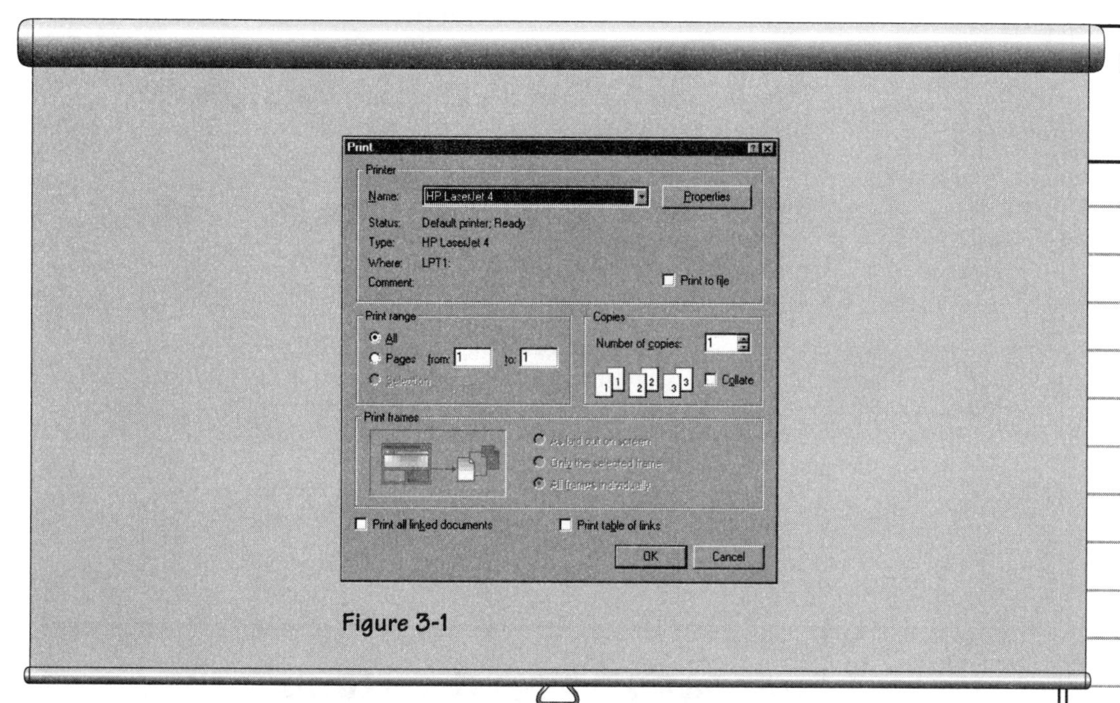

Figure 3-1: Use the Print dialog box to print the contents of a Web page.

5 Choose File⇨Print.

Alternatively, press Ctrl+P. In either case, a Print dialog box like the one in Figure 3-1 appears. The dialog box contains a Print Range box that lets you print All the contents of the current Web page; a range of paper Pages (for example, From 1 To 2 prints only the first two paper pages); or a Selection, which lets you print a highlighted section of the Web page.

The dialog box also lets you switch to a different printer; set the Number Of Copies to print; Collate your pages by printing them in reverse order, or last page first; and Print To File, in case you want to save the output to disk (for example, if you're using a laptop and won't be able to print until later).

Many Web pages are composed of several individual sections called *frames*. Therefore, the dialog box additionally lets you print a page As Laid Out on Screen (that is, the same as the image you see in your browser), Only the Selected Frame (that is, just the section of the Web page that you clicked before popping up the dialog box), or All Frames Individually (meaning one section of the page after another, which can be handy if you want to see how a Web page was constructed).

Finally, the dialog box provides a Print Table of Links option that can list all the links on the page; a Print All Linked Documents option that can print all the pages linked to the current page; and a Properties button that lets you set such things as paper size, and how fonts and graphics are handled.

For now, accept the default settings by leaving the Print dialog box as it is.

to pop up the Print dialog box, choose File→Print or press Ctrl+P

6 Click the OK button.

The dialog box closes, and the Web page starts printing. (***Note:*** If printing doesn't begin, double-check both your printer's status and the settings in the Print dialog box.)

Notes:

to print a Web page immediately, click the Print button

7 After the page is printed, check the paper sheets against the contents of the Web page.

The text and graphics on your paper pages should look the same as the text and graphics that appear on the electronic page.

To sum up, you can print the contents of a Web page by performing two simple steps: choosing File⇨Print or pressing Ctrl+P, and clicking OK.

But there's an even easier method available — if you aren't interested in changing the Print dialog box's defaults, simply click the Print button on the Standard Buttons toolbar. Internet Explorer skips displaying the Print dialog box and immediately begins printing the Web page. This allows you to print a Web page with a single mouse click!

Because printing is relatively effortless, be sure to take advantage of this feature.

Changing print settings

If you ever need to adjust Internet Explorer's standard print settings, you can do so in a couple of ways:

- Choose File⇨Page Setup to adjust such formatting features as page margins, page numbering, and headers and footers.
- Choose File⇨Print⇨Properties to switch to a different paper size, paper tray, and/or paper orientation (Portrait prints across the width of a page, and Landscape prints across the long side of a page). The Properties dialog box also lets you set how fonts and graphics are printed.

Detailing these options is beyond the scope of this book, but you may want to play around with them on your own.

Printing a Web page has many advantages; but it also has drawbacks, such as the cost in paper and ink, the clutter that paper creates, and the difficulty of manipulating paper data (not to mention the possibility of nasty paper cuts). That's why Internet Explorer also lets you save information to disk, which you'll take on next.

Saving the contents of a Web page to disk

For long-term use, saving Web data to disk is often better than printing it, because electronic text takes up much less space than paper and is significantly easier to search through and organize.

In addition, you can easily manipulate and reuse electronic data. For example, you can save stock prices from a Web page to a disk file, and then import the file into a spreadsheet program or other analysis tool to crunch the numbers.

As another example, you can periodically dump Web data that's pertinent to your job onto your hard disk, and then edit the information in your word processor to produce savvy and timely office reports.

You can save Web data in two file formats: text and HTML. The text format (which is also called *plain text,* or *ASCII*) is understood by all PC programs, but it achieves that universality by ignoring formatting such as underlining, boldfacing, margins, fonts, and colors — basically, anything outside of standard words, numbers, and punctuation. Saving information as text allows you to view and edit it in any program, but at the cost of the "look" of the Web page.

Conversely, saving a Web page as an HTML file preserves the look of the page (except for pictures, which are represented in the file by copies of a simple placeholder image). However, you can view HTML files properly only from a browser program such as Internet Explorer. If you load HTML files into another type of program instead, you see a messy jumble consisting of Web page text mixed together with confusing looking formatting codes set in <brackets>. (For more information about HTML, read Unit WP, which is a bonus unit stored on your *Dummies 101* CD. To access this document, see Appendix B.)

on the test

Because of these technical differences, save Web information in text format when you want to view and edit the data using other programs (such as your favorite word processor). Save in HTML format when you just want archival records of Web pages that you can reexamine at your convenience via Internet Explorer.

Saving Web data as a text file

To save your data as a text file, turn once again to the *Hamlet* page.

1. **If you aren't still on the *Hamlet* Web page, move there now.**

   If you need help finding the page, refer to Lesson 2-4.

2. **Choose File⇨Save As.**

   A Save HTML Document dialog box like the one in Figure 3-2 appears. You use this box to select the format of your disk file and to specify where on your hard disk you want to save the file.

   The dialog box's large middle section is a *file list* that shows you the files in your current disk folder. To display the contents of a different folder, you can click inside the Save In box (above the file list) to display all your drives, click the drive that you want, and then double-click the folder that you want. Alternatively, you can click in the File Name box below the file list, type a new drive letter and folder name (for example, C:\MyFolder), and press Enter.

   The dialog box also contains five buttons in its upper-right corner. You can use these buttons to move up one folder level (that is, to move from your subfolder to its parent folder); to move to the highest, or desktop, level; to create a new folder; to list files by name only (which lets you see more of them at a time); or to list each file followed by its size, type, creation date, and creation time.

   Finally, a Save as Type box near the bottom lets you specify the format that Internet Explorer uses to save your Web page. This box's setting also determines the type of files that you see in the file list.

to save the contents of a Web page, choose File→Save As

Figure 3-2: Use the Save HTML Document dialog box to save the contents of a Web page as either a text file or an HTML file.

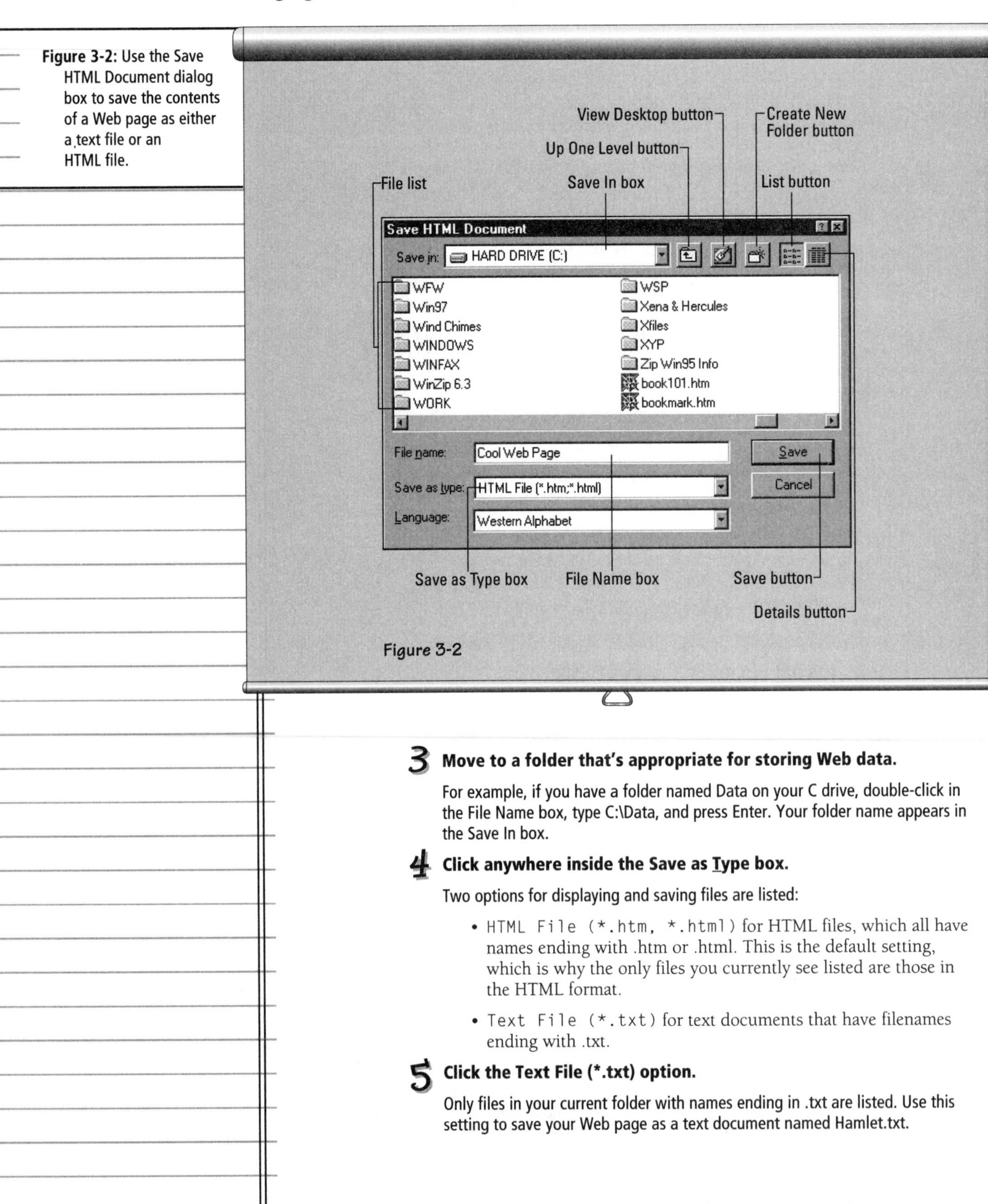

Figure 3-2

3 Move to a folder that's appropriate for storing Web data.

For example, if you have a folder named Data on your C drive, double-click in the File Name box, type C:\Data, and press Enter. Your folder name appears in the Save In box.

4 Click anywhere inside the Save as Type box.

Two options for displaying and saving files are listed:

- `HTML File (*.htm, *.html)` for HTML files, which all have names ending with .htm or .html. This is the default setting, which is why the only files you currently see listed are those in the HTML format.
- `Text File (*.txt)` for text documents that have filenames ending with .txt.

5 Click the Text File (*.txt) option.

Only files in your current folder with names ending in .txt are listed. Use this setting to save your Web page as a text document named Hamlet.txt.

6 **Double-click in the File Name box to highlight any text that's already there and then type** Hamlet.txt.

Your filename Hamlet.txt replaces any previous filename in the box.

7 **Press Enter or click Save.**

The text of your Web page is saved to the current drive and folder in the file Hamlet.txt, and the Save HTML Document dialog box closes.

8 **Choose File⇨Save As.**

The Save HTML Document dialog box reopens.

9 **Click in the Save as Type box and click the Text File (*.txt) option.**

You should now see the file Hamlet.txt listed, verifying that your text save was successful.

Saving your data as an HTML file

Next, perform a similar operation to save your Web page as an HTML file. The Save HTML Document dialog box should still be open.

1 **Click in the Save as Type box and click the HTML File (*.htm, *.html) option.**

Only files with names ending in .htm or .html in the current folder are listed. Use this setting to save your Web page as an HTML document.

2 **Double-click in the File Name box to highlight any text that's already there and then type** Hamlet.htm.

Your filename is entered in the box.

3 **Press Enter or click Save.**

Both the text and formatting of your Web page are stored to the current drive and folder in the file Hamlet.htm, and the Save HTML Document dialog box closes.

Checking your saved text and HTML files

You've now finished saving your Web page in both text and HTML versions, so check out the files that you created.

1 **Open Notepad, WordPad, or some other word processing program.**

Both your word processor and Internet Explorer should be running, with your word processor in the foreground.

2 **Load the file Hamlet.txt into the word processor you're using.**

Specifically, for most word processors, choose File⇨Open; specify the appropriate drive letter, folder name, and filename (for example, type C:\Data\Hamlet.txt); and press Enter.

You should see a plain, all-text version of the current Web page. (If you notice any extraneous pieces of text, they're probably leftover HTML codes, which you should delete.) You can now use this Web data in the same way that you would any other word processing document.

Notes:

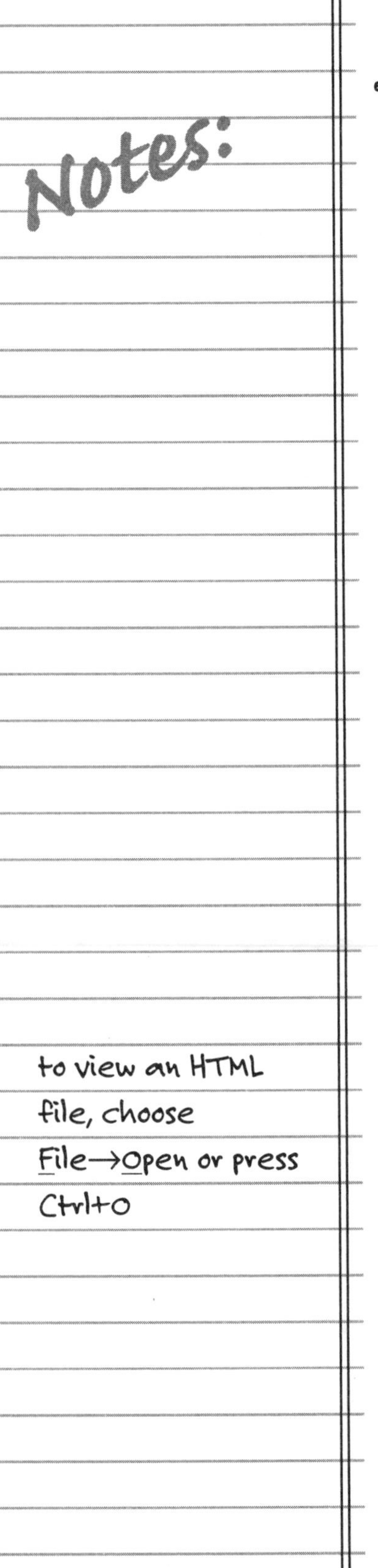

Saving Web page text using the Clipboard

One other way that you can save Web data is by highlighting it and then copying it to the Windows 98 Clipboard. This technique is especially handy when you're interested in only a portion of the Web page, because it spares you from having to save the entire document. Here's how to manage it:

1. **Click the beginning of the Web text that you want to copy.**
2. **While holding down your mouse button, drag over the section of text until all of it is highlighted and then release your mouse button.**
3. **Press Ctrl+C to copy the highlighted text to the (invisible) Clipboard.**
4. **Open a document in a word processor or other program where you want to use the text.**
5. **Click the spot where you want to insert the text and then press Ctrl+V to paste it in.**

   You can now work with the text.
6. **After you're done editing the data, save your document.**

You may also find it easier to save an entire Web page using the Clipboard, since the whole operation can be accomplished with a few keystrokes. Specifically, press Ctrl+A (or choose Edit⇨Select All) to select all the text on the page; press Ctrl+C to copy the text; click the spot in the window where you want to insert the text; and press Ctrl+V to paste. Finally, after you've edited the text, save it from its new window.

3 Save any revisions you made to the document (for example, by choosing File⇨Save), and exit your word processor.

Both the document and the word processor close, returning the Internet Explorer window to the front of your screen. Now examine the HTML file that you created, which you can do by using Internet Explorer's Open option.

4 Choose File⇨Open or press Ctrl+O.

An Open dialog box appears that prompts you to enter the name of a file or Web page.

5 Specify the appropriate drive letter, folder name, and filename (for example, type C:\Data\Hamlet.htm), and press Enter or click OK.

The HTML file that you created appears in the Internet Explorer window. The file looks very similar to the Web page that generated it. In place of the graphics on the Web page, however, the file has only copies of a simple placeholder image to represent the missing pictures.

6 Click the Back button.

You move back to the *Hamlet* Web page.

Whew! These file-saving exercises took a while to get through because they contain a lot of new material. Now that you have it all under your belt, though, you should have no trouble saving Web data. You'll typically choose

File⇨Save As to open the Save HTML Document dialog box, set the format to Text File (*.txt), type an appropriate filename in the File Name box, and press Enter. Easy as pie.

Using some discretion when preserving Web information is necessary, because cluttering your desk or disk with nonessentials hinders your locating the facts you really need. (Comedian Steven Wright made this point succinctly when he observed, "You can't have everything. Where would you put it?") But as long as you restrict printing and saving to genuinely useful data, you'll find these features to be great aids on your journey along the Web.

☑ Progress Check

If you can do the following, you've mastered this lesson:

- ❑ Print a Web page's contents.
- ❑ Save a Web page's contents as a text file.
- ❑ Save a Web page's contents as an HTML file.
- ❑ Open text and HTML files that you've created.

heads up

Keeping copyright issues in mind

As this lesson demonstrates, you can print or save to disk virtually any information you find on a Web page. However, that doesn't mean you're free to use the information without restraint. The text and pictures on Web pages are owned by the authors of those pages, and they're protected by copyright laws in the same way that the contents of books and magazines are protected (even if the pages don't display copyright notices). For example, you can't publish large portions of text from a Web page without obtaining permission from the author, just as you can't publish long sections from a book or magazine article without permission.

If you need more information about copyright laws, a good place to start your research is the United States Copyright Office. To visit the Web site of the Copyright Office, click in the Address bar, type the URL `lcweb.loc.gov/copyright` and press Enter.

Downloading Files from the Web

Lesson 3-2

In Lessons 2-5 and 3-1, you learned how to search Web pages for text information and save the data to disk. You can also search for and copy *files* from the Web to disk. The files may be programs (such as a new version of Internet Explorer), pictures (ranging from the Mona Lisa to a Madonna poster), digital sounds (ranging from a Mozart sonata to the theme from *The Twilight Zone*), digital video (such as a clip of Neil Armstrong's famous first steps on the moon), or any other kind of data that you can use on your PC.

downloading = transmitting files to your computer

on the test

Getting files from another computer is called *downloading,* because the data is typically loaded from a much larger computer system down to the hard disk of your PC. (Similarly, sending files from your PC to another computer is called *uploading.*)

uploading = transmitting files from your computer

Notes:

To locate files to download, you can employ the same Web search programs that you used in Lesson 2-5 for text research. Alternatively, if you aren't sure what's available, you can cruise over to one of the many Web sites that specialize in distributing the latest and greatest program, picture, sound, and video files.

After you locate a file that you want, click the file's link. Internet Explorer first displays a File Download dialog box that includes a Save This Program to Disk option (which is the default) and an OK button. After you click OK, Internet Explorer pops up a standard Save As dialog box which is almost identical to the dialog box you used in Lesson 3-1 to save text and HTML files. Use the dialog box's file list or Save In box to specify where you want to store the file on your hard disk, and then click the dialog box's Save button to begin downloading the file.

This downloading process may seem complicated, but it really isn't — as we hope the next section demonstrates.

Searching for and downloading a file

You can find thousands of fun and useful files on the Internet. One of the most popular is WinZip, which is a data compression/decompression program — that is, it employs special tricks to shrink files by up to 90 percent of their usual size and then restores the files to normal size when needed.

Most of the files you'll encounter on the Internet are compressed to cut down on the amount of space needed to store them and, more importantly, the amount of time needed to download them. After you transfer a file to your hard disk, you therefore typically need to run a program like WinZip to decompress it and make it useable.

Because WinZip is so handy, we feel that you should have a copy. We've already included it on this book's CD, just in case you don't feel like spending the time and phone charges to download the program. However, if you're willing to go the extra mile to learn about the downloading process — and get the guaranteed latest version of WinZip in the bargain — then follow these steps:

1. **If you aren't still connected to the Internet, dial in again now.**

   Your browser should be maximized and displaying a Web page.

2. **Click the Links bar button that you created in Lesson 2-3 to move to the *Searching the Web* page.**

   You also can reach this page by clicking in the Address bar, typing the URL `net.gurus.com/internet101/search.htm` and pressing Enter.

3. **Locate the HotBot search box and then click in the box.**

   A blinking cursor appears in the box to indicate that you can enter your search text.

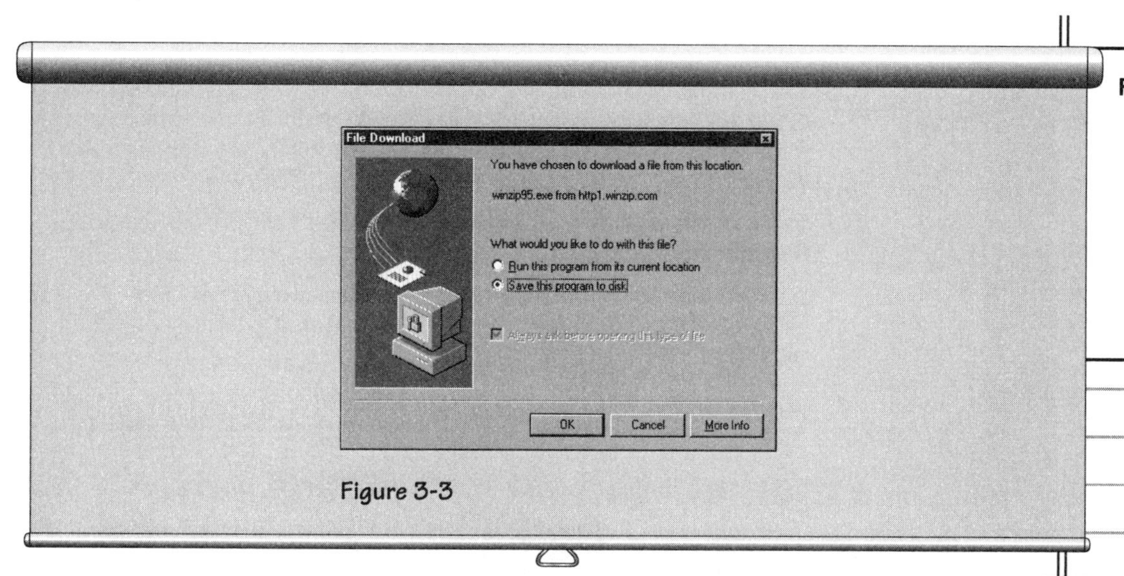

Figure 3-3

Figure 3-3: When you click a link to download a file using Internet Explorer, a File Download dialog box appears. Accept the selected Save This Program to Disk option and click OK to download the file.

4. **Type** winzip home page **and press Enter to find the Web site of the publisher of WinZip.**

   You jump to a HotBot list of Web pages that distribute — or, at minimum, *mention* — WinZip. The WinZip home page (which, at the time of this writing, has the URL `www.winzip.com`) should be listed at least once among the first batch of matches. (If you don't see the WinZip home page at first, try looking at additional matches by clicking the right-pointing arrow near the bottom of the page.)

5. **When you locate a link to the WinZip home page, click the link.**

   If you can't locate the link, just click inside the Address bar, type the URL **www.winzip.com** and press Enter. You should move to the WinZip site.

6. **Locate the link that leads to the WinZip file (for example, a Download WinZip button or Download Evaluation Version graphic), and click the link.**

   You move to another page that offers narrower options leading to the file.

7. **Continue clicking appropriate options until you work your way to the link that lets you download the latest version of WinZip for Windows. After you find the link, click it.**

   A File Download dialog box like the one in Figure 3-3 appears. Notice that the Save This Program to Disk option is selected and an OK button appears near the bottom of the box.

8. **Click the OK button.**

   A Save As dialog box appears that's almost identical to the Save HTML Document dialog box you used in Lesson 3-1 to save Web page data. Notice that the name of the file you want has been entered for you automatically in the File Name box.

9. **Use your mouse to select a folder for temporarily storing the compressed file (or accept whatever folder is currently selected), write down the folder location and filename (for example, jot it down in the margin of this book), and press Enter or click Save to initiate the download.**

The file begins to be copied to your hard disk, as indicated by a status box that continually tells you how much data has been transmitted and how much time is left for the transfer. After the entire file has been copied, the status box goes away.

10 **Using Windows Explorer, switch to the folder that contains your downloaded file.**

Locate your file, which is actually a collection of many compressed files packaged with an installation program. To make WinZip useable, first run the current file.

use WinZip to decompress zipped files

Ensuring efficient downloads with GetRight

Downloading a small file is generally quick and easy. However, downloading a large file can take a long time, which increases the likelihood of something going wrong with your Internet connection during the process. For example, you might spend an hour downloading 95 percent of a large file and then helplessly watch a mishap on the Web site sever your Internet connection. If this occurs, the hour will have been wasted, because you'll have to start the download again from scratch. Worse, you'll have to risk the same thing happening all over again, which can be extremely frustrating.

To avoid such problems, use a shareware program named GetRight, which is included on your *Dummies 101* CD. After installing GetRight following the instructions in Appendix B, run the program by clicking the Start button in the lower-left corner of your screen and then choosing Programs➪GetRight➪GetRight Monitor from the menus that appear.

To use GetRight, locate a link that downloads the file you want, as usual; but instead of clicking the link and releasing your mouse button, click the link and, while keeping your mouse button held down, drag the link to the small GetRight Monitor window. (If the Monitor window isn't visible, first move your mouse to the GetRight button on the taskbar, which will pop up the window.) Alternatively, right-click the link and then choose Copy Shortcut from the menu that appears.

After you either click-and-drag the link or click Copy Shortcut, a GetRight — Save As dialog box appears. As usual, use the Save As dialog box to specify where you want to store the file and press Enter. GetRight then begins the download but also saves special information about the file. If you're disconnected before the downloading has completed, simply dial back into the Net and click GetRight's Resume button; GetRight will magically pick up the downloading from where it left off! This spares you from having to restart a long download from scratch.

One caveat is that GetRight can perform this trick only for those sites that support its "resume" feature; but most modern sites do. And even for sites that don't support it, GetRight saves you a little time by letting you restart the download with a mouse click instead of forcing you to find the download link again and select a folder again.

For more information about GetRight, see Appendix B.

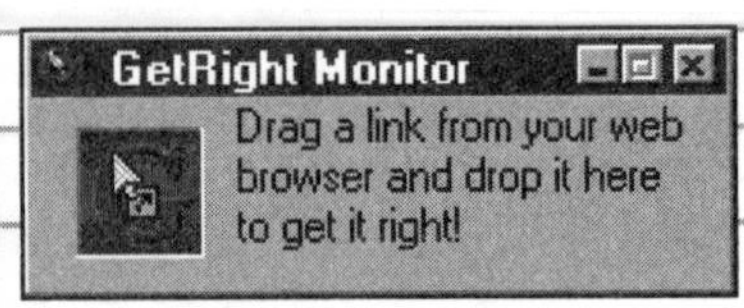

GetRight Monitor window

11 Double-click the WinZip file.

The file runs a setup program. Follow the prompts that appear on your screen to complete your installation of WinZip, and/or see Appendix B for more information. In addition, see Appendix B for instructions on using WinZip to decompress files.

Congratulations! You've successfully downloaded one of the hottest programs on the Internet! Just as importantly, you can use the same procedure to find and download thousands of *other* popular files. And when the files you download are zipped (and it's likely that lots of them will be), you can now use WinZip to decompress them quickly and make them useable.

Notes:

Poking around Web sites for files

As efficient as Web searchers are, you shouldn't rely on them entirely to find files. That's because new kinds of files that you may not even dream exist, let alone think to search for, come out all the time. Therefore, you should also occasionally nose around Web sites devoted to program and data files and see whether anything new catches your fancy. In fact, why not try that now?

1 If you aren't still connected to the Internet, dial in again now.

The favorites you installed in Lesson 2-1 include a folder named Software Libraries. Use this folder now to visit a few software collections.

2 Choose Favorites⇨+Hy's and Margy's Favorites+⇨Software Libraries⇨Clicked.Com Top 20 Shareware Gallery (which is at URL `www.clicked.com/shareware`**).**

You move to what this site considers to be the top 20 Windows programs in each of several categories, including Internet, graphics, multimedia, and games. As of this writing, the site includes the versatile graphics viewer/editor L-View Pro, the business flowchart and diagram generator SmartDraw, the cutting-edge music and words player RealAudio, and the classic game Duke Nukem 3D. Explore the site at your leisure, and download any files that you think would be genuinely useful (but avoid cluttering your disk with files that you don't really need).

3 Choose Favorites⇨+Hy's and Margy's Favorites+⇨Software Libraries⇨SHAREWARE.COM (which is at URL `www.shareware.com`**).**

You move to the SHAREWARE.COM site, which offers thousands of different kinds of files, including word processors, electronic spreadsheets, database programs, picture files, sound files, and more. Snoop around the site's many different areas, including its What's Hot list.

4 Choose Favorites⇨+Hy's and Margy's Favorites+⇨Software Libraries⇨JUMBO! (which is at URL `www.jumbo.com`**).**

You move to JUMBO!, a lighthearted site that also offers tens of thousands of files. Poke around its nooks and crannies, and download any files that you feel may bring you joy.

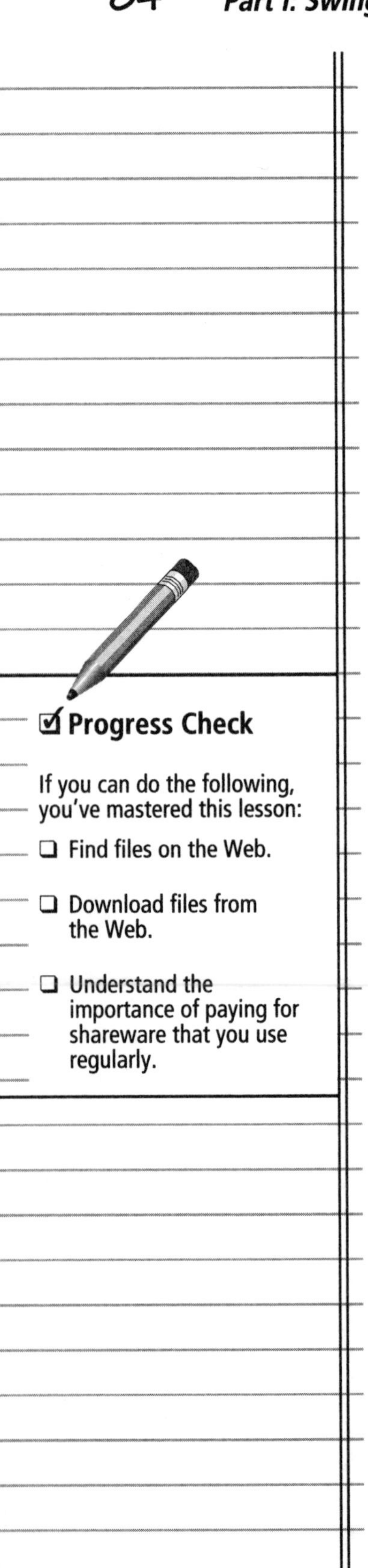

5 Choose Favorites⇨+Hy's and Margy's Favorites+⇨Software Libraries⇨Happy Puppy Games (which is at URL `www.happypuppy.com`**).**

You move to Happy Puppy Games, a site devoted to games that (presumably) will make you as happy as a playful puppy. Sniff around until you're satisfied.

These four sites are by no means the only ones with interesting files available for downloading. For example, arguably the best Internet-related software library is The Ultimate Collection of Winsock Software, or TUCOWS (`www.tucows.com`), which reviews, rates (on a scale of one to five cows), and lets you download fabulous programs that help you exploit the many resources available on the Net.

And if all those sites still don't fulfill your craving for data, you can use links, magazine articles, and the advice of friends to find more. In addition, check in periodically with the *Dummies 101: The Internet for Windows 98* home page (`net.gurus.com/net101`) for recommendations of new software distribution sites as they pop up.

As you download programs and other files, you should keep in mind that many of them are *not* free. Instead, they're *shareware,* which means that these programs are available to you for an evaluation period (typically, anywhere from 30 to 90 days). If you decide that you like a shareware program and want to keep using it, you're expected to send a registration fee to its publisher, which entitles you to technical support and notifications about new versions.

Most shareware operates on an honor system, so the programs continue working even if you don't register them. However, it's a good idea to support the shareware concept and encourage the continued production of quality low-cost software by sending in your payment for the programs you use. For more information about paying for your shareware software, see the registration information that's included with each program.

One last thing to keep in mind when downloading a program is the tiny risk that running it will infect your hard disk with a computer virus. Contrary to the hype from the popular press, the odds of encountering a virus are very low, especially if you stick to well-maintained Web sites that test each program before offering it for downloading. Still, viruses that can infect and destroy your hard disk's data *do* exist, so running a virus-detection program before launching any new software is sensible. You can buy a virus checker from a software store, or you can download one from the Web. Alternatively, you can simply install ThunderBYTE Anti-Virus, which is supplied on your *Dummies 101* CD (as detailed in Appendix B).

Recess

Before you start downloading scores of programs and multimedia files that will keep you at your computer for hours, go out and get some fresh air, smell some flowers (even if you have to walk to a florist to do so), visit some local trees, and feed a squirrel. When you're rejuvenated, return to tackle the following quirky quiz questions.

Unit 3 Quiz

Notes:

For each of the following questions, circle the letter of the correct answer or answers. Remember, each question may have more than one right answer.

1. **Printing a Web page is helpful because:**

   A. The Web is constantly changing, and there's always a chance that the information on a given Web page will suddenly disappear.

   B. Printing preserves the look of a Web page, including its graphics.

   C. Reading from paper pages is often easier on the eyes than reading from a computer screen.

   D. You can carry paper pages anywhere and read them at any time, even when you don't have access to a computer.

   E. All of the above.

2. **To print a Web page:**

   A. You must first obtain a printing license.

   B. Press Ctrl+P and Enter.

   C. Choose File⇨Print and click OK.

   D. Click the Download To Printer button on the toolbar.

   E. Click the Print button on the toolbar.

3. **Saving Web page information to disk is helpful because:**

   A. Limiting paper usage saves both money and trees.

   B. Electronic data is easier to analyze, edit, and reorganize than paper data.

   C. Storing electronic data requires much less space than storing paper data.

   D. Your computer will start acting up if you don't appease it by regularly feeding it interesting new data.

   E. All of the above (except for D).

4. **To save a Web page:**

   A. Pray for it nightly.

   B. Keep it away from direct sunlight.

   C. Click the Save button on the toolbar.

   D. Choose File⇨Save As, select a file type by using the Save as Type box, type a filename in the File Name box, and press Enter.

   E. Sock away a little bit of Web data every day and be patient.

5. **To get, or *download*, a file from the Web:**

   A. Swipe it when nobody's looking and hope you don't get caught.

   B. Offer one of your own files to the Web and try to work out a trade.

   C. Click the Download button on the toolbar, select a folder, and click OK.

   D. Click the file's link, accept the Save This Program to Disk option by clicking the File Download dialog box's OK button, select an appropriate folder using the Save As dialog box, and press Enter or click Save.

   E. You don't get down from a load, you get down from a duck.

Unit 3 Exercise

In this exercise, apply what you've learned about finding files and copying them from the Web by downloading a program that you'd enjoy.

1. Run Internet Explorer and connect to the Net.
2. Click the Links bar button that you created in Lesson 2-5 to move to this book's Searching the Web page (or just use the Address bar to go to `net.gurus.com/internet101/search.htm`).
3. Use a Web searcher such as Yahoo! or HotBot to locate a program devoted to a subject that fascinates you (say, genealogy, or financial investing, or arcade games — whatever you like).
4. Find a few Web pages that describe programs dealing with your subject that sound interesting.
5. Print the pages.
6. Save the pages' contents as text files.
7. Pick the program that you want the most, and locate the link that downloads the program.
8. Click the link to download the file to your hard disk. (***Extra credit:*** Use the GetRight program to ensure an efficient download.)
9. Close Internet Explorer and disconnect from the Net.
10. Double-click the file you downloaded to decompress it and to install your new program.
11. Enjoy!

Note: You've now tackled all the exercises that require your Links bar to have buttons for the *Dummies 101: The Internet for Windows 98* home page and Searching the Web page. If you'd like to eliminate these buttons, open the Organize Favorites dialog box, open the Links folder, delete the two *Dummies 101* favorites from the folder, and close the dialog box.

Unit 4

Customizing the Browser

Objectives for This Unit

- ✓ Cruising the Web without viewing pictures to speed up performance
- ✓ Using multiple browser windows to speed up performance
- ✓ Hiding window elements to expand the browser's Web page display
- ✓ Using menu options or keystrokes in place of the toolbar buttons and Address bar
- ✓ Adjusting other Internet Explorer settings

Prerequisites

- Cruising the Web with Internet Explorer (Lesson 1-2)
- Creating and using favorites (Lessons 2-1 and 2-2)
- Entering URLs (Lesson 2-3)
- Using the Standard Buttons toolbar (Lessons 1-2, 1-3, 2-1, 2-5, and 3-1)

Now that you're an expert at getting around the Web, you're ready to take a closer look at the program that you're using to do your cruising. This final section on the Web therefore concentrates on special features of Internet Explorer.

In this unit, you'll learn how to change Internet Explorer's settings to help you get to Web pages more quickly. You'll also find out how to adjust Internet Explorer's appearance to make it more attractive and more efficient for your particular needs.

Lesson 4-1

Enhancing Internet Explorer's Performance

If you haven't been frustrated by how *l-o-n-g* Web pages take to be transferred to your screen, you're probably using a super-fast computer system and don't have much need for this lesson (although we recommend that you at least skim it to see whether any of the options discussed interest you).

If Web pages *do* take an awfully long time to appear on your screen, your system may have some limitations. For example, your modem may be slower than the current standard speeds of 36,600 or 56,000 bits per second (or *bps*), which puts a ceiling on how rapidly your computer can receive data.

Another possibility is the amount of electronic memory in your system. Modern PCs tend to come with 32MB or 64MB of memory. If your system has less memory, your computer operates less efficiently, and that affects its performance on the Web.

A third factor is the speed of your computer's "brain," which is called a *central processing unit* chip, or *CPU.* Modern PC CPUs include the Pentium and the Pentium Pro, which are faster than such older models as 486 and 386 CPUs.

Upgrading your computer system isn't your only option for boosting performance, though; you can choose to take advantage of some special Internet Explorer features. The next two sections tell you how.

Cruising without pictures

If you don't care to spend lots of money making your computer system faster, you can still improve your cruising speed on the Web dramatically by making one simple adjustment to Internet Explorer: Tell it to skip the pictures.

to prevent Web page pictures from being transmitted, choose View→Internet Options, click the Advanced tab, and click Show Pictures to turn the option off

on the test

Specifically, you can choose View➪Internet Options, click the Advanced tab from the dialog box that appears, and click the Show Pictures option to tell Internet Explorer to *not* transmit any images that appear on a Web page and instead show only a simple "placeholder" graphic for each image. This setting makes transfers go a lot faster because text can move rapidly over the Web. Delays are caused almost entirely by graphics, which require much more data to be displayed on a computer than text does (proving once again that a picture is worth a thousand words).

When the Show Pictures command is turned off, you still have the option of seeing any picture on a Web page, but only when you explicitly *force* Internet Explorer to send the data. You accomplish this by right-clicking the placeholder of the image you want to view and then choosing Show Picture from the menu that appears.

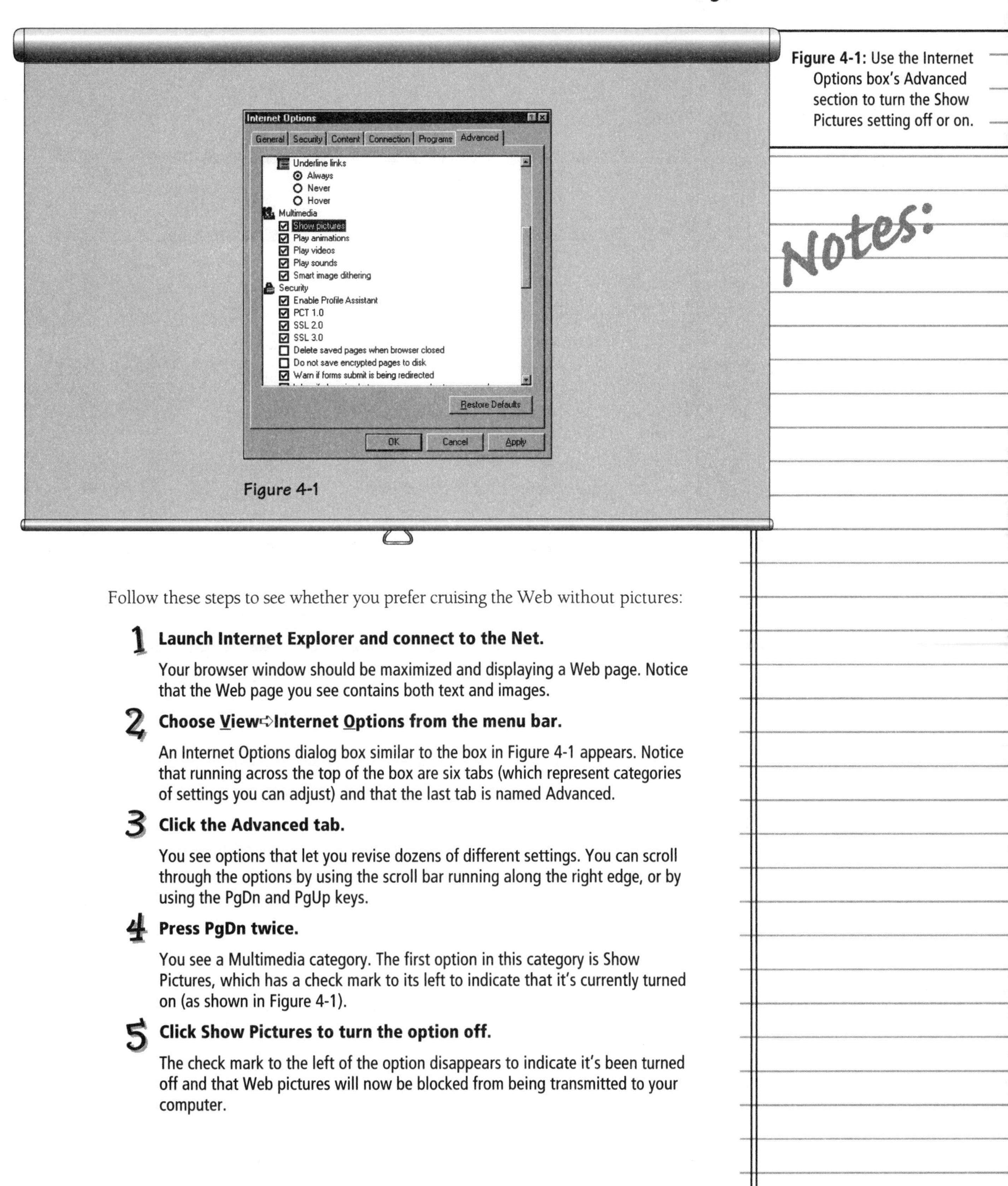

Figure 4-1

Figure 4-1: Use the Internet Options box's Advanced section to turn the Show Pictures setting off or on.

Follow these steps to see whether you prefer cruising the Web without pictures:

1. **Launch Internet Explorer and connect to the Net.**

   Your browser window should be maximized and displaying a Web page. Notice that the Web page you see contains both text and images.

2. **Choose View⇨Internet Options from the menu bar.**

   An Internet Options dialog box similar to the box in Figure 4-1 appears. Notice that running across the top of the box are six tabs (which represent categories of settings you can adjust) and that the last tab is named Advanced.

3. **Click the Advanced tab.**

   You see options that let you revise dozens of different settings. You can scroll through the options by using the scroll bar running along the right edge, or by using the PgDn and PgUp keys.

4. **Press PgDn twice.**

   You see a Multimedia category. The first option in this category is Show Pictures, which has a check mark to its left to indicate that it's currently turned on (as shown in Figure 4-1).

5. **Click Show Pictures to turn the option off.**

   The check mark to the left of the option disappears to indicate it's been turned off and that Web pictures will now be blocked from being transmitted to your computer.

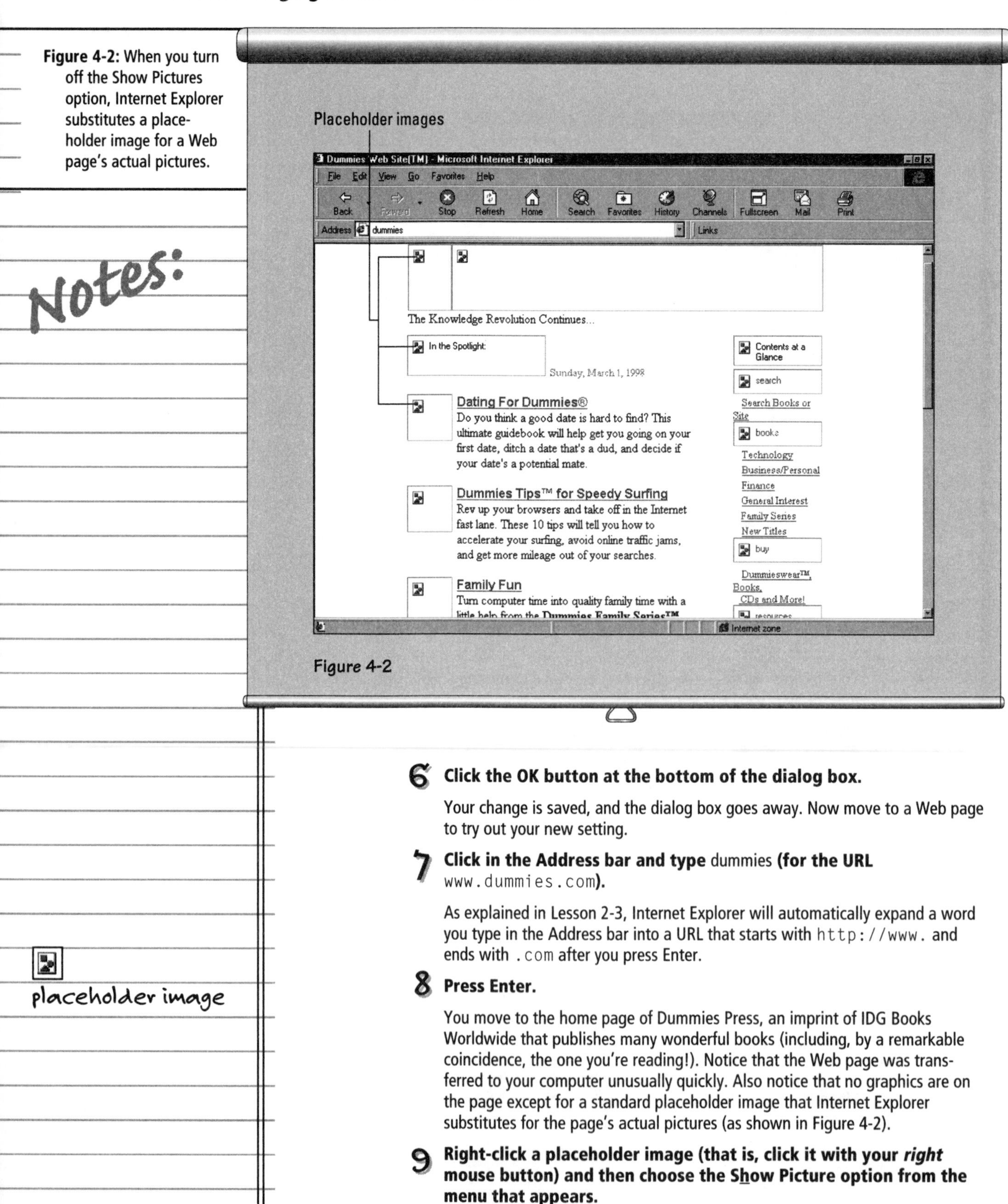

Figure 4-2: When you turn off the Show Pictures option, Internet Explorer substitutes a placeholder image for a Web page's actual pictures.

Figure 4-2

6 **Click the OK button at the bottom of the dialog box.**

Your change is saved, and the dialog box goes away. Now move to a Web page to try out your new setting.

7 **Click in the Address bar and type** dummies **(for the URL** `www.dummies.com`**).**

As explained in Lesson 2-3, Internet Explorer will automatically expand a word you type in the Address bar into a URL that starts with `http://www.` and ends with `.com` after you press Enter.

8 **Press Enter.**

You move to the home page of Dummies Press, an imprint of IDG Books Worldwide that publishes many wonderful books (including, by a remarkable coincidence, the one you're reading!). Notice that the Web page was transferred to your computer unusually quickly. Also notice that no graphics are on the page except for a standard placeholder image that Internet Explorer substitutes for the page's actual pictures (as shown in Figure 4-2).

9 **Right-click a placeholder image (that is, click it with your *right* mouse button) and then choose the Show Picture option from the menu that appears.**

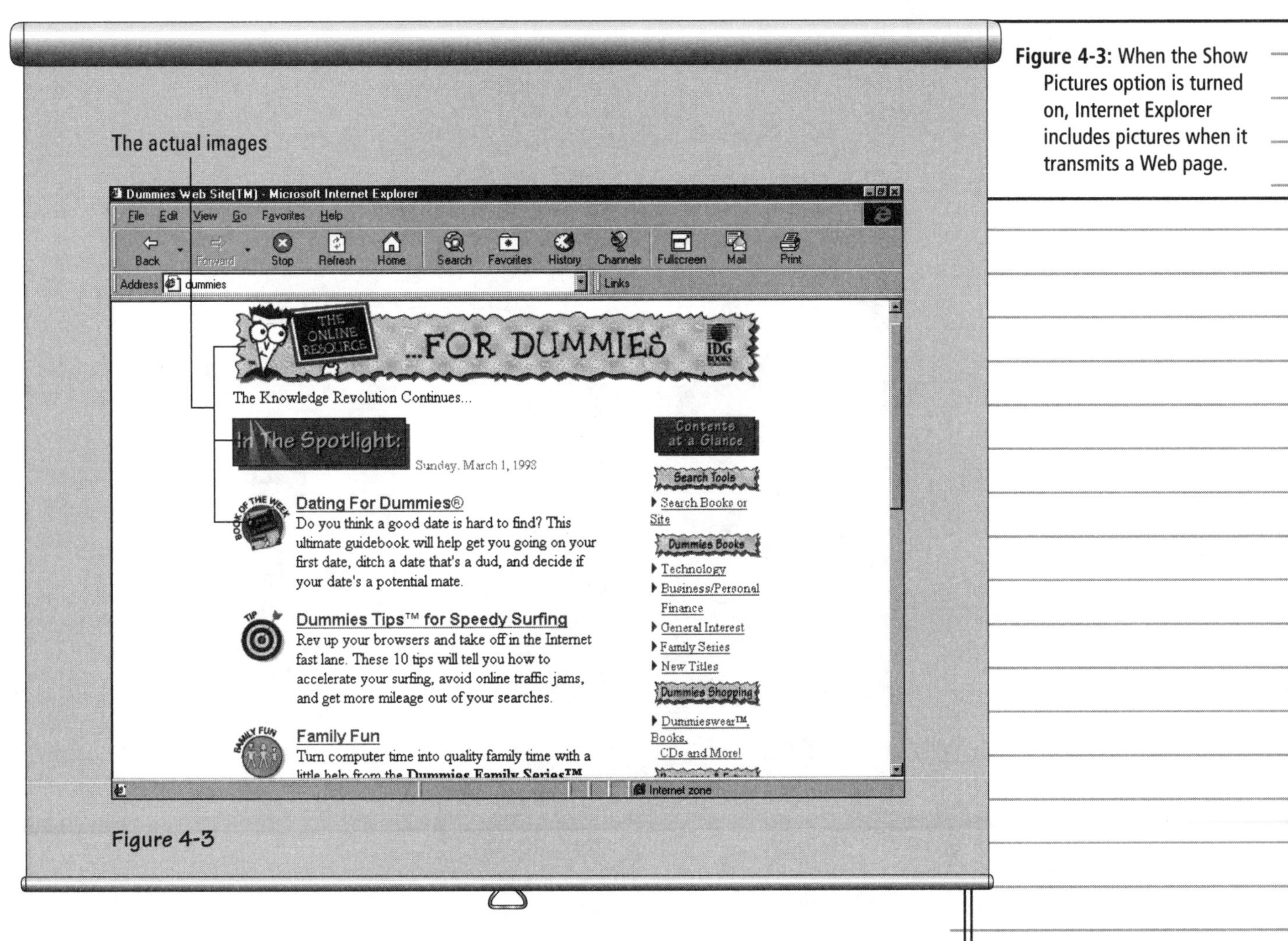

Figure 4-3

Figure 4-3: When the Show Pictures option is turned on, Internet Explorer includes pictures when it transmits a Web page.

After a pause, Internet Explorer replaces the placeholder you clicked with the actual picture the placeholder represented.

10 **Explore the Dummies Press Web site by clicking various interesting links. Whenever you see a placeholder representing an image that intrigues you, right-click the placeholder and choose Show Picture to see the actual image.**

If you find that moving from page to page without having to wait for pictures to be transmitted makes Web cruising more enjoyable, consider keeping the Show Pictures option turned off in the future. To perform the remaining exercises in this unit, however, turn the option back on.

11 **Choose View⇨Internet Options, click the Advanced tab, press PgDn twice, click the Show Pictures option to turn its check mark back on, and click the OK button.**

The dialog box disappears. You're now set to display pictures on Web pages again.

12 **Click in the Address bar, type** dummies **to return to the Dummies Press home page, and press Enter.**

Unless you have a very fast system, the data transfer takes noticeably longer to complete this time. On the other hand, the Web page is now much more lively and attractive (see Figure 4-3).

to force the display of a Web page picture, right-click its placeholder image and choose Show Picture

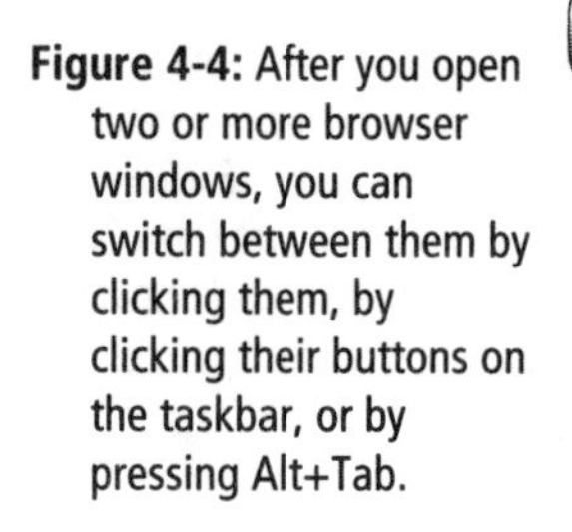

Figure 4-4: After you open two or more browser windows, you can switch between them by clicking them, by clicking their buttons on the taskbar, or by pressing Alt+Tab.

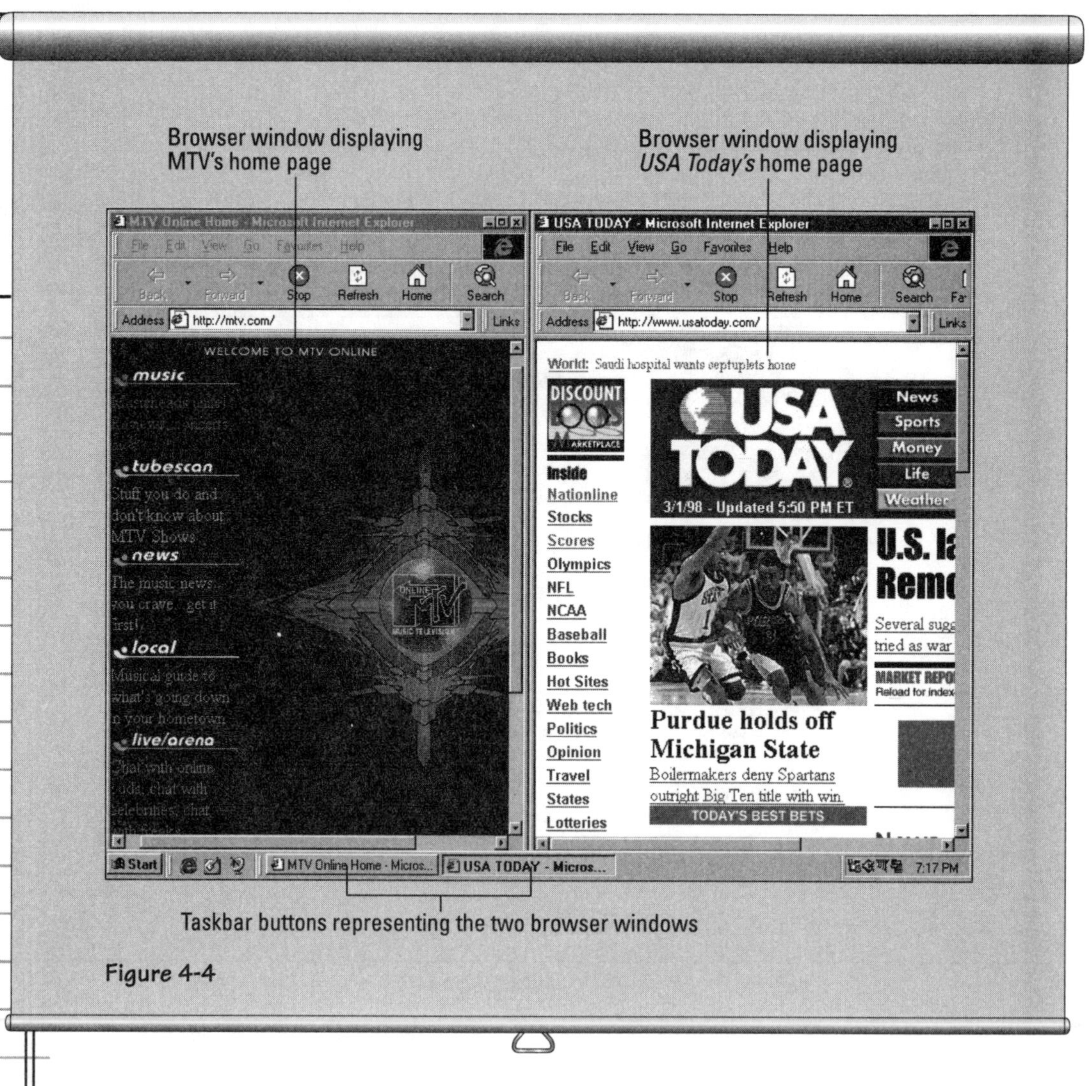

Figure 4-4

To sum up, the Show Pictures command lets you choose between the pleasure of Web graphics and the pleasure of speedy cruising. Which you opt for depends in part on the reason that you're using the Web — for example, pictures aren't as important for research as they are for entertainment — and on just how exasperated you are by the amount of time Web pages take to appear on your screen. If you *do* decide to run with the Show Pictures option turned off, don't forget that you can still display any image by right-clicking its placeholder and choosing Show Picture.

Using multiple browsers

People say that two heads are better than one. After reading this section, you may decide that the same is true of browsers! That's because you can increase your efficiency by using two (or more) Internet Explorer windows at the same time.

Running multiple browsers allows you to study the information on one Web page while Web data is being transferred in the background to a different Internet Explorer window. It also lets you switch between several Web pages without having to wait for any of the pages to reload.

Opening a new browser is a snap; just choose File➪New➪Window or press Ctrl+N. You can do so as often as you like (up to the limits of your computer's memory), but it's generally best to avoid running more than two or three browsers at a time to avoid confusion. After you open your browser windows, you can switch between them by pressing Alt+Tab, or by clicking them, or by clicking their buttons on the Windows 98 taskbar.

To explore the advantages of using multiple browser windows, follow these steps:

1. **If you aren't still connected to the Internet, dial in again now.**

   Your browser window should be open and displaying a Web page.

2. **Choose File➪New➪Window or press Ctrl+N.**

   A second browser window opens on top of your first one. If the second window is maximized (that is, completely covering your initial window), it may not be obvious that you have two browsers running. However, you can verify it by noticing that the Windows 98 taskbar at the bottom of your screen now has two Internet Explorer window buttons to represent the two browsers (as shown in Figure 4-4). You can also verify it by resizing the windows so that both are visible at the same time (as also shown in Figure 4-4).

3. **Access the home page of *USA Today* — which gives you the day's news — by clicking in the Address bar, typing** usatoday **(for the URL** `www.usatoday.com`**), and pressing Enter.**

   In your second browser window, you move to the *USA Today* Web site.

4. **On the Windows 98 taskbar, click the button representing your first browser window (that is, the button that is *not* currently pushed in).**

   You switch to your first browser window, which still displays your initial Web page, proving that your two browser windows are operating independently of each other. Now that you have two browsers open, you can read the information in one while transferring Web data to the other.

5. **Access the home page of MTV (a Web site that typically contains a lot of graphics) by clicking in your first browser's Address bar, typing** mtv **(for the URL** `www.mtv.com`**), and pressing Enter.**

   Your first browser connects to the MTV site and begins transmitting its Web page data. MTV typically crams lots of pictures on its pages, though, so instead of waiting for the process to complete, make good use of your time by switching to your second browser window.

6. **On the taskbar, click the button representing your second browser window (that is, the button that is *not* currently pushed in).**

   The *USA Today* home page is displayed again. Spend a minute or two scrolling through the page to read today's headlines and see what articles are available.

Notes:

to open another Internet Explorer window, choose File→New→Window or press Ctrl+N

☑ Progress Check

If you can do the following, you've mastered this lesson:

- ❑ Prevent Web page pictures from being transmitted.
- ❑ Force a Web page picture to be transmitted by right-clicking its placeholder image.
- ❑ Open and use multiple Internet Explorer windows.

7 On the taskbar, click the button representing your first browser window (that is, the button that is *not* currently pushed in).

You should see the complete MTV home page. While you were reading today's news, all the data on this Web page was transmitted in the background. Examine the MTV page until you're ready to exit it.

8 Press Ctrl+W (or choose File⇨Close) to close your second browser window.

The window exits, returning you to the first browser window.

9 If your browser window is no longer maximized, click its Maximize button.

The window fills the screen, providing you with a large Web display.

This exercise demonstrates only one use of multiple browsers. As you become comfortable juggling several browser windows simultaneously, you're likely to find additional uses suited to your particular work habits that help you save time and avoid frustrating waits.

Lesson 4-2

Adjusting Internet Explorer's Settings

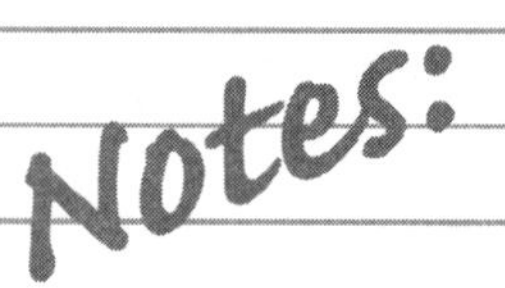

Internet Explorer is extremely flexible in the ways that it lets you display both itself and Web data. For example, you can hide and expand parts of its window, adjust how links appear, select different fonts and colors, and even choose to operate in a different language! This lesson shows you how to use such options to tailor Internet Explorer's settings to your personal tastes.

Hiding the browser window's toolbars

Only about three-quarters of your Internet Explorer window is normally available for displaying Web pages. The rest of the window is taken up by such elements as the Standard Buttons toolbar, which houses buttons that help you navigate, locate, and print Web pages; the Address bar, which lets you enter URLs; and the Links bar, which houses buttons you've created to quickly move you to your favorite Web sites.

on the test

Although these elements in your Internet Explorer window are convenient, they are *not* necessities. That's because the functions they provide are all duplicated by Internet Explorer menu options and/or special keystrokes. As a result, you may want to consider eliminating some or all of these toolbars to make more room in the window for your Web page display. Here's how:

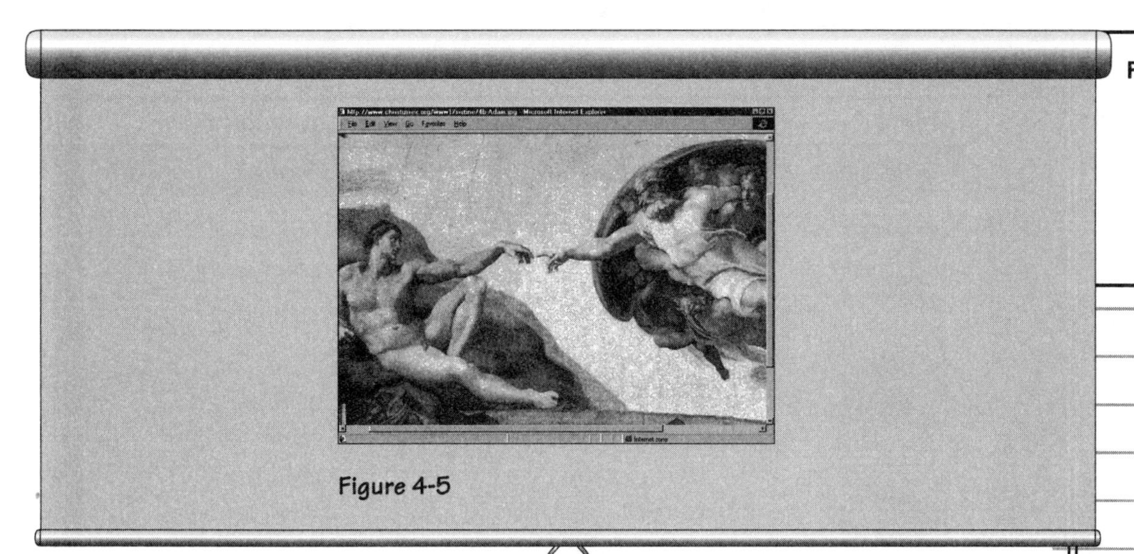
Figure 4-5

Figure 4-5: When you hide the Standard Buttons, Address, and Links bars in an Internet Explorer window, you provide more room for Web pages to be displayed.

1. **If you aren't still connected to the Internet, dial in again now.**

   Your browser window should be maximized and displaying a Web page. In addition, you should see the Standard Buttons toolbar, Address bar, and Links bar displayed near the top of the window.

2. **Choose View⇨Toolbars.**

   The View menu spawns a submenu with the options Standard Buttons, Address Bar, Links, and Text Labels (the latter controlling whether the buttons on the toolbar display text labels as well as pictures to identify their respective functions). Notice that each bar has a check mark to its left, which indicates that it's currently turned on.

3. **Click the Standard Buttons option to turn off its check mark.**

   The Standard Buttons toolbar disappears. Also, the Web page display expands to take advantage of the additional space you created in the window.

4. **Choose View⇨Toolbars⇨Address Bar.**

   The Address bar goes away, and the Web page expands again to exploit the extra space. Also, your Links bar now either appears on its own line . . . or has jumped into the right side of the menu bar!

5. **Choose View⇨Toolbars⇨Links.**

   The Links bar evaporates. Also, the Web page expands to take up most of the window (as shown in Figure 4-5).

to hide or display an Internet Explorer toolbar, choose View→Toolbars and then click the pertinent toolbar option

Running Internet Explorer this way doesn't require sacrifices in functionality, because you can still access all the usual commands by using menu options or keystrokes. For example, instead of using a constantly available Address bar, you can choose File⇨Open or press Ctrl+O to open a temporary Address bar that exits after you type a URL and press Enter. As another example, instead of clicking the Back button, you can choose Go⇨Back or press Alt+← (that is, Alt and the left arrow key). You can also do without your Links bar buttons by choosing Favorites⇨Links and then clicking whatever favorite you're after. A complete list of toolbar button, Address bar, and Links bar equivalents appears in Table 4-1.

to open a temporary Address bar, choose File→Open or press Ctrl+O

Notes:

Table 4-1 Internet Explorer Toolbar Button Equivalents

Toolbar Button	*Menu Option*	*Keystroke(s)*
Back	Go⇨Back	Alt+←
Forward	Go⇨Forward	Alt+→
Stop	View⇨Stop	Esc
Refresh	View⇨Refresh	F5
Home	Go⇨Home Page	Alt+G, H
Search	View⇨Explorer Bar⇨Search	Alt+V, E, S
Favorites	View⇨Explorer Bar⇨Favorites	Alt+V, E, F
History	View⇨Explorer Bar⇨History	Alt+V, E, H
Channels	View⇨Explorer Bar⇨Channels	Alt+V, E, C
Fullscreen	View⇨Full Screen	F11
Mail	Go⇨Mail	Alt+G, M
Print	File⇨Print	Ctrl+P

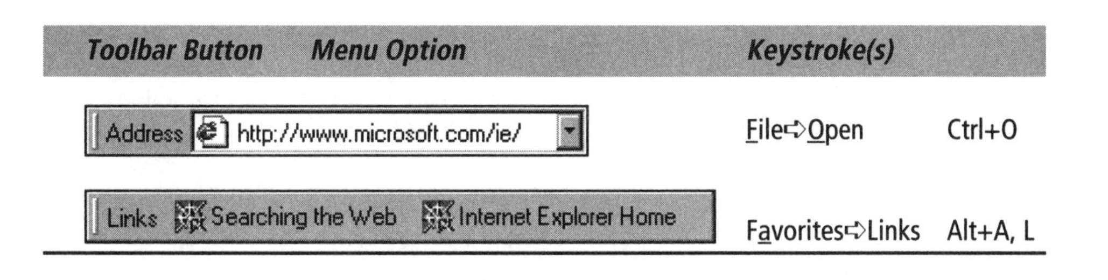

Toolbar Button	Menu Option	Keystroke(s)
Address http://www.microsoft.com/ie/	File⇨Open	Ctrl+O
Links Searching the Web Internet Explorer Home	Favorites⇨Links	Alt+A, L

The Refresh button

If you tend to visit Web pages that change frequently, or if you sometimes have trouble with Web pages loading, you should become familiar with the Refresh button on the Standard Buttons toolbar. As its name implies, Refresh forces your current Web page's contents to be retransmitted, or *refreshed*. This button is useful because the Web transfers only a "snapshot" of a page at the moment you access it, so what you're viewing doesn't reflect subsequent changes that occur on the Web page. If you're connected to, say, a page of stock quotes that's updated every minute, you need to click Refresh periodically to get the latest information from the page.

Another reason that you may be viewing old Web data is that Internet Explorer uses a portion of your hard disk, called a *disk cache*, to temporarily store pages you've recently traveled to. When you tell Internet Explorer to return to a page that you've visited, it checks its storage area and, if the page is there, loads the page from your hard disk immediately instead of making you wait for it to be recopied from the Web. This is a great time-saver when you're accessing Web pages that don't change frequently. If you suspect that a page has changed since your last visit, though, clicking Refresh makes Internet Explorer check for changes and, if it finds them, retransmit the page from the Web.

Finally, if a Web page that you cruise to doesn't transfer properly for some reason, you can click Refresh to make Internet Explorer resend the page to your computer.

Refresh button

The Mail and Channels buttons

The only two elements on the Standard Buttons toolbar that we haven't covered yet are the Mail and Channels buttons.

The Mail button lets you launch an e-mail manager or newsgroup reader directly from your browser window. For more information about e-mail and newsgroup programs, see Units 5, 6, and 7 in this book, and Unit ML on your *Dummies 101* CD. To learn how to tell Internet Explorer which particular programs to run when you use the Mail button, see the "Changing Internet Explorer Settings" section later in this lesson.

Similarly, the Channels button lets you launch the channels feature built into Windows 98. For more information about using channels, see Unit 8.

Mail button

Channels button

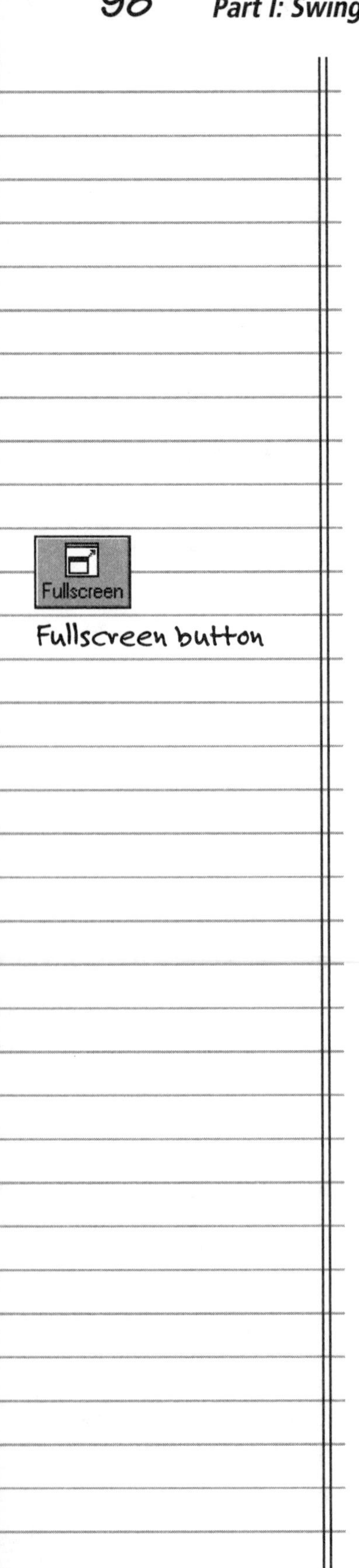

Fullscreen button

Although you don't *need* to include the Standard Buttons toolbar, Address bar, and Links bar in your browser window, you may prefer the one-click convenience these bars provide to having a larger Web page display. Happily, you can always restore any bar by just turning its menu option on again:

1. **Choose View⇨Toolbars⇨Standard Buttons.**

   The Web page display shrinks to provide some extra room in the window, and the Standard Buttons toolbar reappears.

2. **Choose View⇨Toolbars⇨Address Bar.**

   The Web page display shrinks some more, and the Address bar comes back.

3. **Choose View⇨Toolbars⇨Links.**

   The Web page display returns to its standard size, and the Links bar reappears.

Even if you keep all the bars turned on, you can still achieve a large Web page display when needed by clicking the Fullscreen button on the Standard Buttons toolbar. This button hides all window elements except for scroll bars and the Standard Buttons toolbar — which Internet Explorer shrinks to half-size by removing the text labels from the buttons — providing the most amount of room possible for showing a Web page. A disadvantage of this view is that it hides the menu bar; but when you need to click a menu, you can instantly switch back to your previous window layout by just clicking the Fullscreen button again.

Whether you decide to devote a larger area of your browser window to the Web page display or accept the standard window is entirely a matter of taste. Therefore, simply choose a window arrangement that you're comfortable with and that pleases your eye.

Rearranging the browser window's toolbars

In addition to deciding whether the Standard Buttons toolbar, Address bar, and Links bar appear, you can choose the *order* in which they appear. Even better, you can do so with just a few clicks and drags of your mouse! Here's how:

1. **Move your mouse pointer over the ridge on the left edge of the Standard Buttons toolbar.**

   When the pointer is positioned properly, it changes from its usual single arrowhead shape to two arrowheads pointing left and right.

2. **Click the ridge and, while keeping your mouse button held down, drag the toolbar down as far as it will go; then release your mouse button.**

   The Standard Buttons toolbar, which is normally above the Address and Links bars, slides down to reside below them.

3. **Click the ridge on the left edge of the Address bar and, while keeping your mouse button held down, drag the bar down as far as it will go; then release your mouse button.**

   The Address bar settles down below the Standard Buttons toolbar again.

4 Click the ridge at the left edge of the Links bar and, while keeping your mouse button held down, drag the bar to the right side of the Address bar; then release your mouse button.

Each of the bars can resize itself to share space with any other bar (including the menu bar!). Therefore, the Links bar settles into the right side of the Address bar. You can adjust how much space a bar occupies by clicking and dragging the bar's ridge sideways.

5 Click the ridge at the left edge of the Links bar and, while keeping your mouse button held down, drag to the left or right until you're satisfied with the amount of space allocated to both the Address bar and Links bar; then release your mouse button.

Alternatively, click and drag the Links bar down to allow both it and the Address bar to fully stretch across the window.

You can order and combine the Standard Buttons toolbar, Address bar, and Links bar in almost any way — for example, you can place all the bars on the same line alongside the menu bar! So if you ever get bored with the way your browser bars look, don't hesitate to give them a makeover. All it takes is a few mouse clicks.

Notes:

Changing Internet Explorer settings

on the test

In addition to rearranging the elements in your browser window, you can adjust how links appear, what colors and fonts you see in your Web display, which Web page pops up when you run Internet Explorer, and dozens of other settings. You can revise any or all of these options by choosing View⇨Internet Options and then selecting the appropriate category tab. To discover the many varied and astounding choices that Internet Explorer offers you, follow these steps:

1 Choose Help⇨Contents and Index.

An Internet Explorer Help window appears that contains extensive information about the browser's options. To look up an option, click the Index tab near the top of the window (as shown in Figure 4-6); type an appropriate word or phrase in the text box below the tab; press Enter to display a list of mini-articles about your topic; and double-click an article to view its contents. Keep this Help window open and turn to it any time you want to learn more about the options you encounter in this exercise.

You can also get quick information about an option by simply right-clicking it and choosing a What's This? command (as you'll see shortly).

Now that you have help at hand, you're ready to explore the browser's settings.

2 Choose View⇨Internet Options.

The Internet Options dialog box in Figure 4-7 appears. As you may recall from Lesson 4-1, this dialog box has six tabs running across its top for the settings categories General, Security, Content, Connection, Programs, and Advanced.

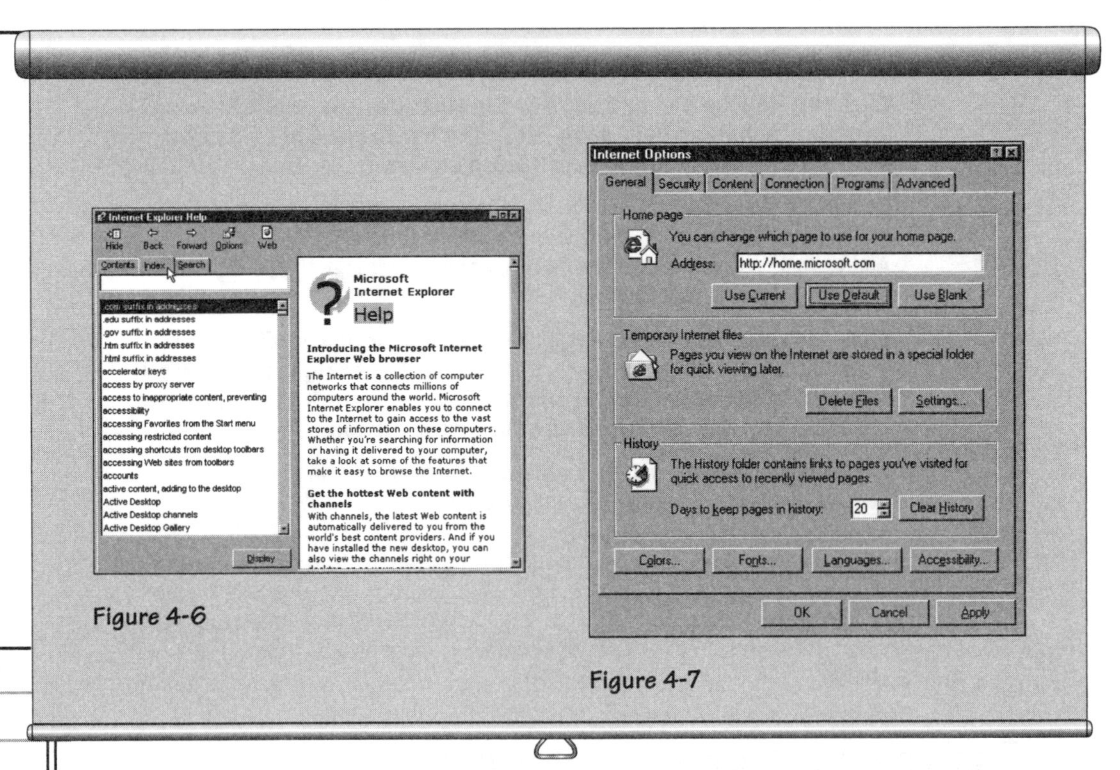

Figure 4-6: The Internet Explorer Help window lets you look up information about virtually any option provided by the browser program.

Figure 4-7: The Internet Options dialog box lets you adjust dozens of different Internet Explorer settings, including the Web address of your home page, the size of your disk cache, and the number of days the History bar remembers your Web page visits.

You start off in the General category, which contains most of the settings you'll normally care about, and is itself divided into a number of sections.

The top section is named Home Page, because it lets you choose which Web page is displayed when you start your browser or click the Home button. With a mouse click, you can set the home page to be the Web page you're currently visiting; the default page (which is typically either the home page of your ISP or the Microsoft Internet home page at `home.microsoft.com`); or a blank page. Alternatively, you can specify any Web page you want by typing its URL in the Address text box.

The bottom section of the dialog box is titled History, because it lets you set the number of days that the History bar will store the names and URLs of Web pages you've visited (the default being 20 days). This section also lets you delete the contents of the History bar by clicking a Clear History button.

Make any changes that you desire, or just accept the current settings. In addition, if you aren't sure what an option does, right-click it.

3 Right-click (that is, click with your *right* mouse button) the Days To Keep Pages In History option and then click the What's This? command that appears.

A brief description of the option pops up. As we mentioned previously, you can right-click any option in the dialog box to learn the option's function. If you want further details, you can look up the option in the Internet Explorer Help window. Don't hesitate to exploit these information resources whenever you want to know more about an option.

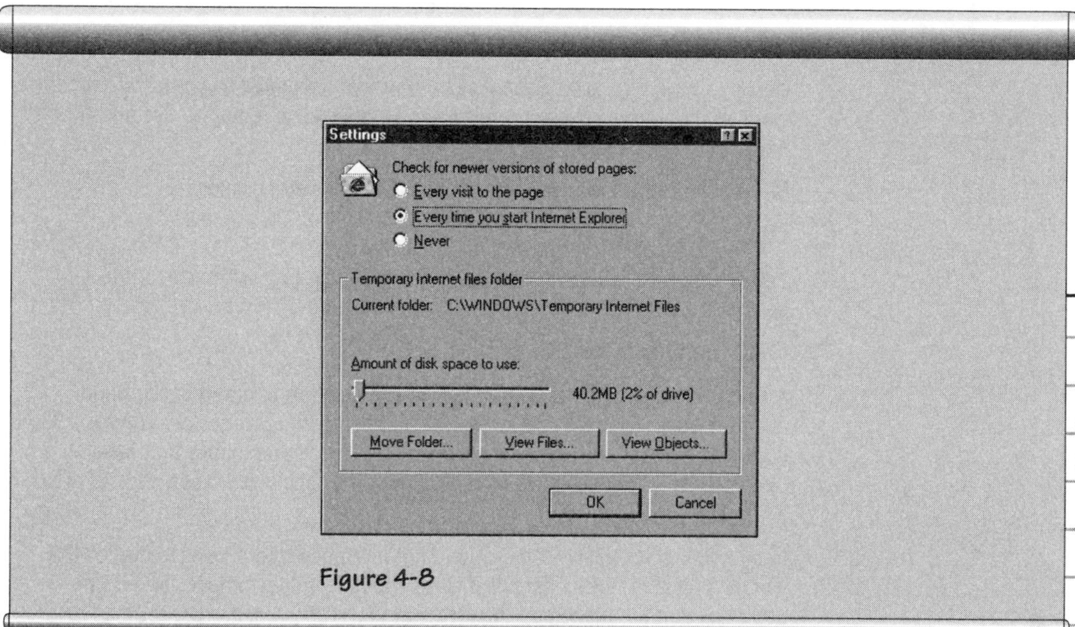

Figure 4-8

Figure 4-8: The Settings dialog box lets you adjust the size of Internet Explorer's disk cache, which is a temporary storage space that helps speed up your Web cruising.

Notes:

Click any blank area of the dialog box.

The description of the option goes away, giving you a clear view of the dialog box again. Notice that the dialog box's middle section is named Temporary Internet Files. This section lets you adjust a temporary storage area on your hard disk — called a *disk cache* — that saves recent data, such as the text and graphics of the last few Web pages you've visited. Whenever you revisit a Web page, Internet Explorer checks to see whether the page is already present in your disk cache. If it is, Internet Explorer displays the page immediately from the cache instead of making you wait for the page to be retransmitted from the Web. If you're ever running short of disk space, however, you can erase the contents of the cache by clicking the Delete Files button and clicking OK. In addition, you can adjust the size of the disk cache by using the Settings button.

5 **Click the Settings button.**

A dialog box appears that provides several cache-related options, including buttons that let you view the files currently in the cache and select a different folder for storing the cache (as shown in Figure 4-8).

A Web page's contents may change between the time that it's stored in the cache and the time you next visit it, so you're also given the options of having Internet Explorer check the cache data against Web data on Every Visit to the Page (which is slowest), Never (which is fastest), or Every Time You Start Internet Explorer (meaning once per session, which is the default). Even if you choose Never, keep in mind that you can always update a Web page by clicking the toolbar's Refresh button.

Also notice that the middle of the dialog box contains a special control called a *slider* that you can move to the left to decrease the amount of disk space allocated to the cache or move to the right to increase the cache's size. A large cache improves Internet Explorer's chances of being able to load Web pages directly from your hard disk when you revisit them, which speeds up your Web cruising; but a big cache also takes up space you could be using to store other types of files. A typical compromise is to set the cache to two to five percent of a hard disk's total size.

Make any changes that you like, or just leave the settings alone.

6 **Click the OK button.**

You return to the General settings. Now notice the four buttons near the bottom named Colors, Fonts, Languages, and Accessibility.

7 **Click the Colors button.**

A Colors dialog box pops up that lets you choose the Text and Background colors of your browser window, the default being whatever colors Windows 98 is set to. (***Note:*** These settings normally affect only Web pages that haven't already been assigned colors by their authors. To apply your color choices to *all* Web pages, see Step 10.)

In addition, you can select the colors that Internet Explorer uses to display links you haven't clicked (the default is blue) and links that you have clicked (the default is purple). Make any changes that you want, or leave the settings as they are.

8 **Click OK to exit the Colors box, and click the Fonts button (near the bottom of the dialog box).**

Options that let you select which fonts Internet Explorer uses to display Web page text appear. The top option lets you select the language of the font letters and offers such choices as Baltic Alphabet, Central European, Cyrillic, Turkish Alphabet, and Western (which includes the English alphabet and is the default).

The other options let you select a Proportional Font (a font that adjusts the spaces between letters to enhance readability, and is used for most text); a Fixed-Width Font (a font that maintains the same space between each letter, and is used for special text such as computer programming code); and the size of the fonts (ranging from Smallest to Largest). The respective defaults are Times New Roman, Courier New, and Medium.

Click inside each box that interests you to drop down a list of choices, and then click the new setting you want. On the other hand, if you're comfortable with the current font settings, simply let them stand.

9 **Click OK to exit the Fonts box, and click the Languages button (near the bottom of the dialog box).**

You're asked to specify which languages Internet Explorer should display (that is, in addition to the one you're using). This option is handy if you expect to access Web pages written in other languages. Add languages by clicking the Add button, or just leave the language list as it is.

10 **Click OK to exit the Language Preference box, and click the Accessibility button (near the bottom of the dialog box).**

You see options that let you override the color and font settings of Web pages with the settings you selected in Steps 7 and 8. This option is useful if you have difficulty distinguishing between certain colors or seeing small letters; or if you're using a notebook PC that doesn't display colors or text clearly. Otherwise, we suggest that you leave these options turned off so you can view each Web page the way it was designed to look.

11 Click OK to exit the Language Preference box.

You've completed exploring the dialog box's General category, which includes most of the settings you'll normally want to adjust. Now take a brief look at the remaining five categories.

12 Click the Security tab (near the top of the dialog box).

Options appear that let you set up different security levels, or *zones*. For each zone, accept the default Medium option if you want to be warned every time Internet Explorer thinks you're about to send or receive sensitive data; click the Low option if you want to skip seeing warning messages; or click the High option if you want to bar even the possibility of viewing certain types of data. For more information about security, right-click each option in the dialog box and/or look up *security* in the Internet Explorer Help window.

13 Click the Content tab (near the top of the dialog box).

Options appear that let you turn on a Content Advisor program that helps block out the racier areas of the Net (in case children have access to your PC); set up electronic IDs that can be used to identify you for financial transactions over the Net; and create an electronic business card that you can attach to e-mail messages (see Lesson 6-1 for details). For more information about any option, right-click the option and/or look it up in the Internet Explorer Help window.

14 Click the Connection tab (near the top of the dialog box).

Technical settings appear that tell Internet Explorer how you're connected to the Net. If you dial into the Net using a modem and phone line, the Connect to the Internet Using a Modem setting is selected. Otherwise, speak to your system administrator if you're having problems getting Internet Explorer to connect to the Net.

15 Click the Programs tab (near the top of the dialog box).

You see options that let you identify your favorite e-mail manager (Mail), newsgroup reader (News), Internet conference manager (Internet Call), electronic appointment manager (Calendar), and electronic address book (Contact List). When you try to perform a task from Internet Explorer that requires one of these extra programs, or when you click an option from the Mail button on the Standard Buttons toolbar, Internet Explorer can use the information supplied in this dialog box to run the particular program you want immediately instead of having to first ask you to specify the program.

For additional information about any option, right-click the option and/or look it up in the Internet Explorer Help window. You can also learn more about e-mail managers and electronic address books in Units 5 and 6 in this book, and Unit ML on this book's CD; and you can learn more about newsgroup readers in Unit 7.

16 Click the Advanced tab (near the top of the dialog box).

Dozens of miscellaneous settings appear. Some of these settings can have major effects, as you saw in Lesson 4-1 when you used the Show Picture option to block Internet Explorer from transmitting pictures from Web pages.

The meaning of most of these options is self-evident. However, the options involving Java and cookies (which, contrary to appearances, have nothing to do with after-dinner treats) require special explanations.

Notes:

Java is the main programming language used on the Internet. The default is to allow Java programs to run automatically whenever you encounter a Web page that includes them, because they can make Web browsing a lot more fun. However, if you'd rather not be slowed down by such programs, or if you're nervous about the security aspects of having programs run automatically (even though Java programs have safeguards built-in), you can turn off Internet Explorer's ability to run Java.

Cookies are small bits of information that help Web sites remember previous choices you've made. For example, if you were visiting an online mall, you might select several items to place in your electronic shopping basket but then go to another Web site to compare prices before actually making your purchases. Your first Web site would ordinarily store your shopping basket selections as cookies on your hard disk so that they'd be waiting for you when you returned to the site. Unless you're concerned about the security aspects of Web sites that you visit writing data to your hard disk, let stand the default selection of Always Accept Cookies. (Needless to say, this option is also the appropriate choice if you have a sweet tooth.)

Covering every setting in the Advanced category is beyond the scope of this book, but we encourage you to examine them on your own. If you need more information about any option, right-click it and/or look it up in the Internet Explorer Help window.

17 If you're satisfied with all the settings changes that you've made, click the Internet Options box's OK button; otherwise, click the box's Cancel button to abandon your changes.

The dialog box closes, and, if you clicked OK, your changes go into effect. If you aren't satisfied later with the way everything turned out, simply choose View⇨Internet Options again, adjust your settings as needed, and click OK again.

Wow! We haven't seen so many choices since Ben and Jerry started making ice cream! All these options may be a little overwhelming at first, but as you continue to work with Internet Explorer, you'll probably come to appreciate the flexibility they offer. You can always simply accept the default settings — many people do — but if you find yourself dissatisfied with an aspect of Internet Explorer's appearance or performance, don't hesitate to use the Internet Options dialog box to tailor the browser to your personal tastes and needs.

☑ Progress Check

If you can do the following, you've mastered this lesson:

- ❑ Hide and restore the Standard Buttons toolbar, Address bar, and Links bar.
- ❑ Move and resize the Standard Buttons toolbar, Address bar, and Links bar.
- ❑ Pop up the Internet Options dialog box.
- ❑ Adjust any of Internet Explorer's dozens of different settings.

Recess

You've just completed this book's course on the World Wide Web, and you've done it superbly! You can now impress your friends by slinging around intimidating phrases like *URL* and *Web link* and *Yahoo! search engine*, and by saying cool things like, "Hey dudes, wanna cruise on down to my fave home page?" Relax a spell by taking a long, leisurely walk, going for a swim, or riding your bike. When you're fully refreshed, fly through these quiz questions on fiddling with Internet Explorer.

Unit 4 Quiz

Notes:

For each of the following questions, circle the letter of the correct answer or answers. Remember, each question may have more than one right answer.

1. **To access Web pages more quickly, you can**
   A. Lure the pages toward you with sweets.
   B. Say the magic words "open sez me" five times fast.
   C. Upgrade your system by adding memory, installing a speedier modem, and/or buying a machine with a faster CPU.
   D. Choose View➪Internet Options, click the Advanced tab, click Show Pictures to turn this option off, and click OK.
   E. Type faster.

2. **If the Show Pictures option is turned off, you can still view a Web page picture by:**
   A. Wearing those crazy 3-D glasses that are now packaged with all new computers.
   B. Clicking the Show Me button.
   C. Clicking the placeholder image.
   D. Right-clicking the placeholder image and choosing Show Picture.
   E. Choosing View➪Load Thousand Words.

3. **To open another Internet Explorer window:**
   A. Buy another computer, install another copy of Internet Explorer, place your second computer next to your first one, and go wild.
   B. Choose File➪New➪Window.
   C. Press Ctrl+N.
   D. Trick question; you can't open more than one Internet Explorer window at a time.
   E. You *can* open more than one Internet Explorer window at a time, but doing so makes your computer explode.

4. **Elements that you can adjust on an Internet Explorer window include**
   A. The lace curtains.
   B. The Standard Buttons toolbar.
   C. The Address Bar.
   D. The Links bar.
   E. The bug-proof screen.

5. The Internet Options dialog box lets you:

A. Choose which Web page you move to when you start up Internet Explorer.

B. Set the size of Internet Explorer's disk cache.

C. Select the fonts and colors that appear in your browser window.

D. Set the number of days the History bar remembers your Web page visits.

E. Change the Internet Explorer logo's rotating planet to flying toasters.

6. A new scene that appears in the revamped *Star Wars* trilogy is

A. Jabba the Hut walking and talking in the first film.

B. Luke Skywalker initially blowing up the wrong Deathstar.

C. Yoda reminiscing about his early days working for a furniture moving company.

D. Han Solo revealing that he's really Chewbacca's father.

E. Miss Piggy's light saber battle with Darth Vader.

Unit 4 Exercise

1. Run Internet Explorer and connect to the Internet.
2. Open a second browser window.
3. In the second window, prevent Web pictures from being transmitted automatically.
4. In the second window, eliminate the Standard Buttons toolbar and Links bar.
5. Cruise the Web by using your first window and then by using your second window, and see which you prefer.
6. Enlarge the size of Internet Explorer's disk cache, and then cruise the Web again to see whether you notice a significant speed increase.
7. When you're done, exit both browser windows and disconnect from the Internet.

Part I Review

Unit 1 Summary

- **Preparing to go online with Internet Explorer:** Make sure that you have the right equipment (primarily a PC running Windows 98, a 14,400 bps or faster modem, and a phone line to connect to the modem), sign up for an account with an Internet service provider, and make sure that you have a copy of Internet Explorer Version 4.0 or higher installed.
- **Starting Internet Explorer:** On the taskbar, click Launch Internet Explorer Browser (the button directly to the right of the Start button). Alternatively, double-click the Internet Explorer icon on your desktop; or click the Start button and choose Programs⇨Internet Explorer⇨Internet Explorer from the menus that appear.
- **Moving on a Web page:** Click the up and down arrows, or drag the scroll box, of the vertical scroll bar; or press the PgDn and PgUp keys.
- **Identifying a link:** Move your mouse pointer over an area that's marked in some special way (for example, underlined text that's colored blue or purple), and see if the pointer's shape changes into a hand.
- **Identifying a link's electronic address:** Point to the link and look at the status bar at the bottom of the browser window, which displays the link's URL.
- **Switching between a few Web pages:** Click the browser's Back, Forward, and/or Home buttons from the Standard Buttons toolbar.
- **Switching between many Web pages:** Click the File menu and then click the page you want. Alternatively, click the History button from the Standard Buttons toolbar to display a History bar; click folders to open them until you see the page you want; and then click the page.

Unit 2 Summary

- **Using a favorite to move to a Web page:** Click the Favorites menu, click the folder that contains the favorite you're after, and then click the favorite. Alternatively, click the Favorites button from the Standard Buttons toolbar to display a Favorites bar, and then locate and click the favorite from the bar.
- **Creating a favorite:** First, move to the Web page for which you want to create a favorite. To then create the favorite quickly, press Ctrl+D. To create and file the favorite at the same time, click and drag the page icon from the Address bar to the Favorites menu, drag the icon to the folder where you want to store the favorite, and release your mouse button. To optionally file, rename, and subscribe to the favorite at the same time you create it, choose Favorites⇨Add to Favorites and then use the Add Favorite dialog box that appears.
- **Moving a favorite:** Open the Organize Favorites dialog box, locate and click the favorite, press Ctrl+X to place the favorite into the (invisible) Windows Clipboard, double-click the folder into which you want to move the favorite, click anywhere inside the open folder, and press Ctrl+V. The favorite is inserted into the folder and deleted from its original location.
- **Copying a favorite:** Open the Organize Favorites dialog box, locate and click the favorite, press Ctrl+C to copy the favorite to the (invisible) Windows Clipboard, double-click the folder into which you want to copy the favorite, click anywhere inside the open folder, and press Ctrl+V. A copy of the favorite is inserted into the folder, while the original favorite is unchanged.
- **Renaming a favorite:** Open the Organize Favorites dialog box, locate and click the favorite, press the Rename button, type a different name, and click anywhere outside the favorite to save your change.

Part I Review

- **Deleting a favorite:** Open the Organize Favorites dialog box, locate and click the favorite, and press the Del key.
- **Undeleting a favorite:** If you change your mind immediately after deleting a favorite, press Ctrl+Z to recover the favorite.
- **Adjusting Links bar buttons:** Open the Organize Favorites dialog box and adjust the favorites in the Links folder.
- **Entering a URL to move to a Web page:** Click anywhere inside Internet Explorer's Address bar to highlight the current text, type a URL to replace the text, and press Enter to move to the Web page located at the URL.
- **Searching for information on your current Web page:** Choose Edit⇨Find or press Ctrl+F to open the Find dialog box, type an appropriate word or phrase in the Find What text box, and then click the Find Next button until you locate what you're after.
- **Searching for information across the Web:** Move to a page that lets you access a Web search program — for example, click the Search button on the Standard Buttons toolbar, or go to this book's Searching the Web page at `net.gurus.com/internet101/search.htm`. Type an appropriate word or phrase in a search text box, and press Enter to generate a list of topic categories or Web pages.
- **Searching for a broad popular topic:** Use a category-based Web searcher such as Yahoo!.
- **Searching for a narrow or obscure topic:** Use an open-ended Web searcher such as HotBot or AltaVista.
- **Searching via several different programs:** Use a "meta-search" program, such as Savvy Search, that plugs your text into several popular Web searchers and then gives you all the initial matches together on the same page and organized by program.

Unit 3 Summary

- **Printing the contents of a Web page:** Make sure that your printer is ready to print, choose File⇨Print or press Ctrl+P to pop up the Print dialog box, adjust any settings you need to change, and click OK. Alternatively, click the Print button from the Standard Buttons toolbar to print immediately.
- **Saving the contents of a Web page as text:** Choose File⇨Save As to open the Save HTML Document dialog box; click inside the Save as Type box and click the Text File (*.txt) option; double-click inside the File Name box to highlight the current text (if any); type the drive letter, folder name, and filename you want to use (for example, C:\WebData\HotNews); and press Enter.
- **Saving both the contents and "look" of a Web page:** Choose File⇨Save As to open the Save HTML Document dialog box; make sure that the Save as Type box is set to the HTML File (*.htm, *.html) option; double-click inside the File Name box to highlight the current text (if any); type the drive letter, folder name, and filename you want to use (for example, C:\WebData\HotNews.htm); and press Enter.
- **Downloading a file from the Web:** Locate and click a link to the file to open the File Download dialog box; make sure that the Save This Program to Disk option is selected; click OK to open a Save As dialog box; use the dialog box's file list or Save In box to specify where you want to store the file on your hard disk; and click the Save button or press Enter to begin downloading the file.
- **Making compressed files useable:** Follow the directions in Appendix B to install WinZip, which is a program on the *Dummies 101* CD included with this book. You can then decompress each file using WinZip.

Part I Review

Unit 4 Summary

- **Preventing Web page pictures from being transmitted:** Choose View➪Internet Options, click the Advanced tab from the dialog box that appears, locate and click a Show Pictures option to turn the setting off, and click the dialog box's OK button. Repeat these steps to turn the option back on.
- **Receiving a Web page picture when the Show Pictures option is turned off:** Right-click the picture's placeholder image and then choose the Show Picture option from the menu that appears.
- **Opening additional browser windows:** Choose File➪New➪Window or press Ctrl+N. You can open as many browser windows as you want (up to the limits of your computer's memory).
- **Switching between multiple browser windows:** Press Alt+Tab, or click each window's button on the taskbar, or simply click each window directly.
- **Eliminating the Standard Buttons toolbar, Address bar, and/or Links bar:** Choose View➪Toolbars and then click the bar you want to hide. Repeat this step to display the bar again.
- **Moving the Standard Buttons toolbar, Address bar, and/or Links bar:** Click the ridge on the left edge of the bar you want to move and, while keeping your mouse button held down, drag the bar to a different position. When you're done, release your mouse button.
- **Forcing the current Web page to be retransmitted:** Click the Refresh button on the Standard Buttons toolbar, choose View➪Refresh, or press function key F5 to update the page.
- **Adjusting various Internet Explorer settings:** Choose View➪Internet Options to bring up the Internet Options dialog box; click any of the six category tabs running across the top to access the options in which you're interested; adjust the settings you want to change; and click the dialog box's OK button to save your new settings and close the box.

Part I Test

The questions on this test cover all the material presented in Part I, Units 1-4.

True False

T F 1. Popular Internet service providers, or ISPs, include America Online, AT&T WorldNet Service, and MindSpring.

T F 2. Internet Explorer is sometimes called a *carouser* because it lets you party on the World Wild Web.

T F 3. The World Wide Web didn't even exist until 1990, but now provides access to tens of millions of Web pages from around the globe.

T F 4. To find a link on a Web page, click Internet Explorer's Find button, type **link**, and press Enter.

T F 5. To use a link, simply click it. Internet Explorer will then use the link's URL to move you to the appropriate Web page.

T F 6. If you want to return to your current Web page during future sessions, you can create a favorite for it by pressing Ctrl+D, dragging the page icon from the Address bar to the Favorites menu, or choosing Favorites⇨Add to Favorites.

T F 7. You can get information about virtually any subject by using a Web search program to list sites that cover the subject.

T F 8. If you don't mind skipping the pictures, you can move to Web pages more quickly by choosing View⇨Internet Options, clicking the Advanced tab from the dialog box that appears, locating and clicking a Show Pictures option to turn the setting off, and clicking OK.

T F 9. You can run no more than three browser windows at the same time.

T F 10. You can switch between browser windows by pressing Alt+Tab, by clicking each window's button on the taskbar, or by clicking each window directly.

Multiple Choice

For each of the following questions, circle the correct answer or answers. Remember, there may be more than one right answer for each question.

11. The World Wide Web:

A. Was predicted by HAL 2000 in the film *2001: A Space Odyssey*.

B. Is run by an international committee headed by the Duke of URL.

C. Is just another name for the Internet, and the two terms can be used interchangeably.

D. Is a subset of the Internet, along with other Internet features such as electronic mail and newsgroups.

E. Is owned by no one and available to virtually everyone, which is why the Web is so chaotic, enormous, and fascinating.

12. Internet Explorer allows you to:

A. Cruise the colorful and fascinating World Wide Web.

B. Find information about virtually any topic in minutes.

Part I Test

C. Download any of thousands of programs you can run to make your PC use more productive or more fun.

D. Shop for virtually any item from the comfort of your home or office.

E. All of the above.

13. Links:

A. Was the character played by Clarence Williams III on *The Mod Squad.*

B. Display URLs in the status bar when you point to them.

C. Was the symbol used in the 1950s to identify Iron Curtain Web sites.

D. Are a great tool for rambling around the Web and discovering pages you might not have even thought to look for.

E. Is a wild cat inhabiting the northern U.S. that has thick soft fur, a short tail, and tufted ears.

14. The best way to handle the vast amount of information on the Web is to:

A. Hide your head under the blankets and hope it all goes away.

B. Tell endless stories about the good old days when people just watched TV.

C. Stay on the Web every waking hour so you miss as little as possible.

D. Save it all to disk because tomorrow it may be gone.

E. Take what you can use and let the rest go by.

15. If you want to preserve a Web page, you can

A. Print it.

B. Save it to disk as a text file.

C. Save it to disk as an HTML file.

D. Print it or save it, but not both.

E. Wrap Mylar around your screen.

16. Files you can download from the Web include

A. Business programs such as spreadsheets, database managers, and presentation software.

B. Fun programs such as games and educational software.

C. Pictures such as illustrations, paintings, and photographs.

D. Audio and video clips such as music, speeches, and movie sequences.

E. Steel tools with hardened ridged surfaces used for smoothing, grinding down, and boring.

17. You *can't* use the Internet Options dialog box to specify:

A. Which Web page Internet Explorer jumps to when you launch it.

B. How many days the History bar will remember the Web pages you've visited.

C. The size of the browser's disk cache.

D. Which fonts and colors to use for Web page text.

E. Which letter to display in the Internet Explorer logo.

18. Famous personalities who probably would have used the Web if given the chance include

A. Cleopatra.

B. Michelangelo.

C. James Joyce.

D. Little Miss Muffett.

E. All of the above; the Web's for everyone (though Little Miss Muffett would probably have been a little put off by its name).

Part I Test

Matching

19. Match the following toolbar buttons with their corresponding commands:

A. Back	1. View➪Full Screen
B. Fullscreen	2. File➪Print
C. Print	3. View➪Explorer Bar➪History
D. Search	4. Go➪Back
E. History	5. View➪Explorer Bar➪Search

20. Match the following descriptions with the corresponding toolbar buttons:

A. Moves you to the next Web page.

B. Displays your favorites in a vertical bar.

C. Cuts off data being transmitted from a Web page.

D. Returns you to your initial Web page.

E. Forces the current Web page to be retransmitted.

1. Home

2. Refresh

3. 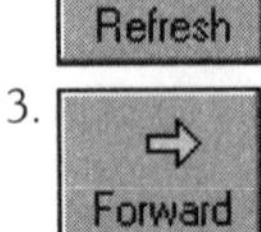

4. Favorites

5. Stop

21. Match the following keyboard shortcuts with their corresponding actions:

A. Ctrl+D	1. Expands the Web display to fill the browser window.
B. Esc	2. Forces the current Web page to be retransmitted.
C. Ctrl+P	3. Creates a favorite for the current Web page.
D. F11	4. Pops up a dialog box for printing the current Web page.
E. F5	5. Stops data being transmitted from a Web page.

22. Match each explorer with the land that he's best known for reaching:

A. Christopher Columbus	1. Moon
B. Eric the Red	2. Florida
C. Robert Edwin Peary	3. Southwest coast of Greenland
D. Juan Ponce de Léon	4. America
E. Neil A. Armstrong	5. North Pole

Part I Lab Assignment

Create your own list of cool Web sites by following these steps:

Step 1: Run Internet Explorer and connect to the Net.

Step 2: Peruse Web guides to uncover cool Web pages.

You can start with Yahoo's guide at `www.yahoo.com/Entertainment/Cool_Links`, Cool Central's guide at `www.coolcentral.com`, and this book's own guide at `net.gurus.com/internet101/sites.htm`. Preserve each list by printing it and/or saving it to disk.

Step 3: Discover more Web guides.

Use some Web search programs, such as Yahoo! or HotBot, or a "meta-searcher," such as Savvy Search. Again, preserve each list by printing it and/or saving it to disk.

Step 4: Compile a list of the most promising-looking Web pages.

Study the paper pages and/or files you've generated to do so.

Step 5: Investigate each Web page on your list by moving to it.

Visit each page by either clicking its link or typing in its URL. If you decide you like the page and will want to return to it in the future, create a favorite for it.

Step 6: When you've worked your way through your list, organize your new favorites.

Create a folder with the name of your topic and then move all your new favorites into the folder.

Part I Lab Assignment

Step 7: Visit some of the most interesting sites you've discovered . . . and enjoy yourself!

Step 8: After you've finished, disconnect from the Internet.

And give yourself a treat as a reward for mastering the World Wide Web.

Reading
E-Mail and
Usenet
Newsgroups
Part
II

In this part . . .

Now that you know how to browse the Web, it's time to explore the other key use for the Internet: electronic mail. In Units 5 and 6, you'll learn how to use the Outlook Express program to compose and send e-mail, retrieve and read e-mail, reply to and file messages, maintain an electronic address book, and transmit and receive data files by e-mail. After you're done, you'll be able to send messages in seconds to friends and colleagues around the word for the price of a local call.

Another way to communicate with people on a global scale is by joining some of the tens of thousands of online discussion groups that take place in Usenet newsgroups.

In Unit 7, you'll use the Outlook Express program to also exploit this terrific resource.

In Unit 8 you'll learn how to set your PC to receive streams of Web content, called channels, that are transmitted on a specified schedule and in the background through your Internet connection. You can view channels via Internet Explorer or display them directly on your desktop; and you can even assign certain channels to be screen savers that appear automatically when your PC is idle.

Finally, Appendix A gives you the answers to the test questions that appear at the ends of Parts I and II, and Appendix B tells you how to install and use the programs that are stored on the *Dummies 101* CD.

Unit 5

Getting Started with E-Mail

Objectives for This Unit

- ✓ Setting up Outlook Express to send and receive e-mail
- ✓ Sending your first e-mail message
- ✓ Reading e-mail messages
- ✓ Replying to e-mail messages
- ✓ Forwarding messages
- ✓ Printing messages
- ✓ Deleting messages
- ✓ Following the rules of e-mail etiquette

Prerequisites

- Establishing an Internet e-mail account (Lesson 1-1)
- Connecting to the Net (Lesson 1-1)

- Outlook Express

use Outlook Express to send and receive e-mail

The Internet is famous for its World Wide Web — as you learned in Part I of this book — but the single most-used Internet service is still e-mail. *E-mail* (or *electronic mail*) allows you to type messages on your computer, connect to the Internet, and send the messages to anyone with an Internet e-mail address. While you're connected, you can also receive e-mail messages. Windows 98 includes an excellent e-mail program named Outlook Express, so you've already got everything you need to start sending and receiving e-mail.

Note: Lesson 1-1 tells you how to confirm that your version of Windows 98 has Outlook Express. If you discover that you don't have this program, you can install Outlook Express from the CD that comes with this book. For more information, see Appendix B.

In this unit, you'll first set up Outlook Express to communicate with your Internet e-mail account. You'll then learn how to create, spell-check, and send e-mail messages. You'll also learn how to retrieve the messages from your electronic mailbox and how to read, reply to, forward, delete, and print these e-mail messages.

Lesson 5-1 Telling Outlook Express How to Get Your Mail

ISP = Internet service provider

server = computer that provides a service to a number of people

POP server = computer that stores e-mail until you collect it

SMTP server = computer that accepts outgoing messages for delivery over the Internet

You didn't have to provide Internet Explorer with any special information to browse the Web because Web pages are a public resource available to everyone. But your e-mail account is private; the only person allowed to use it is you. As a result, Outlook Express needs to know a few things about your particular Internet account before it can handle your e-mail.

The software you used to sign up with your Internet service provider, or *ISP*, may have already tailored Outlook Express to work with your e-mail account. Otherwise, we'll guide you through entering the necessary information yourself. Either way, by the end of this lesson, Outlook Express will be ready to receive and send your e-mail.

To process your e-mail, Outlook Express needs four pieces of information. First, it needs to know your e-mail address, which identifies your electronic mailbox; and your password, which is the secret code word that you use to "unlock" your mailbox. In addition, Outlook Express needs to know the names of two computers, or *servers:*

- The computer at your ISP that stores incoming mail for you to pick up. This computer is called a *POP* or *POP3* server, which stands for Post Office Protocol Version 3.
- The computer at your ISP that accepts outgoing mail from you and sends it along to its intended destination. This computer is called an *SMTP* server, which stands for Simple Mail Transfer Protocol.

To find out whether your copy of Outlook Express already has the e-mail information it needs, tackle the exercise in the next section.

Can Outlook Express get your mail?

The best way to find out whether your copy of Outlook Express knows how to get your e-mail is to try it! Outlook Express is stored in your Internet Explorer folder, so follow these steps to put the program through a trial run:

1. **Click the Windows 98 Start button (in the lower-left corner of your screen), click Programs from the first menu that appears, click Internet Explorer from the second menu that appears, and click Outlook Express from the third menu that appears.**

   After a few moments, Outlook Express launches.

   If you see an error message, or an Internet Connection Wizard dialog box like the one in Figure 5-1, then Outlook Express needs some information from you before it can handle your e-mail. Click the Cancel and Yes buttons to make the dialog box go away, and then skip to the next section, "Finding out where your mail is."

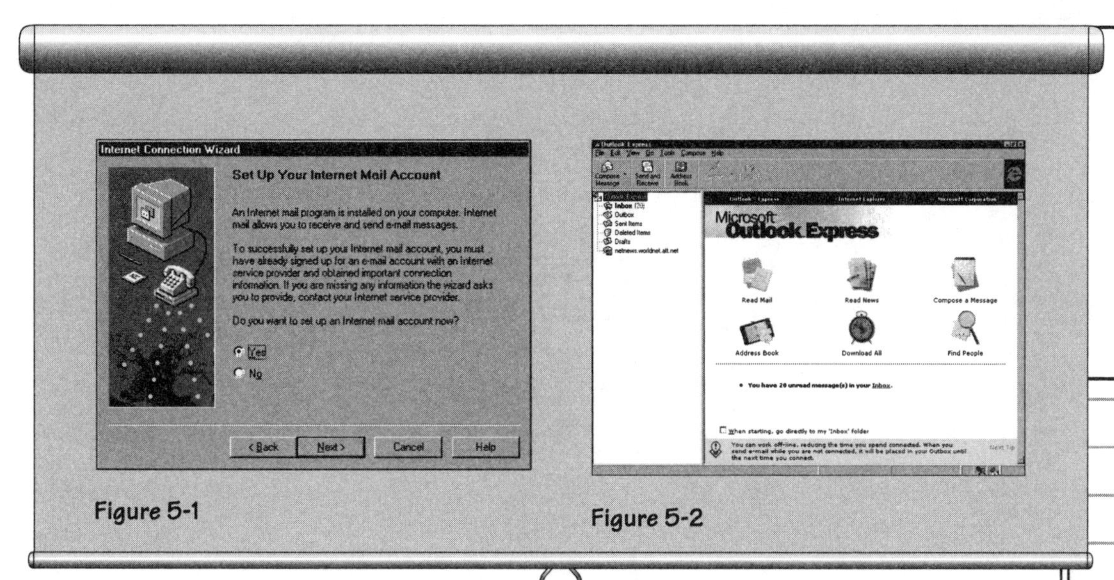

Figure 5-1

Figure 5-2

Figure 5-1: If you see the Internet Connection Wizard dialog box, Outlook Express needs some setup information from you before it can handle your e-mail.

Figure 5-2: Use the Outlook Express window to collect your e-mail.

Notes:

If all you see is the program in Figure 5-2, however, you can proceed to test Outlook Express by telling it to collect your mail.

2 Connect to the Internet.

If you aren't sure how, see Lesson 1-1. Alternatively, choose File⇨Connect from the Outlook menu bar and then click the name of your ISP.

After you're connected, notice the large Outlook toolbar near the top of the window. One of the buttons on this toolbar is named Send and Receive, because clicking it makes Outlook Express both send out the messages you've previously created and receive the new messages in your electronic mailbox.

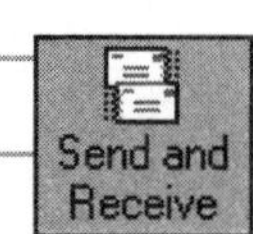

Send and Receive button

3 Click the Send and Receive button on the Outlook toolbar.

Outlook Express responds by trying to retrieve your e-mail.

to pick up your e-mail, click the Send and Receive button on the Outlook toolbar

4 If no error message appears, then Outlook Express knows everything it needs to handle your mail. Skip to Lesson 5-2, "Sending a Message."

You're in luck; Outlook Express is already set up to receive and send your e-mail.

If a dialog box flashing by tells you it's checking for new messages and then just as quickly disappears, it means that Outlook Express successfully connected to your POP server, but no messages were waiting for you. Don't worry — we'll arrange for you to get mail in Lesson 5-2.

5 If a Logon dialog box like the one in Figure 5-3 asks for your user name and password, first type your user name, which is the portion of your e-mail address that appears before the @ sign.

For example, if your e-mail address happened to be `Nikita@aol.com`, you'd type *Nikita* for your user name.

Figure 5-3: If you see the Logon dialog box, it means Outlook Express requires you to supply your e-mail user name and password before it can get your e-mail.

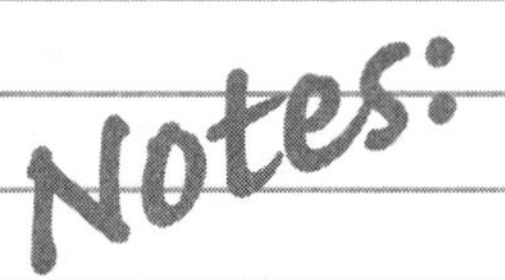

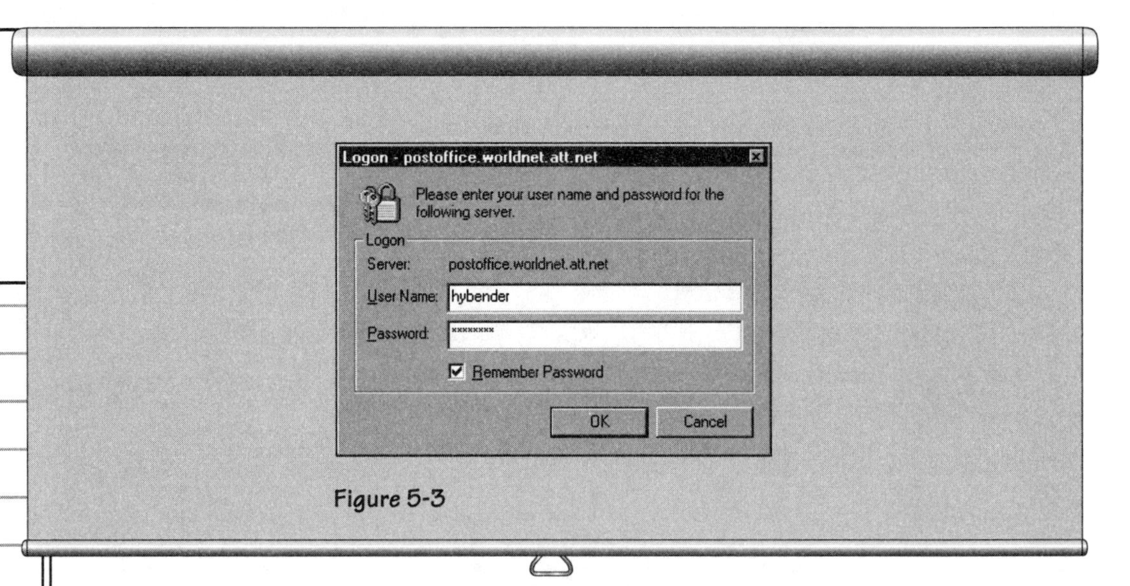

Figure 5-3

6 **Press Tab.**

You move to the Password text box.

7 **Carefully type your e-mail password, paying attention to lowercase and uppercase differences.**

As you enter your password, only asterisks appear so that someone who may be glancing over your shoulder can't read what you're typing.

8 **Click the OK button.**

Outlook Express tells the POP server your password. If you supplied the correct password, Outlook Express succeeds in connecting to the POP server and copies all your incoming e-mail to your PC. (You'll learn how to read these messages in Lesson 5-3.) You're all set! Proceed to Lesson 5-2, "Sending a Message."

If a dialog box appears but then disappears almost instantly, it means that Outlook Express successfully connected to your POP server, but no messages were waiting for you. Even though getting messages is more fun, this is still good news — it means that Outlook Express is now ready and able to handle your e-mail. Go to Lesson 5-2, "Sending a Message."

9 **If you didn't type the right password, Outlook Express repeats its request; try typing your password again and clicking OK.**

The asterisks can make it hard to type accurately, so retype your password slowly and carefully before clicking OK. If that doesn't work, try typing the password that lets you log on to the Internet (as opposed to the password specific to your e-mail account). If that doesn't work either, call your ISP to ask how you can get your e-mail password. (***Note:*** If your password isn't available somewhere on your hard disk, you may need to wait until your ISP resends it to you by paper mail.)

Finding out where your mail is

If a Wizard dialog box similar to Figure 5-1 appeared when you opened the Outlook window, then Outlook Express is missing the data it needs to check for mail on your ISP's computer. Don't panic! Here's the information you need to gather:

- **Your e-mail address:** The address you chose (or were assigned) through your ISP to establish the name of your electronic mailbox. For example, if you chose the user name *janedoe* for an AT&T WorldNet e-mail account, your e-mail address is `janedoe@worldnet.att.net`. This means that everyone who wants to send you e-mail can do so by addressing messages to `janedoe@worldnet.att.net`. All the e-mail that *you* send displays this address near the top of each message to identify you.
- **Your e-mail password:** The secret code that, like a key, unlocks access to your e-mail account (so that you can pick up your messages and send messages) and simultaneously locks everyone else out of your e-mail account. Your e-mail password may be the same as the password that you use to log on to the Internet, or it may be different.

  If you don't already know your password, your ISP's staff may not be willing to tell you what it is over the phone for security reasons. (Makes sense — how do they know it's really you?) If necessary, they may mail it to you (using paper mail, of course), and you'll have to wait until you receive it to use e-mail.
- **Your Internet service provider's POP (Post Office Protocol) server:** The computer that stores your incoming mail; its name is a series of words separated by periods. Many ISPs use the word *pop* followed by the provider's Internet name, such as `pop.sover.net` for SoVerNet (Margy's ISP in Vermont). Others use the word *mail,* such as `mail.tiac.net` for TIAC (an ISP in Boston).
- **Your Internet service provider's SMTP (Simple Mail Transfer Protocol) server:** The computer that handles your outgoing mail; its name is also a series of words separated by periods. Your provider's SMTP server may have the same name as its POP server, because it's not uncommon for both server programs to run on the same computer. However, many providers use separate computers for incoming and outgoing mail — for example, AT&T WorldNet's POP server is named `postoffice.worldnet.att.net`, and its SMTP server is named `mailhost.worldnet.att.net`.
- **Your Internet service provider's NNTP (Network News Transfer Protocol) server:** The computer that stores the messages of Usenet newsgroups. (You won't use newsgroups until Unit 7, but you might as well get this information at the same time you're getting the e-mail data.)

You can probably find what you need by reading the information your ISP sent you when you signed up for an account. If you never received this information or can't find it, call your ISP and ask. Write down the answers in Table 5-1 and on the Cheat Sheet in the front of this book. Write your e-mail password on a separate sheet of paper and store the sheet in a safe place.

Notes:

Table 5-1 Information from Your Internet Service Provider

What You Need to Know	*Write Your Information Here*
E-mail address	
E-mail password	(write on a separate sheet of paper)
POP server	
SMTP server	
NNTP server	

Note: Don't try to use the POP or SMTP server of an Internet service provider for which you haven't established an e-mail account. If you do, you'll just end up with an error message.

Setting up Outlook Express to handle your e-mail

Terrific! Now that you have all the information you require, follow these steps to set up Outlook Express for handling your e-mail (referring to Table 5-1 or the Cheat Sheet at the front of this book as needed):

1. **If Outlook Express isn't already running, launch it now.**

   If a Wizard dialog box pops up, close it temporarily by clicking its Cancel and Yes buttons. (You'll be running this Wizard shortly, but in a more orderly manner.)

   Notice that one of the menus at the top of the Outlook Express window is named Tools. This menu includes an Accounts command that lets you enter e-mail account data.

2. **Choose Tools⇨Accounts from the menu bar.**

   An Internet Accounts dialog box appears. To set up new account data, use the Add button in the upper-left section of the box.

3. **Click the Add button.**

   A menu appears that displays the options News (for reading Usenet newsgroups, which you'll learn about in Unit 7); Directory Service (which lets you search for e-mail addresses, as explained in the "How to find out someone's e-mail address" sidebar near the end of this lesson); and Mail.

4. **Click the Mail option.**

   An Internet Connection Wizard dialog box like the one in Figure 5-4 appears. The box first asks you for your name.

to set up Outlook Express to handle e-mail, choose Tools→Accounts→Add→Mail

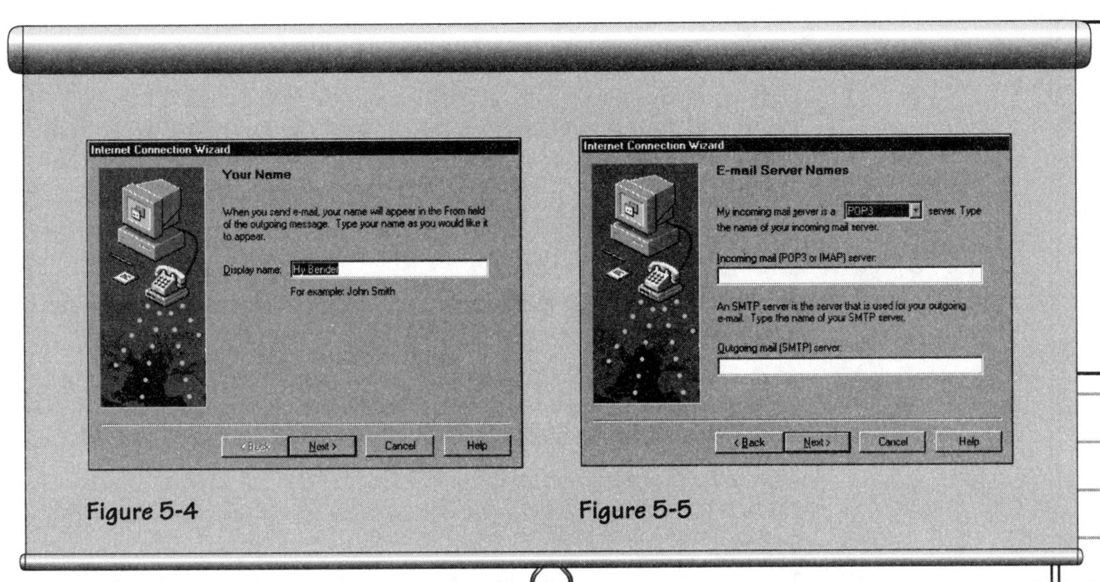

Figure 5-4

Figure 5-5

Figure 5-4: Use the Internet Connection Wizard dialog box to enter your e-mail setup information.

Figure 5-5: Identify the names of the POP and SMTP servers that your Internet service provider uses to handle incoming and outgoing e-mail.

5. **Type your full name as you'd like it to appear in your e-mail messages.**

   For example, if you were Elvis, you'd type *Elvis Presley*. If you make a mistake, press the Backspace key to correct the error and then type the correct text.

   After you're done with each dialog box, proceed to the next one via the bottom Next button.

6. **Click the Next button.**

   You're now asked for your e-mail address.

7. **Type your e-mail address and then click Next.**

   For example, if you were Elvis and had an e-mail account with MindSpring, you'd type *elvis@mindspring.com.*

   After you click Next, you're asked for the names of your ISP's mail servers, as shown in Figure 5-5. The type of server that you're using is already correctly identified as POP3, so skip to naming your account's POP server.

8. **Press Tab and then type the name of your ISP's incoming mail, or POP, server.**

   Make sure that you put all those pesky periods in the right places! After you're done, name your account's SMTP server.

9. **Press Tab and then type the name of your ISP's outgoing mail, or SMTP, server.**

   Type this name carefully, too, again making sure that you plant all the periods in their proper spots.

10. **Click Next.**

    You're asked to provide your e-mail user name and password.

Notes:

11 First type your user name, or POP account name, which is the portion of your e-mail address that appears before the @ sign; then press Tab.

For example, if your e-mail address happened to be `AllyMcBeal@aol.com`, you'd type *AllyMcBeal* for your user name. After you press Tab, you move to the Password text box.

12 Carefully type your e-mail password, paying attention to lowercase and uppercase differences; then click Next.

As you enter your password, only asterisks appear so that anyone who may be glancing over your shoulder can't read what you're typing. The asterisks can make typing accurately difficult, so enter your password slowly and carefully.

After you click Next, you're asked for a "Friendly Name" to represent all the e-mail setup information that you've just supplied. You can later use this name to display and edit your settings.

13 Type any name that's likely to remind you of your current e-mail account; then click Next.

The name can be up to 255 letters, numbers, and spaces. For example, if your ISP was IBM Internet Connection, you could use *IBM Internet Connection account* as the name.

After you click Next, you're asked to identify which method you're using to connect to the Internet.

14 If you're using a phone line, click the top option, Connect Using My Phone Line; then click Next.

Lastly, you're asked to identify which dial-up connection to use.

15 Click the second option, Use an Existing Dial-Up Connection, and then click the name of the connection you normally use to log on to the Net. After you're done, click Next.

You're told that the Wizard has all the information it needs. All right!

16 Click the Finish button.

Your setup information is saved to your hard disk so that Outlook Express can use it in future sessions. The Internet Connection Wizard then exits, returning you to the Internet Accounts dialog box.

17 Click the Mail tab near the top of the dialog box.

Notice that the name you chose to represent your setup data is now listed in the dialog box. If the word *(default)* doesn't already appear to the name's right, click the name and then click the Set as Default button to activate your setup.

You can review and revise your information at any time by clicking the name you chose and then clicking the dialog box's Properties button. For now, though, simply exit the box.

18 Click the Close button near the bottom of the dialog box.

The box closes, returning you to the Outlook Express window.

Great work! Outlook Express is now ready to tackle your e-mail!

☑ Progress Check

If you can do the following, you've mastered this lesson:

- ☐ Check whether Outlook Express is set up for handling your e-mail account.
- ☐ If necessary, gather and then enter the setup information that Outlook Express requires to send and receive your e-mail.

Sending a Message

Lesson 5-2

Now that Outlook Express is set up to handle your e-mail account, we'd like you to send us a message. Before you can write to someone over the Net, however, you need to know his or her *e-mail address.* E-mail addresses look like this:

```
username@computername
```

e-mail address format = username@computername

The *username* part is the name used to identify the person on the computer system that he or she uses. The *computername* part is the name of the computer on which the person's mail is stored. For example, Peter Pan might have this e-mail address:

```
peterpan@neverland.com
```

The user name is *peterpan,* and the computer that stores the mail is named *neverland.com.*

To create an e-mail message from Outlook Express, first click the Compose Message button from the Outlook toolbar to open a blank New Message window. Next, enter one or more e-mail addresses, a subject line, and the text of your message. After checking your message for errors (such as typos), click the Send button on the New Message toolbar; this transmits the message to your ISP, which in turn sends it out over the Internet to the party you're trying to reach. For your very first e-mail message, that party will be us, the authors of this book!

In this lesson, you'll open a New Message window, create a test e-mail message, spell-check the message, and send the message. You'll also learn the best way to obtain someone's e-mail address.

Composing, spell-checking, and sending a message

To test that your e-mail is working, and to make sure that you have mail to read in Lesson 5-3, send a message to Internet For Dummies Central, where a tireless *mail robot* (a program that automatically responds to messages) stands ready to receive your words. The address to use is

```
net101@gurus.com
```

We set up this address especially for the readers of this book!

Figure 5-6: Use the Outlook Express window to send and receive e-mail messages.

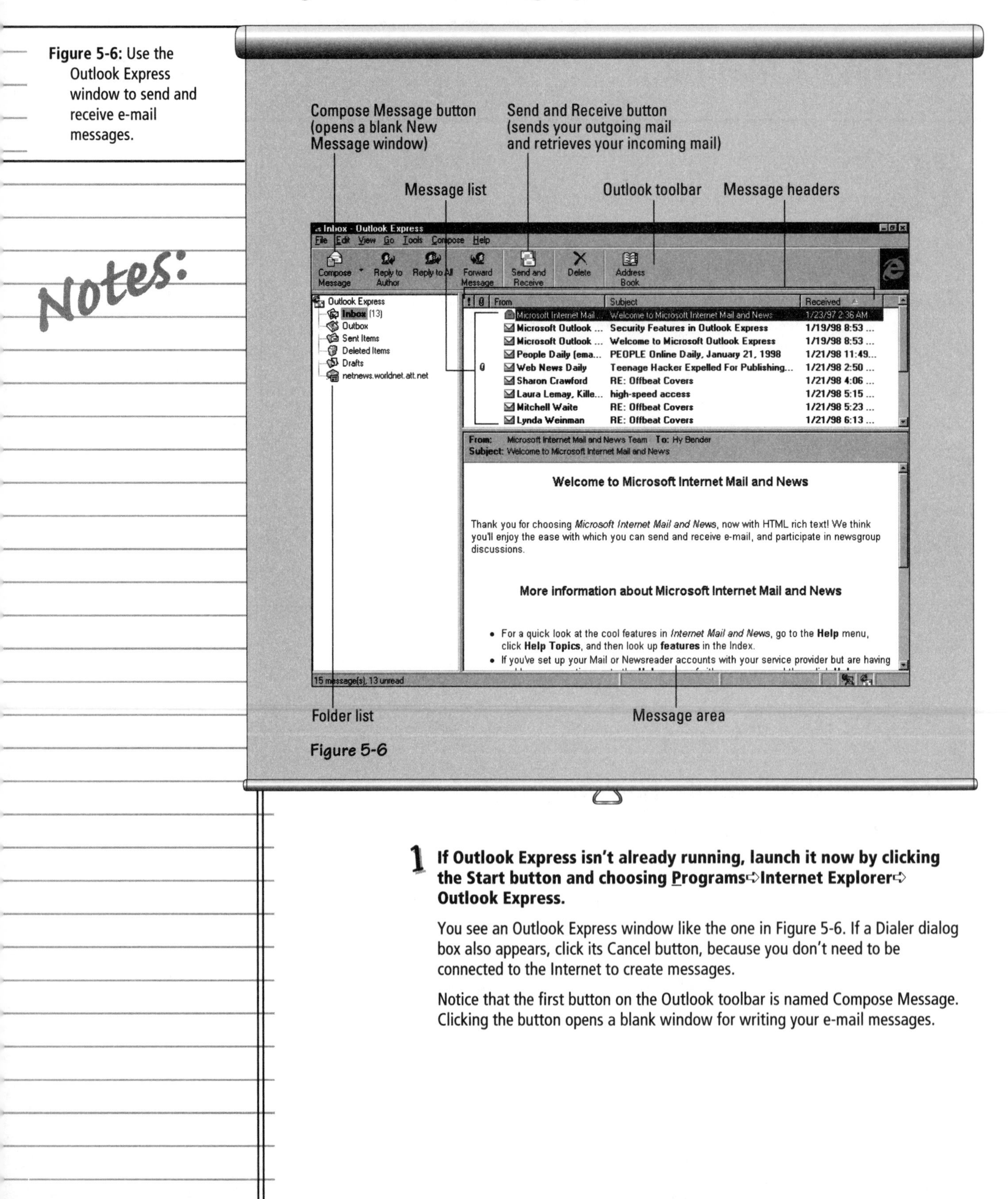

Figure 5-6

1 If Outlook Express isn't already running, launch it now by clicking the Start button and choosing Programs⇨Internet Explorer⇨ Outlook Express.

You see an Outlook Express window like the one in Figure 5-6. If a Dialer dialog box also appears, click its Cancel button, because you don't need to be connected to the Internet to create messages.

Notice that the first button on the Outlook toolbar is named Compose Message. Clicking the button opens a blank window for writing your e-mail messages.

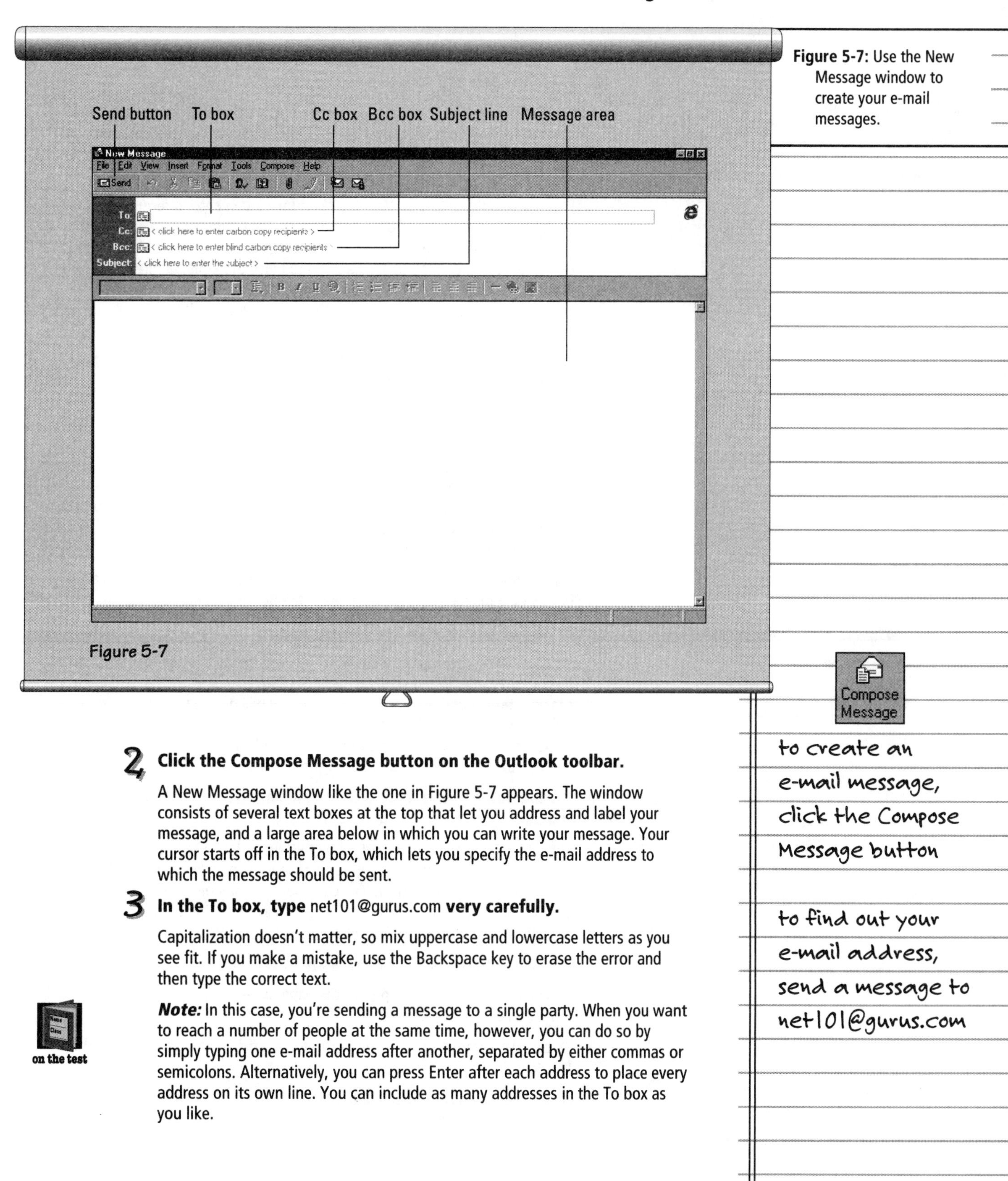

Figure 5-7: Use the New Message window to create your e-mail messages.

2. **Click the Compose Message button on the Outlook toolbar.**

   A New Message window like the one in Figure 5-7 appears. The window consists of several text boxes at the top that let you address and label your message, and a large area below in which you can write your message. Your cursor starts off in the To box, which lets you specify the e-mail address to which the message should be sent.

3. **In the To box, type** net101@gurus.com **very carefully.**

   Capitalization doesn't matter, so mix uppercase and lowercase letters as you see fit. If you make a mistake, use the Backspace key to erase the error and then type the correct text.

   Note: In this case, you're sending a message to a single party. When you want to reach a number of people at the same time, however, you can do so by simply typing one e-mail address after another, separated by either commas or semicolons. Alternatively, you can press Enter after each address to place every address on its own line. You can include as many addresses in the To box as you like.

to create an e-mail message, click the Compose Message button

to find out your e-mail address, send a message to net101@gurus.com

press Tab to move to the next text box and Shift + Tab to move to the previous text box

4. **Press the Tab key to move to the Cc box.**

   You can always move to the next text box by pressing Tab and to the previous box by pressing Shift+Tab. *Don't* press Enter to move to a text box, because doing so will just create a blank line in your current box. If you press Enter by mistake, simply remove the blank line by pressing the Backspace key.

   You're now in the Cc box (*Cc* being short for *carbon copy,* referring to a method of copying messages used back in the Stone Age). When you're sending a message that's primarily directed at one person or group but which may also be of interest to other people, it's common to place the e-mail addresses of your main audience in the To box and place the addresses of your secondary audience in the Cc box. Just as with the To box, you can include as many addresses as you like (separated by commas or semicolons) in the Cc box.

   This particular message isn't likely to interest anyone but us and our robot, though, so leave the Cc box blank.

5. **Press Tab to move to the Bcc box.**

   You're now in the Bcc, or *blind carbon copy,* box. Like the Cc box, the Bcc box can be used to address your message to a secondary audience. The difference is that everyone who receives your message will see the addresses you've placed in the To and Cc boxes, but no one will see the addresses in the Bcc box. The latter therefore lets you include someone in an e-mail transmission without any of the other recipients knowing about it.

   Again, though, your current message probably won't be compelling to anyone but us (and maybe your mom), so leave the Bcc box blank, too.

6. **Press Tab to move to the Subject line.**

   You're now on the Subject line, which lets you briefly identify the topic covered by your message. When someone receives your e-mail, he or she will initially see your e-mail address and Subject line, and will decide whether to bother reading your message based on that information. Further, some e-mail systems display only the first 30 letters or so of the Subject. You should therefore try to make your Subject line both as descriptive and as concise as possible.

7. **On the Subject line, type** Net101 Test Message **or whatever you'd like the subject of the message to be.**

   This message is going to a mail robot, but we authors read these messages too, so be polite. As you type the subject, notice that your text is echoed in the title bar at the top of the window. You can open as many message windows at a time as you want, so this feature makes it easy for you to identify the contents of each window by its title bar name.

8. **Press Tab to move to the message area.**

   You've arrived at the main part of the window — the one that lets you actually write and edit your message!

9. **Compose a message to our mail robot and to the authors of this book.**

   How about saying whether you like (or don't like) this book? The message can be as long as you want.

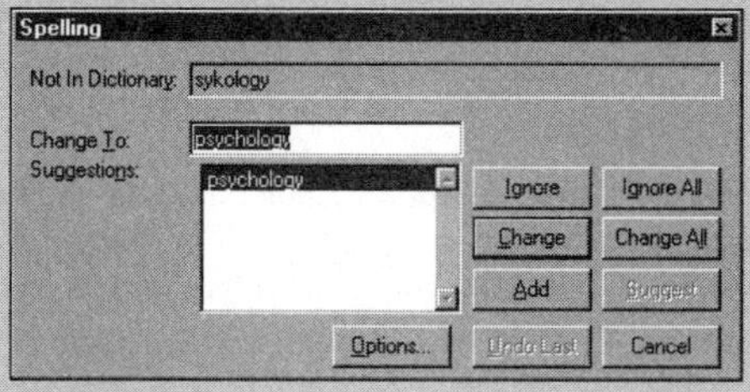

Figure 5-8

Figure 5-8: Use the Spelling dialog box to catch and correct your message's typos and misspellings.

Notice that the Composition window behaves like a simple word processor. For example, you don't have to press Enter at the end of each line — your cursor moves to the beginning of the next line as you fill up each line. As a result, you have to press Enter only at the ends of paragraphs and to create blank lines.

press Enter only at the end of each paragraph

Similarly, you can erase mistakes using the Backspace or Del key, and undo your last editing change by pressing Ctrl+Z.

Also, like a word processor, the Composition window lets you check your spelling. Try it!

10 After you're done writing your message, click Tools from the menu bar and choose the Spelling option.

to spell-check your message, choose Tools→Spelling or press F7

If a box pops up that says `The spelling check is complete`, then your text didn't contain any questionable words. In this case, skip to Step 12.

Otherwise, a Spelling dialog box like the one in Figure 5-8 appears.

11 Spell-check your message by responding to each word that the spelling checker doesn't recognize.

When the checker finds a word that isn't in its dictionary (such as *sykology*), it displays the word in a Change To box so that you can edit it, and also lists suggested alternatives (such as *psychology*).

If a suggested word is the one you want, click it to select it (if it isn't already highlighted) and then click the Change button to replace that one word. Alternatively, click the Change All button if you want to replace *all* occurrences of the word in your message.

On the other hand, if you want to leave the word as it is, click the Ignore button to skip over that one word; or click the Ignore All button to skip over all occurrences of the word in your message; or click the Add button to permanently add the word to the spelling checker's dictionary. You can also simply click in the Change To text box and revise the word manually.

After you've dealt with all the words flagged by the spelling checker, a box pops up telling you that `The spelling check is complete`.

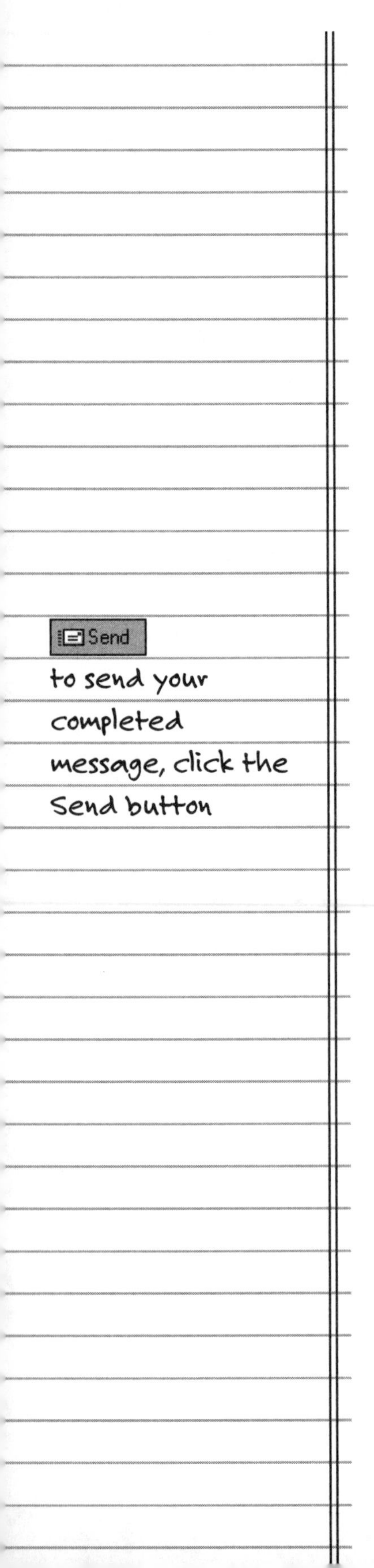

12 Click the OK button.

The box disappears, returning you to the now perfectly spelled text. Just one task remains — sending your message! You can do this a couple of different ways.

If you want to send your message immediately, simply click Send, which is the first button on the window's toolbar. If you're connected to the Internet, the message is sent out instantly; if you're not connected, Outlook Express automatically dials into the Net for you and then sends your message.

If you're not ready to transmit your message right away, however — for example, if you'd like to create several messages offline and then send them all simultaneously — choose File➪Send Later from the menu bar. This command saves your message in an e-mail folder named *Outbox*. When you're ready, you can send all the messages in the Outbox folder by connecting to the Net and clicking the Send and Receive button from the Outlook toolbar. Alternatively, if you change your mind before sending, you can click the Outbox folder to list its messages, and then double-click any message to reopen it and revise its contents . . . or click a message and press the Del key to eliminate it.

In this case, we recommend that you go for it and send your message immediately.

13 Click the Send button (the first button on the window's toolbar).

If you were already connected to the Internet, your message is transmitted in seconds. Otherwise, Outlook Express first activates your dialing program and connects to the Net for you! (Cool!) The program then transmits your message over the Net.

After your e-mail is sent, the message window — its job completed — closes and returns you to the Outlook Express window.

Congratulations! You just sent your first e-mail! It's pretty exciting, we must admit.

Eventually, you'll want to send messages to people besides us. When you do, you'll encounter a variety of e-mail addresses. Taking a quick look at the structure of e-mail addresses is worthwhile so that you know what to expect when you start sending e-mail all over the Internet.

All major online services and ISPs are connected to the Internet, so you can send e-mail to people with accounts on America Online, AT&T WorldNet Service, CompuServe, Concentric, IBM Internet Connection, Microsoft Network, MindSpring, Prodigy, and just about anyplace else. See Table 5-2 to find out how to write to friends belonging to some of the most popular national online services and ISPs.

Notes:

Table 5-2 Internet Addresses of Online Services and Internet Service Providers

Service or Provider	*E-Mail Address Format*
America Online	Add *@aol.com* to the screen name; if someone has the screen name *SteveCase,* address mail to `SteveCase@aol.com`
AT&T WorldNet Service	Add *@worldnet.att.net* to the user name; if someone has the user name *Michaelangelo,* address mail to `michaelangelo@worldnet.att.net`
CompuServe	Change the comma in the user ID to a period and add *@compuserve.com* to the end; if someone has the user ID *76543,210,* address mail to `76543.210@compuserve.com`
Concentric	Add *@cris.com* to the end; if someone has the user name *BruceWayne,* address mail to `BruceWayne@cris.com`
IBM Internet Connection	Add *@ibm.net* to the user name; if someone has the user name *BigBlue,* address mail to `BigBlue@ibm.net`
Microsoft Network	Add *@msn.com* to the user name; if someone has the user name *BillGates,* address mail to `BillGates@msn.com`
MindSpring	Add *@mindspring.com* to the user name; if someone has the user name *RockNRoll,* address mail to `RockNRoll@mindspring.com`
Prodigy	Add *@prodigy.com* to the service ID; if someone has the service ID *ABC123,* address mail to `ABC123@prodigy.com`

Exiting Outlook Express

When you're done creating and sending messages, here's how to quit Outlook Express:

Choose File⇨Exit from the menu bar, or click the Close button in the window's upper-right corner.

If you have no unsent messages, Outlook Express immediately disappears.

Otherwise, if you have any messages in your Outbox folder (that is, as a result of using the File⇨Send Later command from the message window), Outlook Express asks whether you want to send them now.

2. **Click the Yes button if you want your pending messages transmitted or the No button if you don't.**

   After you click a button, Outlook Express exits.

Now you know how to get in and out of Outlook Express — mission control for e-mail. And you've sent an e-mail message to Internet For Dummies Central. (You'll receive a reply in the next lesson.) Nice work!

How to find out someone's e-mail address

You hear that your aunt has an e-mail address and you want to send her a message. Here's the best way to find out your aunt's address:

Call and ask.

True, this method is neither zoomy nor high-tech, but it's by far the quickest and surest way.

But what if you don't know your aunt's phone number? Quite a few people directories have sprung up on the World Wide Web. Using the Internet Explorer browser, you can try searching for the e-mail address — and, while you're at it, the phone number — that you need at such superb Web sites as WhoWhere (www.whowhere.com), Switchboard (www.switchboard.com), Four11 (www.four11.com), and Bigfoot (www.bigfoot.com).

Alternatively, you can access certain lookup services directly from Outlook Express! To do so, first connect to the Net and choose Edit⇨Find People from the Outlook menu bar to display a Find People dialog box. Click in the Look in box to view a list of directory services (which includes the four that we mentioned in the previous paragraph); click the service you want to use (for example, WhoWhere or Switchboard); type the person's name in the Name box; and click the Find Now button to launch the search. After a few moments, you're furnished a list of matching names and their respective e-mail addresses.

Recess

You've sent your first message over the Internet. Take a walk around the block while your e-mail winds its way back to you. Before you go, though, disconnect from the Net. Hanging up on your ISP is a good idea whenever you'll be away from your desk for more than a few minutes — especially if you pay by the hour. When you return, you can dial back into your Internet account.

☑ Progress Check

If you can do the following, you've mastered this lesson:

- ☐ Use Outlook Express to open a New Message window.
- ☐ Enter the e-mail address of a person to whom you want to send a message.
- ☐ Compose, edit, and spell-check the text of your e-mail message.
- ☐ Send your e-mail message.
- ☐ Exit Outlook Express.

Including names with e-mail addresses

If you'd like to make your messages a bit classier, include people's names along with their e-mail addresses. You can set a name and address apart by enclosing the latter with angle brackets (< and >). For example, instead of addressing your message to us previously at `net101@gurus.com`, you could've typed the following in the To box:

```
Hy and Margy <net101@
  gurus.com>
```

The only thing to be wary of is including any punctuation, such as periods, in the name. If you need to do so, then enclose the entire name with quotation marks (" and "). For example, if the late Dr. Martin Luther King Jr. had the e-mail address `king@freedom.com`, you could've addressed messages to him as follows:

```
"Dr. Martin Luther King
  Jr." <king@freedom.com>
```

Including someone's name with his or her e-mail address isn't necessary, but it's a nice touch that helps make your computer-transmitted messages feel personal.

Reading E-Mail Messages

Lesson 5-3

Reading e-mail is a lot easier than sending it because you don't have to do any typing. When you receive messages over the Internet, your ISP's computer — specifically, its POP server — holds them for you until you pick them up via an e-mail program such as Outlook Express. The POP server then copies your waiting e-mail to your hard disk, allowing you to read the messages, compose replies, and file any messages that you want to keep.

e-mail folders hold groups of messages

To retrieve your e-mail, launch Outlook Express and click the Send and Receive button on the window's toolbar. After Outlook Express gets your messages, it stores them in one or more *folders* — that is, areas that hold groups of messages. The main folder is named *Inbox,* and that's where your incoming messages are typically stored. Outlook Express also has other folders, including an Outbox folder for holding messages you've created to be sent out (as mentioned in the preceding lesson); a Sent Items folder for storing messages you've already sent; a Drafts folder for temporarily saving messages you're still in the process of editing; and a Deleted Items folder for housing messages that you've thrown away. In addition, you can create your own folders to organize your messages more precisely (for example, a *Joe* folder for storing messages from your friend Joe), which you'll learn to do in Lesson 6-2.

new e-mail is typically stored in your Inbox folder

All the e-mail folders in Outlook Express are listed on the left side of the program's window. To switch to any folder, simply click it. After you do so, the messages in the folder are listed in the upper-right section of the window.

Notes:

Maximize button

display the contents of a folder by clicking it from the folder list

To read any listed message, again, just click it. After you do so, the message's contents are displayed in the lower-right section of the window.

In this lesson, you'll use Outlook Express to both retrieve and display your mail.

Picking up and reading your e-mail

Here's how to get your e-mail and read it:

1. **Launch Outlook Express and connect to the Internet.**

   If the Outlook Express window doesn't already fill your screen, click the Maximize button, which is the middle of the three buttons residing in the window's upper-right corner. Enlarging the window will make it easier for you to list and read your messages.

2. **Click the Send and Receive button on the Outlook toolbar to retrieve your messages.**

   Outlook Express checks your mailbox for new messages. While the program is retrieving your mail, status phrases flash by, such as `finding host` (*host* referring to your ISP), `connecting`, `authorizing`, and (if you have mail) `receiving message`. When all your mail has been collected, the Inbox folder is boldfaced to indicate that it contains unread mail. In addition, a number in parentheses appears to the folder's right, telling you exactly how many unread messages are waiting for you.

   In this case, you should have received a reply to the message that you sent in Lesson 5-2. You may have also received messages from anyone to whom you've revealed your e-mail address. (***Note:*** If you didn't get mail, you may want to wait an hour and try again. If you still don't receive a reply to your previous message, send a message to yourself and then work with that mail instead.) To view the messages in your Inbox, click the folder.

3. **Click the Inbox folder (in the upper-left portion of the window).**

   All the messages in the folder are now listed in the upper-right portion of the window, as shown in Figure 5-9. This e-mail roster is called the *message list.* You can scroll through the list by clicking the arrows on the vertical scroll bar along its right edge.

   Notice that each message is represented by a line that tells you whom the message is from, the subject of the message, and when the message was received by your ISP's server.

   In addition, the line tells you the message's priority (via a "!" icon for high priority or a down arrow icon for low priority); whether the message has a file attached (via the presence or absence of a paperclip icon); and whether the message is unread (via both boldfacing and a closed envelope icon) or read (by the lack of boldfacing and by an open envelope icon).

   To read a message, simply click it.

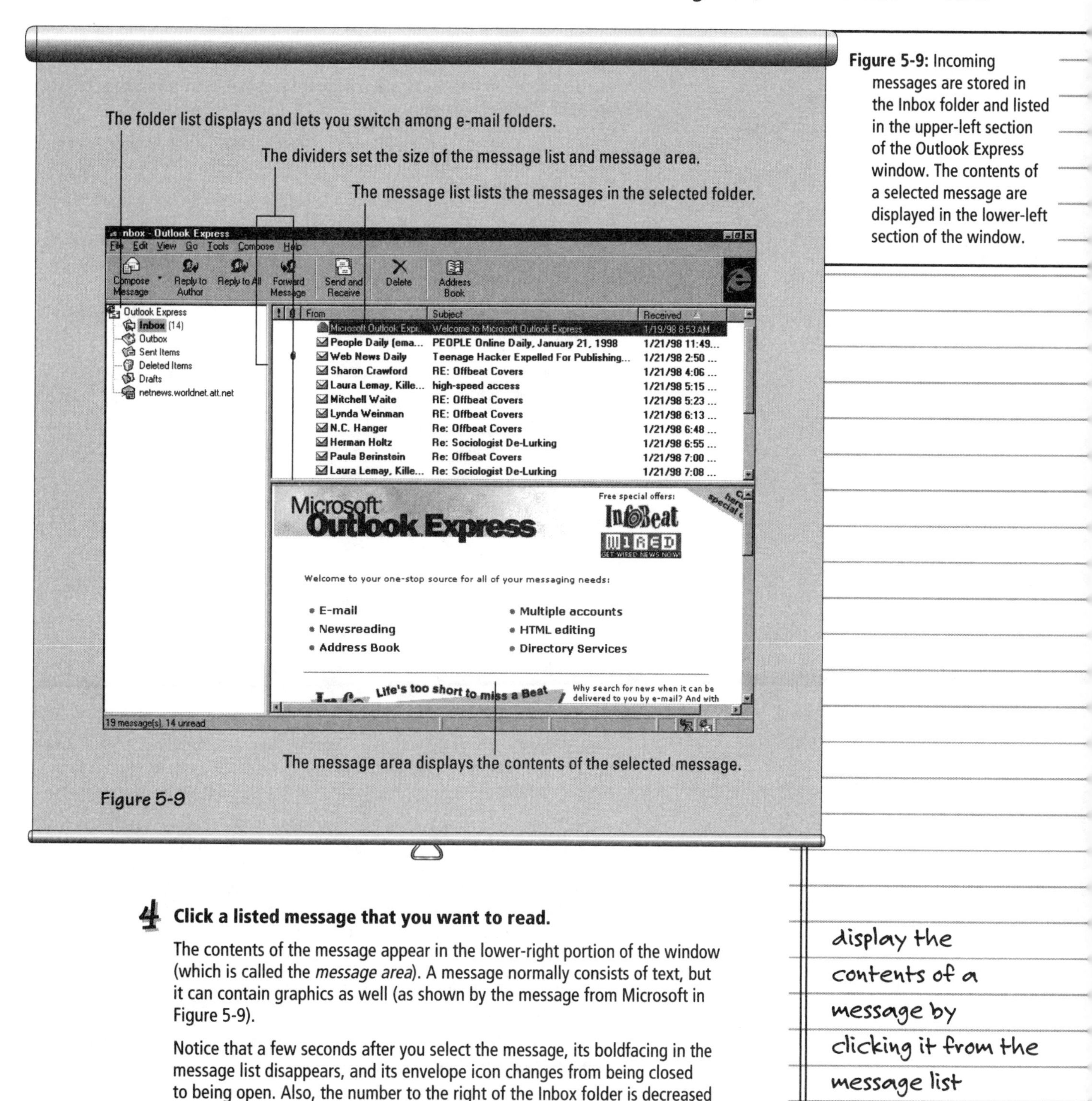

Figure 5-9

Figure 5-9: Incoming messages are stored in the Inbox folder and listed in the upper-left section of the Outlook Express window. The contents of a selected message are displayed in the lower-left section of the window.

4 Click a listed message that you want to read.

The contents of the message appear in the lower-right portion of the window (which is called the *message area*). A message normally consists of text, but it can contain graphics as well (as shown by the message from Microsoft in Figure 5-9).

Notice that a few seconds after you select the message, its boldfacing in the message list disappears, and its envelope icon changes from being closed to being open. Also, the number to the right of the Inbox folder is decreased by one.

display the contents of a message by clicking it from the message list to read long messages, scroll through the message area using your mouse or arrow keys

5 **Click another listed message you're interested in (if you have another e-mail message).**

The contents of the message that you've selected replace those of the previous message in the message area. You can read any message by simply clicking its line on the message list.

If a message is longer than the message area, you can scroll through its contents by clicking the vertical scroll bar along its right edge. You can also click anywhere inside the message area to select it, and then move through the message using your arrow keys or PgDn and PgUp keys.

Alternatively, you can display a message in its own window! To do so, double-click the message in the message list.

6 **Double-click (that is, click twice in rapid succession) a message in the message list.**

A new window opens, displaying the contents of the message. You can maximize this window and make the message fill your screen, which is a convenient way to read long messages.

You can keep open as many message windows as you like simultaneously and flip between them by pressing Alt+Tab. For now, though, quit your current window.

7 **Click the Close box in your message window's upper-right corner, or choose File⇨Close, to exit this view.**

You're returned to the Outlook window.

8 **For each message in your Inbox, first select the message from the message list and then read the message from the message area.**

When you reach the message that you received from Internet For Dummies Central, notice that it tells you your official Internet e-mail address, in case you weren't sure what it was. (And you know that the address works because this message arrived!)

Note: If you don't receive a reply from our mail robot, you may instead get a message saying that your mail was undeliverable. Such messages are generated automatically by your ISP's own mail robot whenever an e-mail address can't be located. Study the e-mail address that the message reports as being incorrect. If the address is something other than `net101@gurus.com`, then return to Lesson 5-2 and try sending another message, making sure to get every character in the e-mail address exactly right.

After you're done reading messages, quit both the Internet and Outlook Express. You can accomplish both tasks using the File menu.

9 **Choose File⇨Hang Up to disconnect from the Net and then choose File⇨Exit to quit Outlook Express.**

Your connection is terminated, and the program disappears.

Adjusting how the message list is displayed

Outlook Express gives you lots of flexibility in determining how messages are listed.

To list your messages in a particular order, simply click the appropriate header at the top of the message list. For example, to sort your messages from most recent to least recent, click the Received header. To sort your messages from least recent to most recent (that is, the reverse order), just click Received again. You can follow the same procedure to sort messages alphabetically by Subject, by sender (via the "From" header), or by Priority (via the "!" header).

You can also adjust the length of each header's column. To do so, click the divider at either side of the column and, while holding your mouse button down, drag the divider to make the column wider or narrower, and then release your mouse button.

You can rearrange the order in which the headers appear, too. To do so, simply click a header and, while holding your mouse button down, move it to where you want it. (Neat!)

In addition, you can adjust the size of the message list using the gray horizontal and vertical dividers. For example, to make the message list longer, click the horizontal divider below it and, while holding your mouse button down, drag the divider down. This action also makes the message area *contract*, so you must balance having a longer message list with having a shorter message area.

Alternatively, you can eliminate the message area entirely. To do so, choose View⇨Layout from the menu bar to open a Layout dialog box; click the Use Preview Pane option to turn off its check mark; and click the OK button at the bottom of the dialog box. The message area disappears, allowing the message list to fill the right section of the window. To read a message, though, you now have to double-click it from the list to make the message's contents appear in a separate window. Some people like this arrangement because it provides the maximum amount of space for both listing and reading messages. If you prefer the convenience of having the message list and message area in the same window, though, again choose View⇨Layout, click the Use Preview Pane option, and click OK to return to a standard display.

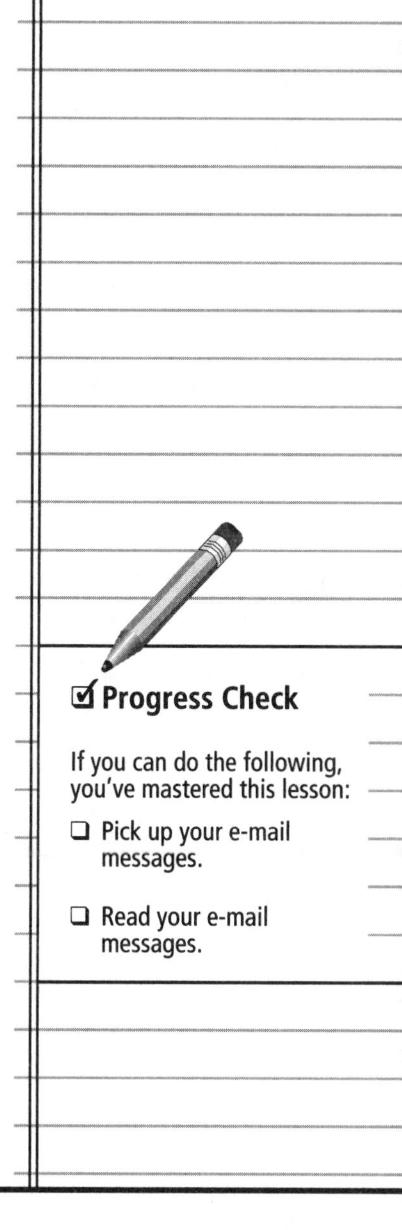

☑ Progress Check

If you can do the following, you've mastered this lesson:

- ❑ Pick up your e-mail messages.
- ❑ Read your e-mail messages.

Replying to, Forwarding, Printing, and Deleting Messages

Lesson 5-4

Some messages are destined for oblivion; others demand a reply or need to be passed along to someone else. In this lesson, you'll learn how to reply to messages, forward messages to other people, print messages, and delete unwanted messages.

Reply to Author

respond to a message by clicking either the Reply to Author button or Reply to All button

quoted text appears with a > at the beginning of each line

Replying to a message

Personal messages deserve a reply, and creating one is easy. First, make sure that the message you want to answer is selected. Next, click the Reply to Author button on the Outlook toolbar to respond to the person who wrote the message; or click the Reply to All button to respond to the message's author *and* to everyone else who received the message. Either way, a message window that's pre-addressed to the person(s) you've specified appears. In addition, the window's Subject line is already filled in with the original message's subject text (plus a *Re:* prefix).

The original message's text appears in the new window, too, but in *quoted* format; that is, to distinguish it from the new text that you'll supply, each line of the original text is preceded by either a > character or a vertical line. (Whether > or a vertical line is used depends on the format of the original message. For more information, see the "HTML and e-mail" sidebar that appears later in this lesson.)

Quoting the interesting parts of a message is a good way to help you and the person you're writing to remember what the heck you were both talking about. Deleting the boring parts or the parts to which you aren't replying is polite.

To practice answering e-mail, reply to our robot's Internet For Dummies Central message:

1. **Fire up Outlook Express.**

   You don't have to connect to the Internet yet.

2. **Click the Inbox folder to list the messages you've received.**

   You see the folder's contents in the message list.

3. **Click the message you received from Internet For Dummies Central, which has the sender name `Automated response`.**

   Or reply to a different message, if you prefer. After you click the message, its contents appear in the message area.

4. **Click the Reply to Author button on the Outlook toolbar.**

   A message window appears that's already addressed to the sender of the message — in this case, `Automated response <net101@gurus.com>`. The subject of the message is the same as the subject of the original message, with *Re:* added to the front. (*Re* is short for the Latin *in re,* in case you were wondering, which means *about the thing.*) You can optionally change the latter by clicking the Subject line and then revising its text.

   The message area begins with a blank line, which is where you can start writing your reply. Underneath it is a line that says

   ```
   ---Original Message---
   ```

This line marks the spot at which the text of the message you're answering begins. Following the marker are several lines that identify the original message's sender, recipient(s), date, and subject. Finally, the quoted text of the original message appears, with each line preceded by a >.

5 **With your cursor at the top of the message area, type a response (such as *Thanks for the nice message*).**

If you're writing to us, you might add how long it took for our first message to get to you. (Minutes? Hours? Days? Just a rough idea is fine.)

6 **Delete most or all of the original message.**

When you reply to a message, it's considerate to your audience to delete everything from the original message that isn't pertinent. If the quoted text includes salutations, lots of blank lines, and other unnecessary text, eliminate the excess verbiage by highlighting it with your mouse and pressing the Del key.

7 **Click the Send button to transmit your reply.**

Outlook Express first connects to the Internet automatically and then sends your message. In addition, it files a copy of the message in your Sent Items folder so that you have a record of your outgoing mail.

The next time you pick up your e-mail, you'll receive another reply from Internet For Dummies Central — our mail robot just can't leave a message unanswered!

Nice work! If you're like most people, you'll spend as much time replying to messages as you do writing new ones.

Notes:

include only the relevant parts of the original message in your reply

HTML and e-mail

Whether you see vertical lines or > characters when quoting a message depends on the format of the message you're answering. Some messages use a formatting language called *HTML*, which (as explained in Lesson 3-1) allows the inclusion of special effects such as colors, fonts, graphics — and vertical lines for marking quoted text. Other messages are in plain text, which is an older format that can't handle special effects but that, unlike HTML, all programs understand. Outlook Express supports both the HTML and plain text formats, so it automatically sets your message to be in the same format as the message to which you're replying.

The format of messages you create from scratch, however, is up to you. To select either HTML or plain text, choose Tools⇨Options from the Outlook menu bar to open an Options dialog box; click the Send tab, which is the second tab at the top of the box; click either the HTML option or the Plain text option in the Mail section near the top of the box; and click the OK button at the bottom of the box to save your setting.

Forward Message

to forward a selected message, click the Forward Message button

Forwarding a message

If you receive an interesting message or one that really should have been sent to someone else, you can easily forward it. First, select the message and click the Forward Message button on the Outlook toolbar. Outlook Express opens a window with a blank line, then a line that says `--Original Message---`, and then the entire contents of the original message. You can simply jot down a quick explanation on the blank line, such as *FYI* or *Here's what Bill says!*; or you can write as much of an introduction as you like, as well as edit the original message. The window's Subject line is already filled in (with the prefix `Fw:`, for *forward*, followed by the original subject text), so you can then just address the message and send it off.

Try forwarding a message to yourself (which doesn't make a lot of sense in real life but is a good way to practice):

1. **From the message list, click a message that you want to forward.**

   Unless you have a better candidate, select the message that you received from us.

2. **Click the Forward Message button on the Outlook toolbar.**

   A message window opens with a Subject line that says something like `Fw: Re: Net101 Test Message`. Underneath is a blank line, an `Original Message` line, and then the original message's header information and contents.

3. **Address the message by typing your e-mail address in the To box.**

   If you don't remember what your e-mail address is, look in the message that you received from us.

4. **Press Tab four times to move to the message area.**

   Supply a brief introduction to the message you're forwarding.

5. **Type** Check this out!

   Or write something a bit more refined; it's up to you.

6. **Click the Send button.**

   Outlook Express transmits the message.

Nice going! Since you were working with a copy, the original message remains unchanged in your Inbox, allowing you to reply to it, forward it to someone else, or file it. (You'll learn how to file messages in Lesson 6-2.)

to print a selected message, choose File→Print or press Ctrl+P

Printing a message

Sometimes you need to print a message to store it in a manila folder, to give it to someone, or to carry it around in your pocket. (Perhaps you just received a love letter by e-mail.) Printing e-mail is easy — just click the message you want to print, choose File⇨Print or press Ctrl+P, and click OK.

Before you try to print, make sure that your printer is connected to your computer, is turned on, has its on-line light on, and is loaded with paper. Then you can begin.

1. **From the message list, click the message that you want to print.**

   Check the message area to make sure that what you selected is the message you want to get on paper.

2. **Choose File⇨Print or click Ctrl+P.**

   A Print dialog box appears that gives you such standard options as choosing which pages to print and how many copies to print of each page.

3. **Click OK to print one copy of the entire message.**

   The data is transmitted to your printer and then voilà! Your message is on paper.

Outlook Express automatically prints a page number at the top of every page and the current date at the bottom of each page. It also begins the first page with the message's sender, recipients, date, and subject, followed by the contents of the message itself.

If you want to print only part of a long message, click the Pages option on the Print dialog box and fill in the range of pages that you want. Because you can't see on-screen where pages start and end, this option is useful mainly for printing just the beginning of a long message — for example, for printing only pages 1 through 1.

Deleting a message

After reading a message, you may want to place it carefully in the circular file or in the Great Big Bucket in the Sky. In Outlook Express, you put such important messages in the Deleted Items folder by first selecting the message from the message list, and then clicking the Delete button on the Outlook toolbar or pressing the Del key.

1. **From the message list, click a message that you want to eliminate.**

   You can delete the message from us, or any other message that's sitting in your Inbox folder. When you select the message, its contents appear in the message area.

2. **Click the Delete button on the Outlook toolbar or press the Del key.**

   The message disappears from the Inbox folder. The message wasn't actually erased, though; it was just transferred to the Deleted Items folder. If you suddenly decide that you want the deleted message back, you can undelete it.

3. **Click the Deleted Items folder to display its contents.**

   Wonder of wonders! Your trashed message is in the Deleted Items folder, and it's not covered with old coffee grounds like when you throw something away in your off-screen trash.

Notes:

Delete

to delete a selected message, click the Delete button or press the Del key

the Deleted Items folder contains messages you've deleted

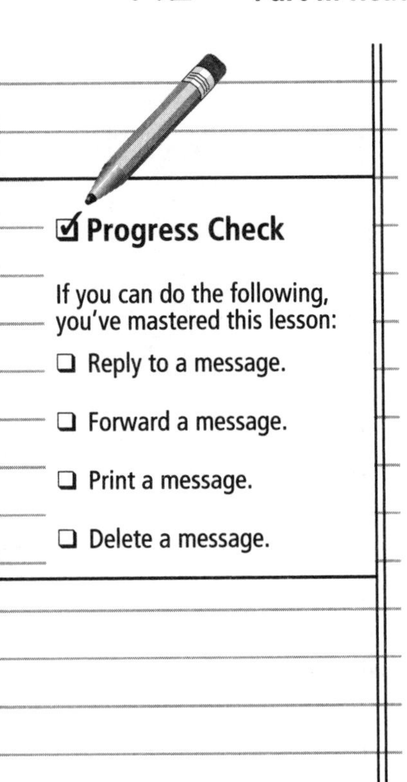

☑ Progress Check

If you can do the following, you've mastered this lesson:

- ❑ Reply to a message.
- ❑ Forward a message.
- ❑ Print a message.
- ❑ Delete a message.

heads up

You can read messages in your Deleted Items folder by clicking them, just like messages in any other folder. You can also save a message from oblivion by clicking it from the message list and, while keeping your mouse button held down, dragging the message from the Deleted Items folder to some other folder, and then releasing your mouse button. (You'll learn more about storing messages in other folders in Lesson 6-2.)

Messages lie around in your Deleted Items folder until you take out the garbage by clicking the folder with your right (not left) mouse button and choosing the Empty Folder option from the menu that appears. Your deleted messages are then *really* deleted, freeing up space on your hard disk for new messages.

Tip: If you're the type of person who does crossword puzzles with a pen, you can set the Deleted Items folder to empty itself automatically every time you exit Outlook Express. To accomplish this, choose Tools➪Options from the menu bar to open an Options dialog box; click the General tab at the top of the box (if it isn't already selected); click the third option, Empty Messages From the 'Deleted Items' Folder on Exit, to turn its check mark on; and click the OK button at the bottom of the box. This setting reduces your chances of later recovering a message that you've mistakenly deleted, but it also frees you from having to remember to periodically purge erased messages.

Recess

You now know nearly all the basics of e-mail! Take a quick breather and then come back to learn some rules of e-mail etiquette. After the next lesson, your messages will look like they're from an e-mail veteran.

Lesson 5-5 E-Mail E-tiquette

heads up

Something about e-mail makes people take offense easily and forget that they're corresponding with a living, breathing human being with feelings. Perhaps it's because you can't see the other person's face or hear a live voice, or perhaps it's a side effect of our pent-up hostility to computers. Whatever the cause, ticking people off by e-mail is remarkably easy. This lesson doesn't have any steps, but don't skip over it, because this stuff is really important.

So here are some words of advice about e-mail etiquette:

- **Use specific subjects.** Your subject appears in the listing of messages in the recipient's Inbox. Make it easy for your correspondent to decide what to read first by typing a very short summary of your message.

- **Don't use all capital letters in e-mail.** It looks like SHOUTING.
- **Avoid sarcasm.** In e-mail, it can be hard to tell when someone is joking. (If you insist on trying, however, see the "Emoticons and e-mail abbreviations" sidebar in Lesson 6-1.)
- **Check your spelling and punctuation before sending messages.** People who don't know you can judge you only on the content of your message, so make it impressive!
- **Avoid writing anything in e-mail that would embarrass you if distributed widely.** You never know who may decide to forward your message to others.

on the test

- **If you get a truly offensive message and you're tempted to shoot off a truly offensive response, don't.** Take a walk instead and calm down. The person is probably just having a bad day. As Margy's mother used to say, "His feet probably hurt." If you feel that you need to respond, write the message and then delete it. Or send it to `nobody@gurus.com`, which gives your message the attention it deserves by automatically throwing your message away.
- **Don't flame.** An angry message is called a *flame.* Sending angry messages is called *flaming,* and an exchange of flames is called a *flame war.* Try to stay out of them — flame wars are bad for your blood pressure and for your reputation on the Net.
- **Don't get ticked off at someone for not responding to your e-mail.** The Internet eats e-mail from time to time, so you may want to send a follow-up message asking whether your correspondent got the first message.
- **Don't believe everything you read.** Just because you get e-mail from someone claiming to be a female 20-something aerobics instructor doesn't mean that you didn't actually just hear from a lonely 12-year-old boy looking for friends.

Here's another piece of advice: Never pass along chain letters by e-mail. A few well-known chain letters (that is, messages that tell you to pass the message along to lots of friends and coworkers) to avoid include messages announcing the Good News virus (the virus doesn't exist), get-rich-quick schemes (the most famous of which has the subject line *MAKE MONEY FAST*), messages about a nonexistent modem tax, and messages claiming that a dying boy in England wants to receive greeting cards. (He got well a decade ago.)

Just read chain letters and delete them. Optional: Skip reading them.

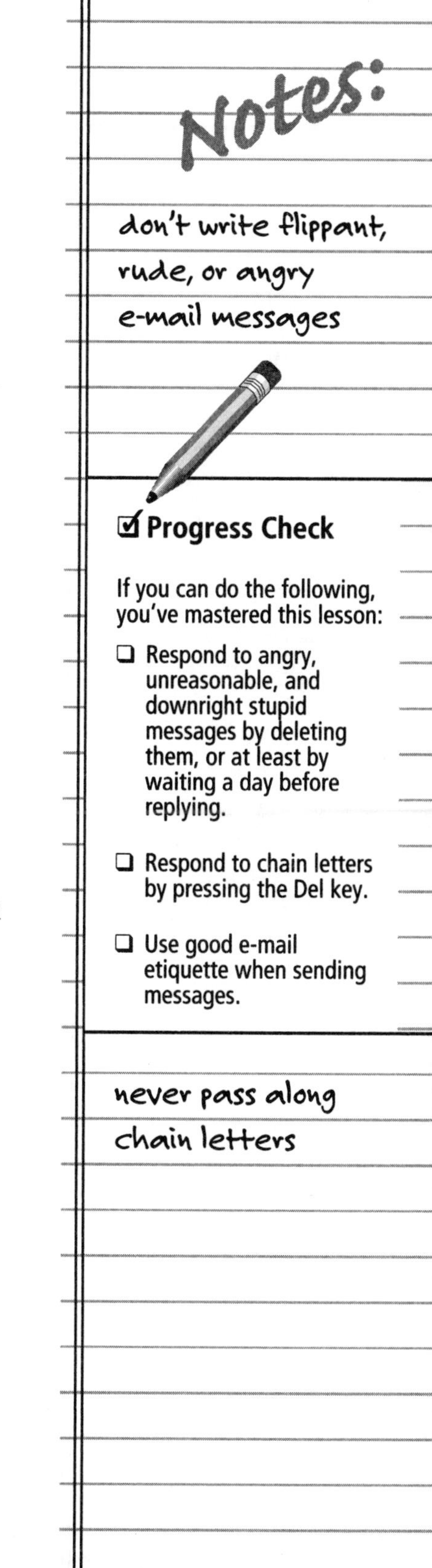

☑ Progress Check

If you can do the following, you've mastered this lesson:

- ❑ Respond to angry, unreasonable, and downright stupid messages by deleting them, or at least by waiting a day before replying.
- ❑ Respond to chain letters by pressing the Del key.
- ❑ Use good e-mail etiquette when sending messages.

Unit 5 Quiz

For each of the following questions, circle the letter of the correct answer or answers. Remember, each question may have more than one right answer.

1. **An Internet e-mail address looks like this:**

   A. `username@computername`

   B. `username@hostname`

   C. `yourname@myname`

   D. `vegetable@mineral`

   E. `net101@gurus.com`

2. **You can use Outlook Express to:**

   A. Read e-mail messages addressed to you.

   B. Send e-mail messages to anyone with an Internet account.

   C. Send e-mail messages to anyone with an account on America Online, CompuServe, or an Internet service provider, among others.

   D. Reply to e-mail messages you receive.

   E. Impress your friends.

3. **Clicking the Compose Message button on the Outlook toolbar:**

   A. Lowers your message's blood pressure.

   B. Opens a blank New Message window.

   C. Sends your message over the Internet.

   D. Lets you write an e-mail message.

   E. Is a good index finger exercise.

4. **To send a message to several people:**

   A. Type the same message over and over, sending it to one person at a time.

   B. Type all the pertinent e-mail addresses in the To box, separating each address with a comma or semi-colon.

   C. Type all the pertinent e-mail addresses in the To box, pressing Enter to place each address on its own line.

   D. Type the message once, print it out, photocopy the printout, and mail the message to each person using envelopes and stamps.

   E. Tell it to one really gabby person and swear that person to secrecy.

5. **When creating a message, you should avoid**
   A. Writing in haste or anger.
   B. TYPING IN ALL CAPS.
   C. Saying something that you might regret later.
   D. Not checking for proper spelling and punctuation.
   E. Playing disco music in the background.

Unit 5 Exercise

1. Call a friend who has an Internet or online service e-mail account. Ask for your friend's e-mail address. Write it down very carefully, including the @ and all the dots (or type it right into a New Message window). Don't worry about capitalization because it rarely matters in e-mail addresses.
2. Fire up Outlook Express and create a new e-mail message. Address the message to your friend.
3. In the text of the message, ask your friend to send back a reply.
4. Send the message.
5. Wait a day, or at least an hour or two, and check your incoming e-mail.
6. Read your friend's message.
7. Send your friend a reply.

Unit 6

More Mail Maneuvers

Objectives for This Unit

- ✓ Creating and using an e-mail address book
- ✓ Filing messages in e-mail folders manually
- ✓ Filing messages automatically using filters
- ✓ Sending attached files by e-mail
- ✓ Receiving attached files

Prerequisites

- Running Outlook Express (Lesson 5-1)
- Sending and receiving e-mail (Lessons 5-2, 5-3, and 5-4)

- Leo.jpg

You've joined the world of online communications — you can send and receive e-mail. When your friends and colleagues exchange e-mail addresses, you can toss yours into the conversation. Why not put your e-mail address on your business cards and stationery?

Now that you know e-mail basics, it's time to learn some advanced features. In this unit, you'll create an e-mail address book, organize your messages using e-mail folders, and send data files (such as pictures, spreadsheets, and databases) along with your messages.

Using Your Address Book

Lesson 6-1

Typing e-mail addresses is painstaking and annoying work. One period or at sign (@) out of place and you're sunk. Luckily, you don't have to type any e-mail address more than once — just enter it right into your Outlook Express Address Book. Along with a person's e-mail address, you can enter her name, company, title, business address, home address, telephone numbers, and fax numbers. You can also supply a nickname and display name of your choosing.

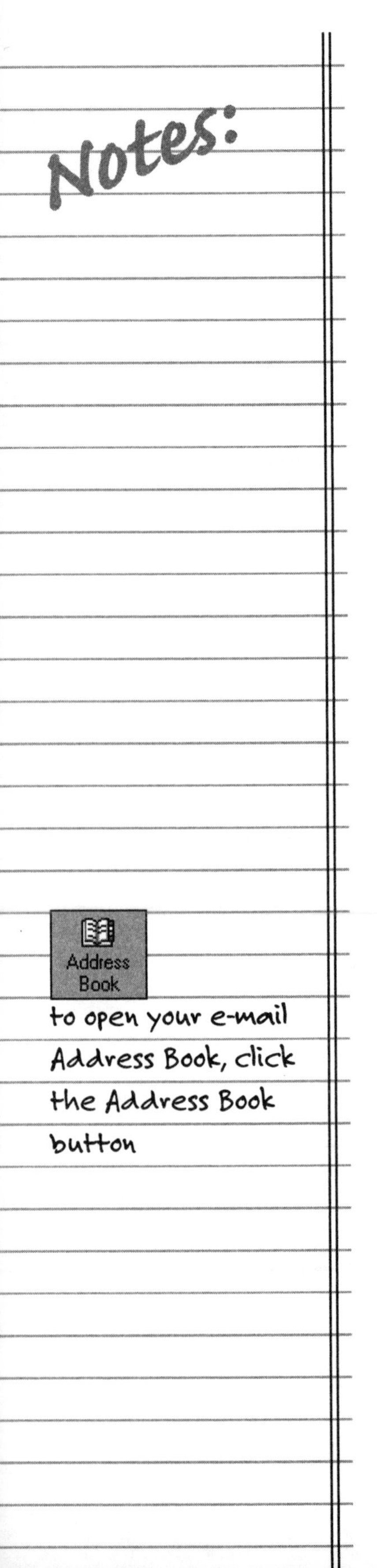

In Outlook Express, a *nickname* is an abbreviated name that you pick to stand for a person who will receive your e-mail. When you open a message window to compose e-mail, you can type the person's nickname in a To, Cc, or Bcc address box in place of the person's e-mail address.

For example, for your mother, you might choose the nickname *Mom*; for your friend Herbert Pickleherring, you might assign the nickname *Herb*; and for a salesman you regularly deal with at WhizBang Gizmo Corporation, you could pick the nickname *Gizmo*. After you click the message window's Send button, Outlook Express automatically converts each nickname into the full name and e-mail address the nickname represents. A *display name* is similar to a nickname, except that it's typically a person's full name and is used by the Address Book as a label to represent the person's collection of information. Therefore, it's faster to type a nickname than a display name.

Outlook Express doesn't stop with these address substitutes, however; the program also automatically types out entire display names, e-mail addresses, and even nicknames for you as you start to enter them! Specifically, when you type a first letter (say, the letter *D*) in an address box, Outlook Express automatically checks that letter against all the entries in your Address Book.

If Outlook Express finds a display name, nickname, or address that starts with the same letter (say, the display name *Daisy Angelus*), it immediately places that text in the address box. If two or more entries start with the same letter (for example, *Daisy Angelus* and *Dorothy Knoxhuddle*), Outlook Express inserts the first entry it encounters (in this case, *Daisy Angelus*). If that entry's not the one you want, simply keep going; when you type enough to match a different entry (say, *Do*), the program instantly replaces the old text with the new text (in this case, *Dorothy Knoxhuddle*).

Similarly, if none of the Outlook Express suggestions are what you want, no problem; just keep typing (for example, type *Don*), and the program eventually runs out of suggestions and simply accepts what you type.

You can open your Address Book by clicking the Address Book button on the Outlook Express toolbar. You can then create a new entry by clicking the New Contact button on the Address Book toolbar. In this lesson, you'll create an entry or two in your Address Book and then use a nickname to address a message.

Adding people to your Address Book

The first person you should put in your Address Book is *you*. You can then use your nickname to easily send messages to yourself whenever you want to test your e-mail account. To add the entry, follow these steps:

1. **Launch Outlook Express.**

   You don't have to connect to the Internet yet.

2. **Click the Address Book button on the Outlook toolbar.**

   You see the Address Book window — which is initially empty — in Figure 6-1.

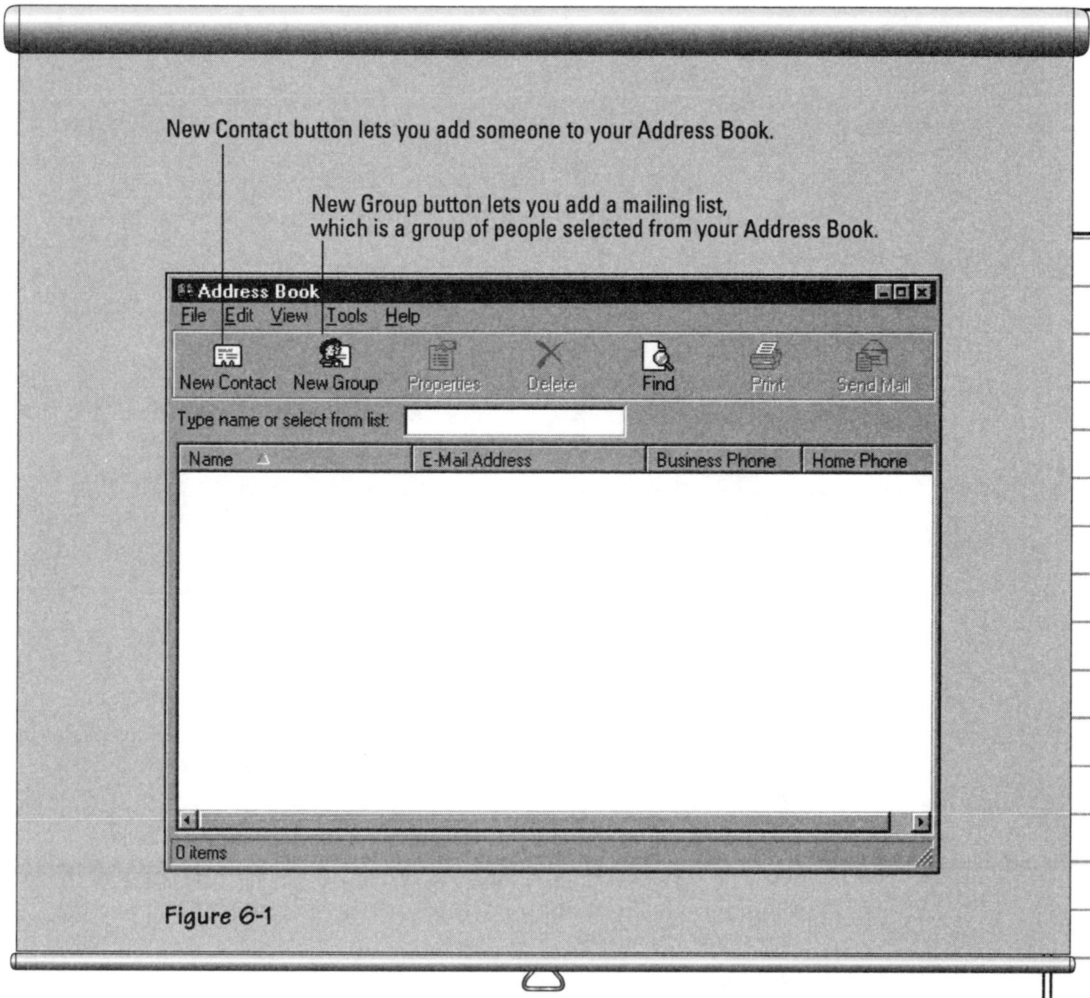

New Contact button lets you add someone to your Address Book.

New Group button lets you add a mailing list, which is a group of people selected from your Address Book.

Figure 6-1

Figure 6-1: The Address Book lets you maintain a collection of names, e-mail addresses, and nicknames that spare you unnecessary typing.

Notice that the first button on this window's toolbar is named New Contact. This button allows you to add an entry to your Address Book (similar to the way you'd add a new card to a Rolodex).

3 Click the New Contact button (the first button on the Address Book toolbar).

You see the Properties dialog box in Figure 6-2. Notice that the box has six tabs across its top: Personal, Home, Business, Other, NetMeeting (or Conferencing), and Digital IDs. You start off with the Personal tab selected and with your cursor in a First name text box.

to add someone to your Address Book, click the New Contact button

4 Type your first name.

This name will appear in each message that you send to the person (in this case, yourself), so type it carefully. If you make a mistake, use the Backspace key to erase the error and then type the correct text.

As you type, notice that your text is echoed both in the Display box directly below and in the title bar at the top of the window. The display name is a label used by the Address Book to represent all the information you enter about the person. The display name is normally the person's full name, so what you type in the First, Middle, and Last name boxes is automatically inserted in the Display box.

Figure 6-2: Use the Properties dialog box to add a person's contact information to your Address Book.

Figure 6-3: Use the Home form to enter such contact data as a home address, a home phone number, a home fax number, and a personal Web page address.

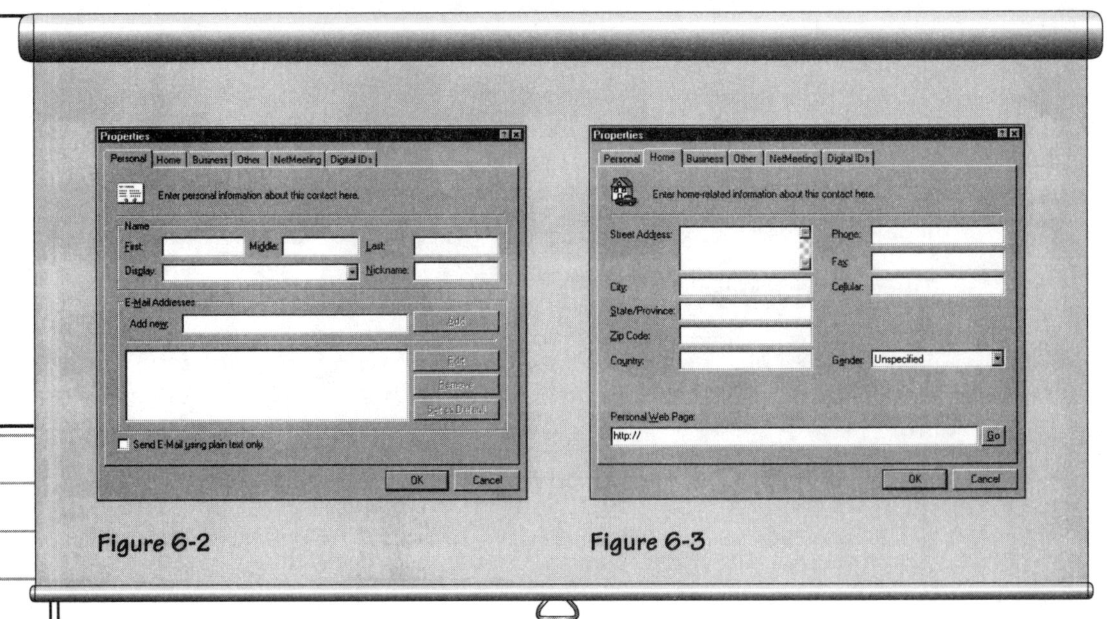

Figure 6-2

Figure 6-3

5 Press the Tab key.

You move to the Middle box, which lets you enter a middle name or initial. You can always move to the next text box by pressing Tab and to the previous box by pressing Shift+Tab.

6 Optionally type a middle name or initial, and then press Tab.

If the person doesn't normally use a middle name or initial, then just leave this box blank. After you press Tab, you move to the Last box, which lets you enter the person's last name.

7 Type your last name and then press Tab.

Again, this name will appear in all the messages that you send to the person, so type it carefully.

After you press Tab, you move to the Display box — which now contains the text you entered in the First, Middle, and Last name boxes.

8 Optionally revise the display name and then press Tab.

A full name is the clearest way to label a person's contact information, so we recommend that you leave the display name as is. If you have a special reason to use a different display name, though, you can change the text to anything you like. Your revisions are reflected in the window's title bar.

After you press Tab, you move to the Nickname box, which lets you assign a short name you can type in place of the person's full name and e-mail address.

9 Choose a nickname that will be easy to remember and type. When you're ready, carefully type the nickname and then press Tab.

You can type your first name, or the word *me*, or some cute name that you've been called since childhood. Every time you click the Send button to transmit a message, Outlook Express will automatically look for this nickname in the To, Cc, and Bcc address boxes, and will replace each occurrence with the full name and e-mail address the nickname represents.

After you press Tab, you move to the Add New box, which lets you enter one or more e-mail addresses for the person.

10 Carefully type your e-mail address.

This entry is critical, so be sure to get all those pesky at signs (@) and periods right.

11 Click the Add button (to the right of the Add New box).

The e-mail address you typed is inserted into a box that's large enough to store multiple addresses. Some people have more than one electronic mailbox — for example, one for business and one for personal mail. If the person (in this case, you) has precisely one e-mail address, however, then skip to Step 14.

12 Type another e-mail address in the Add New box and then click the Add button.

Repeat this step until you've entered all the person's e-mail addresses.

13 Click the address you'll normally use to send yourself messages and then click the Set as Default button.

The phrase `(Default E-Mail)` appears to the right to indicate that Outlook Express will use this address whenever you enter the person's nickname or display name in an address box.

14 Review the Send E-Mail Using Plain Text Only option in the lower-left section of the dialog box.

For more information about formatting, see the sidebar "HTML and e-mail" in Lesson 5-4. The plain text only option should be turned on if you know that the person's e-mail program can't handle HTML. Since you receive e-mail via Outlook Express, which supports both plain text and HTML, leave the option turned off.

You've now finished entering all the data Outlook Express needs to handle the person's e-mail. The Address Book provides a few additional forms, however, in case you'd like to consolidate all of the person's contact information.

15 Click the Home tab near the top of the dialog box.

You see a form (shown in Figure 6-3) that lets you enter the person's home address, phone number, fax number, cellular number, gender, and personal Web page URL. Optionally fill in the form.

16 Click the Business tab near the top of the dialog box.

You see a form that lets you enter the person's business address, job title, department name, office location, business phone number, fax number, pager number, and business Web page URL. Optionally fill in the form.

17 Click the Other tab near the top of the dialog box.

You see a box that lets you enter miscellaneous notes about the person — for example, where you first met, the person's birthday, the names of the person's spouse and children, and so on. Optionally type a few facts into the box.

18 Click the next tab, which is named either NetMeeting (if you've installed Microsoft NetMeeting) or Conferencing (if you haven't).

You see a dialog box that helps you include the person in electronic conferences. If this option interests you, see your company's computer manager for more information.

Notes:

Properties

to change an entry in the Address Book window, double-click the entry, or click it and click the Properties button

Delete

to delete an Address Book window entry, press the Del key or click the Delete button, and click Yes

19 Click the Digital IDs tab near the top of the dialog box.

You see a dialog box devoted to electronic IDs, which can be used to encode and decode messages for enhanced security. Digital IDs are beyond the scope of this book, but you can find more information about them on the Web (via the instructions in Lesson 2-5) by searching for phrases such as *digital ID* and *certifying authority*.

You've now thoroughly explored the Properties box, so save your contact information and exit.

20 Click the OK button near the bottom of the dialog box.

The contact data you typed is saved to your hard disk, the dialog box goes away, and you see the Address Book window again. Notice that you now appear as the first entry in the window!

21 If you already know other people who have e-mail addresses and whom you intend to correspond with, repeat Steps 3 through 17 for each person (substituting the person's information for your own).

After entering each person's contact information, click the OK button to save the information. The entry appears in your Address Book window.

22 After you're finished adding entries, choose File⇨Close to exit the Address Book.

The Address Book window disappears.

Great work! You now have a useful Address Book that will spare you lots of extra typing in the future.

If you later need to revise an Address Book entry, you can simply open the Address Book and double-click the entry. Alternatively, you can click the entry to select it and click the Properties button on the toolbar. Either way, the Properties dialog box appears with the information you previously supplied. Click in any text box that you want to change, edit the information appropriately, and click the OK button to save your changes.

You can also easily delete an Address Book entry that's become obsolete. To do so, click the entry in the Address Book window, press the Del key or click the Delete button on the toolbar, and click the Yes button to confirm the deletion. Think twice before using this option, however, because you can't get the entry back after it's deleted.

Notes:

Don't retype e-mail addresses!

If you receive a message from someone who you want to add to your Address Book, don't retype the person's address. Instead, let Outlook Express do it for you:

1. **Double-click the message from the message list.**

   The message opens in its own window.

2. **Right-click (that is, click with your *right* mouse button) the address in the From box.**

   A menu appears that includes an Add To Address Book option.

3. **Click the Add To Address Book option.**

   A Properties box dialog box pops up that lets you add a new Address Book entry. Further, the e-mail address you clicked has automatically been inserted in the Add New box.

4. **Use the dialog box to fill in the rest of the person's contact information. After you're done, click OK.**

   Your new entry is saved, with its critical e-mail address entered perfectly.

5. **Choose File⇨Close to exit the message window.**

Use the Add To Address Book command whenever possible to avoid making typos while inserting those pesky e-mail addresses.

Creating mailing lists

Using your Address Book is convenient for sending e-mail to one person, but it's a virtual necessity when you need to repeatedly send e-mail to a group of people (for example, when it's part of your job to notify coworkers about upcoming meetings). To handle this chore, open your Address Book and click the New Group button, which is the second button on the toolbar. This opens a dialog box that lets you add an unlimited number of display names from your Address Book — and also lets you assign a display name to represent the entire list! After you save the list by clicking OK, you can simply type the list's display name in a To, Cc, or Bcc address box. Outlook Express automatically inserts all the e-mail addresses that the list represents after you click the Send button.

Tip: If you have a lot of people on your list, don't put the list's display name in the To box because it will force each recipient to wade through a bunch of e-mail addresses before getting to your message. Instead, type your own display name or nickname in the To box, and type the list's display name in the Bcc (Blind Carbon Copy) box. This ensures that each recipient sees only your name and e-mail address in the message's headers.

Notes:

Addressing messages using the Address Book

Now that you've created an entry for yourself in the Address Book, send a test message using your new nickname:

1. **Click the Compose Message button on the Outlook toolbar.**

   A New Message window appears, with your cursor in the To box.

2. **Start typing your nickname, slowly, until Outlook Express fills in the rest of it for you.**

   When you've typed enough letters to uniquely identify your nickname (which, depending on the entries in your Address Book, may require only a first letter), Outlook Express supplies the remaining letters. If the program types out your display name instead of your nickname, that's fine, too. After you click the Send button, your full name and e-mail address will replace the current nickname or display name.

3. **Press the Tab key three times.**

   You move to the Subject line.

4. **Type a subject for your message, like *Address Book Test*, and press Tab.**

   You move to the window's message area.

5. **Type a short message, such as *Checking out the nickname feature!***

   Or whatever you want; you're the only one who will see this message.

6. **Click the Send button (the first button on the toolbar).**

   Outlook Express dials into the Net (if you aren't already connected). The program then transmits the message (poof!), and the message window disappears.

Easy, no? As you've just seen, all you need to remember to send someone e-mail is the first few letters of her nickname or real name.

But what if you *can't* remember the beginning of the person's name? That's no problem, either, because you can always conduct more extensive searches of the Address Book by clicking either the Check Names button or Select Recipients button on the message window's toolbar. Try that now to create a second test message:

1. **Click the Compose Message button again.**

   Another New Message window pops up. Pretend for a moment that you remember only a fragment of your name — for example, your last name but not your first name.

2. **Type a few letters from the beginning of your last name.**

   Notice that Outlook Express fails to suggest you as the intended audience, because your text doesn't match the start of your display name or nickname. You can still find yourself in the Address Book, however, by clicking the Check Names button, which is the sixth button on the toolbar.

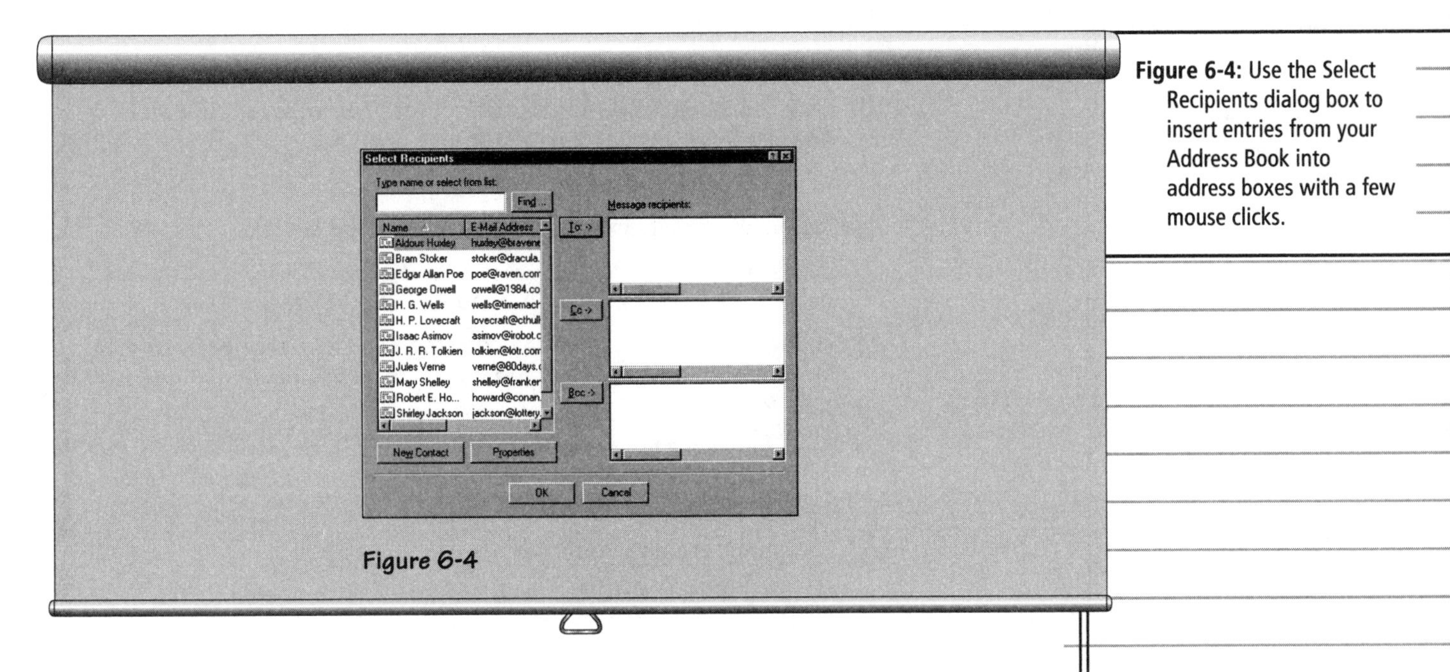

Figure 6-4: Use the Select Recipients dialog box to insert entries from your Address Book into address boxes with a few mouse clicks.

3 Click the Check Names button (the toolbar button that looks like a person next to a check mark).

Outlook Express instantly searches through your Address Book for *any* match of the letters you've typed, locates your last name, and inserts your display name in the To box! (That is, unless a different name was matched first — in such a case, press Backspace to delete the incorrect suggestion, type additional letters to ensure the match you want, and click Check Names again.)

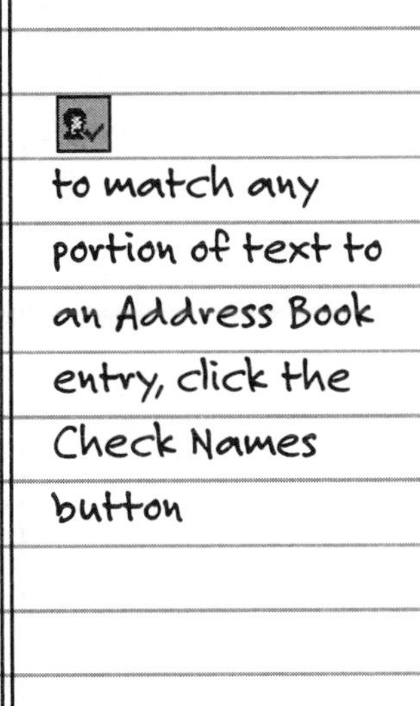

Finally, what if you don't remember a person's name at all, but you'd know it if you saw it? That's no problem, either; simply pop up your Address Book entries by clicking the Select Recipients button, which is the seventh button on the toolbar.

4 Click the Select Recipients button (the toolbar button that looks like an open book).

You see a Select Recipients dialog box that lets you scroll through all your Address Book entries (as shown in Figure 6-4).

5 Locate your name in the list and then click the name to select it.

The list is normally ordered alphabetically by first name, but you can click the Name header (directly above the list) twice to instead display the names alphabetically by last name. You can also jump to any group of names beginning with a particular letter by just typing the letter. After you locate and click a name, you can insert it into an address box by clicking one of the buttons to the right of the list.

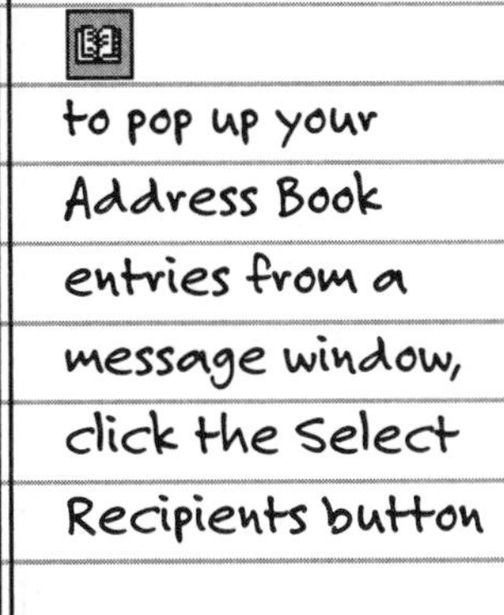

6 Click the To button to the right of the list.

The selected name is copied into the To box. If you want to send your message to additional people, simply continue clicking names and address buttons.

7 After you're done inserting names, click the OK button at the bottom of the dialog box.

The box goes way, returning you to the message window.

Notes:

8 Click the Subject line, type a subject for your message such as *Address Book Test,* and press Tab.

You move to the window's message area.

9 Type a short message and then click the Send button.

Something like *You're terrific!* is always appropriate. After you click Send, the message window exits, returning you to the Outlook Express window.

10 Wait a few minutes, and then click the Send and Receive button on the Outlook toolbar. If you get new mail, check the Inbox folder for your test messages.

If your mail doesn't show up right away, try again a little later. Eventually, your test messages should arrive, proving how effectively you can use your Address Book to send messages.

11 Disconnect from the Internet.

And pat yourself on the back; you're now an Address Book expert!

Attaching a business card and using stationery

You can share the Address Book information you've entered about yourself with others via e-mail by including a *business card,* which appears in your message as an icon that looks like a Rolodex card. If the recipient is using a program that supports HTML, she can typically view the contents of the business card by double-clicking its icon and then clicking an option such as Open.

To include your electronic business card in messages, first choose Tools⇨Stationery from the Outlook menu bar; click the Signatures button from the dialog box that appears; click in the Card text box (near the bottom) from the second dialog box that appears; click your own Address Book entry from the list that pops down; make sure that the Attach card to all outgoing messages option is turned off, because you want to be selective about who receives your contact data; and click OK twice. You can then attach your business card to any message by opening a New Message window and choosing Insert⇨Business Card from the menu bar.

You can also include prepared pictures, called *stationery,* as background images for your messages. This Outlook Express feature won't necessarily work for people reading your messages with programs other than Outlook Express. If you'd like to play around with stationery, though, simply click the narrow button directly to the right of the Compose Message button on the Outlook toolbar, and then click one of the options that appears (such as Balloon Party Invitation or Holiday Letter) to open a New Message window that contains the stationery. Alternatively, you can open a blank New Message window and then insert stationery by choosing Format⇨Apply Stationery from the menu bar.

Emoticons and e-mail abbreviations

E-mail messages contain lots of mysterious things, such as *emoticons* (or *smileys*), which are pictures of faces drawn with punctuation. To read an emoticon, tip your head to the left. Here are a few emoticons, as well as some widely used abbreviations:

:-)	A happy face
:-(	A sad face
8-)	A happy face with glasses
:-o	A shocked face
=|;-)	A winking happy face wearing a top hat
<g>	Grin
BTW	By The Way
TIA	Thanks In Advance
IMO	In My Opinion
IMHO	In My Humble Opinion
IMNSHO	In My Not-So-Humble Opinion
RTFM	Read The, er, Fine Manual
YMMV	Your Mileage May Vary

Recess

Tilt your head and take another look at the "Emoticons and e-mail abbreviations" sidebar. Play around by typing a few. (You may even want to try creating a few of your own.) Emoticons and e-mail abbreviations aren't for everyone's tastes, but if you decide that you like them, enjoy <g>.

☑ Progress Check

If you can do the following, you've mastered this lesson:

- ❑ Enter e-mail addresses and other contact information for your relatives, friends, and coworkers into your Address Book.
- ❑ Address e-mail messages by using nicknames or display names.
- ❑ Address e-mail messages by popping up Address Book entries.

Filing Messages in Folders — Lesson 6-2

When you receive important correspondence on paper, you file it in folders for safekeeping. (Yeah, right — who are we kidding? You probably just stack it on top of all those other important papers, like we do.) The same is true when you receive an important e-mail message — except that the folders are on your hard disk rather than in a filing cabinet. Outlook Express automatically provides you with the following five e-mail folders:

Notes:

- **Inbox:** Stores messages you receive.
- **Drafts:** Stores messages you've created and are in the process of editing.
- **Outbox:** Stores messages you've completed and plan to send off shortly.
- **Sent Items:** Stores copies of messages you've already sent.
- **Deleted Items:** Temporarily stores messages you've deleted.

You aren't stuck with using only the handful of folders that Outlook Express creates, though. You can make as many folders as you want and use them to store messages based on such criteria as who sent the e-mail or the subject matter of the e-mail. You can then transfer messages from one folder to another manually; or you can tell Outlook Express to *automatically* direct incoming messages to appropriate folders!

In this lesson, you'll create e-mail folders, move messages between folders, and set Outlook Express to automatically sort your incoming messages into folders.

Creating folders

create folders by project or for each person you correspond with

Outlook Express normally throws all your incoming mail into the Inbox folder. If you get a lot of messages, however, it's more convenient to organize them into a number of different folders. You can create a folder for each project that you're working on (say, Annual Budget, or Novel in Progress). You can also make folders for people or groups with whom you correspond frequently (for example, Shawna Epstein, or Gigantcorp Marketing).

to create an e-mail folder, choose File→Folder→New Folder

on the test

To create a folder, choose File⇨Folder⇨New Folder from the Outlook menu bar; type a name for the folder; choose whether you want to create a first-level folder or a subfolder within an existing folder; and click OK. The folder is instantly created and displayed on the folder list.

Take a few moments now to pick a folder name. (If you have trouble deciding, just use *Personal,* which can serve to store e-mail from your friends.) When you're ready, go ahead and create the folder:

1. **Fire up Outlook Express, if it's not already running.**

   You don't have to connect to the Internet in this exercise; all the action takes place on your hard disk.

2. **Choose File⇨Folder⇨New Folder from the menu bar.**

   You see the Create Folder dialog box in Figure 6-5. Near its top is a Folder Name text box that lets you type the name of your folder. The rest of the dialog box displays the folder list, which lets you specify where you want to place your new folder.

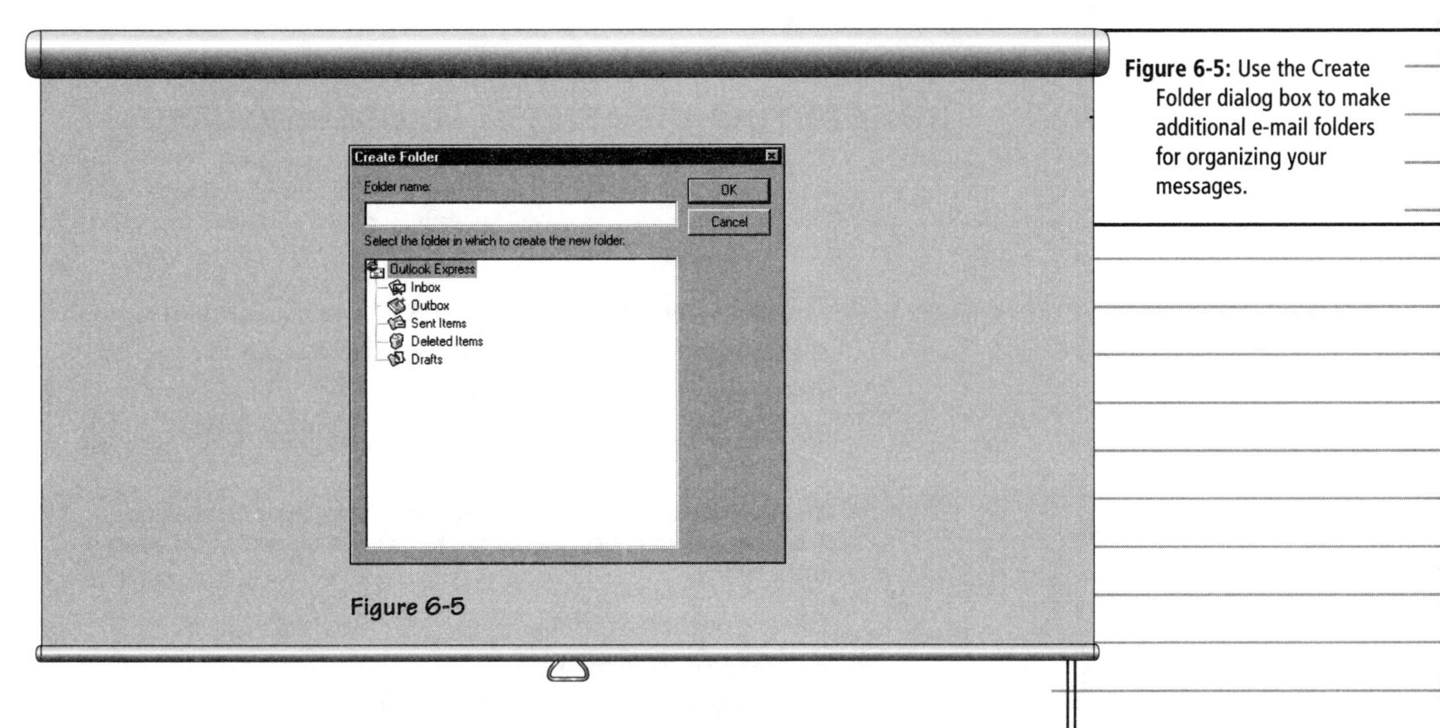

Figure 6-5: Use the Create Folder dialog box to make additional e-mail folders for organizing your messages.

3. **In the Folder Name box, type the name you picked for your new folder (for example, type *Personal*).**

   After you're done typing, notice that you can create a first-level folder — that is, on the same level as Inbox, Outbox, Drafts, and so on — by clicking Outlook Express at the top of the folder list. Alternatively, you can click any other folder to place your new folder within it as a subfolder. The latter option is useful if you have lots of messages that are related but different — for example, within a Music folder, you might want to create subfolders named Classical, Rock, and Country & Western. For now, though, make your folder first-level.

4. **Click Outlook Express at the top of the folder list.**

   You've set both the name and location of your new folder, so give Outlook Express the green light to create it.

5. **Click the OK button in the upper-left section of the dialog box.**

   The dialog box exits . . . and your folder is created! You should now see your folder as part of the folder list in the upper-left section of the Outlook Express window.

6. **Click your folder to switch to it.**

   The contents of the folder are displayed in the message list in the upper-right section of the window.

Folders start out empty, so all you see in the message list at the moment is blank space. You can fix that by transferring messages from other folders to your new folder — which is exactly what you'll do in the next exercise.

Tip: If a folder stops being useful, you can delete it by clicking it to select it, clicking the Delete button on the Outlook toolbar or pressing the Del key, and clicking the Yes button to confirm the deletion. Be sure to think twice before deleting a folder, however, because doing so permanently eliminates both the folder and all the messages it contains.

Transferring messages to other folders

Moving a message from one folder to another is quick and easy. Simply click the folder that contains the message you want, and then click and drag the message to the destination folder. Try it!

1. **Click the Inbox folder on the folder list.**

   The contents of the Inbox folder are displayed in the message list.

2. **Click a message that you want to move.**

   The message is selected, as indicated by its contents appearing in the message area in the lower-right section of the window.

3. **While keeping your mouse button held down, drag the message from the message list over to the folder you created in the preceding exercise.**

   Your new folder is highlighted to show it's selected.

4. **Release your mouse button.**

   The message is moved to your new folder, as indicated by its contents disappearing from the message area and being replaced by the next message in your Inbox.

5. **Click your new folder.**

   You switch to your new folder and — lo and behold! — you see the message that you moved.

In other words, moving a message around is a snap. By creating folders and transferring messages, you can ensure that your e-mail stays well organized.

Tip: You can also *copy* a message to a folder. To do so, simply click and drag the message to the folder while holding down the Ctrl key. A copy of the message is placed in the destination folder, while the original message is unaffected.

Adjusting the folder list

If you don't care for the small, branchlike icons in the folder list, you can change them to large, box-like buttons with a few mouse clicks. First, choose View⇨Layout from the Outlook menu bar to open a Layout dialog box. Next, click the Folder List option to turn it off; click the Outlook Bar option to turn it on; and click OK. The folder list changes from a tree with small icons to a vertical bar with large buttons!

You can use the Layout dialog box to change other elements of the Outlook Express window, as well. Play around with the dialog box until you've tailored the window to your tastes.

Filtering messages

If you receive e-mail only occasionally, manually transferring messages isn't much of a chore. However, if you start conducting a lot of business via e-mail, or if you begin subscribing to mailing lists (which distribute interesting information and ongoing discussions via e-mail; see Unit 7 and Unit ML on your *Dummies 101* CD for details), you can end up getting dozens of messages a day. Having to transfer so many messages to appropriate folders by hand can consume a lot of time and effort. In addition, when all those unrelated messages are dumped into the same Inbox folder, the clutter may cause you to accidentally overlook important and timely messages.

A better way to go is to take advantage of the terrific *message filtering* feature. Filtering automatically sorts messages based on text you specify that appears in any portion of the message you choose. For example, you can tell Outlook Express to send all messages with *Gobhackle* in the From line to a folder that you've created for your friend Bob Gobhackle. As another example, you can direct all messages with the word *taxes* in the Subject line to a folder that you've created named *This Year's Taxes*. After you've set up your filters, download your mail as usual, and then look at the folder list. You can identify folders containing unread messages because Outlook Express displays them in boldface, with the number of unread messages to the right of the folder. Click each boldfaced folder to switch to it and read the new mail it contains.

To set up an e-mail filter, first create the folder to which you'll be directing messages (if the folder doesn't already exist). Next, choose Tools⇨Inbox Assistant from the menu bar. From the dialog box that appears, click the Add button, define the filter's rules, and click OK twice. All your subsequent incoming e-mail is filtered through the rules that you've created. Those that match a rule are redirected to the appropriate folder, while the rest get dropped (as usual) into your Inbox.

To get a better sense of how filters work, create a folder for someone with whom you'll be corresponding and then direct that person's messages to the folder:

1. **Choose File⇨Folder⇨New Folder from the menu bar.**

   The Create Folder dialog box appears.

2. **In the Folder name box, type the name of a friend or colleague with whom you expect to chat frequently via e-mail.**

   For example, if you were friends with Sean Connery, you might type *Sean* (or something more informal, like *Bond, James Bond*) for the folder name.

3. **Click *Outlook Express* at the top of the folder list and then click OK.**

   The dialog box closes, and your folder is created. You're now ready to create your filter.

4. **Choose Tools⇨Inbox Assistant from the menu bar.**

   An Inbox Assistant dialog box appears. To create a filter, click the Add button in the lower-left section of the box.

Notes:

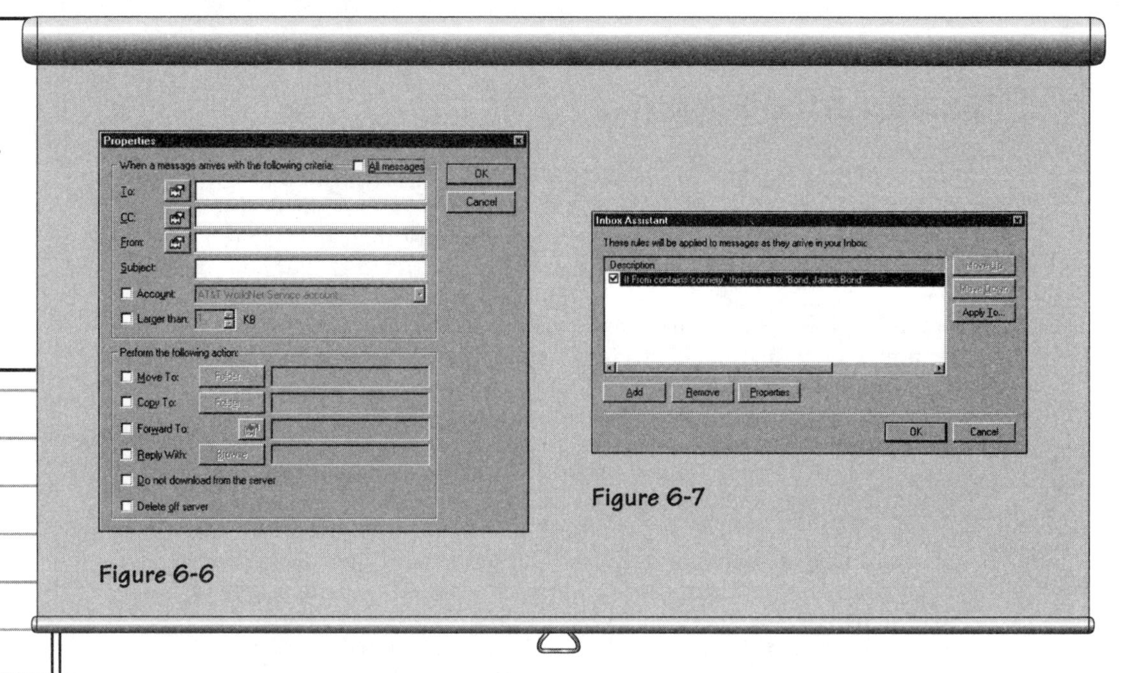

Figure 6-6

Figure 6-7

Figure 6-6: Create e-mail filters to automatically file your new messages into appropriate folders.

Figure 6-7: The Inbox Assistant dialog box displays the e-mail filters you've created to sort your incoming messages.

5 Click the Add button.

You see the Properties dialog box in Figure 6-6. The top half of the box lets you specify what to search for in an incoming message's To, Cc, From, or Subject text. The bottom half of the box lets you pick which folder should receive messages that fit your search criteria.

In this case, you want the filter to find incoming messages from a particular person, so start by entering the person's e-mail address into the From box.

6 Click the text box to the right of the From option, and then carefully type some or all of your friend's e-mail address.

You don't have to type the entire address, just enough text to uniquely match the address.

Alternatively, if your friend is in your Address Book, click the button directly to the right of the From option to pop up the Select Recipients dialog box; locate and click your friend's name; click the From button; and click OK. Your friend's e-mail address is inserted into the From box, enclosed in quotation marks.

After you define what the filter should look for, tell the filter where to direct your friend's messages.

7 Click the Move To option to direct your friend's messages to a particular folder.

A check mark appears to the left to indicate you've turned the option on. Also, the Folder button to the right, which was grayed out, is now activated.

8 Click the Folder button.

A list of your e-mail folders appears.

9 Click the folder you created to store your friend's messages and then click OK.

The name of the folder in entered in the Move To box, indicating that Outlook Express will automatically move all incoming messages from your friend into her folder.

You've now established both your filter's search rule and the action the filter should take when the rule is met, so you're done.

10. **Click the OK button in the upper-right section of the Properties dialog box.**

    The box closes, returning you to the Inbox Assistant dialog box. Notice that the filter rule and action you've defined now appear in the dialog box in the form of a "if *this*, then *do this*" sentence, as shown in Figure 6-7.

    If you later want to revise this filter, simply double-click it to pop up the Properties box again. You can also temporarily turn the filter off by clicking to its left to make its check mark disappear; or you can permanently delete the filter by clicking it and clicking the Remove button. For now, though, simply save your filter and exit.

11. **Click the OK button in the upper-right section of the Inbox Assistant dialog box.**

    The box goes away, and your filter is saved. The next time that you receive e-mail from your friend, her messages will appear in the special folder you created instead of the Inbox folder.

If you want to create folders and filters for other friends or projects, go ahead and do so now, following a similar procedure to the one you just performed.

After you've set up your e-mail filters, follow these steps to find and read your incoming messages:

1. **Click the Send and Receive button from the Outlook Express toolbar to retrieve your new mail.**

   Your incoming messages are filtered through the rules you've established and then filed in the appropriate folders, rather than just being deposited as one disorganized group into the Inbox folder.

   Notice that some of the folders in the folder list appear in boldface. The boldfacing means that these folders contain unread messages.

2. **Click a folder that contains messages you want to read.**

   You're switched to the folder, and you see the unread messages in it boldfaced in the message list.

3. **Click each boldfaced message from the message list until you've read all the new mail in the folder.**

   After you've read all your new messages, the folder loses its boldfacing.

4. **Repeat Steps 2 and 3 until you've read all your new messages.**

   You'll know that you've gone through all your mail when none of your e-mail folders appear in boldface.

Notes:

folders containing unread messages appear in boldface

unread messages appear in boldface

Notes:

If you're in a hurry, though, just open the folders that are likely to contain important messages. If you've set up your mail filters effectively, you can skip examining the rest of your folders until you have more time because you know the messages in them can wait. You can also feel assured that you won't accidentally overlook critical messages that might otherwise have been buried amidst unimportant ones in the Inbox folder.

Outlook Express' message filtering is a powerful feature that can revolutionize how you interact with your e-mail. We recommend that you play around with it and find creative uses for it tailored to your e-mail needs.

Even if you don't use filtering, though, try to file your important messages in e-mail folders rather than printing each message and filing it in a manila folder. Save a tree!

Creating a signature

Many e-mail users like to include a *signature* — that is, a few lines of text that are automatically added to the bottom of every message. For example, instead of typing your name and e-mail address at the end of every message, you can have Outlook Express do it for you.

Your signature can also contain a pithy statement that's fun or piques your reader's interest. However, don't use long sentences, verbose quotations, or cute pictures created from letters and punctuation marks (also known as *ASCII art*). These can be interesting the first time someone sees them, but they get old fast after a recipient reads your second or third message. Your entire signature should be no more than four lines long.

To create a signature, do the following:

1. **Choose Tools⇨Stationery from the Outlook menu bar.**

   A Stationery dialog box appears.

2. **Click the Signatures button (in the lower-right section of the dialog box).**

   A Signature dialog box appears.

3. **Click in the large text box (near the top of the dialog box).**

4. **Type something both concise and informative that can stand up to repeated viewings.**

5. **Click the Add This Signature To All Outgoing Messages option (near the top of the dialog box).**

   A check mark appears to the left of the option.

6. **Click OK twice.**

   Both dialog boxes close, and your signature is saved.

You can perform similar steps at any time to revise your signature text or to turn off the automatic signature feature. If you do the latter, you can still manually add your signature to any message by choosing Insert⇨Signature from the New Message menu bar.

extra credit

What happens to dead letters?

If you type an e-mail address incorrectly, the Internet can't deliver your message. Instead, the message is bounced back to you with a large, scary-looking notice from a Mail Delivery Subsystem (or some other official-sounding program). Don't panic! Simply do the following:

1. **Read through the returned mail to spot the error you made in the e-mail address.**
2. **Use your mouse to highlight the text of your original message (which typically appears below the error notice).**
3. **Press Ctrl+C to copy the highlighted text to the (invisible) Windows Clipboard.**
4. **Click the Compose Message button on the Outlook toolbar to open a New Message window.**
5. **Click the window's message area, and press Ctrl+V to paste your original text into the window.**
6. **Click the To box and carefully type the correct e-mail address.**
7. **Click the Send button.**

With any luck, the second time's the charm.

☑ Progress Check

If you can do the following, you've mastered this lesson:

- ❑ Create a new folder.
- ❑ Move a message into a folder.
- ❑ Create a message filter.

Sending Files Along with Your Messages

Lesson 6-3

We love e-mail, and we use it for just about everything, including submitting the units in this book to our fabulous editor Kelly Ewing at IDG Books Worldwide. But e-mail messages are limited to just two formats: plain text and HTML (and, as mentioned in Lesson 6-1, some e-mail programs can handle only plain text). So to submit units with all the formatting that Kelly needs, we *attach* word-processing documents to our e-mail messages. In fact, you can attach any file to a message — word-processing documents, spreadsheets, data files, graphics files — you name it! The only qualifier is that some e-mail systems choke on extremely large files, so if you encounter problems, call both your ISP and the ISP you're sending to and ask what their size limits are for e-mail.

on the test

Why send a file by e-mail? Here are some common reasons:

- Someone wants to know what you look like, so you promise to send a graphics file containing a scanned picture of yourself.
- Your business partner needs to get your company's sales figures, which are stored in a spreadsheet file.
- You ran across a great public domain program for creating genealogy charts that you'd like to share with your sister.
- You've created an inventory of your jazz collection with a database program and now want to get it to a dealer who's interested in buying rare music albums.

attachment = file that's sent as part of an e-mail message

To send a file, you attach it to an e-mail message. The file that you send is therefore called an *attachment*.

In this lesson, you'll learn how to send a message with an attachment. In Lesson 6-4, you'll learn what to do when you receive an attached file.

Understanding how a file is attached

To attach a file to a message, your e-mail program automatically converts the file into specially encoded text. The e-mail program of the person who receives the message then automatically decodes the special text to restore the file to normal.

Since the conversion process is automatic on both ends, in an ideal world, you wouldn't have to be aware of it. Unfortunately, there isn't just one standard way of performing this conversion, but three entirely different formats named MIME, uuencoding, and BinHex. (Think of them as tape, staples, and glue.) All three formats result in the same thing: your file arriving along with your e-mail message. The problem is that not all e-mail programs and online services support all three formats, and if both the sender and the receiver of a message can't handle the same conversion format, the file transfer doesn't work.

Outlook Express sends files using MIME

Outlook Express uses MIME (the most modern, up-to-date format) when sending attached files. Outlook Express can also handle incoming messages that use any of the three attachment formats. So you can receive attached files from anyone; but if you want to *send* an attached file, you should first find out whether your intended recipient uses a program that can handle the MIME format — or be prepared to find out by trial and error. (***Fair warning:*** If you send a message with an attached file to folks whose e-mail programs can't deal with the attachment, the message will appear as a long series of incomprehensible gibberish when they open it, and you may get some complaints.)

on the test

Which attachment format to use isn't the only consideration to keep in mind before you e-mail a file. Here are some others:

ask before sending files via e-mail

- **Make sure that your recipient can deal with the file that you want to send.** For example, if you plan to send a WordPerfect document or an Excel spreadsheet, first ask whether the person can read WordPerfect documents or Excel spreadsheets. You may need to save your file in a special format that he or she can handle. Most word processors, spreadsheet programs, and database programs can save files in a wide variety of formats.
- **Make sure that the addressee wants to receive it!** We get a lot of e-mail from people we don't know, and we find it annoying when people send us files, especially large ones. A large file can take several minutes to download, tying up the phone line and making the recipient wait around to read her other incoming mail. If the recipient pays by the hour to connect to the Internet, this costs her money as well. Ask before you send!

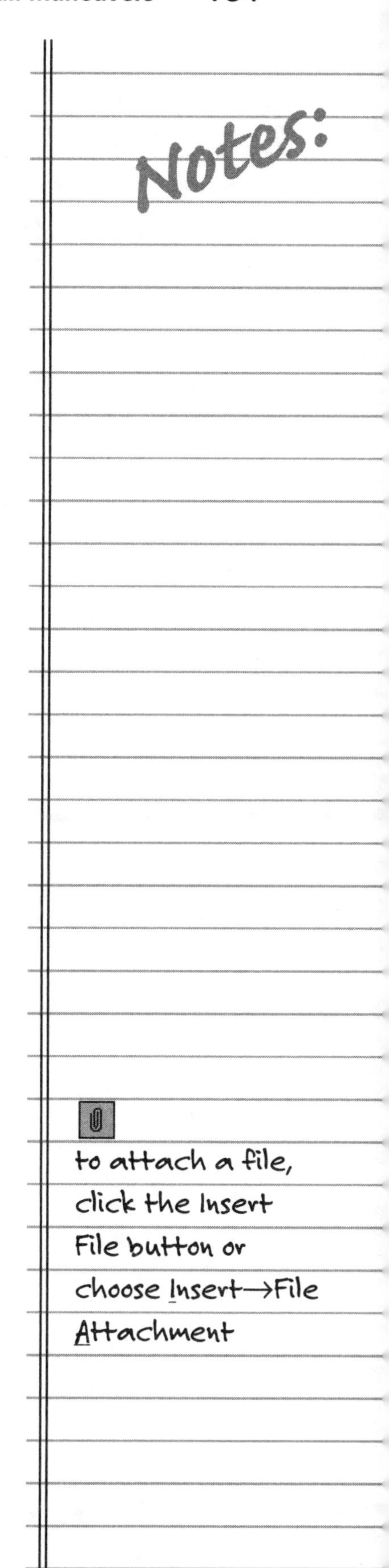

- **Consider compressing the file before sending it.** Appendix B describes how to install and use WinZip, a wildly popular and invaluable file compression program that's on your *Dummies 101* CD. (But make sure that your recipient knows how to decompress the file!)

If you're certain that the person to whom you plan to send a file both wants it and can deal with it, you're ready to e-mail the attachment.

Attaching and sending a file

After you determine that e-mailing a particular file is a good idea, all that's left to do is actually attach and send it. Follow these steps to send a picture file on the *Dummies 101* CD to yourself, just for practice:

1. **Insert the CD that came with this book into your CD-ROM drive.**

   Be careful to touch only the sides of the CD and to insert it with its printed side up.

2. **Launch Outlook Express (if it isn't already running) and then click the Compose Message button on the Outlook toolbar.**

   You see the New Message window.

3. **In the To box, type your e-mail nickname (which you created in Lesson 6-1); then press Tab three times.**

   You move to the Subject line.

4. **Type** Self-portrait by Leonardo da Vinci **and then press Tab.**

   One of history's greatest artists drew himself late in his career. This image is stored in a file on your *Dummies 101* CD using a graphics format named JPEG. Electronic pictures are stored in a bewildering variety of formats with unpronounceable names. JPEG is a format that's especially popular on the Internet.

5. **In the message area, type** Leonardo da Vinci self-portrait, stored in graphics file Leo.jpg in JPEG format.

   Always provide information about the file you're attaching, including what the file is about and what format the file is in. Otherwise, the recipient may not know what to do with it!

   After you finish typing, notice the eighth button on the toolbar, which looks like a paper clip. This is the Insert File button, and it lets you attach a file.

6. **Click the Insert File button (the paper clip button on the toolbar).**

   If you prefer, you can choose Insert⇨File Attachment from the menu bar. Either way, an Insert Attachment dialog box like the one in Figure 6-8 appears. This is a standard file dialog box, similar to what you see after choosing a File⇨Open or File⇨Save As command.

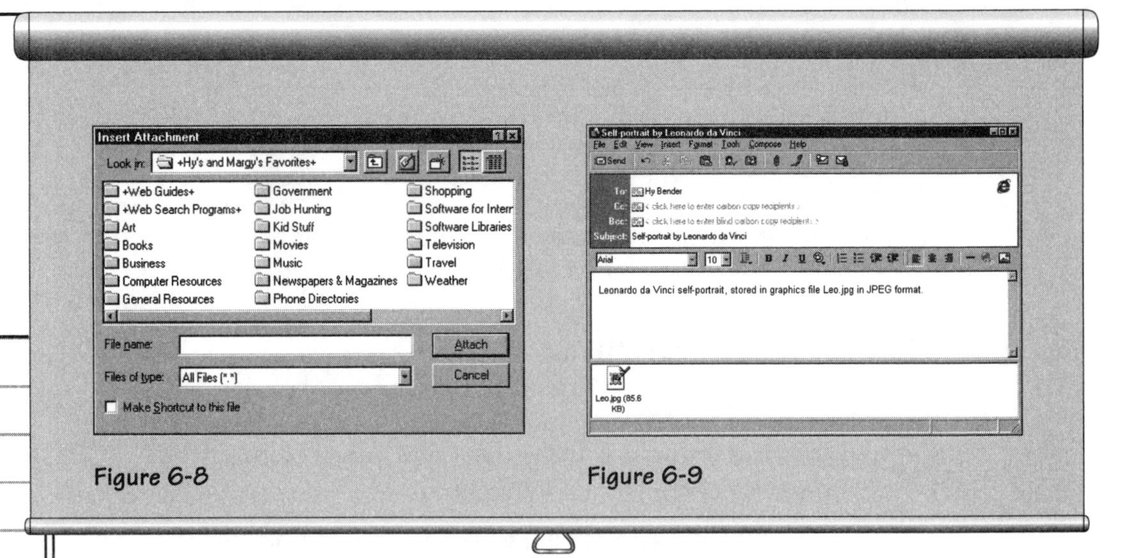

Figure 6-8: Use the Insert Attachment dialog box to attach a file to your e-mail message.

Figure 6-9: After you attach a file, an icon representing the file is inserted at the bottom of your message.

Notes:

7. **Click in the File Name box and type** d:\Leo.jpg **(that is, the letter** d**, a colon, a backslash, and the filename** Leo.jpg**).**

   If your CD-ROM drive isn't drive D, type the letter appropriate for your drive.

8. **Click the Attach button.**

   The dialog box goes away, and an icon representing the Leonardo file is inserted at the bottom of your message window, as shown in Figure 6-9. In this case, the icon looks like a picture being painted because Outlook Express recognizes the file's *jpg* extension as belonging to a graphics file. Underneath the icon is the file's name and, in parentheses, the file's size (which determines how long the file will take to transmit). Your message is now complete, so send it off.

9. **Click the Send button on the toolbar.**

   Outlook Express dials into the Net (if you aren't already connected) and starts transmitting your message. Because the Leo.jpg file is of moderate size (about 86K), sending it should take a minute or two. When the transmission is completed, the message window closes and you're returned to the Outlook Express window.

Sending a file by e-mail is relatively easy: Compose a message, attach the file to the message, and send your message as usual. Receiving and viewing an attached file is just as easy — as you'll see shortly.

Sending links

If someone uses an e-mail program that supports HTML, you can send the person links to Web pages. When your message arrives, each link appears as underlined and in color, just like links on the Web; and when the recipient clicks a link, the person's default browser program runs and displays the Web page! To insert a link in a message, follow these steps:

1. **Open a New Message window and choose Format⇨Rich Text (HTML) from the menu bar.**

   This setting ensures that your link will be created properly.

2. **In the message area, type a short phrase to represent the link.**

   For example, if the link will point to your personal Web page, you might type *My Home Page.*

3. **Highlight the link text with your mouse and then choose Insert⇨Hyperlink from the menu bar.**

   Alternatively, click the Hyperlink button, which is the next-to-last button on the Formatting toolbar directly above the message area. Either way, a dialog box appears that prompts you to type the URL of a Web page.

4. **Type the URL of the Web page to which you're establishing a link and then click OK.**

   The dialog box closes, and the text you selected is turned into a link. You can repeat Steps 2 through 4 to create as many links as you desire.

5. **Complete your message as usual and then click the Send button.**

   When your message is received, the recipient will be able to travel to each Web page you've referenced by just clicking its link!

☑ Progress Check

If you can do the following, you've mastered this lesson:

- ❑ Attach a file to a message.
- ❑ Send the message.

Receiving an Attached File

Lesson 6-4

In the preceding lesson, you sent yourself an attached file. Now follow these steps to receive the file:

1. **Run Outlook Express and connect to the Internet (if you aren't already connected).**

2. **Click the Send and Receive button on the Outlook Express toolbar. If you receive mail, check the Inbox folder for your Leonardo message.**

   If the message doesn't show up right away, try again a little later. Eventually, the message you sent to yourself should arrive in your Inbox.

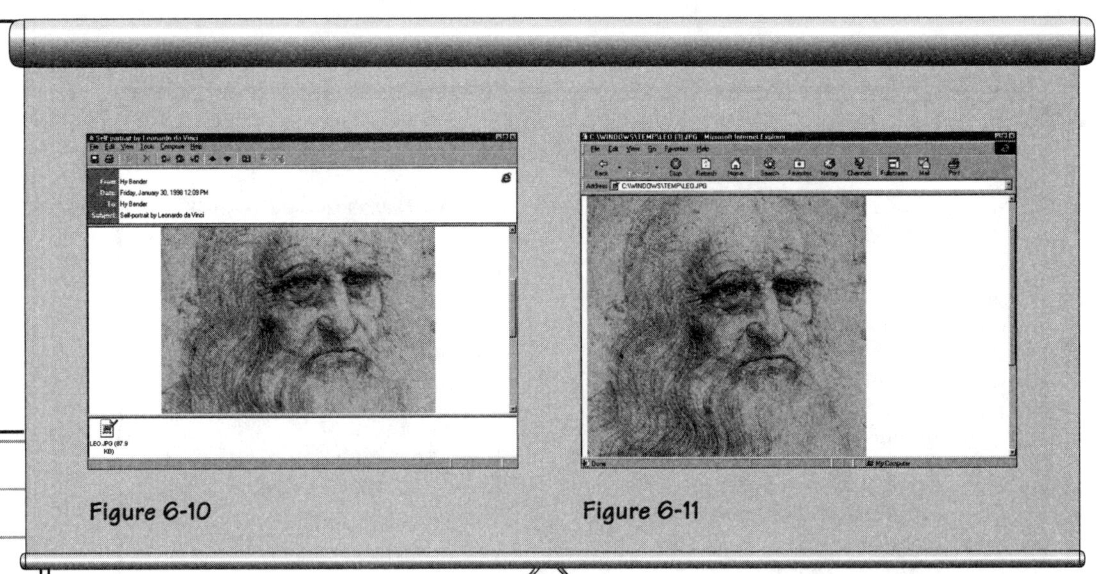

Figure 6-10: If you receive a graphics file in a format that Outlook Express supports, the program displays the image directly in the message area.

Figure 6-11: Internet Explorer displays your attached picture in its browser window — cool!

3 Click the Leonardo message from the message list.

The text of the message appears in the message area, and . . . look at that! A self-portrait by one of the world's master illustrators appears, as well! That's because Outlook Express happens to support the JPEG format used by this file. Otherwise, you'd see only an icon representing the file.

Now get a better view of the image by putting the message in its own window.

4 Double-click the Leonardo message from the message list.

The message opens in a separate window.

5 Maximize your new window so that it fills the screen and then scroll through the message.

You see more of the Leonardo picture, as shown in Figure 6-10.

In addition, you see an icon at the bottom of the message that represents the file. If the file was in a format that Outlook Express doesn't support — for example, a spreadsheet or a database — then this icon is all you would see of the file.

6 Right-click the file icon (that is, click it with your *right* mouse button).

A menu appears that includes the options to print the file; save the file under a different filename and/or folder (that is, create a copy of the file); and open the file. The latter option runs whatever program on your hard disk is likely to handle the file's format and then directs the program to load the file.

7 Click the Open option to load the file into a program designed to display it.

Your hard disk probably has several programs on it that can handle JPEG images; but because you're opening the image from Outlook Express, Internet Explorer launches and loads the picture. Therefore, after a few moments, you see Leonardo in an Internet Explorer browser window (as shown in Figure 6-11).

☑ Progress Check

If you can do the following, you've mastered this lesson:

- ❑ Receive a message with an attached file.
- ❑ Load an attached data file into a program designed to display it.

You can follow the same procedure — that is, right-clicking the file's icon and clicking the Open option — to deal with any attached file you receive. If the file is a program, your PC runs it. If it's a data file, Windows 98 tries to recognize the format and run the appropriate program for displaying that type of file (assuming that you have the necessary program on your hard disk). If you ever get stuck, just call the person who sent you the file and arrange to receive it in a different format.

Practice safe computing

If someone sends you a program by e-mail, should you go ahead and run it? Depends on who sends it to you! If you don't know and trust the sender, don't run the program unless you run a virus checker first. See Lesson 3-2 for information about checking programs for viruses.

Unit 6 Quiz

For each of the following questions, circle the letter of the correct answer or answers. Remember, some questions may have more than one right answer.

1. **A nickname is**

   A. A computer term created by a guy named Nick.

   B. Something you type into the Outlook Express Address Book.

   C. A cute name that only your childhood friends can get away with calling you.

   D. From the Middle English *eekname,* meaning "also name."

   E. A name you can use when addressing e-mail messages so that you don't have to type a person's actual e-mail address.

2. **To make an e-mail folder:**

   A. It takes a village.

   B. Click the New button from the Outlook Express toolbar.

   C. Choose File➪Folder➪New Folder from the Outlook Express menu bar.

   D. Choose File➪New➪Folder from the Outlook Express menu bar.

   E. Buy the appropriate materials at a hardware store and start sawing.

Notes:

3. **If you want to filter messages about making money into a Get Rich folder, you can tell Outlook Express to search for text in:**

   A. The sender header.

   B. The subject header.

   C. The message's body.

   D. The message's soul.

   E. The sender's bank account.

4. **Reasons to attach a file to an e-mail message include**

   A. Sending word processing documents to colleagues who are collaborating on a writing project.

   B. Sending pictures of your kids to your parents.

   C. Sending spreadsheets to your company's accounting department with your expense reports.

   D. Wanting to show off how much you know about the Internet.

   E. Sending a file full of vital top-secret information to yourself just before enemy agents break down your door so that you can delete the original file from your hard disk and claim that you don't know what file they're talking about.

5. **Before sending a file to someone, you should be sure that:**

   A. The person's e-mail program can handle MIME attachments, because Outlook Express attaches files using MIME.

   B. The person has software that can read the type of file you're sending; for example, the appropriate word processor, spreadsheet, or presentation program.

   C. The person feels like dealing with the whole subject of attached files.

   D. The person wants to receive the file.

   E. Your sun sign is compatible with the sign of the person receiving the file.

6. **In the children's classic *A Wrinkle in Time,* the main characters are helped by three beings (Mrs. Who, Mrs. Which, and Mrs. Whatsit) who used to be**

   A. Stars.

   B. Planets.

   C. Tesseracts.

   D. Evil, but now they are good.

   E. Tabloid journalists.

Unit 6 Exercise

1. Remember that friend with whom you exchanged messages in the exercise at the end of Unit 5? Get hold of that person's e-mail address. You can find it by opening the message you sent to your friend, if the message is still in the Sent Items folder in the folder list.

   Note: If you skipped the Unit 5 exercise, call your friends until you find someone with an e-mail address. Write it down very carefully.

2. In the Address Book, create an entry for your friend.

   Extra credit: Use cut-and-paste commands to copy your friend's address from the message in the Sent Items folder to the Address Book entry.

3. Create a new message and address it to your friend by using the Address Book.

4. Type a message to your friend. Be sure to mention that you're reading this wonderful book about how to use the Internet with Windows 98.

   Extra credit: Find out whether your friend's mail program can handle MIME attachments and, if it can, attach the Leo.jpg file to your message.

5. Send the message.

Unit 7

Joining Usenet Newsgroups

Objectives for This Unit

- ✓ Understanding what Usenet newsgroups are all about
- ✓ Listing newsgroups
- ✓ Subscribing to newsgroups
- ✓ Reading newsgroup articles
- ✓ Finding newsgroups and newsgroup articles of interest

Prerequisites

- Entering a URL to go to a Web page (Lesson 2-3)
- Setting up Outlook Express to handle e-mail (Lesson 5-1)
- Reading, sending, and replying to e-mail messages (Lessons 5-2, 5-3, and 5-4)
- E-mail etiquette (Lesson 5-5)

on the CD

- Maillist.pdf

Among the best resources of the Internet are its tens of thousands of ongoing discussion groups, which conduct lively conversations devoted to virtually every subject under the sun (and even a few beyond it).

newsgroup = ongoing discussion or series of announcements

on the CD

Some of the most useful and interesting discussions take place via e-mail mailing lists. More information about this form of discussion group appears in Unit ML, "Joining Discussions by E-Mail," which is stored on the CD that came with this book under the filename Maillist.pdf. You can read and print this file by using the Acrobat Reader program, which is also stored on the CD. (For more information, see Appendix B.)

Usenet = Internet distribution system used by thousands of newsgroups

on the test

Another way to participate in online discussions is to join newsgroups. A *newsgroup* is an ongoing discussion of a particular topic that takes place via an area of the Internet called *Usenet.* More than 30,000 newsgroups exist, so you can find discussions on virtually any topic you can think of, ranging from baseball (`rec.sports.baseball`) to orthopedic surgery (`sci.medicine.orthopedic`), and from pantyhose (`alt.pantyhose`) to the afterlife (`alt.life.afterlife`). Over 50,000 new messages — or, as they're referred to on Usenet, *articles* — pour into newsgroups every day, making these collective talkfests a rich resource for both learning and fun.

article = message that's distributed by a Usenet newsgroup

Notes:

Each newsgroup has a name consisting of a bunch of words (or parts of words) strung together by dots.

The first word in a newsgroup name tells you the general category the newsgroup falls under (for example, `rec` for recreational or `sci` for scientific). The word or words following the first word in the name further define the newsgroup's topic. Depending on how specific the newsgroup is and how many similar newsgroups exist, the name may have several words or only two. For example, precisely one U.S. newsgroup discusses the joy of flying kites, so the name of the newsgroup is `rec.kites`. However, lots of newsgroups talk about pets, so the name of the dogs newsgroup is `rec.pets.dogs`.

newsgroups are organized into hierarchies

All the newsgroups that start with the same initial word or words are called a *hierarchy*. The following are the seven major hierarchies — that is, the seven types of newsgroups that are the most widely distributed:

- `rec`: Recreational topics, such as sports, games, collecting, music, and art
- `soc`: Both social issues (such as politics, religion, and human rights) and socializing (such as singles and pen-pal newsgroups)
- `talk`: Impassioned debate about topical and controversial issues (though often more heat than light is shed here)
- `sci`: Scientific topics, such as physics, chemistry, biology, and medicine
- `comp`: Computer-related topics, including discussions of PC software and hardware
- `news`: Topics concerning Usenet and newsgroups themselves
- `misc`: Miscellaneous topics that don't fit neatly under the other six hierarchies, such as health and fitness, screenwriting, job hunting, and for-sale notices.

Many newer or more narrow hierarchies aren't as "official" but are of great interest anyway. The most notable of these by far is `alt` (short for alternative), which contains over 4,000 wildly diverse newsgroups. These range from the benign (`alt.sewing`, `alt.algebra.help`, `alt.comedy.slapstick.3-stooges`) to the serious (`alt.adoption`, `alt.alcohol`, `alt.censorship`, `alt.save.the.earth`) to the off-the-wall (`alt.alien.visitors`, `alt.fan.lemur`, `alt.barney.dinosaur.die.die.die`).

Other newsgroup hierarchies include those devoted to a particular company (for example, `microsoft` for Microsoft or `netscape` for Netscape Communications) or region (for example, `ca` for topics related to California, or `fr` for topics related to France *and* discussed in French).

Because keeping up-to-date on all these newsgroups consumes a huge amount of an Internet provider's computer resources, some ISPs choose to not carry hierarchies outside the seven long-established ones we just mentioned. However, a full-service ISP is likely to carry most of the Usenet newsgroups available.

In Units 5 and 6, you learned how the Outlook Express program included in Windows 98 can handle your e-mail. But Outlook Express is multitalented; it can also let you read and participate in newsgroups! In this unit, you'll use Outlook Express to search for newsgroups, join newsgroups, read newsgroup articles, and post your own newsgroup articles.

Outlook Express = program that lets you read newsgroups

What's the difference between newsgroups and mailing lists?

If you've read Unit ML, "Joining Discussions by E-Mail," you may wonder how getting involved in newsgroups differs from joining mailing lists.

Newsgroups are similar to mailing lists in that they let you read and participate in focused discussions along with other nice people on the Internet. Also, like mailing lists, newsgroups can be *announcement only* (just one person posts articles to the newsgroup), *moderated* (one person acts as a censor, approving articles before making them public), or *open discussion* (anyone can post articles).

However, a mailing list is managed at one computer, by one person or program, and sends each of its messages directly from the list manager to the subscriber. In contrast, newsgroup articles aren't sent directly to subscribers, but are passed along all over the Internet by various computers (called *news servers*) that are especially assigned to receive them, with no central management. This means that you can reach out and grab articles from any newsgroup at any time, without providing any notification to the people who run the newsgroup. In fact, when you subscribe to a newsgroup, that action affects only the behavior of your copy of Outlook Express, not other computers. (Specifically, your subscribing to a newsgroup makes Outlook Express list the newsgroup in the folder list along with your e-mail folders, allowing you to switch to the newsgroup and read its articles in the same way that you switch to and read your e-mail messages. Subscribing to a newsgroup also allows Outlook Express to keep track of your unread articles in the newsgroup.)

The bottom line, however, is that both mailing lists and newsgroups let you share information with millions of other knowledgeable people around the world. What you should concentrate on isn't picking which message distribution system you prefer (there's no reason not to use both), but discovering which discussions taking place on the Internet are the most likely to help you out or make you happy.

Setting Up Outlook Express to Read Newsgroups

Lesson 7-1

To show you available newsgroups, Outlook Express has to connect to the computer your Internet provider uses to store newsgroup articles. This computer is variously referred to as a *news server*, *news host*, or *NNTP (Network News Transfer Protocol) server*.

Notes:

to set up Outlook Express to handle newsgroups, choose Tools→Accounts→Add→News

Each news server has a unique name that identifies its location on the Net (similar to the way that URLs identify Web pages and e-mail addresses identify electronic mailboxes). To connect to newsgroups, you therefore first have to tell Outlook Express the name of the news server used by your ISP. If you followed the instructions in Lesson 5-1, you already know this server name. If you skipped Lesson 5-1, call your Internet service provider now and obtain the name of its NNTP server.

After you have the name of your ISP's news server, follow these steps to provide it to Outlook Express:

1. **Click the Start button (in the lower-left corner of your screen) and choose Programs⇨Internet Explorer⇨Outlook Express from the menus that appear.**

   After a few moments, Outlook Express launches.

   Notice that one of the menus near the top of the window is named Tools. This menu includes an Accounts command that lets you enter newsgroup data.

2. **Choose Tools⇨Accounts from the menu bar.**

   An Internet Accounts dialog box appears. Notice that there are four tabs across the top of the box named All, News, Mail, and Directory Service.

3. **Click the News tab.**

   You see a dialog box that stores news server names. If your ISP's news server already appears in this box, you're all set and can skip to Step 16. Otherwise, proceed to create an entry for the server.

4. **Click the Add button (in the upper-right section of the dialog box).**

   A menu appears that displays the options Mail (which sets up Outlook Express to handle your e-mail, as covered in Lesson 5-1); Directory Service (which lets you search for e-mail addresses, as explained in Lesson 5-1); and News (which sets up Outlook Express to handle newsgroups).

5. **Click the News option.**

   The Internet Connection Wizard dialog box shown in Figure 7-1 appears and asks for your name.

6. **Type your full name as you'd like it to appear in your newsgroup messages, or accept the suggested name that appears.**

   For example, if you were starring on a TV series as a teen vampire slayer named Buffy, you'd type *Sarah Michelle Gellar.* If you make a mistake, press the Backspace key to correct the error and then type the correct text.

   After you're done with each form, use the Next button to proceed to the following form.

7. **Click the Next button.**

   You're now asked for your e-mail address, which people who read your newsgroup postings can use to send you feedback.

8. **Type the e-mail address you want to appear in your newsgroup messages, or accept the suggested address that appears; then click Next.**

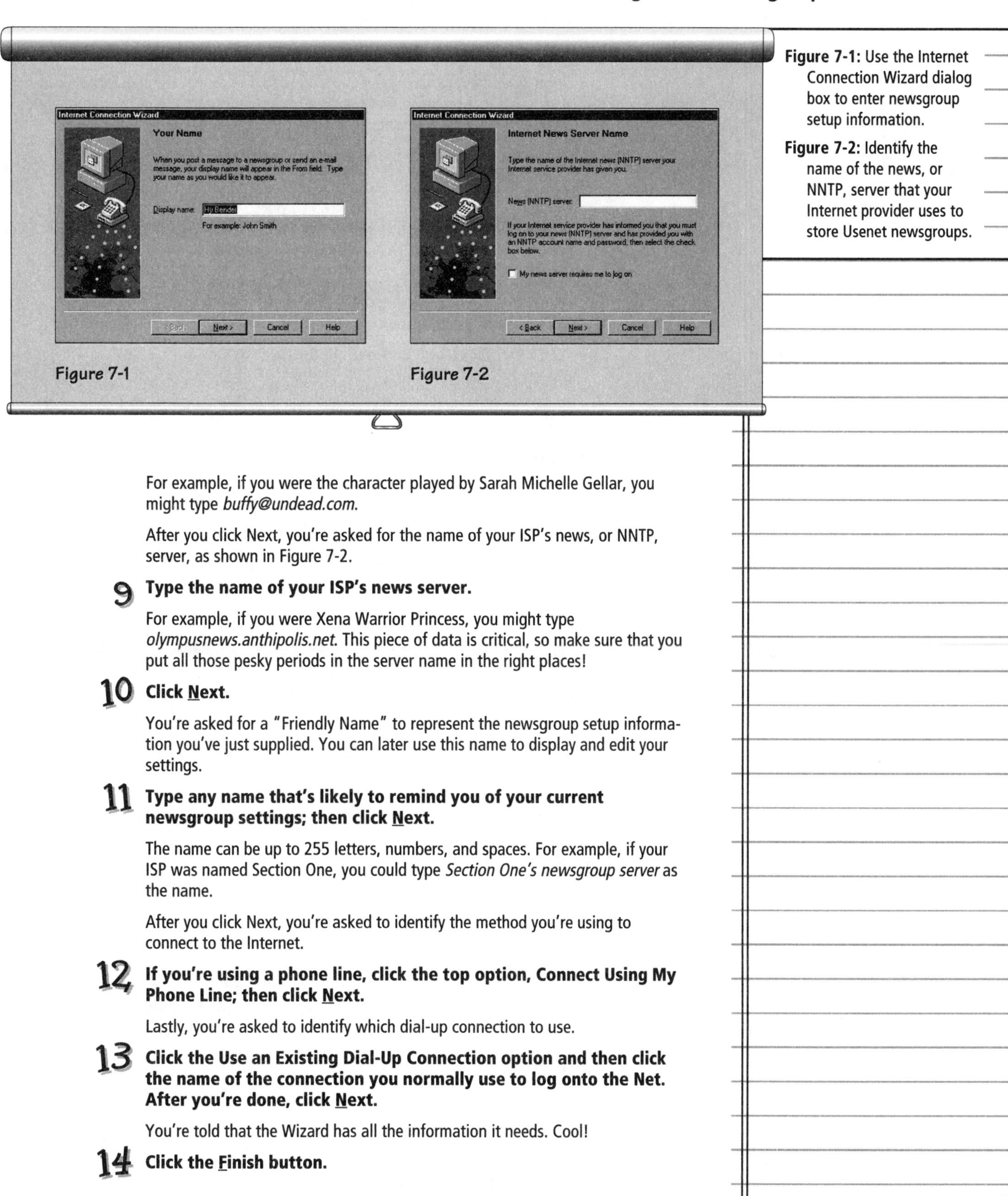

Figure 7-1

Figure 7-2

Figure 7-1: Use the Internet Connection Wizard dialog box to enter newsgroup setup information.

Figure 7-2: Identify the name of the news, or NNTP, server that your Internet provider uses to store Usenet newsgroups.

For example, if you were the character played by Sarah Michelle Gellar, you might type *buffy@undead.com*.

After you click Next, you're asked for the name of your ISP's news, or NNTP, server, as shown in Figure 7-2.

9. **Type the name of your ISP's news server.**

   For example, if you were Xena Warrior Princess, you might type *olympusnews.anthipolis.net*. This piece of data is critical, so make sure that you put all those pesky periods in the server name in the right places!

10. **Click Next.**

    You're asked for a "Friendly Name" to represent the newsgroup setup information you've just supplied. You can later use this name to display and edit your settings.

11. **Type any name that's likely to remind you of your current newsgroup settings; then click Next.**

    The name can be up to 255 letters, numbers, and spaces. For example, if your ISP was named Section One, you could type *Section One's newsgroup server* as the name.

    After you click Next, you're asked to identify the method you're using to connect to the Internet.

12. **If you're using a phone line, click the top option, Connect Using My Phone Line; then click Next.**

    Lastly, you're asked to identify which dial-up connection to use.

13. **Click the Use an Existing Dial-Up Connection option and then click the name of the connection you normally use to log onto the Net. After you're done, click Next.**

    You're told that the Wizard has all the information it needs. Cool!

14. **Click the Finish button.**

☑ **Progress Check**

If you can do the following, you've mastered this lesson:

❑ Find out the name of your ISP's news server.

❑ Provide the name of your ISP's news server to Outlook Express.

Your setup information is saved to your hard disk so that Outlook Express can use it in future sessions. The Internet Connection Wizard then exits, returning you to the Internet Accounts dialog box.

15. **Click the News tab near the top of the dialog box.**

    Notice that the name you chose to represent your setup data is now listed in the dialog box. If the word `(default)` doesn't already appear to the name's right, click the name and then click the Set as Default button to activate your setup.

    You can review and revise your information at any time by clicking the name you chose and then clicking the dialog box's Properties button. For now, though, simply exit the box.

16. **Click the Close button near the bottom of the dialog box.**

    The box goes away, and you're asked if you want to download newsgroups from the news server you just added. You'll be doing precisely that in the next lesson, so hold off for now.

17. **Click the No button.**

    You're returned to the Outlook Express window.

Terrific work! If you look at the upper-left section of the Outlook Express window, you should now see the name of your ISP's news server added to the bottom of the folder list. Outlook Express is ready to retrieve and display your newsgroups!

Lesson 7-2 Listing and Subscribing to Newsgroups

In the preceding lesson, you added the name of your Internet service provider's news server to the bottom of the Outlook Express folder list. You can click this name to access the server's newsgroups. Outlook Express first downloads a list of the newsgroups available, and then lets you explore the list and subscribe to the newsgroups that sound interesting. After you're done subscribing, the newsgroups you selected are added to the folder list (indented below the server name). You can then simply click a newsgroup to list and read its articles.

In this lesson, you'll retrieve a list of available newsgroups from your ISP's news server, explore the list, and subscribe to a few newsgroups.

Listing newsgroups

To see a list of the newsgroups you can join through your ISP, follow these steps:

1. **Connect to the Internet and launch Outlook Express (if it isn't already running).**

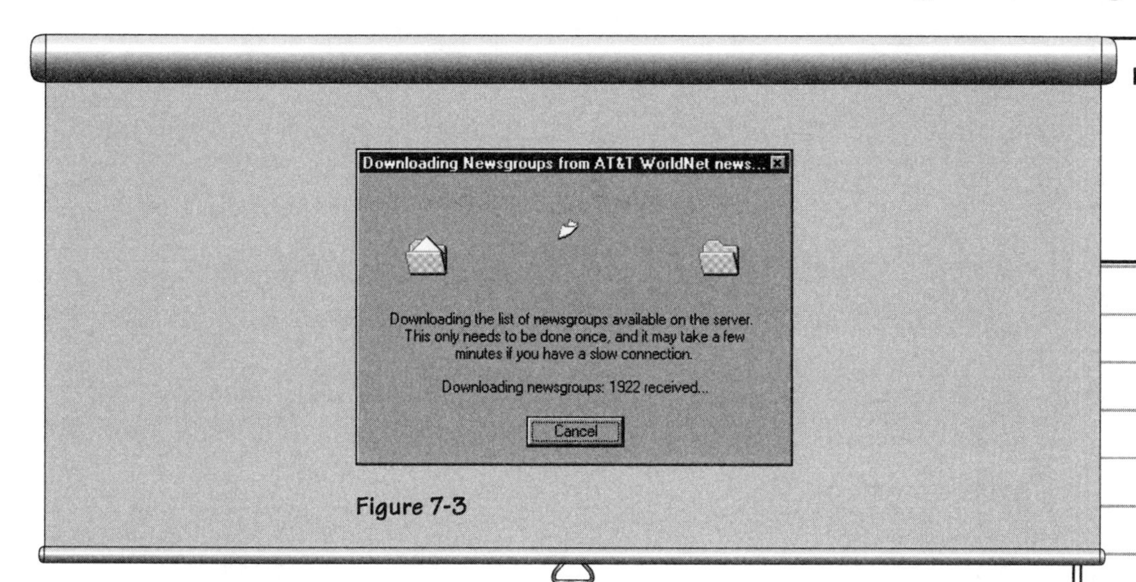

Figure 7-3

Figure 7-3: Outlook Express shows you its progress as it downloads the names of available newsgroups from your ISP's news server.

Notes:

You see the Outlook Express window, which contains a folder list in its upper-left section that displays both your e-mail folders and the name of your ISP's news server.

2. **Click your ISP's news server, which is the last item on the folder list.**

   Because you've never accessed this news server before, a box pops up that says `You are currently not subscribed to any newsgroups. Would you like to view a list of available newsgroups now?`

3. **Click the Yes button.**

   Outlook Express proceeds to download a list of available newsgroups from your news server. Depending on the speed of your connection and the number of newsgroups on the server, this process can take anywhere from a few minutes to half an hour. A status box like the one in Figure 7-3 continuously shows you the progress of the download; but if you don't feel like watching it, feel encouraged to get up and enjoy a cup of coffee (or maybe some nice herbal tea).

   After the names of all the newsgroups are retrieved, the status box is replaced by the Newsgroups window shown in Figure 7-4, which is the Outlook Express mission control center for newsgroups. In the middle of the window is the *newsgroup list*, which is a collection of your available newsgroups in alphabetical order.

to access a news server, click it from the folder list

Nice going! You now have a huge collection of newsgroups to work with. Your next step is to explore the list.

Exploring your newsgroup list

You should still be viewing your newsgroup list. To investigate the list and get a sense of the many different types of newsgroups that are available, follow these steps:

Figure 7-4: Use the Newsgroup dialog box to list and subscribe to newsgroups.

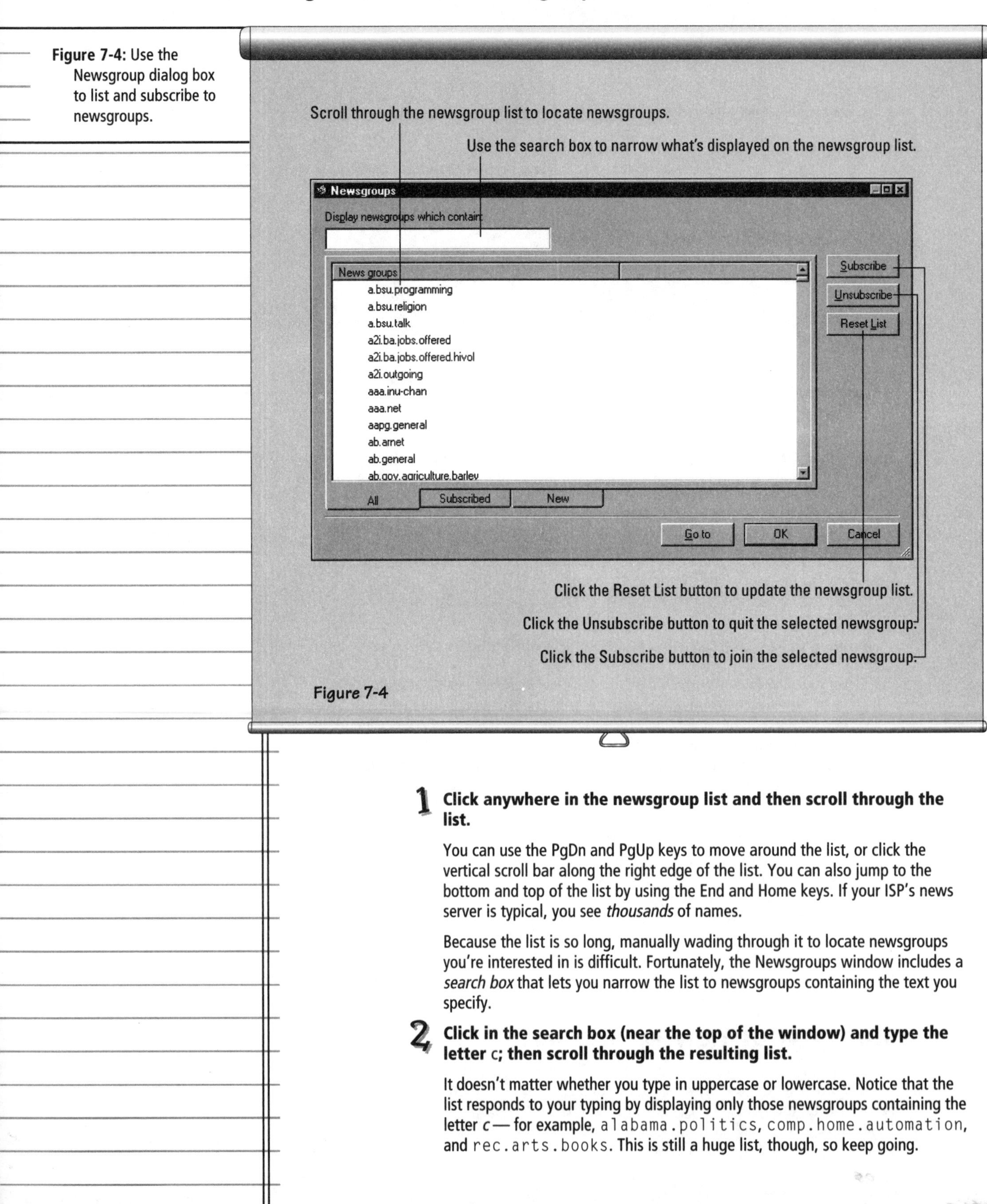

Figure 7-4

1 Click anywhere in the newsgroup list and then scroll through the list.

You can use the PgDn and PgUp keys to move around the list, or click the vertical scroll bar along the right edge of the list. You can also jump to the bottom and top of the list by using the End and Home keys. If your ISP's news server is typical, you see *thousands* of names.

Because the list is so long, manually wading through it to locate newsgroups you're interested in is difficult. Fortunately, the Newsgroups window includes a *search box* that lets you narrow the list to newsgroups containing the text you specify.

2 Click in the search box (near the top of the window) and type the letter c**; then scroll through the resulting list.**

It doesn't matter whether you type in uppercase or lowercase. Notice that the list responds to your typing by displaying only those newsgroups containing the letter *c* — for example, `alabama.politics`, `comp.home.automation`, and `rec.arts.books`. This is still a huge list, though, so keep going.

Notes:

3. **Click in the right side of the search box and type the letters at; then scroll through the resulting list.**

   The search box now contains *cat*, and the list changes to display only newsgroups containing that sequence of letters — for example, `alt.art.caricature`, `misc.education.adult`, and `rec.scuba.locations`. The list is now more manageable, but it's still pretty long.

4. **Click in the right side of the search box and type the letter s; then examine the resulting list.**

   The search box now contains *cats*, and the list changes to display only newsgroups containing that word — for example, `alt.cats`, `rec.pets.cats`, and `rec.pets.cats.anecdotes`. This list is short enough to deal with, while still being broad enough to give you a number of interesting choices.

5. **Double-click in the search box to highlight your old text, and then type a word that represents a topic dear to your heart.**

   For example, type *startrek* or *skiing* or *arts;* the first letter you type replaces the highlighted text. After you're done typing, you see a list of newsgroups that contain the text you've specified.

6. **Scroll through the list you've created, and carefully write down the names of any newsgroups that look intriguing.**

   Repeat Steps 5 and 6 a few times to learn what newsgroups are available covering your areas of interest. You can make use of your written list in the next section, which deals with subscribing to newsgroups.

Take some time to further explore the newsgroup list on your own. Don't hesitate to type anything in the search box, no matter how improbable; you may be surprised at the results. Again, write down the names of any newsgroups that interest you.

After you're done, you should have a solid feel for the vast number and diversity of Usenet newsgroups. Some of these newsgroups are relatively quiet, garnering only a few articles a week; but some of the more popular ones can draw scores of articles a day. To see for yourself, push on to the next exercise, in which you subscribe to a bunch of newsgroups.

Subscribing to and unsubscribing from newsgroups

If you want to read a newsgroup, you *subscribe* to it. This adds the newsgroup to the Outlook Express folder list, indented below the server name. You can then display the newsgroup's articles by simply clicking it from the folder list. Your subscribing allows Outlook Express to keep track of which articles you've read in the newsgroup, sparing you from accidentally reading an article twice.

subscribe = join a newsgroup

You should still be displaying the newsgroup list. To subscribe to a few helpful newsgroups, follow these steps:

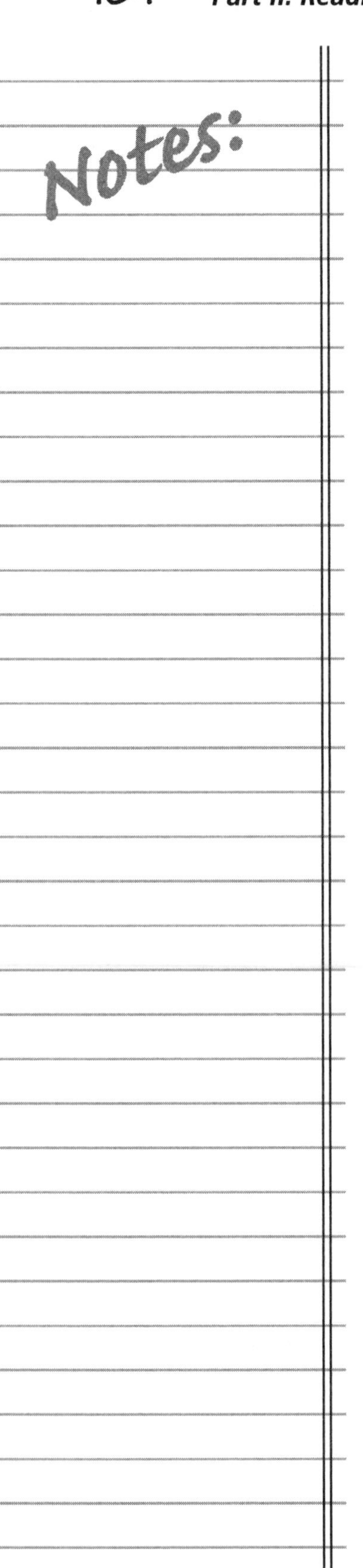

1 Double-click inside the search box and type news.announce.newusers **very carefully**.

Be sure to include both dots in the newsgroup name. After you're done typing, the `news.announce.newusers` newsgroup should be highlighted. (If it isn't, click it to select it.) This newsgroup is devoted to providing basic information and guidelines to Usenet novices.

2 Click the Subscribe button (in the upper-right section of the window).

An icon appears to the left of the newsgroup to show that you've joined it.

3 Click the Unsubscribe button (directly below the Subscribe button).

The icon next to the newsgroup disappears, indicating that you've canceled your subscribe command. You can quit a newsgroup you've joined at any time by simply selecting it and then clicking the Unsubscribe button.

4 Click the Subscribe button again.

The icon reappears to show that you've rejoined the newsgroup.

5 Double-click inside the search box again, type news.newusers.questions **carefully, and click the Subscribe button.**

A subscribe icon appears to the left of the `news.newusers.questions` newsgroup, which is devoted to taking the questions of new Internet users and providing answers.

6 Double-click inside the search box again; type news.answers **carefully; click the** `news.answers` **newsgroup that appears (if it isn't already selected); and click the Subscribe button.**

A subscribe icon appears next to the `news.answers` newsgroup, which is devoted to carrying the *FAQs* (that is, *F*requently *A*sked *Q*uestions list) of other newsgroups. (For more information, see the sidebar "Just the FAQs, ma'am" that appears later in this unit.)

7 Optionally repeat Step 6 to subscribe to a few newsgroups you're personally interested in.

For example, subscribe to some of the newsgroups you wrote down in the preceding exercise. (***Tip:*** As an alternative to clicking a newsgroup and clicking the Subscribe button, simply double-click the newsgroup.) Restrict yourself to two or three additional newsgroups for now. Life is too short to be reading newsgroups all day!

After you're done, notice that three tabs appear below the newsgroup list:

- **All:** Displays all available newsgroups on the news server.
- **Subscribed:** Displays only the newsgroups you've joined.
- **New:** Displays only newsgroups that haven't appeared before on the news server.

You've been working with the All box, which is why you've been able to view all the newsgroups.

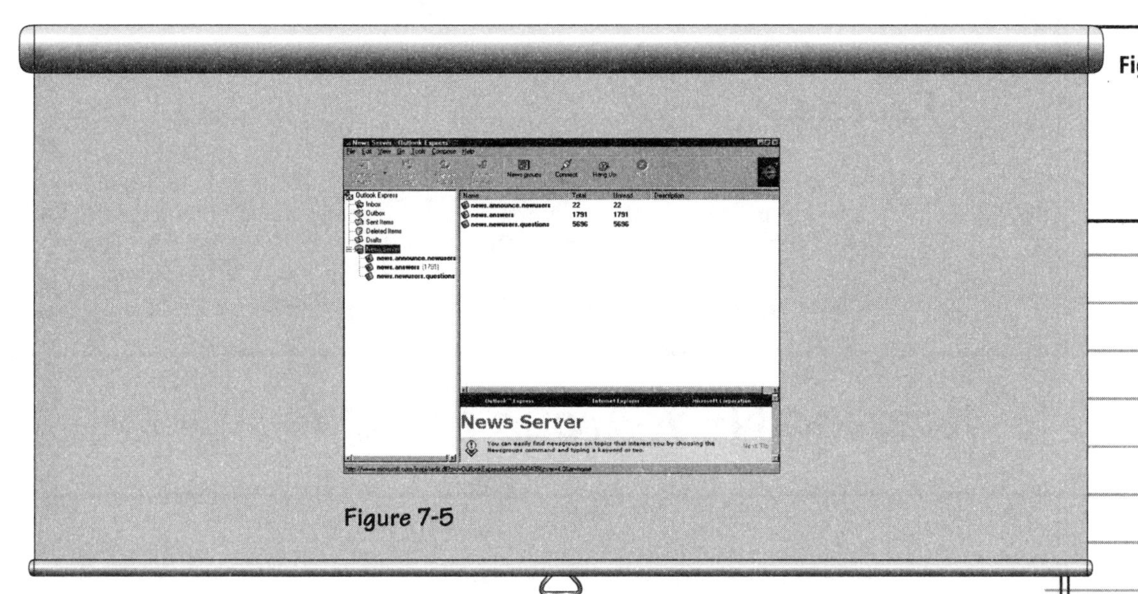

Figure 7-5: After you subscribe to a newsgroup, its name is listed on the folder list under its news server.

8 Click the Subscribed tab (below the newsgroup list); then clear the search box by double-clicking inside it and pressing Backspace.

You now see a list of the newsgroups to which you're currently subscribed. Use this view whenever you want to see which newsgroups you've joined or when you want to quickly unsubscribe from a newsgroup. For now, keep all the newsgroups you've joined and just exit the window.

9 Click the window's OK button (in the lower-right section).

Your subscription choices are saved, and the Newsgroups window disappears.

News groups button

You now see the Outlook Express window again. There are some additions to the folder list since you last viewed it, though — under your ISP's server are the names of all the newsgroups to which you just subscribed! If you don't see them, click the plus (+) sign to the left of the news server name, which will cause the list of newsgroups to expand from the server name (as shown in Figure 7-5). You'll read articles from these newsgroups in the next lesson.

on the test

Note: If you later want to subscribe to additional newsgroups, simply click the News groups button on the Outlook Toolbar. This brings up the Newsgroups window, allowing you to further explore the newsgroup list.

on the test

Tip: If you get tired of a newsgroup to which you've subscribed, you can quit it directly from the folder list. To do so, right-click the newsgroup (that is, click it with your *right* mouse button); choose the Unsubscribe From This Newsgroup option from the menu that appears; and click the Yes button to confirm the deletion. The newsgroup and all its articles are instantly removed from the Outlook Express window. (We'll go through these steps again in the next lesson.) If you later change your mind, just subscribe to the newsgroup again.

☑ Progress Check

If you can do the following, you've mastered this lesson:

- ❑ Retrieve a list of newsgroups from your ISP's news server.
- ❑ Open the Newsgroups window.
- ❑ Scroll through the newsgroup list.
- ❑ Search for particular types of newsgroups on the newsgroup list.
- ❑ Subscribe to and unsubscribe from newsgroups.

Recess

Now that you know how to list and subscribe to newsgroups, you're ready for more advanced instruction. But first, take a stretch. Be sure to disconnect from your Internet service provider so that you don't tie up your phone line. Then focus on something far away — out the window, if possible. Focusing on something close up for hours at a time is bad for your eyes!

Lesson 7-3 Reading Newsgroup Articles

to list a newsgroup's articles, click it from the folder list

to read an article, click it from the message list

All the newsgroups to which you've subscribed now appear on the folder list, indented directly below their news server.

on the test

As we indicated earlier in this unit, the Outlook Express window lets you read the articles in a newsgroup similar to the way you read the messages in an e-mail folder. First, click the newsgroup from the folder list; the newsgroup's articles are displayed in the message list in the upper-right section of the window. Next, scroll through the list until you see a subject heading that looks interesting. Finally, click the article you want; its contents are displayed in the message area in the lower-right section of the window.

To read a few newsgroup articles, follow these steps:

1. **Launch Outlook Express (if it isn't already running) and connect to the Internet.**

   If your Outlook Express window doesn't already fill the screen, click the window's Maximize button so there's plenty of room for listing and reading your newsgroup articles.

2. **If the newsgroups to which you subscribed aren't already displayed on the folder list, click the plus (+) sign to the left of their news server.**

   If the newsgroups are already displayed, a minus (-) sign appears to the left of the news server instead. You can always display or hide newsgroups on the folder list by clicking the sign to the left of their news server.

   When a newsgroup is displayed, you can tell how many unread articles it contains by looking at the number in parentheses at its right. After you select a newsgroup, you can also tell both how many unread messages and how many total messages it contains by looking at the left corner of the status bar at the bottom of the window.

   One of the newsgroups you should see listed is `news.announce.newusers`. Start by reading the articles in this newsgroup.

3. **Click the `news.announce.newusers` newsgroup to switch to it.**

   After a few moments, the articles in `news.announce.newusers` are displayed in the message list (in the upper-right section of the window).

Notes:

4 Click an article that looks interesting.

The contents of the article appear in the message area (in the lower-right section of the window). Click anywhere in the message area and then read the article, using the PgDn key or your mouse to scroll down the text.

heads up

Note: In place of an article's contents, you may sometimes see the statement `This message is not cached. Please connect to your server to download the message.` This means that the article's contents haven't been stored on your hard disk, and that the article is no longer set to be retrieved from the news server (typically because some time has passed since you last accessed the news server). To solve the problem, make sure that you're connected to the Internet; click your news server on the folder list to reestablish your connection; and then click the newsgroup again and click the article in the message list again. After a moment, Outlook Express retrieves the article and displays its contents in the message area.

5 Click another article that looks interesting.

Notice that each time you select an article, after about five seconds the article loses its boldfacing in the message list to indicate that it's been read. Also, both the number to the right of the newsgroup and the second number on the status bar decrease by one to reflect there's now one less unread article in the newsgroup.

6 If you haven't already done so, locate and click an article with the subject heading *Answers to Frequently Asked Questions about Usenet.* (Since this is a long heading, you may see only its first few words in the message list.)

This article is the *FAQ* (*F*requently *A*sked *Q*uestions list) about Usenet newsgroups. The article lists 50 questions at its top and then repeats each question followed by an answer. First read through the list of questions to identify the ones that interest you and then scroll down the article to read the pertinent answers. For more information about FAQs, see the "Just the FAQs, ma'am" sidebar later in this unit.

You may occasionally see an article with a plus (+) sign to its left. This indicates that the article is the start of a *thread*. A thread is an article that begins a discussion, followed by responses to that article, followed by responses to the responses, and so forth. If you click the plus sign next to the initial article, the subsequent articles appear indented below it.

thread = series of articles responding to one original article

7 Locate a thread, click its plus sign to display the thread's articles, and read each article in the thread.

Sometimes the first article in a thread is no longer present, because news servers typically don't keep articles for more than about three days. If the first articles in the thread are older than that, they vanish, leaving behind the later articles in the thread. You can usually figure out what the earlier articles said, though, because responses frequently quote parts of the original article.

8 Continue looking through the articles in the newsgroup.

Outlook Express initially retrieves only the first 300 articles in a newsgroup. If you run out of the first batch of articles, get more by choosing Tools⇨Get Next 300 Headers. (If there *aren't* any more articles available, the Get Next 300 Headers option is grayed out on the menu.)

When you've had enough of the current newsgroup, move on to another one.

9. **Click another newsgroup on the folder list.**

   After a few moments, the articles in the newsgroup are displayed in the message list. Click any article that looks interesting to read its contents in the message area.

That's about all there is to reading newsgroups!

As you just saw, after you subscribe to a newsgroup, you can read any article in it with just a few mouse clicks. New messages in your newsgroups arrive automatically, so the only hard part is figuring out which articles you want to take the time to read — and that's a skill you'll develop with practice.

If you decide that you're enjoying your current newsgroups, simply stay subscribed to them. If you get bored with a newsgroup, however, you can quit it quickly by doing the following:

1. **Right-click the newsgroup you want to quit.**

   That is, click the newsgroup from the folder list with your *right* mouse button. After you do so, a menu with newsgroup commands appears.

2. **Click the Unsubscribe From This Newsgroup option.**

   You're asked to confirm the command, because it will remove both the newsgroup and all its articles from the window.

3. **Click the Yes button.**

   The newsgroup is deleted from the folder list, and its articles disappear from the message list.

Alternatively, you can quit a newsgroup by clicking it from the folder list, choosing Tools➪Unsubscribe From This Newsgroup, and clicking the Yes button.

If you later change your mind, you can subscribe to a newsgroup again at any time by clicking the News groups button from the Outlook toolbar to open the Newsgroups window; clicking the newsgroup you want; clicking the Subscribe button; and clicking OK.

☑ Progress Check

If you can do the following, you've mastered this lesson:

- ❑ Switch to a newsgroup on the folder list.
- ❑ Retrieve the newsgroup's articles.
- ❑ Read the newsgroup's articles.

extra credit

Just the FAQs, ma'am

A *FAQ* is a list of frequently asked questions and their answers. Many newsgroups create FAQs that include the questions that come up over and over and that folks on the newsgroup are sick of answering. If you pose one of these questions, you're likely to get responses that say, *Read the $%#(* FAQ!*

How do you read the FAQ for a newsgroup? If the FAQ appears on the list of articles for the newsgroup, read it like any other article. If you don't see the FAQ among the articles in the newsgroup, go to the `news.answers` newsgroup. This newsgroup contains the FAQs for many newsgroups that have FAQs, listed in no particular order. Many FAQs are really long and have been divided into several parts. Long FAQs appear as a series of articles, with titles like *alt.backyard.chickens FAQ, Part 2 of 5.*

Searching for Newsgroups of Interest

Lesson 7-4

Notes:

You can find many interesting newsgroups using the Newsgroups window, but you can miss a lot of them, too. For example, in Lesson 7-2, you typed *cats* in the search box and turned up such pertinent newsgroups as `alt.cats` and `rec.pets.cats`. However, you passed over such equally pertinent newsgroups as `alt.animals.felines`, as well as marginally related newsgroups such as `alt.support.depression` and `rec.arts.theatre.musicals`, simply because the latter newsgroups don't happen to include the word *cats* in their names. Isn't there a better way to locate the newsgroups you're looking for?

There is; use the Web! This lesson will show you how to use specialized Web search programs to turn up newsgroups devoted to your favorite topics.

One of the best Web sites for newsgroup information is Deja News. This site looks at not only the names of newsgroups but also the content of their articles, and so can supply you with a comprehensive list of newsgroups devoted to your favorite subjects. To exploit this resource, follow these steps:

1. **Launch Internet Explorer and connect to the Net.**

   If you aren't sure how, review Lesson 1-2.

2. **Click in the browser window's Address bar, type** dejanews **and press Enter.**

   Internet Explorer takes you to `www.dejanews.com`, and you see the Deja News home page shown in Figure 7-6.

3. **Click the Interest Finder link (which, at the time we write this, is on the left side of the page).**

   If you use the home page's Find box, Deja News will respond by listing all newsgroup articles mentioning your topic, which is a terrific service but isn't quite what you're after right now.

   After you move to the Interest Finder page, you see a Find box that offers to locate groups based on the topic you specify.

4. **Click in the Find box, type a word or phrase (like** cooking **or** baseball **or** dating**), and press Enter.**

   You see a page listing newsgroups that typically discuss your topic (as in Figure 7-7). Each newsgroup name is blue and underlined, which means that it's a link.

5. **Click a newsgroup that looks promising.**

   You see a page listing articles from the newsgroup that include the word or phrase you typed. For each article, you see the date it was posted, the article's subject (which is a link), the newsgroup the article was posted to, and the name of the author of the article. If more matches are found than can fit on the page, you can click a *Next* link near the bottom of the page to see additional matches.

Figure 7-6: Use the Deja News site to find newsgroups devoted to your favorite subjects.

Figure 7-7: After *chocolate* is entered as a search word, Deja News lists newsgroups that tend to discuss chocolate.

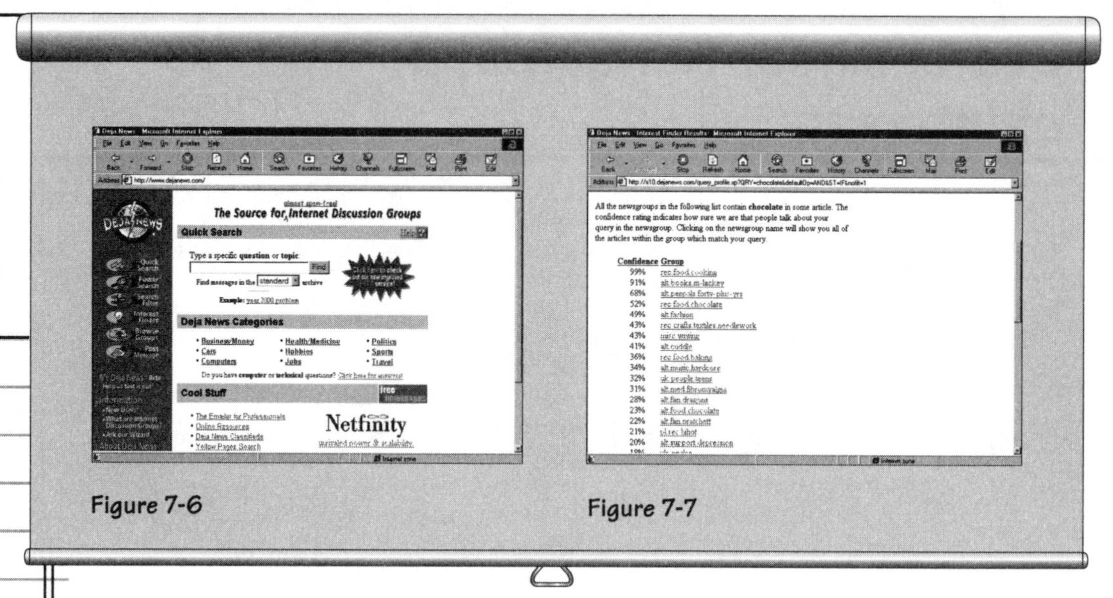

Figure 7-6

Figure 7-7

6 Click the subject of an article that looks interesting.

Deja News displays the article right in your browser window. The Newsgroups heading of the article tells you which newsgroup the article comes from.

extra credit

Other ways to find newsgroup articles

Two other Web pages that help you search for newsgroups and articles are

- **The AltaVista page you used in Lesson 2-5 to search for Web pages:** Near the top of its home page (at `altavista.digital.com`), AltaVista says something like "Search the Web for documents in any language," and the phrase "the Web" appears in a box. First, click inside the box to display a short menu and choose the Usenet option. Next, type a word or phrase in the search box and press Enter. When you see a list of articles, click the subject link to read the article; AltaVista displays the text in your browser window.
- **The Liszt of Newsgroups page:** Go to `www.liszt.com/news`, type a word in the search box on the page, and press Enter. Liszt searches only in the names and descriptions of newsgroups, not the text of their articles. After you see a list of the newsgroups that Liszt found, you can write them down and then subscribe to them using Outlook Express. (***Note:*** Liszt is also a wonderful resource for finding electronic mailing lists. For more information, see Unit ML in file Maillist.pdf on your *Dummies 101* CD.)

☑ Progress Check

If you can do the following, you've mastered this lesson:

- ❑ Find newsgroups devoted to your favorite subjects using the Deja News Web site.
- ❑ Find newsgroup articles covering a particular topic using the Deja News Web site.
- ❑ Read the articles that Deja News finds.

7 Click your browser's Back button to return to the list of articles.

Continue clicking articles to get a feel for the newsgroup. If what you see convinces you that you'd enjoy reading the newsgroup regularly, subscribe to the newsgroup. Otherwise, use your browser's Back button to return to the original list of newsgroups and repeat Steps 5 through 7 until you find a newsgroup that satisfies you.

Pretty cool! If you want to return to this site later, you can use the favorites you installed in Lesson 2-1; the Deja News link is stored under the Web Search Programs category.

Notes:

Replying to Newsgroup Articles

Lesson 7-5

After you read the articles in a newsgroup for a while, you may be ready to chime in. You have two ways to respond to an article that you read in a newsgroup:

- **By e-mail:** If your response is of interest only to the person who posted the original article, your message is a bit personal and you don't want to share it with the whole newsgroup, or the original article requested replies by e-mail, respond with an e-mail message directly to the person who wrote the article.
- **With your own article:** If your response is of interest to lots of people who read the newsgroup, you're sure of your facts, and you have the time to write a clear, concise reply, then respond by posting your own article to the newsgroup. Remember, thousands of people around the world may read your article, so make sure that you really have something to say!

You can also post an article that, rather than responding to another article, starts a new thread by bringing up a fresh topic.

In this lesson, you'll create an article using the Outlook Express New Message window. You'll then send your article to the `misc.test` newsgroup, which is designed precisely for the purpose of letting people try out their posting skills. You'll also respond to your test article by e-mail.

Posting a test article

Here's how to post an article on a newsgroup:

1 Run Outlook Express and connect to the Internet.

2 Click the News groups button on the Outlook toolbar.

The Newsgroups window appears. Use this box to subscribe to `misc.test`, which is a newsgroup whose sole purpose is to allow people starting out on Usenet to practice by posting test articles.

3. **In the search box, type** misc.test **(that is, type** misc, **a period, and** test**).**

   The newsgroup list narrows to display just a few newsgroups.

4. **Click the** `misc.test` **newsgroup to select it and then click the Subscribe button.**

   An icon appears to the left of `misc.test` to indicate that you've joined this newsgroup.

5. **Click OK.**

   The Newsgroups window closes, and you're returned to the Outlook Express window. Notice that `misc.test` now appears on the folder list.

6. **Click** `misc.test` **from the folder list.**

   The articles in `misc.test` should be displayed in the message list. (If they aren't, click your news server on the folder list to reestablish your connection and then click `misc.test` again.) Because this newsgroup is provided exclusively for the purpose of letting folks practice their skills at posting articles, nothing in `misc.test` is really worth reading. To make ignoring the newsgroup's articles easy, and to help you quickly find your own article after you post it, use a little trick: Mark all the existing messages as read.

to mark all articles as read, choose Edit→Mark All as Read

7. **Choose Edit⇨Mark All as Read from the menu bar.**

   All the articles in `misc.test` are marked as read, as indicated by the boldfacing being cleared from both the newsgroup on the folder list and the articles in the message list. Now start creating your test article.

8. **Click the Compose Message button on the Outlook toolbar.**

   A New Message window similar to the one you use for writing e-mail appears. The name of the current newsgroup, `misc.test`, has been automatically inserted in the first address box, which is labeled *Newsgroup* to remind you that you aren't writing to an individual or a handful of people but to a large audience. Your cursor is on the Subject line.

9. **For your subject, type** Test: Please ignore **(or something like that).**

   The article you're about to post isn't going to be of interest to anyone but you. (And maybe your mother.)

10. **Press tab to move to the message area and then type** This is a test posting from Outlook Express **(or something like that).**

    Type whatever you'd like to see when you read the article later.

Post

to post an article you've written, click the Post button

11. **When the article looks satisfactory, click the Post button (the first button on the window's toolbar).**

    Outlook Express posts the article to the `misc.test` newsgroup. If a dialog box appears telling you that your message has been posted, click the OK button.

Your article is winging its way to newsgroup readers around the world!

If you start composing an article and then think better of it, you can close the New Message window by clicking its Close button. When Outlook Express asks whether you're sure you want to discard your changes, click the Yes button.

Rules and regulations for posting articles

All the rules of e-mail netiquette that you learned in Lesson 5-5 apply to newsgroup articles, too. Follow the rules in the sidebar "Mailing list do's and don'ts" in Unit ML as well, because mailing lists and newsgroups have a lot in common. In addition, follow these rules to avoid getting flamed by angry newsgroupies:

- Read a newsgroup for at least a week before posting anything, to be sure that your posting is appropriate for the newsgroup.
- Read the newsgroup's FAQ before posting anything. (See the sidebar "Just the FAQs, ma'am" earlier in this unit.)
- Don't post ads! If you have a product that relates directly to the subject of the newsgroup, you can post a brief article about it *once*, but you'll have better luck if the article is short and informational rather than salesy and vague. Be sure to include an e-mail address to which people can write for more information.
- Never post an article to a newsgroup you don't read regularly.
- Don't post the same article to lots of newsgroups. (This is called *crossposting*, and it's frowned upon.) Sometimes an article is of interest to two or three newsgroups, but think long and hard before you crosspost.

Reading the article you posted

In a few minutes, the article you just posted should appear in the `misc.test` newsgroup. You should still be in Outlook Express with `misc.test` selected. Here's how to see whether your post was sent successfully:

1. **Click the news server on the folder list to reestablish your connection and then click the `misc.test` newsgroup again.**

   Outlook Express retrieves the latest articles, including yours. You'll probably be able to spot your article quickly because it's boldfaced, unlike the old articles that you previously marked as read. To make locating your article even easier, though, tell Outlook Express to display only unread articles.

2. **Choose View⇨Current View⇨Unread Messages from the menu bar.**

   Now only unread articles appear in the message list. If the article you posted doesn't appear, wait a few more minutes and then repeat Step 1 to try again. (If your article doesn't show up within a half hour, call your Internet provider to find out what's amiss.) Eventually, you see your test article.

3. **Click your test article.**

   The text of your article appears in the message area.

Cool! You posted an article to a newsgroup! When you next have something reasonably interesting and wise to say, consider following the same procedure to post articles to the newsgroups you read regularly.

to list only unread articles, choose View→Current View→Unread Messages

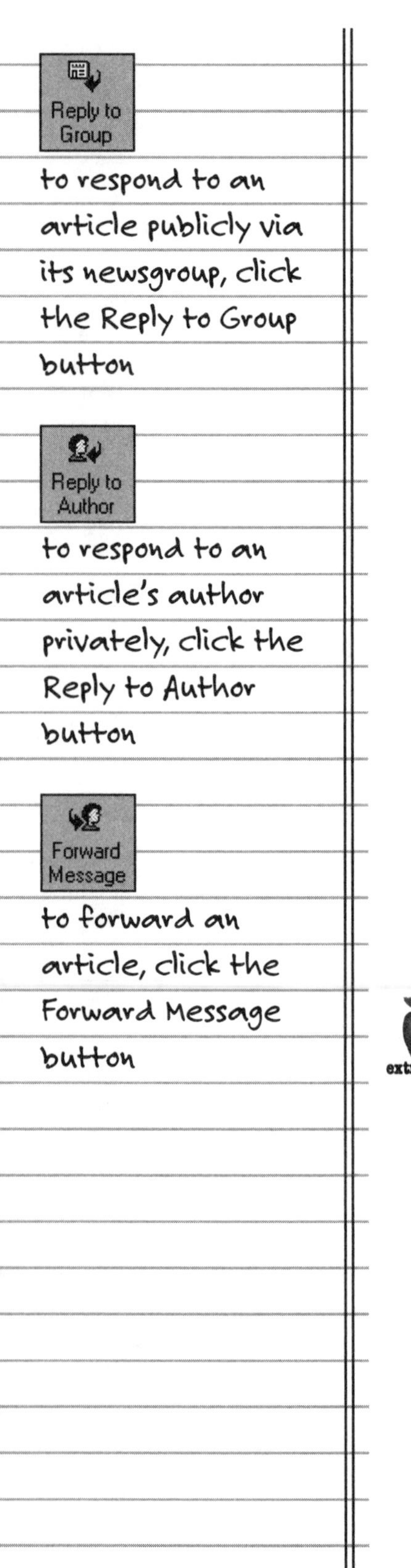

If you read an article and want to publicly reply to it with an article (because what you have to say is of interest to others in the newsgroup), click the Reply to Group button on the Outlook toolbar. A message window appears that's addressed to the newsgroup and contains the subject line of the original message. Use this window to compose and post your article.

If your response isn't of interest to most of the group, however, reply to an article privately by clicking the Reply to Author button on the Outlook toolbar, which brings up a message window addressed only to the article's author. Always use e-mail when replying to an annoying, clueless, or downright stupid article — there's no point embarrassing people in the public arena of a newsgroup.

Forwarding, printing, and saving articles

Here are a few other things you can do with newsgroup articles:

- **Forward an article by e-mail:** If you see an article that would interest a friend, send her a copy by clicking the article to select it and then clicking the Forward Message button on the Outlook toolbar.
- **Print an article:** Click the article to select it; choose File⇨Print or press Ctrl+P to display the Print dialog box; make sure that your printer is on and has paper in it; and click OK.
- **Save the article in a text file:** Click the article to select it; choose File⇨Save As to bring up a Save As dialog box; click in the Save as Type box and choose the Text Files (*.txt) option from the menu that appears; optionally select a different folder using the Save In box; and then click the Save button. The article is stored as a plain text file in the folder you selected.

Receiving files from newsgroups

A few newsgroups specialize in distributing programs and graphics files. For example, the `alt.binaries.pictures.fractals` newsgroup distributes fractal graphics. (If you don't know what a fractal is, try reading the newsgroup's FAQ!)

Because files tend to be too large to fit in a single article, they usually appear as a series of articles, with titles like *Dancer - dancer3.gif 1/3,* meaning that the graphics file is named dancer3.gif and that this article is article one of three. Article 0 of a set of articles is the header article, with information about the file. Articles 1, 2, and so on contain the actual file.

To download a file, click article 1 of the series. Outlook Express downloads the entire series of articles, decodes the file, and displays it. You can save the picture in a separate file by right-clicking the image and then choosing the Save Picture As option from the menu that appears.

Other programs of interest

Outlook Express isn't the only tool available for reading and participating in newsgroups. Another is Free Agent, which is an excellent free newsreader that's stored on the *Dummies 101* CD that came with this book. If you're interested in trying out an alternative approach to handling newsgroups, you won't go wrong with the acclaimed Free Agent program (or with its commercial version, Agent). For more information, see Appendix B.

Another way you can participate in group discussions on the Net is by talking live with others through a worldwide system called *Internet Relay Chat*, or *IRC*. IRC enables anyone in a group to write messages that are instantly seen by everyone else in the group, creating the equivalent of a global party line on your screen. To experience IRC, you must use a program such as the terrific mIRC, which is also stored on your *Dummies 101* CD. For additional information, see Appendix B.

☑ Progress Check

If you can do the following, you've mastered this lesson:

- ❑ Post a test article.
- ❑ Receive and read your test article.

Recess

Congratulations! You now know how to read articles in newsgroups, find articles by topic, and post your own articles to newsgroups. You are an amazing person, and we're pleased to know you! Don't get a swelled head, though; you still have to face the Unit 7 quiz!

Unit 7 Quiz

For each of the following questions, circle the letter of the correct answer or answers. Remember, there may be more than one right answer for each question.

1. **A newsgroup:**

   A. Is a collection of journalists such as Clark Kent, Lois Lane, and Jimmy Olsen.

   B. Is an ongoing discussion devoted to a particular topic that takes place over the Internet.

   C. Provides the daily headlines and sports scores with your morning coffee.

   D. Has a name consisting of words, or parts of words, separated by dots.

   E. Consists of articles posted by Internet users around the world.

2. The seven major newsgroup hierarchies include

A. news and comp

B. rec and misc

C. Doc and Sneezy

D. soc and sci

E. *Star Trek* and *Star Wars*

3. To subscribe to a newsgroup:

A. Double-click its FAQ.

B. Click the newspaper icon to its right.

C. From the Newsgroups window, click the newsgroup and then click the Subscribe button.

D. From the Newsgroups window, double-click the newsgroup. (Try it!)

E. Pay an extra dollar a week to the newsgroup delivery boy.

4. To unsubscribe from a newsgroup:

A. Double-click its FAQ.

B. Click the Quit icon to its left.

C. From the Newsgroups window, click the newsgroup and then click the Unsubscribe button.

D. Right-click the newsgroup from the folder list, click the Unsubscribe From This Newsgroup option, and click the Yes button.

E. Stop paying the newsgroup delivery boy.

Unit 7 Exercise

1. Launch Internet Explorer and go to the Deja News Interest Finder Web page.
2. Search for something you're interested in, like mangos or lizards or antiques. Carefully write down the names of the newsgroups that appear promising.
3. Subscribe to a newsgroup you found.
4. Read the newsgroup's articles for a week or so.
5. Look in the news.answers newsgroup for the FAQ on the newsgroup you joined, and read the FAQ.
6. When you have a question to ask or want to contribute an answer or comment, post an article to the newsgroup. (But make sure that the question isn't answered in the FAQ!)
7. Continue reading the newsgroup to see how your article looks and what reaction it causes.

Unit 8

Tuning in to Channels

Objectives for This Unit

✓ Viewing channels

✓ Subscribing to channels

✓ Adding channels to your desktop

✓ Assigning a channel to be a screen saver

✓ Managing channels

Prerequisites

- Browsing the Web (Units 1, 2, 3, and 4)

In Part I of this book, you found information and entertainment on the Web by traveling to Web pages, similar to the way you might look up pages from books or magazines in a massive library.

on the test

There's also another way to interact with the Web, which is to direct certain kinds of data — such as stock prices, weather reports, and sports scores — to automatically come to *you*. More specifically, you can set your PC to receive streams of Web content, called *channels,* that are transmitted on a specified schedule and in the background via your Internet connection. Then whenever you want to get a certain piece of information, you can simply click the channel that carries it, similar to the way you flip to a channel on your TV or radio.

channel = Web site data that can be periodically transmitted to your PC

You don't have to be connected to the Net when you view channel content, because the most recent data the channel sends is automatically saved to your hard disk. This means that, for example, you can schedule your PC to dial into the Net and receive the latest content from your favorite channels at night, and you can then browse the new data quickly and conveniently from your hard disk each morning.

Since a channel is basically a Web site that's been optimized to transmit information on a regular basis, you can view channels using Internet Explorer. Alternatively, however, you can set channel data to be constantly displayed on

Notes:

your desktop. For example, later in this unit, you'll create a news ticker on your desktop that continually displays news headlines from *The New York Times*.

You can even designate certain channels to be screen savers — that is, have them pop up after your PC has been idle for a set period of time to prevent a static image from burning into your screen.

Windows 98 channels, or *Active Channels,* are sometimes referred to as *push technology* because their information is periodically *pushed* at your PC, similar to the way broadcast signals are continually beamed into your TV and radio. In contrast, the method you've used so far to cruise the Web is called *pull technology* because it requires you to move to a Web site and immediately copy, or *pull,* the content from the site to your browser window.

In this unit, you'll learn how to view channels, add channels, and manage your channels.

Lesson 8-1 Viewing Channels

Since channels are Web sites, you can move to a channel by simply typing its URL in the Address bar and pressing Enter. However, you'll generally find it more convenient to use the Windows 98 *Channel bar,* which lets you display a channel with a mouse click. The Channel bar comes with a number of channels already installed to get you started, but you can freely add other channels and delete obsolete channels (as you'll see in Lesson 8-2).

Channels button

You can pop up the Channel bar in several ways:

- **Click Internet Explorer's Channels button:** If you're already running Internet Explorer, click the Channels button (which looks like a satellite dish) on the Standard Buttons toolbar. The Channel bar appears along the left side of the window, as shown in Figure 8-1. You can view channels by clicking the buttons on this bar.
- **Click the taskbar's View Channels button:** The taskbar normally displays a Quick Launch toolbar in its left corner that has three buttons named Launch Internet Explorer Browser, Show Desktop, and View Channels. You used the first button in previous units to run Internet Explorer. Alternatively, you can click the View Channels button (which looks like a satellite dish) to open an Internet Explorer window that's tailored to display channels. Specifically, the browser opens as maximized and with its Fullscreen button turned on, which ensures that you see as much Web content as possible (as in Figure 8-2). Also, the Channel bar is activated but remains hidden until you move your mouse to the left edge of the window; the bar then temporarily slides out so that you can use it to click the channel you want.

View Channels button

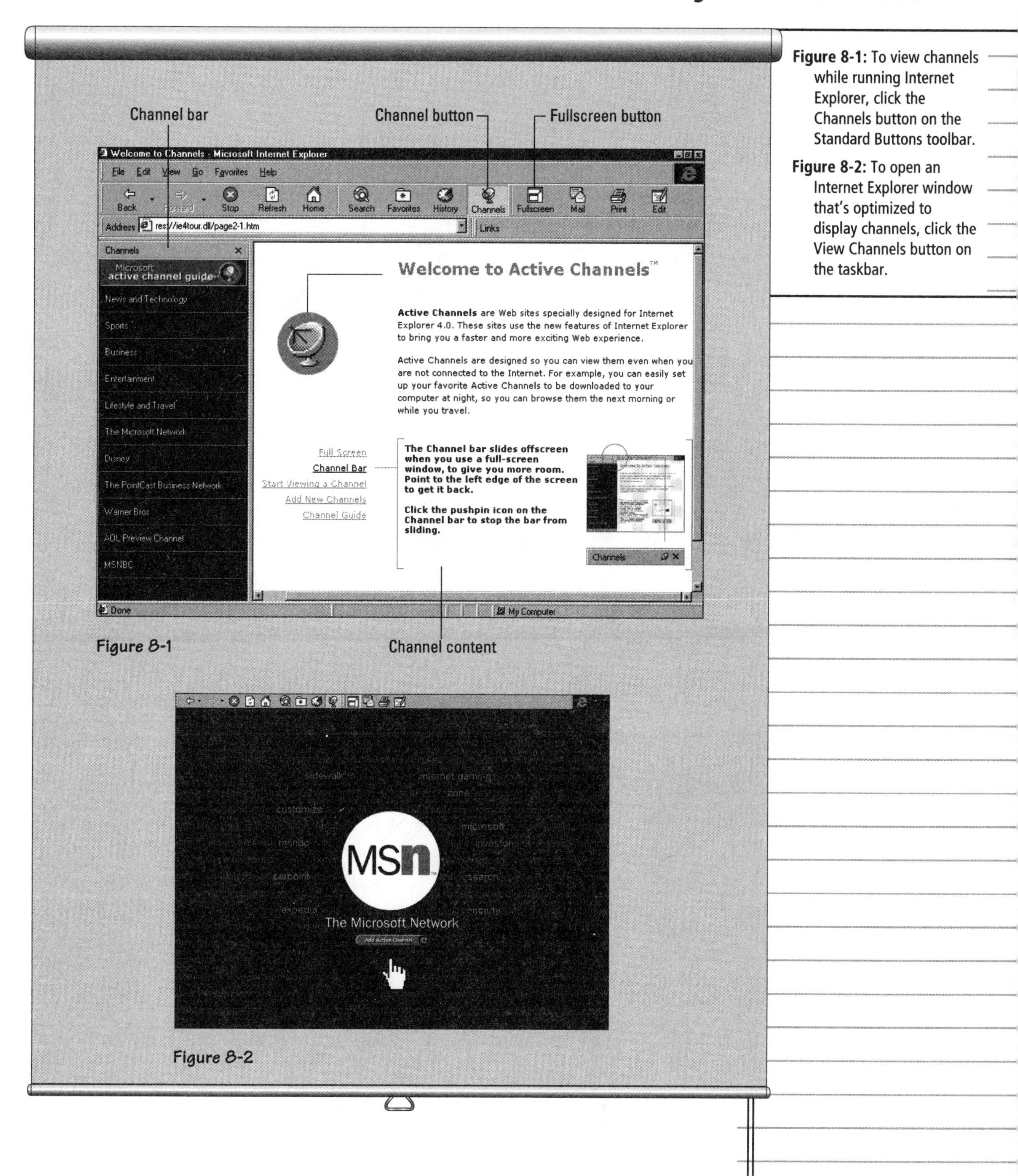

Figure 8-1

Figure 8-2

Figure 8-1: To view channels while running Internet Explorer, click the Channels button on the Standard Buttons toolbar.

Figure 8-2: To open an Internet Explorer window that's optimized to display channels, click the View Channels button on the taskbar.

Figure 8-3: When you turn on the Active Desktop option, a Channel bar pops up directly on your desktop.

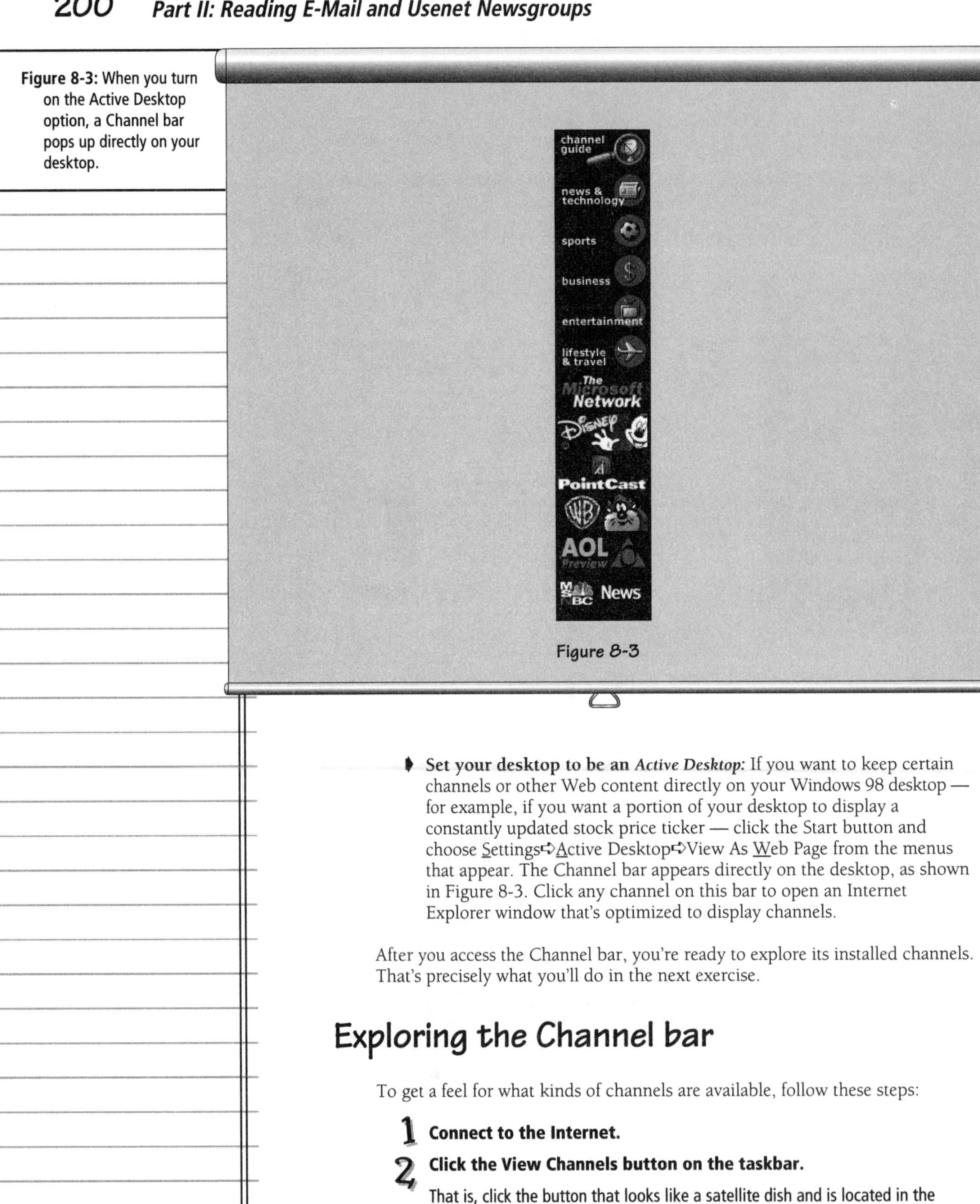

Figure 8-3

- **Set your desktop to be an *Active Desktop:*** If you want to keep certain channels or other Web content directly on your Windows 98 desktop — for example, if you want a portion of your desktop to display a constantly updated stock price ticker — click the Start button and choose Settings➪Active Desktop➪View As Web Page from the menus that appear. The Channel bar appears directly on the desktop, as shown in Figure 8-3. Click any channel on this bar to open an Internet Explorer window that's optimized to display channels.

After you access the Channel bar, you're ready to explore its installed channels. That's precisely what you'll do in the next exercise.

Exploring the Channel bar

To get a feel for what kinds of channels are available, follow these steps:

1. **Connect to the Internet.**
2. **Click the View Channels button on the taskbar.**

   That is, click the button that looks like a satellite dish and is located in the lower-left section of your screen. After you've clicked it, an Internet Explorer window like the one in Figure 8-2 appears that's optimized to display channels.

Notes:

3 **Move your mouse pointer to the left edge of the window.**

You see a Channel bar, like the bar in Figure 8-1, that displays buttons for individual channels, and also for channel categories such as News and Technology, Sports, Business, Entertainment, and Lifestyle and Travel.

4 **Click the News and Technology category.**

A list of channels appears that includes such respected news sources as *The New York Times*, *Time*, and CNN.

5 **Slowly move your mouse pointer over the list.**

Each time you point to a channel, a brief description of it pops up.

6 **Click the channel for *The New York Times* and then move your mouse pointer away from the Channel bar.**

The home page for *The New York Times* channel is transmitted to your window. Also, the Channel bar slides away to provide the maximum amount of space for the Web site you selected to be displayed.

Tip: You can force the Channel bar to remain visible by clicking the pushpin icon at the top of the bar, which is useful if you're quickly flipping between many channels. In general, however, we recommend letting the bar slide out of sight so that you can enjoy an unobstructed view of the channel you're visiting.

7 **Slowly move your mouse pointer over different areas of the Web page.**

You see a page that offers a variety of ways to supply you with information, including (at the time we write this) a one-line continuous stream of news headlines, or *news ticker;* a list of news categories; and a search program that locates *New York Times* articles about any topic you specify.

In addition, you see an Add Active Channel button that lets you *subscribe* to the channel, which means it lets you set the Web site to periodically transmit its data to your PC; and an Add to Active Desktop button that puts the news ticker right on your desktop so that you can look through recent headlines without lifting a finger. You'll pursue these options in the next lesson, but for now continue investigating the different types of channels available.

8 **Move your mouse pointer to the left edge of the window.**

The Channel bar reappears.

9 **Click a different channel in the News and Technology category, and explore the new Web site that appears.**

For example, click the *Time* channel or the CNN channel. Repeat Steps 8 and 9 until you've gotten a sense of what's available in the News and Technology category.

10 **Move your mouse pointer to the left edge of the window and then click the Channel bar's Entertainment category.**

A list of pop culture channels appears that includes such standards as MTV, *People*, and syndicated comic strips.

11 **Click a channel and then explore the new Web site that appears.**

Repeat this step until you've gotten a sense of what's currently available in the Entertainment category.

Notes:

12 Move your mouse pointer to the left edge of the window, click a different category on the Channel bar, and explore its channels.

Repeat this step a few times to get a feel for what other types of categories are available right now on the Channel bar.

As this exercise demonstrates, you can find a number of terrific Web sites just by clicking the channels that came pre-installed on the Channel bar. These channels are only the tip of the iceberg, however. To discover what else is available, tackle the next exercise.

Finding additional channels

To explore a much wider range of channels than the ones initially placed on your Channel bar, follow these steps:

1 Move your mouse to display the Channel bar, and then click Microsoft Channel Guide (typically the top category on the bar).

After a few moments, a Web site named Microsoft Active Channel Guide is displayed. The home page of this site, like the Channel bar itself, lists various categories you can explore.

2 Click the Entertainment category.

You see an initial batch of entertainment channels.

3 Slowly move your mouse pointer over each listed channel.

A description of each channel pops up after you point to it. Explore any channel that interests you by clicking its icon.

Now notice that links appear on the left side of the page. These links lead to more channels in the Entertainment category — in fact, *hundreds* of additional channels (as shown in Figure 8-4). At the time we write this, channels are listed in groups of seven, so the first link — representing the channels you're currently exploring — is named *1-7*, the next link is named *8-14*, the link after that is named *15-24*, and so on.

4 Click the next link on the left side of the page to explore additional channels.

The next set of channels in the Entertainment category is listed. Again, move your mouse pointer over each channel to pop up a description, and explore any channel that interests you by clicking its icon.

5 Click the next link on the left side of the page to explore additional channels.

Yet another group of channels is listed.

Since hundreds of channels are available, it's hard to identify the ones that best address your interests just by clicking links. As a result, this Web site also provides a Find box that lets you quickly locate channels covering a particular topic. If the Find box isn't already visible, you can display it by clicking the Find button that appears near the top of every page on this Web site (as shown in Figure 8-4).

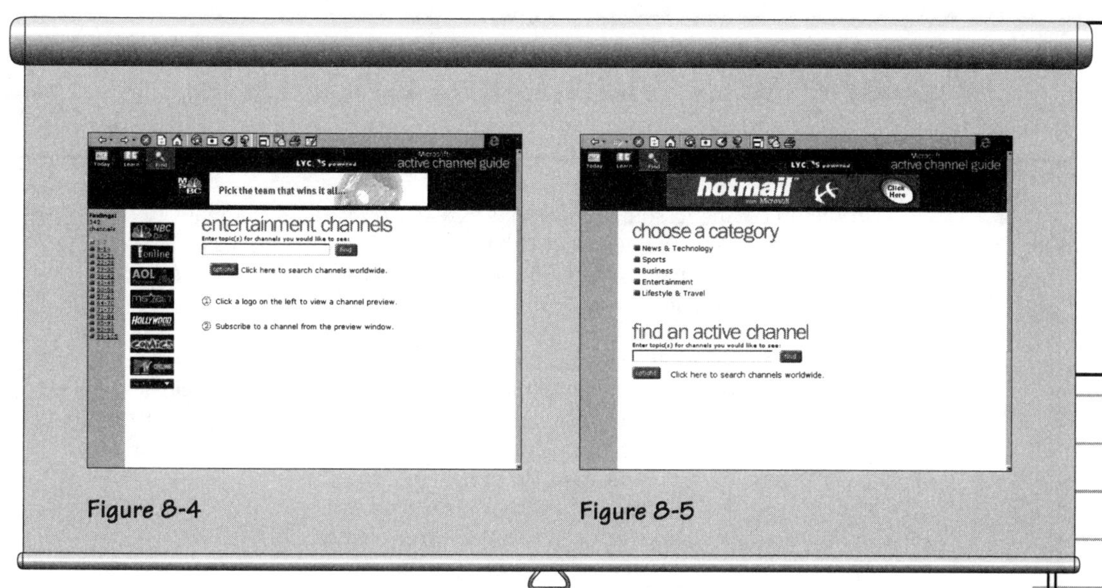

Figure 8-4

Figure 8-5

Figure 8-4: The Microsoft Active Channel Guide site offers hundreds of different channels you can choose from.

Figure 8-5: Use the Find box from the Microsoft Active Channel Guide site to locate channels you're interested in.

6. **Click the Find button in the upper-left section of the Web page.**

   A Find box like the one in Figure 8-5 appears. To try it out, assume that you want to uncover channels that are likely to make you laugh.

7. **Click in the Find box, type** humor **and press Enter.**

   After a few moments, you see an initial batch of channels that involve humor (for example, Comics Channel and Heckler's Online). As usual, move your mouse pointer over each channel to pop up a description, and explore any channel that interests you by clicking its icon.

   Also, notice that links appear on the left side of the page representing additional channels matching your *humor* topic.

8. **Click the link on the left side of the page that represents the next batch of matches.**

   You see another set of channels devoted to humor. Repeat this step until you've listed all the channels that match your topic.

9. **After you're done exploring channels, click the window's Close button (in the upper-right corner) and disconnect from the Net.**

   If the Close button (which looks like an "x") isn't visible initially, point to the right of the Internet Explorer logo in the window's upper-right corner. After you click the Close button, Internet Explorer exits.

Nice going! You've learned how to pop up the Channel bar and explore any channel on the bar. In addition, you've learned how to move to the Microsoft Active Channel Guide site, and how to use the links and the Find box on the site to explore any of hundreds of additional channels.

Now that you know how to locate and select channels of interest, you're ready to actually subscribe to and manage some channels. You'll take on those tasks in the next lesson.

☑ Progress Check

If you can do the following, you've mastered this lesson:

- ❑ Pop up the Channel bar.
- ❑ Select channels from the Channel bar.
- ❑ Select channels from the Microsoft Active Channel Guide site.
- ❑ Search for channels using a site's Find box.

Lesson 8-2 Adding and Managing Channels

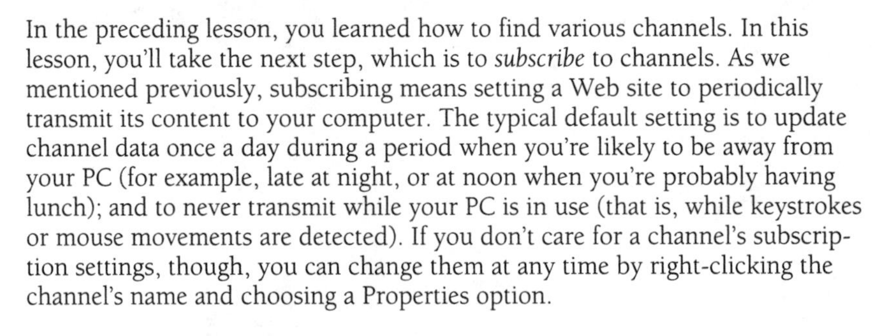

In the preceding lesson, you learned how to find various channels. In this lesson, you'll take the next step, which is to *subscribe* to channels. As we mentioned previously, subscribing means setting a Web site to periodically transmit its content to your computer. The typical default setting is to update channel data once a day during a period when you're likely to be away from your PC (for example, late at night, or at noon when you're probably having lunch); and to never transmit while your PC is in use (that is, while keystrokes or mouse movements are detected). If you don't care for a channel's subscription settings, though, you can change them at any time by right-clicking the channel's name and choosing a Properties option.

There are several ways you can subscribe to a channel:

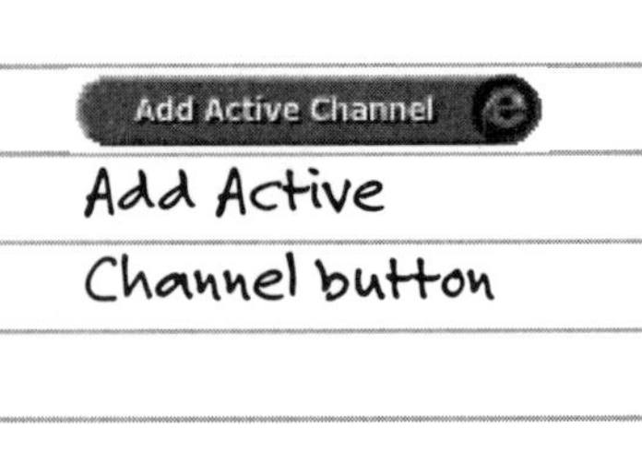

Add Active Channel button

- **Click the site's Add Active Channel button:** A channel's initial Web page typically includes a big blue button that's labeled Add Active Channel. Clicking this button is the most common way to subscribe to a channel. After you subscribe, the channel is added to the Channel bar (if it wasn't already installed on the bar).
- **Right-click the channel name and choose the Subscribe option:** If a channel is already installed on the Channel bar, right-click the channel's name to pop up a menu. If you aren't subscribed to the channel, the menu includes a Subscribe option that you can click to add the channel. (If you *are* already subscribed, the menu instead displays an Update Now option that you can click to make the channel immediately transmit its latest data to your PC.)

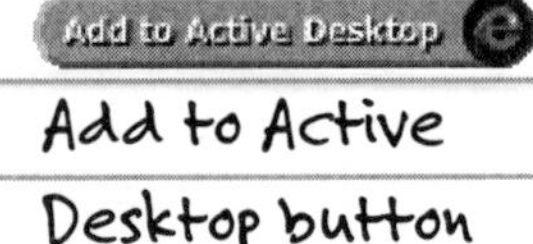

Add to Active Desktop button

- **Click the site's Add to Active Desktop button:** In addition to an Add Active Channel button, the initial Web page of some channels includes an Add to Active Desktop button. Clicking the latter places a special version of the channel — for example, a news ticker that displays stock prices, sports scores, weather conditions, or some other type of timely information — right on your desktop so that it's always available.
- **Add the channel from the Display Properties dialog box:** Even if a Web page doesn't include an Add to Active Desktop button, you can manually place the page on your desktop using the Display Properties dialog box. For more information, see the "Managing desktop channels" section later in this lesson.

When you choose to subscribe to a channel, a dialog box appears that lets you specify the location of the channel on the Channel bar and set how frequently the channel's content is updated. The next exercise takes you through the process step by step.

Subscribing to a channel

Here's how to locate and subscribe to a channel of interest:

1. **Connect to the Internet.**

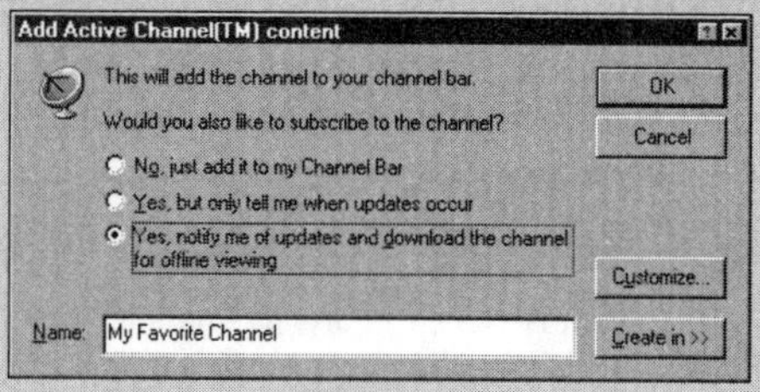

Figure 8-6

Figure 8-6: Use the Add Active Channel Content dialog box to subscribe to a channel and add it to your Channel bar.

Notes:

2 Click the View Channels button (the button on the taskbar that looks like a satellite dish).

An Internet Explorer window appears that's optimized to display channels.

3 Point to the left edge of the window to display the Channel bar, and then click Microsoft Channel Guide (typically at the top of the bar).

The Microsoft Active Channel Guide site is displayed.

4 Click the Find button in the upper-left section of the Web page.

A Find box appears. Use this box to search for channels that deal with a subject near and dear to your heart (for example, *investing* or *cooking* or *dating*).

5 Click in the Find box, type a word or phrase representing a subject that interests you, and press Enter.

An initial batch of channels that cover your topic appears. If your search resulted in more than seven matches, links leading to additional channels are displayed on the left side of the page.

6 Explore the channels that matched your topic until you find one that seems especially fun or useful.

Move your mouse pointer over each channel to pop up a description, and view any channel by clicking its icon. After you've decided on the channel you want, subscribe to it.

7 Locate a blue button labeled Add Active Channel on the Web site you've picked, and click the button.

You see an Add Active Channel Content dialog box like the one in Figure 8-6. This dialog box is very similar to the Add Favorite dialog box you used in Lesson 2-2 when creating Web page favorites. The main differences are that this dialog box adds the Web site you've selected to the Channel bar, not the favorites list; the box's default option is to subscribe to the site, rather than just save its name and URL; and the text in the Name box is chosen with care by the site's publisher and so normally should be left unchanged.

If you want to install your channel as a separate button on the Channel bar, skip to Step 10. Otherwise, use the Create In button to select an existing category on the bar for storing your new channel.

Notes:

8. **Click the Create In button (in the lower-right corner of the dialog box).**

   A list of the primary categories on the Channel bar — Business, Entertainment, Lifestyle and Travel, News and Technology, and Sports — pops down from the bottom of the dialog box.

9. **Click an appropriate category for storing your new channel.**

   After you've chosen a category, its name is highlighted to show that it's been selected. Your channel will be inserted in this category after you've finished using the dialog box and click OK.

   Now notice that directly above the Create In button is a Customize button. You can use the latter to adjust the channel's subscription settings.

10. **Click the Customize button.**

    The first of several Subscription Wizard dialog boxes appears. The current box asks if the data you want transmitted should include only the site's home page or all the Web content selected by the site's publisher. You should normally accept the latter option, which is the default.

11. **Click the Next button (at the bottom) to move to the next dialog box.**

    You're asked if you want to be informed by e-mail whenever the site changes. This option can be useful for a Web site that seldom changes, but most channels are updated at least once a week, so we suggest accepting the default answer of No.

12. **Click the Next button to move to the next dialog box.**

    You see the dialog box that appears in Figure 8-7, which lets you specify when and how often you want the channel to transmit its data to your PC. The default is to accept the schedule created by the site's publisher, which is displayed near the bottom of the dialog box (for example, `Update every day at 3:00 am`).

    If you want to receive the channel's data on a different schedule, click the New button to pop up the Custom Schedule dialog box in Figure 8-8. Use the options from this box to select an update schedule — which can be as frequent as every hour or as seldom as once a month — and then click OK to save your settings.

    The dialog box in Figure 8-7 also contains a Dial as Needed If Connected Through a Modem option. If your PC isn't online at a time when the channel is scheduled to transmit data, this option forces your Internet dialer program to automatically connect to the Net. If you'd prefer to have absolute control over when your PC dials into the Net, leave this option turned off, which is the default.

13. **Click the Finish button.**

    You return to the Add Active Channel Content dialog box. You've now explored all the options of this dialog box, so save your settings and exit.

14. **Click the OK button to subscribe to the channel.**

    The channel is installed on the Channel bar, your subscription settings are saved, and the dialog box closes.

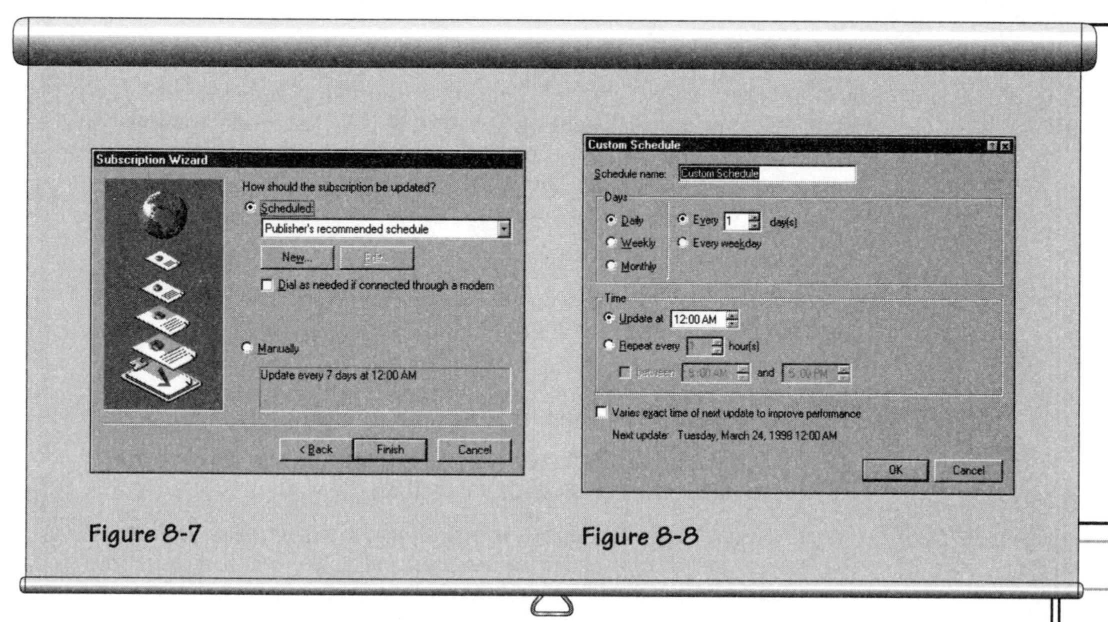

Figure 8-7

Figure 8-8

Figure 8-7: Use the Subscription Wizard dialog box to display a channel's default transmission schedule and to optionally make your PC dial into the Net whenever a transmission is set to occur.

Figure 8-8: Use the Custom Schedule dialog box to set when and how frequently a channel transmits its data to your PC.

In this case, subscribing to a channel took a while because we stepped you through all the available options. If you accept the default settings, however, you can subscribe to a channel rapidly by just clicking its Add Active Channel button and clicking OK. If you later want to revise the channel's settings, simply right-click it from the Channel bar and choose the Properties option from the menu that appears.

After you subscribe to a channel, use the methods you learned in Lesson 8-1 to view it. When you're not connected to the Net, the channel will display the data that it saved to your hard disk during its last scheduled transmission.

Adding a channel to your desktop

Perhaps the most convenient way to use a channel is to keep it on your desktop, because doing so puts the channel's information no more than a mouse click away.

Show Desktop button

Specifically, when your desktop is unobscured, the information of any channel residing on it is constantly viewable. And when your desktop is covered by various program windows, you can click the taskbar's Show Desktop button (which resides between the Launch Internet Explorer Browser and View Channels buttons) to instantly minimize all open windows so that you can see everything housed on your desktop, including its channels.

heads up

Before you can add channels to your desktop, you need to make sure that a Windows feature called *Active Desktop* is turned on. To do this, right-click any blank spot on your desktop, click the Active Desktop option from the menu that appears, and — if a check mark doesn't already appear to its left — click the View As Web Page option from the second menu that appears. This both enables channels to reside on your desktop and puts the Channel bar on your desktop.

Notes:

Tip: If you don't want the Channel bar on your desktop, hide the bar by clicking the Start button, choosing Settings⇨Active Desktop⇨Customize My Desktop from the menus that appear, clicking the box to the left of the Internet Explorer Channel Bar option to make the check mark disappear from the box, and clicking OK. However, keep the Channel bar displayed to perform the next exercise.

One of our favorite channel items is a news ticker from *The New York Times*. To add this never-ending stream of headlines to your desktop, follow these steps:

1. **Connect to the Internet (if you aren't already connected).**

2. **Click the Show Desktop button (the button on the taskbar that looks like a work desk with a pencil on it).**

   Any windows you have open are instantly minimized, providing you with a clear view of your desktop and of the items residing on it — which, because you turned on the Active Desktop, should include the Channel bar.

3. **Click the News and Technology category on the Channel bar.**

   A list of news channels pops down that includes *The New York Times.*

4. **Click the channel for *The New York Times.***

   An Internet Explorer window opens and displays the home page of *The New York Times* channel.

5. **Slowly move your mouse pointer over the options on the page until one or more orange Add to Active Desktop buttons appear.**

   At the time we write this, pointing to an Add to Desktop option on the page makes two Add to Active Desktop buttons appear. One resides next to the phrase *Desktop Edition* and activates a headline news ticker; the other appears next to the phrase *Window on the World* and activates a news photo display.

6. **Click the Add to Active Desktop button that activates a headline news ticker.**

   A confirmation box asks `Do you want to add a desktop item to your active desktop?`

7. **Click the Yes button.**

   The Add Item to Active Desktop dialog box in Figure 8-9 appears. This box is similar to the subscription dialog box you used in the preceding exercise, but it offers fewer options because it requires fewer decisions. (For example, there's no Create In button because this type of subscription doesn't involve installing anything on the Channel bar.)

8. **Click the Customize Subscription button**

   A Subscription Wizard dialog box appears that lets you change the channel's transmission schedule. If you're a news junkie, click the New button, set the channel to transmit updated headlines every hour, and click OK. Otherwise, simply accept the default setting of once a day at 3:00 a.m., which lets you read recent headlines daily over your morning coffee.

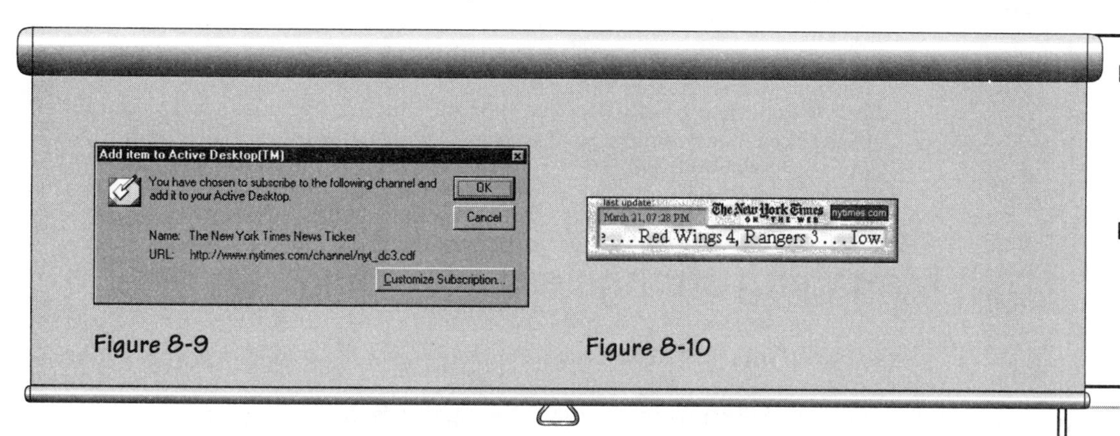

Figure 8-9: Use the Add Item to Active Desktop dialog box to place a channel directly on your desktop.

Figure 8-10: After you finish subscribing to it, a headline news ticker from *The New York Times* appears on your desktop.

9. **Click the Finish button to close the Subscription Wizard dialog box, and click the OK button to close the Add Item to Active Desktop dialog box.**

   Your settings are saved, and a Downloading Subscriptions dialog box briefly appears to indicate that the channel's current data is being sent to your PC. After the transmission is completed, the dialog box exits.

10. **Click the Show Desktop button on the taskbar.**

    You see your desktop again . . . and you now also see the nifty news ticker in Figure 8-10! When you read any headline in the ticker that interests you, click it; an Internet Explorer window opens and displays the full text of the article.

All kinds of interesting desktop channels are available. You can seek out more by visiting Microsoft's Desktop Gallery site at URL `www.microsoft.com/ie/ie40/gallery`.

To learn how to revise, hide, or delete a desktop channel, see the "Managing desktop channels" section later in this lesson.

Setting a channel to be your screen saver

Certain channels offer you the option of using their content as a screen saver via a Channel Screen Saver dialog box that pops up when you choose to subscribe. If you click the dialog box's Yes button, select data from the channel you're adding will automatically appear on your screen whenever your PC is idle for a specified period of time (for example, after you haven't pressed a key or moved your mouse for 15 minutes). In other words, a channel screen saver gives you regularly updated information without requiring you to lift a finger. If you choose more than one channel to be a screen saver, the channels typically take turns displaying their information on your screen.

Some screen savers disappear as soon as you press any key or move your mouse. If you're using a screen saver that doesn't, however, move your mouse pointer to the upper-right corner of your screen, look for a Close button that looks like the letter "X," and click the button to exit the screen saver.

Notes:

Each screen saver has individual options you can adjust. In addition, you can specify how many minutes your PC must remain idle before a screen saver appears. For more information, see the "Managing screen saver channels" section later in this lesson.

Managing channels

After you subscribe to a channel, you may eventually want to revise its settings or, after it's outlived its usefulness, delete it. You can perform these tasks by opening a Subscription window from Internet Explorer. To learn how to manage your channels, follow these steps:

1. **Click the Launch Internet Explorer Browser button on the taskbar.**

   Open a standard Internet Explorer window (as opposed to one optimized to display channels) so that you can access the browser's menu bar.

2. **Choose Favorites⇨Manage Subscriptions.**

   A Subscriptions window like the one in Figure 8-11 appears that lists all the channels to which you've subscribed. The window also has a toolbar near its top that includes the following buttons:

   - **Update:** Forces the selected channel to immediately transmit its latest content to your PC.
   - **Update all:** Forces all your channels to immediately transmit their latest content to your PC.
   - **Properties:** Opens a Properties dialog box that lets you adjust when and how the selected channel transmits its data.
   - **Delete:** Severs your subscription to the selected channel and removes it from your Channel bar, desktop, and/or list of screen savers.

   In addition, you can choose File⇨Rename from the menu bar to change the name of a channel. But the command you're likely to use most often is Properties, which lets you adjust a slew of subscription settings.

3. **Click a channel whose settings you want to examine and/or revise.**

   The channel is highlighted to show that it's been selected.

4. **Click the Properties button.**

   A Properties dialog box appears with three tabs near its top named Subscription, Receiving, and Schedule. You start off on the Subscription tab, which displays such information as the channel's name and URL, the channel's current transmission schedule, the last time the channel's content was updated on your PC, and when the next update is scheduled to occur. This dialog box also includes an Unsubscribe button that you can use to quit the channel.

5. **Click the Receiving tab.**

   You see options that let you set what action the channel takes during a scheduled update. In addition, if the channel requires you to supply a user name and password before performing an update, you can use a Login button to set that information to be provided automatically.

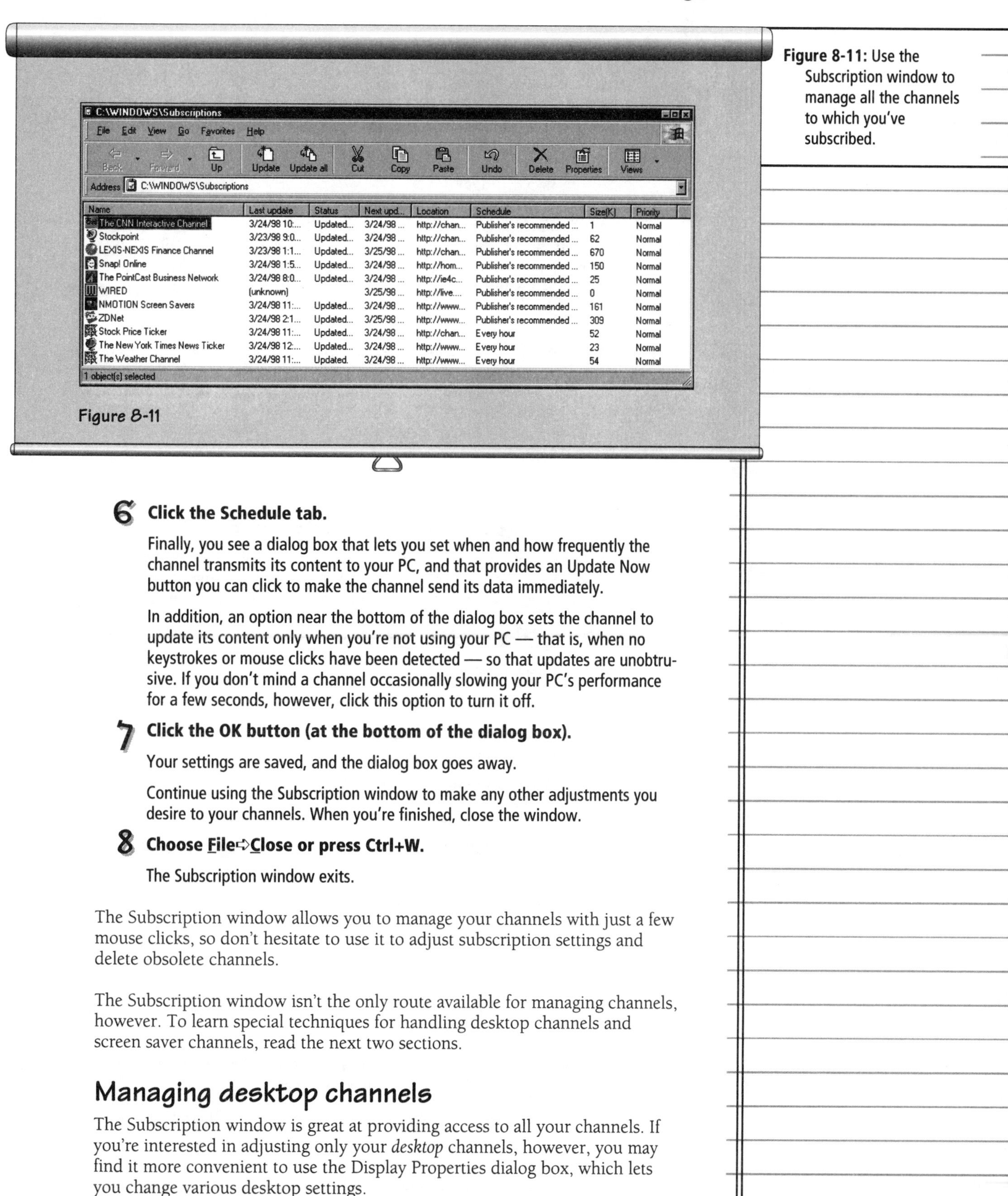

Figure 8-11

Figure 8-11: Use the Subscription window to manage all the channels to which you've subscribed.

6 **Click the Schedule tab.**

Finally, you see a dialog box that lets you set when and how frequently the channel transmits its content to your PC, and that provides an Update Now button you can click to make the channel send its data immediately.

In addition, an option near the bottom of the dialog box sets the channel to update its content only when you're not using your PC — that is, when no keystrokes or mouse clicks have been detected — so that updates are unobtrusive. If you don't mind a channel occasionally slowing your PC's performance for a few seconds, however, click this option to turn it off.

7 **Click the OK button (at the bottom of the dialog box).**

Your settings are saved, and the dialog box goes away.

Continue using the Subscription window to make any other adjustments you desire to your channels. When you're finished, close the window.

8 **Choose File⇨Close or press Ctrl+W.**

The Subscription window exits.

The Subscription window allows you to manage your channels with just a few mouse clicks, so don't hesitate to use it to adjust subscription settings and delete obsolete channels.

The Subscription window isn't the only route available for managing channels, however. To learn special techniques for handling desktop channels and screen saver channels, read the next two sections.

Managing desktop channels

The Subscription window is great at providing access to all your channels. If you're interested in adjusting only your *desktop* channels, however, you may find it more convenient to use the Display Properties dialog box, which lets you change various desktop settings.

Notes:

To do so, click the Start button and choose Settings➪Active Desktop➪Customize My Desktop from the menus that appear. This command pops up a Display Properties dialog box with its Web section selected and your desktop channels listed. Buttons on the right side of the dialog box allow you to delete a selected channel or display the channel's properties (that is, adjust its subscription settings).

In addition, you can click a box to the left of each channel to turn its check mark off, which causes the channel to disappear from your desktop. This is a less permanent way of eliminating a channel than deleting, because you can restore the channel at any time by just clicking to the channel's left again to turn its check mark back on.

Lastly, you can use the dialog box to *create* a desktop channel. Specifically, click the box's New button; click a No button to decline visiting the Microsoft Desktop Gallery site (which is located at `www.microsoft.com/ie/ie40/gallery`); type the URL of the Web page you want to add — which can be *any* page, not just one designed to function as a channel — and click OK twice. The dialog box closes, and a window appears on your desktop that displays the Web page you specified.

Managing screen saver channels

The Subscription window allows you to adjust only some of the settings available for screen saver channels. To access the full range of options available, use the Screen Saver section of the Display Properties dialog box. Here's how:

1. **Right-click a blank spot on your desktop.**

   A menu pops up.

2. **Choose Properties (the bottom option).**

   A Display Properties dialog box appears that has several tabs near its top, including one named Screen Saver.

3. **Click the Screen Saver tab.**

   You see buttons and options that include the following:

   - **Screen Saver:** Click in this box to pop down a list of the screen savers installed on your PC, and then click the screen saver you want to use.
   - **Settings:** Click this button, which appears directly to the right of the Screen Saver box, to examine and revise special settings that vary for each screen saver.
   - **Wait:** Click the arrows to the right of this box to specify how many minutes the screen saver you've selected should wait to appear after your PC becomes idle.
   - **Preview:** Click this button to try out the screen saver you've selected under the settings you've specified.

   Use these options now to revise the dialog box's settings to your tastes.

4 Click in the Screen Saver box to pop down a list of your screen savers, and click the Channel Screen Saver (if it isn't already selected).

Your PC is now set to use the channel screen saver(s) you installed.

5 Click the Settings button to examine and optionally adjust the operation of your channel screen saver(s).

For example, if you've installed more than one channel screen saver, use your mouse to turn on a check mark to the left of each screen saver you currently want activated. (If you turn on multiple channel screen savers, they normally take turns being displayed.)

6 Click the arrows to the right of the Wait box to set the number of minutes your screen saver(s) should wait to appear after your PC becomes idle.

If your monitor has an energy saving feature, also click the Settings button near the bottom of the dialog box to specify how long your monitor should wait after your PC becomes idle to turn itself off.

7 Finally, click the Preview button to check out your screen saver.

With any luck, it looks way cool. When you've seen enough, make the screen saver disappear by (depending on your settings) moving your mouse or clicking the upper-right corner of your screen.

8 After you're satisfied with your screen saver settings, click the OK button.

Your settings are saved, and the dialog box exits.

As you've seen throughout this unit, channels provide a great alternative way of interacting with the Web. Play around with the various options channels offer to make your PC use more productive and more fun.

☑ Progress Check

If you can do the following, you've mastered this lesson:

- ❑ Manage all your channels using the Subscription window.
- ❑ Manage your desktop channels using the Web section of the Display Properties dialog box.
- ❑ Manage your screen saver channels using the Screen Saver section of the Display Properties dialog box.

Recess

Take a break from the Internet and do some channel surfing with your TV remote. After you invigorate yourself by enjoying an episode of *ER, The Practice,* or *South Park,* channel your energies into tackling the following quiz questions.

Unit 8 Quiz

For each of the following questions, circle the letter of the correct answer or answers. Remember, each question may have more than one right answer.

Notes:

1. **Internet channels are**
   - A. TV signals converted into digital data.
   - B. Radio signals converted into digital data.
   - C. Web site data that's transmitted on a specified schedule and in the background via your Internet connection.
   - D. Limited to the channels that appear on the Channel bar.
   - E. Racy Web content that should be viewed only by those over age 18.

2. **To pop up the Channel bar:**
   - A. Click the Start button and choose Programs⇨Channels.
   - B. Click the Channels button from Internet Explorer.
   - C. Click the Channels button from Outlook Express.
   - D. Click the View Channels button from the taskbar.
   - E. Turn on the Active Desktop.

3. **To view a channel:**
   - A. Point your TV remote at your PC screen and start clicking.
   - B. Select it from the Channel bar.
   - C. Select it from the Microsoft Active Channel Guide site.
   - D. View your desktop (if you've placed one or more channels on your desktop).
   - E. Wait until your PC is idle long enough for a screen saver to appear (if you've assigned a channel to be your screen saver).

4. **To subscribe to a channel, you can**
   - A. Click the site's Add Active Channel button and click OK.
   - B. Click the site's Add to Active Desktop button and click OK.
   - C. Right-click the channel, choose the Subscribe option, and click OK.
   - D. Open the Display Properties dialog box, click the Web tab, click the New and No buttons, enter the channel's URL, and click OK twice.
   - E. All of the above.

5. **The following movie is *not* about U.S. politics:**
   - A. *Primary Colors*
   - B. *All the King's Men*
   - C. *Seven Days in May*
   - D. *Wag the Dog*
   - E. *Bedtime for Bonzo*

Unit 8 Exercise

1. Locate a channel that provides a desktop stock ticker — that is, a window that constantly displays the latest stock prices. (***Hint:*** Use the Find box on the Microsoft Active Channel Guide site.)
2. Visit the channel's site and place its ticker on your desktop.
3. Examine and optionally adjust how often the ticker is updated.
4. If you like the stock ticker, keep it. Otherwise, delete it from your desktop.

Notes:

Part II Review

Unit 5 Summary

- **Launching Outlook Express:** Click the Start button (in the left corner of the Windows 98 taskbar) and choose Programs⇨Internet Explorer⇨Outlook Express from the menus that appear.
- **Setting up Outlook Express to handle your e-mail:** Choose Tools⇨Accounts to open the Internet Accounts dialog box, click the Add button, and click the Mail option to pop up an Internet Connection Wizard dialog box. Follow the box's prompts to supply your full name, your e-mail address, the names of your ISP's POP and SMTP servers (that is, the computers of your Internet provider that handle incoming and outgoing mail), your e-mail user name and password, and your connection information. After you're done, click the Finish button to save your e-mail settings, and click the Close button to exit the Internet Accounts dialog box.
- **Creating a message:** Click the Compose Message button on the Outlook toolbar to open a New Message window. Use this message window to create and send your e-mail message.
- **Addressing an e-mail message:** In a message window, type the address of each primary recipient in the To box, type the address of each secondary recipient in the Cc (*carbon copy*) box, and type the address of each person whose name you want to avoid displaying in the message in the Bcc (*blind carbon copy*) box. Separate addresses in the same box using commas or semi-colons.
- **Completing and sending an addressed message:** Click the Subject line and type a brief heading that represents what your message is about. Click in the message area and compose your message, making it as long or short as you want. After you're done editing your message, choose Tools⇨Spelling and follow the prompts to spell-check your text. Finally, click the Send button on the window's toolbar to transmit your message over the Net.
- **Saving a draft message:** If you want to temporarily stop working on a message, choose File⇨Save. The message is stored in the Drafts e-mail folder, where you can resume editing it at any time by selecting the folder and double-clicking the message.
- **Sending e-mail later:** If you've completed a message but don't want to send it right away (for example, if you want to create a number of messages offline and then send them all at the same time), choose File⇨Send Later. Your message is saved in the Outbox e-mail folder. When you're ready to send all the messages in Outbox, click the Send and Receive button on the Outlook toolbar.
- **Retrieving your mail:** Click the Send and Receive button from the Outlook toolbar to both pick up your new messages and transmit any messages in your Outbox folder. The messages are typically stored in the Inbox folder.
- **Selecting an e-mail folder:** Click the folder from the folder list in the upper-left section of the Outlook Express window. After you do so, the contents of the folder are displayed in the message list in the upper-right section of the window.
- **Reading messages:** Select a folder that contains messages you're interested in, and click a message you want to read from the message list. (Unread messages are displayed in boldface.) After you do so, the contents of the message appear in the lower-right section of the window. Continue clicking the message list to read additional messages.

Part II Review

- **Replying to a message:** Click the message to select it, and, from the Outlook toolbar, click either the Reply to Author button (to respond exclusively to the message's author) or the Reply to All button (to respond to the author and also to everyone else who received the message). A message window appears with its address boxes and Subject line filled in, and with the original message quoted (see next item). Type your response in the message area and then click the Send button.
- **Quoting a message:** Remind your correspondent of what he or she said by including parts of the original message in your reply. Quoted material appears with each line preceded by a > or, in e-mail programs such as Outlook Express that support HTML, a vertical line. Include only the relevant parts of the original message and delete the rest.
- **Forwarding a message:** Click the message to select it and then click the Forward Message button on the Outlook toolbar. A message window appears with the Subject line already filled in. Address the message, add your comments at the top of the message area, and click the Send button.
- **Printing a message:** Make sure that your printer is on and has enough paper in it; click the message to select it; choose File⇨Print or press Ctrl+P to pop up the Print dialog box; make any necessary adjustments to the dialog box's settings; and click OK.
- **Deleting a message:** Click the message to select it, and then click the Delete button on the Outlook toolbar or press the Del key. The message is merely transferred to the Deleted Items folder, so you can get it back by moving it from Deleted Items to some other e-mail folder. To permanently eliminate the message, right-click the Deleted Items folder and choose the Empty Folder option from the menu that appears. Your deleted messages are then *really* deleted, freeing up space on your hard disk for new messages.
- **Following Netiquette:** Don't send unnecessarily angry messages, don't distribute chain letters, and don't believe everything you read! Do check your spelling and do think of your correspondents as real people with feelings and foibles.

Unit 6 Summary

- **Opening the Address Book:** Click the Address Book button on the Outlook toolbar. Use the window that appears to enter information on how to contact your friends and colleagues via e-mail.
- **Adding someone to your Address Book:** Click the New Contact button on the Address Book toolbar. A Properties dialog box pops up that lets you enter a variety of contact information, including the person's full name, e-mail address, physical addresses, phone numbers, fax numbers, and Web page addresses. The dialog box also lets you assign the person a nickname that you can type in a message window in place of the person's difficult-to-remember e-mail address, and assign a display name that you can use to reference the entire entry. After you finish entering the contact information, click the OK button to save the entry.
- **Creating a mailing list:** Click the New Group button on the Address Book toolbar. A dialog box appears that lets you enter the display names of entries in your Address Book, and also lets you assign the mailing list itself a display name. After you're done, click the OK button to save your list. You can then enter your mailing list's display name in a To, Cc, or Bcc address box; after you click Send, Outlook Express transmits the message to all the e-mail addresses represented by the mailing list.

Part II Review

- **Editing an Address Book entry:** Double-click the entry, or click the entry to select it and then click the Properties button on the Address Book toolbar. A dialog box pops up with the information you previously entered. Make any necessary revisions and then click the OK button to save your changes.
- **Deleting an Address Book entry:** Click the entry to select it, click the Delete button on the Address Book toolbar or press the Del key, and click the Yes button or press Enter to confirm the deletion. Think twice before using this option, however, because you can't get an entry back after it's deleted.
- **Using your Address Book to address a message:** Open a message window, click in an address box, and type the nickname you assigned to the recipient (or type just the first few letters and let Outlook Express fill in the rest for you). Alternatively, click the Select Recipients button from the message window's toolbar to pop up a list of your Address Book entries. For each recipient, click the person's entry and then click the To, Cc, or Bcc button to the right of the entry. When you're done, click OK; the e-mail addresses of the people you selected are entered into the address boxes you specified.
- **Creating an e-mail folder:** Outlook Express automatically creates Inbox, Drafts, Outbox, Sent Items, and Deleted Items folders to hold, respectively, your incoming, partially written, outgoing, previously sent, and deleted messages. To create an e-mail folder yourself, choose File⇨Folder⇨New Folder from the Outlook menu bar to pop up a Create Folder dialog box; type a name for the folder; choose whether you want to create a first-level folder or a subfolder within an existing folder; and click the OK button. The folder is created and displayed on the folder list.
- **Moving a message to a different e-mail folder:** Click and drag the message from the message list to the folder on the folder list. After you release your mouse button, the message is placed in the folder you selected and deleted from its original folder.
- **Copying a message to a different e-mail folder:** Hold down the Ctrl key and, while keeping the key pressed, click and drag the message from the message list to the folder on the folder list. After you release your mouse button, a copy of the message is placed in the folder you selected, and the original message is unaffected.
- **Creating a message filter:** Choose Tools⇨Inbox Assistant from the Outlook menu bar to pop up an Inbox Assistant dialog box, click the Add button to pop up a Properties dialog box, set the rules for your filter, and click OK twice to save your filter.
- **Reading new messages after setting up message filters:** Both new messages and folders that contain new messages are displayed in boldface. Therefore, click each boldfaced folder from the folder list and click each boldfaced message from the message list until you've read all your new mail.
- **Creating an e-mail signature:** Choose Tools⇨Stationery from the Outlook menu bar; click the Signatures button from the dialog box that appears; click in the topmost text box in the second dialog box that appears; type something both concise and informative, and that can stand up to repeated viewings; click the Add This Signature To All Outgoing Messages option to turn its check mark on; and click OK twice.
- **Attaching a file to an e-mail message**: Click the Insert File button from the message window's toolbar or choose Insert⇨File Attachment; use the Insert Attachment dialog box that pops up to specify the name and folder location of the file you want to transmit; and click the

Part II Review

Attach button to attach the file and exit the dialog box. Address and compose your message as usual, and then click the Send button on the window's toolbar to transmit both your message and the file.

- **Saving or displaying an attached file:** Double-click the e-mail message from the message list to open the message in its own window. If the attached file is a GIF or JPEG picture, then the image is displayed automatically as part of the message. Otherwise, all you see representing the file is an icon near the bottom of the message. Right-click the icon to display a menu, and then either choose the Save As option to pop up a Save As dialog box that lets you save the file to the folder you specify, or choose the Open option to make Windows 98 try to locate and run a program on your hard disk that can display the data file. (If the file is a program itself, Windows 98 simply launches the file.)

Unit 7 Summary

- **Understanding Usenet newsgroups:** *Usenet* is a message distribution system that encompasses over 30,000 ongoing discussions, or *newsgroups*, taking place over the Internet. You can read and participate in these discussions by using Outlook Express. Messages distributed via newsgroups are called *articles*. Sending a message to a newsgroup is called *posting an article*.
- **Understanding hierarchies:** A *hierarchy* is a collection of newsgroups whose names start with the same word. The seven major hierarchies are `rec`, `soc`, `talk`, `sci`, `comp`, `news`, and `misc`. The major unofficial hierarchy is `alt`. Other hierarchies include discussions dedicated to companies, schools, or countries.
- **Launching Outlook Express:** Click the Start button (in the left corner of the Windows 98 taskbar) and choose Programs⇨Internet Explorer⇨Outlook Express from the menus that appear.
- **Setting up Outlook Express to handle Usenet newsgroups:** Choose Tools⇨Accounts to open the Internet Accounts dialog box, click the Add button, and click the News option to pop up an Internet Connection Wizard dialog box. Follow the prompts to provide your full name, your e-mail address, the name of your ISP's news server (that is, the computer of your Internet provider that stores Usenet newsgroup messages), and your connection information. After you're done, click the Finish button to save your newsgroup settings, and click the Close button to exit the Internet Accounts dialog box. You can then immediately begin downloading a list of the newsgroups on the server you specified by clicking a Yes button.
- **Opening the Newsgroups window and listing newsgroups:** Click a news server from the folder list. If you've never accessed the server before, click the Yes button that appears to download the server's newsgroup list. Otherwise, click the News groups button on the Outlook toolbar. In either case, the Newsgroups window opens and displays a list of the newsgroups on the server.
- **Refreshing a newsgroup list:** After you've downloaded a server's newsgroup list, Outlook Express subsequently displays the list from your hard disk whenever you click the News groups button, which saves time but prevents you from seeing new newsgroups. Therefore, occasionally click the Reset List button from the Newsgroups window, which forces Outlook Express to download an updated newsgroup list from the server.

Part II Review

- **Locating a newsgroup by typing its name:** Double-click inside the search box near the top of the Newsgroups window and start entering the newsgroup's name. As you type each letter, the list displays the newsgroup names that most closely match what you're typing.
- **Subscribing to a newsgroup:** Open the Newsgroups window, locate and click the newsgroup you want, and click the Subscribe button. Alternatively, locate and double-click the newsgroup. In either case, an icon appears directly to the left of the newsgroup to show that you've subscribed to it.
- **Unsubscribing from a newsgroup:** From the Newsgroups window, click the newsgroup and click the Unsubscribe button, or double-click the newsgroup; the icon to the left of the newsgroup disappears. From the Outlook Express window, right-click the newsgroup from the folder list, choose the Unsubscribe From This Newsgroup option from the menu that appears, and click a Yes button to confirm quitting the newsgroup.
- **Reading a newsgroup:** If the newsgroups to which you subscribed aren't already displayed on the folder list, first click the plus (+) sign to the left of their news server. Next, click a newsgroup that interests you; its articles appear in the message list in the upper-right section of the window. Finally, click any article from the message list to view its contents in the lower-right section of the window. After you've selected an article for more than five seconds, it loses its boldfacing to indicate you've read it.
- **Searching for newsgroups of interest:** Go to the Deja News Web site at `www.dejanews.com` and click the page's Interest Finder link to access a program that helps you find newsgroups devoted to your favorite topics.
- **Searching for newsgroup articles:** Use the Deja News Web site at `www.dejanews.com` or the AltaVista Web site at `altavista.digital.com` to access programs that help you find newsgroup articles containing a word or phrase you specify.
- **Posting an original newsgroup article:** After you've read a newsgroup for at least a week and have something wise, witty, and wonderful to say, you're ready to post an article. To do so, click the newsgroup from the folder list, click the Compose Message button from the Outlook toolbar to open a pre-addressed message window, type a subject heading on the Subject line, and press Tab to move to the message area. Carefully write and edit your message, being sure to check your spelling, grammar, and tone. When you're ready to transmit your article, click the Post button on the window's toolbar.
- **Responding privately to a newsgroup article:** If what you have to say is of interest primarily to the person who wrote the article or is private, reply to the author via e-mail by clicking the article to select it, clicking the Reply to Author button on the Outlook toolbar, typing your message, and clicking the message window's Send button.
- **Responding publicly to a newsgroup article:** If what you have to say will be of general interest to a newsgroup's readers, respond publicly by clicking the article to select it and clicking the Reply to Group button on the Outlook toolbar. Write your response in the message window that opens, carefully checking your spelling, grammar, and tone, and then click the Post button on the window's toolbar to post your article.

Unit 8 Summary

- **Understanding channels:** An Internet *channel* is Web site content that's designed to be transmitted on a specified schedule and in the background via your Internet connection.
- **Displaying the Channel bar:** If you're running Internet Explorer, click the Channels button on the Standard toolbar. Otherwise, click the View Channels button from the taskbar, or turn on the Active Desktop by right-clicking the desktop and choosing Active Desktop⇨View As Web Page.
- **Viewing a channel:** If the channel has been installed on the Channel bar, click the channel from the bar. Otherwise, click the Microsoft Channel Guide button on the Channel bar and then select the channel from the Microsoft Active Channel Guide site. Alternatively, if the channel is on your desktop, view your desktop; or if the channel is a screen saver, wait until your PC is idle long enough for the channel to automatically appear.
- **Adding a channel to the Channel bar:** First, right-click the channel and choose Subscribe from the menu that appears; or click an Add Active Channel button from the channel's site. Next, use the dialog box that appears to adjust any channel settings you want to change. Finally, click the dialog box's OK button to save your settings and add the channel to the Channel bar.
- **Adding a channel to the desktop:** Click an Add to Active Desktop button from the channel's site, and click a Yes button to confirm adding the channel. Alternatively, if the site doesn't have an Add to Active Desktop button, click the Start button, choose Settings⇨Active Desktop⇨ Customize My Desktop from the menus that appear, click a New button, click No, type the URL of the Web page you want to add, and click OK.
- **Setting a channel to be your screen saver:** If a Channel Screen Saver dialog box pops up while you're subscribing to a channel, click the Yes button to make the channel your screen saver.
- **Managing channels:** To manage channels on the Channel bar, open an Internet Explorer window and choose Favorites⇨Manage Subscriptions. To manage desktop channels, click the Start button and choose Settings⇨Active Desktop⇨Customize My Desktop from the menus that appear. To manage screen saver channels, right-click a blank spot on the desktop, choose Properties from the menu that appears, and click the Screen Saver tab near the top of the dialog box that appears.

Part II Test

The questions on this test cover all the material presented in Part II, Units 5-7.

True False

T F 1. E-mail is like paper mail because it's written and can be kept for future reference.

T F 2. E-mail is like the telephone because it's quick, easy, and informal.

T F 3. `myname@idgbooks.com@dummies.com` is a valid e-mail address.

T F 4. To *flame* someone means to set her heart ablaze with love notes.

T F 5. If you're angry about something, you should take advantage of e-mail's speed and convenience by writing a message quickly and sending it off before you have a chance to calm down.

T F 6. If you delete a message accidentally, you can recover it by simply clicking and dragging it from the Deleted Items folder to a different e-mail folder.

T F 7. You can attach picture files to messages, but you can't attach other files such as word processing documents or spreadsheets.

T F 8. To read a newsgroup, you must first subscribe to it. You can then click the newsgroup from the folder list and click the newsgroup's articles from the message list.

T F 9. If you want to practice posting an article, you can transmit your text to the `misc.test` newsgroup.

T F 10. Internet channels give you easy access to a steady stream of information.

Multiple Choice

For each of the following questions, circle the correct answer or answers. Remember, there may be more than one right answer for each question.

11. To pick up your new e-mail messages, click the following button on the Outlook toolbar:

A. Get Messages

B. New Msg

C. Retrieve Mail

D. Receive Mail

E. Send and Receive

12. To create and send an e-mail message:

A. Click the Compose Message button from the Outlook toolbar to open a New Message window.

B. Address the message to its recipient(s).

C. Type a heading for the message on its Subject line.

D. Write, edit, and spell-check the message's text.

E. Print the message, put it in a stamped envelope, and drop it off at your local post office.

Part II Test

13. When addressing an e-mail message, you can

A. Type multiple addresses in the same address box, separated by commas or semi-colons.

B. Type the addresses of the message's primary recipients in the To box.

C. Type the addresses of secondary recipients in the Cc box or, if you want to suppress their addresses from appearing in the message, the Bcc box.

D. Enter addresses using your mouse by clicking the Select Recipients button to pop up Address Book entries.

E. Use zip-plus-four codes to speed up delivery.

14. The nickname feature of your Address Book:

A. Calls you mean names when you're not looking.

B. Makes you sound tough in your messages.

C. Lets you pick an easy-to-remember word to represent an e-mail address.

D. Spares you from having to constantly type difficult e-mail addresses.

E. Works only with e-mail programs that support HTML.

15. Outlook Express automatically creates the following e-mail folders:

A. E-Mail, Phone Calls, and Letters

B. Inbox, Outbox, and Shoebox

C. Important, Ho-Hum, and Useless

D. Work, Personal, and Top Secret

E. Inbox, Drafts, Outbox, Sent Items, and Deleted Items

16. Steps you can perform to subscribe to a particular newsgroup include

A. Clicking the newsgroup's server from the folder list.

B. Clicking the News groups button to open the Newsgroups window.

C. Typing the newsgroup's name in the search box near the top of the Newsgroups window to display the newsgroup.

D. Clicking the newsgroup to select it and then clicking the Subscribe button, or double-clicking the newsgroup.

E. Sending in a subscription card and waiting six to eight weeks.

17. Internet channels are

A. Broadcast around the clock from specially equipped TV and radio stations.

B. Accessed via a special *Channels Distribution* system on the Internet.

C. Just another name for Usenet newsgroups.

D. Special information sources created by Microsoft Corporation.

E. Web site data that can be transmitted on a set schedule to your PC.

18. Which of the following actresses does *not* play a deadly fighter on TV?

A. Lucy Lawless

B. Hudson Leick

C. Peta Wilson

D. Sarah Michelle Gellar

E. Nana Visitor

Part II Test

Matching

19. Match the following Outlook toolbar buttons with their corresponding descriptions:

A. Reply to Author

B. 

C. Send and Receive

D. 

E. 

1. Open a blank message window that you can use to create a message.
2. Reply to the person who sent the selected message.
3. Reply to the person who sent the selected message *and* to everyone who received the message.
4. Retrieve the new messages that have arrived in your electronic mailbox and transmit any messages you've saved to the Outbox folder.
5. Forward a copy of the selected message to someone who you feel would enjoy and/or benefit from reading it.

20. Match the following newsgroup terms with their corresponding descriptions:

A. Usenet	1. Message that appears in a newsgroup.
B. Article	2. Sending an angry or inflammatory message.
C. Post	3. Global system that distributes newsgroups over the Internet.
D. Flame	4. Series of articles that all respond to the same article and/or to each other.
E. Thread	5. Sending an article to a newsgroup.

21. Match the following message window and Address Book toolbar buttons with their corresponding commands:

A. 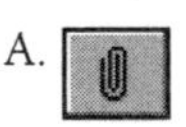

B.

C. Send

D. 

E. New Group

1. Add a person's contact information to your Address Book.
2. Attach a file that will be transmitted with your e-mail message.
3. Add an e-mail mailing list to your Address Book.
4. Pop up your Address Book entries to address a message using your mouse.
5. Transmit your message over the Internet to its intended recipient.

22. Match the following famous newsmakers with their birthdates:

A. Winston Churchill	1. February 12, 1809
B. Martin Luther King, Jr.	2. May 3, 1898
C. Cleopatra	3. January 15, 1929
D. Abraham Lincoln	4. November 30, 1874
E. Golda Meir	5. 69 BC

Part II Lab Assignment

Step 1: Run Outlook Express, connect to the Net, and open the Newsgroups window.

Get ready to do some news-reading!

Step 2: Find and subscribe to a newsgroup that you'll enjoy.

You can find the newsgroups most likely to discuss your favorite topics by examining the newsgroup list or by using the Deja News Web site.

Step 3: Find some interesting articles in the newsgroup.

This step shouldn't take long!

Step 4: Create an e-mail folder for storing the articles.

Give the folder a name that represents your topic.

Step 5: Move the articles into the folder.

You can move each message quickly by clicking and dragging.

Step 6: (optional) Send an e-mail message to the author of an article you especially liked, thanking him or her.

If you have information to add concerning the subject of the article, do so.

Appendix A

Answers

Part I Test Answers

Question	Answer	If You Missed It, Try This
1.	True	Review Lesson 1-1.
2.	False	Review Lesson 1-2.
3.	True	Review Lesson 1-2.
4.	False	Review Lesson 1-2.
5.	True	Review Lesson 1-3.
6.	True	Review Lesson 2-2.
7.	True	Review Lesson 2-5.
8.	True	Review Lesson 4-1.
9.	False	Review Lesson 4-1.
10.	True	Review Lesson 4-1.
11.	D, E	Review Lesson 1-2.
12.	E	Review Lessons 1-2, 2-1, 2-5, and 3-2.
13.	B, D	Review Lessons 1-2 and 1-3.
14.	E	Review Lesson 2-5.
15.	A, B, C	Review Lesson 3-1.
16.	A, B, C, D	Review Lesson 3-2.
17.	E	Review Lesson 4-2.
18.	E	It's a wonderful world we live in.
19.	A, 4	Review Lessons 1-3, 2-5, 3-1, and 4-2.
	B, 1	
	C, 2	
	D, 5	
	E, 3	

Question	Answer	If You Missed It, Try This
20.	A, 3	Review Lessons 1-3, 2-1, and 4-2.
	B, 4	
	C, 5	
	D, 1	
	E, 2	
21.	A, 3	Review Lessons 1-3, 2-1, 3-1, and 4-2.
	B, 5	
	C, 4	
	D, 1	
	E, 2	
22.	A, 4	Review your grade school geography notes.
	B, 3	
	C, 5	
	D, 2	
	E, 1	

Part II Test Answers

Question	Answer	If You Missed It, Try This
1.	True	Review Lesson 5-2 for how to create e-mail and Lesson 6-2 for how to file a message for future reference.
2.	True	Review Lesson 5-2 for how to send e-mail and Lesson 5-5 for rules of e-mail etiquette.
3.	False	Review Lesson 5-2. An e-mail address contains only one at-sign (@), which appears between the user name and the computer name.
4.	False	Review Lesson 5-5.
5.	False	Don't *ever* do this! Review Lesson 5-5.
6.	True	Review Lessons 5-4 and 6-2.
7.	False	Review Lesson 6-3.
8.	True	Review Lesson 7-2.
9.	True	Review Lesson 7-5. Never post test messages to other newsgroups, because you'll just make people mad!
10.	True	Review Lesson 8-1.

Question	Answer	If You Missed It, Try This
11.	E	Review Lesson 5-1.
12.	A, B, C, D	Review Lesson 5-2.
13.	A, B, C, D	Review Lessons 5-2 and 6-1.
14.	C, D	Review Lesson 6-1.
15.	E	Review Lesson 6-2.
16.	A, B, C, D	Review Lesson 7-2.
17.	E	Review Lesson 8-1
18.		Trick question; they *all* portray fierce warriors (and superbly). Lucy Lawless plays the awesome, sword-wielding Xena, Warrior Princess; Hudson Leick plays Xena's deliciously evil nemesis, Callisto; Peta Wilson plays superspy Nikita in *La Femme Nikita;* Sarah Michelle Gellar plays the high-kicking Buffy the Vampire Slayer; and Nana Visitor plays the wondrous spiritual soldier Major Kira Nerys on *Star Trek: Deep Space Nine*.
19.	A, 2	Review Lessons 5-1, 5-2, and 5-4.
	B, 5	
	C, 4	
	D, 3	
	E, 1	
20.	A, 2	Review Lessons 5-2, 6-1, and 6-3.
	B, 4	
	C, 5	
	D, 1	
	E, 3	
21.	A, 3	Review Lessons 5-5, 7-1, 7-3, and 7-5.
	B, 1	
	C, 5	
	D, 2	
	E, 4	
22.	A, 4	Review your grade school history notes (or ask your local kid).
	B, 3	
	C, 5	
	D, 1	
	E, 2	

Appendix B

Using the *Dummies 101* CD

In this final section, we tell you about the programs and other files on your *Dummies 101* CD.

We first provide a brief description of each program and exercise file on the CD. We then explain how to install programs from the CD to your hard disk (which is a necessary step, because the programs can't run directly from the CD), and what equipment you need to use the CD's contents.

We next provide further details about each program, such as installation tips and pointers on where to obtain more information.

Finally, we tell you how to remove any programs you no longer need, and what steps you can take if you encounter any problems with the CD.

So read on; and then have fun playing around with your *Dummies 101* CD!

Programs on the CD

The following is a summary of the programs on your *Dummies 101* CD, in alphabetical order, and a reference to which unit(s) in this book discuss each program:

- **Acrobat Reader:** A free program that lets you view and print portable document format, or *pdf*, files. You'll find several such document files on the CD, including two bonus units for this book: Unit ML, which teaches you how to participate in online group discussions via e-mail mailing lists; and Unit WP, which teaches you how to create your own Web pages. (See the next section, "Document and Exercise Files on the CD.)
- **Eudora Light:** An excellent free electronic mail program that lets you send and receive e-mail messages over the Internet. (See Unit 6.)
- **Free Agent:** An excellent free newsgroup reader program that lets you participate in thousands of ongoing discussions taking place over an area of the Internet called Usenet. (See Unit 7.)
- **FrontPage Express:** A free page composer program that helps you create your own Web pages. (See Unit WP, which is a bonus unit stored on the CD.)

Notes:

- **GetRight:** A shareware program that helps you download files from the Net with maximum efficiency. (See Unit 3.)
- **Internet Explorer:** A superb free browser program that lets you cruise the World Wide Web. (See Units 1, 2, 3, and 4.)
- **MindSpring:** Software that helps you sign up for an Internet account with MindSpring Enterprises, a top-rated service that charges a monthly flat fee for unlimited Internet access. (See Unit 1.)
- **mIRC:** A shareware program that lets you interact live with groups of people on the Internet via your keyboard using Internet Relay Chat, or IRC. (See Unit 7.)
- **Netscape Communicator:** An enormously popular freeware program that lets you cruise the World Wide Web, send and receive e-mail, and participate in newsgroups. (See Unit 1.)
- **Outlook Express:** A free electronic mail program that lets you send and receive e-mail messages over the Internet. (See Units 5 and 6.)
- **Paint Shop Pro:** A versatile shareware graphics program that lets you view just about any image you're likely to encounter on the Web. Paint Shop Pro also enables you to draw and edit images, and convert them into different file formats, which is useful for creating your own Web pages. (See Unit WP, which is a bonus unit stored on the CD.)
- **ThunderBYTE Anti-Virus:** A shareware virus detection program that helps safeguard your data from destructive software. (See Unit 3.)
- **WinZip:** An invaluable shareware decompression utility that lets you make compressed files useable again. (See Unit 3.)
- **WS_FTP LE:** A free (for noncommercial use) File Transfer Protocol, or *FTP*, program that you can use to copy files between your PC and a computer on the Internet. (See Unit WP, which is a bonus unit stored on the CD.)

A few words about free programs versus shareware: Free programs are just that; you can use them as often as you like, for as long as you like, at no charge.

Shareware programs, on the other hand, are available to you to use for an evaluation period (typically, anywhere from 30 to 90 days). If you decide that you like a shareware program and want to keep using it, you're expected to send a registration fee to its author or publisher, which entitles you to technical support and notifications about new versions. (It also makes you feel good.)

Most shareware operates on an honor system, so the programs continue working even if you don't register them. However, it's a good idea to support the shareware concept and encourage the continued production of quality low-cost software by sending in your payment for the programs you use.

Document and Exercise Files on the CD

In addition to programs, the *Dummies 101* CD contains several document and exercise files that we believe you'll find extremely useful. Here's what else is on the CD:

- **MailList.pdf:** Bonus unit for this book (Unit ML, "Joining Discussions by E-Mail") that teaches you how to join and participate in the tens of thousands of ongoing discussions that take place via electronic mailing lists — which are even more numerous than Usenet newsgroups! Read this document using the Acrobat Reader program described later in this appendix.
- **WebPage.pdf:** Bonus unit for this book (Unit WP, "Creating Your Own Web Pages") that teaches you how to communicate with the tens of millions of people who surf the Net by using the FrontPage Express program to compose and publish your own Web pages. Read this document using the Acrobat Reader program described later in this appendix.
- **+Hy's and Margy's Favorites+:** A folder crammed with over 200 Internet Explorer favorites pointing to the very best sites on the World Wide Web. To install this folder, follow the instructions in Lesson 2-1.
- **Leo.jpg:** Self-portrait of Leonardo da Vinci that you use in Lessons 6-3 and 6-4 to learn how to send and receive attached files by e-mail.
- **Fern.gif:** Picture of a fern that you use to help construct a personal Web page in Lesson WP-3 (in document file WebPage.pdf on the CD).
- **Mounts.gif:** Picture of mountains that you use to help construct a personal Web page in Lesson WP-3 (in document file WebPage.pdf on the CD).
- **Rainbow.gif:** Picture of a rainbow that you use to help construct a personal Web page in Lesson WP-3 (in document file WebPage.pdf on the CD).

We hope you enjoy these files!

System Requirements

The following are the minimum requirements needed to run the software on this book's CD:

- A PC that runs Windows 98
- At least 8MB of RAM (though 16MB or more is recommended)
- A 14,400 bps or faster modem (to connect to the Internet)

- A CD-ROM drive (for obvious reasons)
- At least 50MB of available hard disk space *after* installation (primarily for Internet Explorer, which creates a lot of temporary files while it's running)

In addition, if you need some help with the basic operation of your computer, you might want to explore a book such as *Dummies 101: Windows 98* by Andy Rathbone (published by IDG Books Worldwide, Inc.)

Installing the Programs

Before you can use the programs on your *Dummies 101* CD, you need to install them on your hard disk. Follow these steps to run and use the CD's Installer program:

1. **Insert the *Dummies 101* CD into your computer's CD-ROM drive.**

   Be careful to touch only the edges of the CD and to insert the disc with its label side up.

2. **Click the Windows 98 Start button (located in the lower-left corner of your screen) and locate the Run option.**

   If you don't see the Run option, place your mouse pointer on the small down-pointing arrow at the bottom edge of the menu until the menu scrolls up sufficiently to display the Run command.

3. **Click the Run option.**

   A Run dialog box appears that lets you type the name of a program you want to run. If a program name already appears highlighted in the box, ignore it; the text will be replaced as soon as you begin typing.

4. **Type** d:\setup **— that is, the letter d, a colon (:), a backslash (\), and the program name** setup**.**

   If your CD-ROM player isn't at D:, type the letter appropriate for your drive. (If you're not sure what letter to type, see the "If you don't know the letter of your computer's CD-ROM drive" paragraph that appears at the end of this exercise.)

5. **Press Enter or click OK.**

   The Run dialog box closes, and the CD's Installer program launches.

   If this is the first time you're running the Installer, an IDG Books Worldwide, Inc. license agreement is displayed. This is the only time you'll see this document.

6. **Read (or at least skim) the license agreement to make sure that you're comfortable with its terms. When you're ready, click the Accept button.**

If you don't click Accept, you can't use the Installer program. After you click, a message tells you that the CD program is about to be launched.

7 **Click OK.**

After a few seconds, an opening screen appears with two options, Install Favorites Folder and Choose Software. The first option, which installs pointers to over 200 of our favorite sites on the Web, is covered in detail in Lesson 2-1. To install programs, however, choose the second option.

8 **Click the Choose Software option.**

You see a menu consisting of four software categories: Getting Connected (for programs that connect you to the Net); Cruising the Web (for programs that let you interact with the Web); Sending Messages (for programs that let you interact with others on the Net); and Working Offline (for programs that help you work with files you've downloaded from the Net).

9 **Click a category you're interested in.**

A submenu displays the particular programs grouped under the category you selected.

10 **Click a program you're interested in.**

A description of the program appears. Read the description carefully, because it may include steps you need to follow to install and run the program properly.

11 **Click the Continue button in the lower-left section of the window if you want the program to be installed on your hard disk.**

Alternatively, click the Cancel button in the lower-right section of the window to return to the previous menu, and then skip to Step 13.

After you click the Continue button, installation for the program you selected begins.

12 **Follow the prompts that appear on your screen to complete the installation of the program.**

When the installation is finished, you return to the submenu of programs in the last category you selected.

13 **Return to Step 10 to explore another program on the submenu or click the Go Back button to return to the menu of software categories.**

Continue clicking program names until you're done exploring and installing all the programs in which you're currently interested.

14 **When you're finished installing all the programs you currently want, click the Exit button in the lower-right corner of the Installer window, and click the Yes button on the left to confirm you're done.**

The Installer program closes. You can now start using the new software you've installed on your hard disk!

Notes:

Notes:

If you don't know the letter of your computer's CD-ROM drive: Most PCs assign the letter D to a CD-ROM drive. To find out which letter your CD-ROM drive uses, double-click the My Computer icon on your Windows 98 desktop. A window appears that lists all your drives, including your CD-ROM drive (which is usually represented by a shiny disc icon), and shows you the letter of each drive. When you're done examining the My Computer display, exit by clicking the window's Close button in its upper-right corner.

To examine the *Dummies 101* CD's contents: You can use the *Dummies 101* Installer program to install all the software on your CD. However, if you're simply curious about the CD, you can examine its contents after you exit the Installer by opening a Windows Explorer window and double-clicking the CD's icon.

CD Program Descriptions

The following are descriptions of the programs on your *Dummies 101* CD, listed in alphabetical order. Each description tells you the program's version number, the program's publisher, and whether the program is freeware or shareware. In addition, each description tells you how to install the program, run the program, and obtain more information about the program.

Note: If we tell you to choose File⇨Save, this means that you should click File from your program's menu bar to display a list of options and then click the Save option. Similarly, if we tell you to click the Start button and choose Programs⇨Folder Name⇨Program Name, this means that you should click the Start button in the lower-left corner of your screen, click the Programs option from the first menu that appears, click the Folder Name option from the second menu that appears, and click the Program Name option from the third menu that appears.

Acrobat Reader

Acrobat Reader 3.01 from Adobe Systems is a free program that lets you view and print portable document format, or *pdf*, files. The PDF format is used by many programs that you'll find on the Internet for storing documentation because it supports the use of such stylish elements as assorted fonts and colorful graphics, in contrast to the standard plain text format that doesn't allow for any special effects in a document.

For example, your *Dummies 101* CD contains two bonus units for this book that tell you how to participate in Internet mailing lists (Unit ML in file MailList.pdf) and create your own Web pages (Unit WP in file WebPage.pdf). These documents are pdf files, and they require you to use the Acrobat Reader program to view or print them.

Installing Acrobat Reader

To install Acrobat Reader, do the following:

1. **Follow Steps 1 through 8 of this appendix's "Installing the Programs" section.**

   You see the software categories menu.

2. **Click the Working Offline category, click the Acrobat Reader option, read the installation information that appears, and then click the Continue button.**

   The Acrobat Reader installation program is launched.

3. **Click the Yes button to confirm installation.**

   After some initial data copying, the Adobe Acrobat 3.01 Setup screen appears.

4. **Click the Next button.**

   A license agreement appears.

5. **Read or skim the agreement, and then click the Yes button to accept it.**

   You're told that the software will be installed in a default folder (typically, C:\Acrobat3\Reader). If you're comfortable with this folder name and location, skip to Step 7.

6. **Click the Browse button, and use the Choose Directory dialog box that appears to select a different drive and/or folder name to store the software. When you're done, click the OK button.**

   The name of the folder you selected is displayed in the dialog box.

7. **Click the Next button.**

   The software is copied to your hard disk. When the installation is completed, a dialog box appears.

8. **Click the Finish button.**

   A text file shows you last-minute technical notes about the program.

9. **Skim the document for anything that might apply to your particular PC, and then exit the WordPad file and click the OK button that appears.**

   The installation is completed, and you're returned to the *Dummies 101* Installer program.

You can now run Acrobat Reader at any time by clicking the Start button in the lower-left corner of your screen, clicking Programs from the menu that appears, clicking Adobe Acrobat from the second menu that appears, and clicking Acrobat Reader 3.01 from the third menu that appears.

Reading documents with Acrobat Reader

After you run Acrobat Reader, follow these steps to use it:

1. **Choose File⇨Open (that is, click the File menu and then click the Open option).**

   A dialog box prompts you to select the pdf file that you want to view.

2. **Use the dialog box to select the drive and folder that contain the file you want.**

   For example, to access the bonus units on this book's CD, click in the top Look in box to display a list of your drives and then click the shiny disc icon that represents your CD-ROM drive.

3. **Scroll through the list of pdf files until the one you want is listed; then double-click the file's name.**

   For example, if you want to view Unit ML, "Joining Discussions by E-Mail," double-click MailList.pdf; or if you want to view Unit WP, "Creating Your Own Web Pages," double-click WebPage.pdf. After you've double-clicked the name of your desired file, the document appears in the Acrobat Reader window.

   Notice that several VCR-like buttons appear on the window's toolbar near the top of the window. The eighth and ninth buttons that look like single arrowheads are named Next Page and Previous Page, and you can use them to move to the following or preceding page.

4. **Click Next Page (the eighth button on the toolbar) a few times to display different pages in your current document; then click Previous Page (the ninth button on the toolbar) a few times to go back.**

   Acrobat Reader's Next Page button

   Acrobat Reader's Previous Page button

   Using these buttons is similar to clicking the Forward and Back buttons in an Internet Explorer or Windows Explorer window.

   Also notice the seventh and tenth buttons on the toolbar, which look like single arrowheads pointing to a vertical line. These are named the First Page and Last Page buttons, and you can use them to jump to the beginning or end of a document.

5. **Click Last Page (the tenth button on the toolbar) to view the last page in your current document; then click First Page (the seventh button on the toolbar) to jump back to the beginning.**

   Acrobat Reader provides a number of other ways to navigate a document, as well. To read about them, you can press F1 to display the Online Guide, click the Viewing PDF documents option, and click the Navigating pages option. When you're done reading, return to your previous document by clicking the Window menu and then clicking your document's name.

6. **If you want to print the document you're viewing (which we recommend for long documents), make sure that your printer is on and has paper in its paper tray, choose File⇨Print, and click OK.**

   The document is printed, making it easier to read.

7. **If you want to open additional documents, repeat Steps 1 through 3.**

   Each document opens in its own window. You can switch to any document by clicking the window it's in, or by clicking the Window menu and then clicking the name of the file you want (which is listed near the bottom of the menu).

8 When you're done using Acrobat Reader, choose File⇨Exit.

All your PDF documents close, and then the Acrobat Reader program exits.

Getting more information about Acrobat Reader

To learn more about using Acrobat Reader, choose Help⇨Reader Online Guide from the program's menu bar, or press F1 to display the Online Guide. You can also get more information by visiting the Adobe Systems Web site at www.adobe.com.

Eudora Light

Eudora Light 3.0.5 from Qualcomm, Inc. is a free but powerful version of the commercial electronic mail program Eurdora Pro. If you're not entirely satisfied with the Outlook Express program covered in Units 5 and 6, or if you'd simply like to see another approach to e-mail, Eudora Light is an excellent choice.

To install Eudora Light, follow Steps 1 through 8 of this appendix's "Installing the Programs" section. When you see the software categories menu, click the Sending Messages category, click the Eudora Light option, click the Continue button to start the installation, and follow the prompts that appear on your screen to complete the installation.

To run Eudora Light, click the Start button in the lower-left corner of your screen and choose Programs⇨Eudora Light⇨Eudora Light from the menus that appear.

For more information about e-mail, see Units 5 and 6. To learn more about Eudora Light, read the program's manual (which is stored in a pdf file in the Eudora Light folder of the CD) using the Acrobat Reader program described earlier in this appendix. You can also learn more by selecting options from Eudora Light's Help menu and by visiting the program's Web site at www.eudora.com.

Free Agent

Free Agent 1.11 from Forté, Inc. is a free program that lets you read and participate in ongoing group discussions that take place over the Internet via Usenet newsgroups. There are tens of thousands of newsgroups devoted to virtually every topic under the sun, ranging from knitting to high finance and from decoding DNA to dating, and Free Agent is one of the best programs available for accessing them. If you aren't entirely satisfied with the Outlook Express program covered in Unit 7, or if you'd simply like to explore different approaches to reading newsgroups, Free Agent is an excellent choice.

To install Free Agent, follow Steps 1 through 8 of this appendix's "Installing the Programs" section. When you see the software categories menu, click the Sending Messages category, click the Free Agent option, click the Continue button to start the installation, and follow the prompts that appear on your screen to complete the installation.

Notes:

Notes:

To run Free Agent, click the Start button in the lower-left corner of your screen and choose Programs⇨Forté Agent⇨Agent from the menus that appear.

The first time you launch Free Agent, the program asks you to supply basic setup information, such as the name of your newsgroup server (NNTP), outgoing mail server (SMTP), and e-mail address. If you aren't sure what to enter, see Lesson 5-1, "Telling Outlook Express How to Get Your Mail."

For more information about Usenet newsgroups, see Unit 7. To learn how to use Free Agent, choose Help⇨Contents from the program's menu bar to launch its online manual. You can also visit Free Agent's Web site at `www.forteinc.com` to find out more about both Free Agent and its more capable commercial version, which is named Agent.

FrontPage Express

FrontPage Express 2.0 from Microsoft Corporation is a free page composition program that helps you create your own Web pages; it's typically bundled in with Internet Explorer. If you don't already have FrontPage Express, you can install it by first following Steps 1 through 8 of this appendix's "Installing the Programs" section. When you see the software categories menu, click the Cruising the Web category, click the Internet Explorer option, click the Continue button to start the installation, and follow the prompts that appear on your screen. When you're asked whether you want to perform a Minimal, Standard, or Full installation, be sure to select Full, since this is the only option that installs FrontPage Express along with Internet Explorer. Finally, continue following the prompts to complete the installation.

To run FrontPage Express, click the Start button in the lower-left corner of your screen and choose Programs⇨Internet Explorer⇨FrontPage Express from the menus that appear.

For extensive information about using FrontPage Express, see Unit WP (which is stored on the CD in document file WebPage.pdf). You can also learn more by visiting the Internet Explorer Web site at `www.microsoft.com/ie`.

GetRight

GetRight 3.1 from HeadLight Software is an extremely useful shareware program that helps you copy, or *download,* files from the Net efficiently.

The need for GetRight may not be immediately obvious, since downloading files is a straightforward procedure — you click a download link that displays a Save As dialog box, and you use the dialog box to specify a folder on your hard disk for storing the file. After you do so and click the Save button, the file is copied from the Web to your PC. (For more information, see Lesson 3-2.)

The problem is that big files take a long time to download, and Internet connections often aren't reliable. For example, you might spend an hour downloading 95 percent of a large file and then accidentally get disconnected.

If this happens, the hour will have been wasted, because you'll have to start the download again from scratch. Worse, you'll have to risk the same thing happening all over again, which is extremely frustrating.

To avoid such problems, run GetRight and then click and drag each download link to the GetRight Monitor box. GetRight takes control of the downloading and saves special information about each file. If you then get disconnected, simply dial back into the Net and click GetRight's Resume button; GetRight will magically pick up the downloading from where it left off!

One caveat is that GetRight can perform this trick only for those sites that support its "resume" feature; but most modern sites do. And even for sites that don't support it, GetRight saves you a little time by letting you restart the download with a mouse click instead of forcing you to find the download link again and select a folder again.

To install GetRight, follow Steps 1 through 8 of this appendix's "Installing the Programs" section. When you see the software categories menu, click the Cruising the Web category, click the GetRight option, click the Continue button to start the installation, and follow the prompts that appear on your screen to complete the installation.

To run GetRight, click the Start button in the lower-left corner of your screen and choose Programs➪GetRight➪GetRight Monitor from the menus that appear.

For additional information on downloading files, see Lesson 3-2. To find out more about using GetRight, click the button in the upper-left corner of the program's title bar and then click the Help option from the menu that appears. Also, visit the program's Web site at `www.headlightsw.com`.

Internet Explorer

Internet Explorer 4.0 from Microsoft Corporation is a free Web browser that lets you cruise the World Wide Web. Internet Explorer is typically bundled in with Windows 98, but if you don't already have the program, you can install it by first following Steps 1 through 8 of this appendix's "Installing the Programs" section. When you see the software categories menu, click the Cruising the Web category, click the Internet Explorer option, click the Continue button to start the installation, and follow the prompts that appear on your screen.

heads up

If a message appears saying that a version of Internet Explorer has been detected on your hard disk that's newer than the version on the CD, then you already have a recent copy of Internet Explorer installed. In this case, do *not* install the version on the CD. Instead, click the No button on the message dialog box to cancel the installation.

If you don't already have Internet Explorer, however, continue following the prompts that appear on your screen. When you're asked whether you want to perform a Minimal, Standard, or Full installation, be sure to select Full, since this is the only option that installs Outlook Express and FrontPage Express along with Internet Explorer. Finally, keep following the prompts to complete the installation.

Notes:

To run Internet Explorer, simply click the blue "e" button that appears on your Windows 98 taskbar (that is, the button next to the Start button in the lower-left corner of your screen). Alternatively, click the Start button and choose Programs⇨Internet Explorer⇨Internet Explorer from the menus that appear.

For extensive information about using Internet Explorer, see Units 1, 2, 3, and 4. You can also learn more by visiting the program's Web site at www.microsoft.com/ie.

MindSpring

MindSpring Internet Access is a free program you can use to sign up for an Internet account with MindSpring Enterprises, a top-rated Internet service provider, or *ISP*. For a monthly charge, MindSpring supplies you with an Internet e-mail account and full access to all Internet features. MindSpring also provides free technical support via an 800 number that's available 24 hours a day, seven days a week.

To launch the MindSpring sign-up kit, follow Steps 1 through 8 of this appendix's "Installing the Programs" section. When you see the software categories menu, click the Getting Connected category, click the MindSpring option, click the Continue button to start the installation, and follow the prompts that appear on your screen to complete the installation.

To learn more about MindSpring, see Lesson 1-1, and visit the ISP's Web site at www.mindspring.com.

mIRC

mIRC 5.31 is an excellent shareware program from software author Khaled Mardam-Bey. It lets you participate in Internet Relay Chat, or *IRC*, a world-wide system that enables you to receive messages over the Internet within seconds of when other people type them, and vice versa.

Thousands of folks use this Internet feature at a time so, to prevent total chaos, IRC is divided into groups of people, or *channels*. When you participate in a discussion, you see the messages from everyone in your channel, and they all see your messages. It's like having a global party line on your screen.

Each channel has a name that starts with a "#." For example, if a bunch of readers of *...For Dummies* and *Dummies 101* books wanted to get together and chat online, they might create a channel called #dummies. (In fact, the authors and readers of various *...For Dummies* and *Dummies 101* books are sometimes online in that very channel.) Any user can create a channel, and many do, so you get some funky (not to mention downright lewd) channels.

To pass along all the messages and keep track of who is in what channel, dozens of *IRC server* programs run on large computers on the Internet. To use IRC, you connect to an IRC server, look at a list of the channels available on that server, and choose one or two (or more) to join. Not all channels are available on all servers, so you may use some IRC servers more than others based on which channels you like to join.

You can join more than one channel at a time. To do so, simply join one channel, display the Channels folder again, and join another channel. Each channel appears in its own window. Adjust the sizes of the windows so that you can follow the conversations in each channel.

You can do lots of other things using IRC. For example, a system called DCC allows two people to communicate directly rather than as part of a channel. DCC is like two people sneaking off into another room (or, more likely, into a dark closet). You can chat using DCC, and you can even exchange files.

If you're looking for interesting IRC channels to join, try reading the `alt.irc` newsgroup; or ask others in any newsgroups or mailing lists that you participate in whether there are IRC channels devoted to topics that interest you.

Warning: In addition to the interesting, nice people on IRC, some sickos are out there too. Maybe they're just bored, lonely college sophomores — we don't know. But if someone offers to send you a picture, turn him or her down unless you're prepared for something that's likely to be pretty raunchy.

Another warning: If someone asks you to type a string of characters that you don't understand, don't do it! Using IRC commands, it's possible for another user to take over your IRC program and find out what your Internet password is. But doing so requires *you* to type some commands. We won't tell you the exact commands not to type (for obvious reasons, and because we don't know them ourselves), but don't type anything just because some IRCer tells you to!

To connect to IRC, first install mIRC by following Steps 1 through 8 of this appendix's "Installing the Programs" section. When you see the software categories menu, click the Sending Messages category, click the mIRC option, click the Continue button to start the installation, and follow the prompts that appear on your screen to complete the installation.

To run mIRC, click the Start button in the lower-left corner of your screen and choose Programs⇨mIRC v5.31⇨mIRC from the menus that appear.

To learn more about IRC, click the Start button and choose Programs⇨mIRC v5.31⇨IRC Intro from the menus that appear. To learn how to use mIRC, click the program's More info button on the first window that appears; and obtain further information after you're past the opening window by pressing F1, clicking a Help button that looks like a life preserver, or choosing Help⇨Contents. For additional facts about mIRC, visit its home page at `www.mirc.co.uk`.

Netscape Communicator

Netscape Communicator 4.05 from Netscape Communications, Inc. is an extraordinarily popular shareware browser that lets you cruise the World Wide Web, send and receive e-mail, and participate in newsgroups. If you're not entirely satisfied with the Internet Explorer and Outlook Express programs covered in Units 1 through 7, or if you'd simply like to try another approach to exploiting the Internet, Netscape Communicator is a superb choice.

Notes:

To install Netscape Communicator, follow Steps 1 through 8 of this appendix's "Installing the Programs" section. When you see the software categories menu, click the Cruising the Web category, click the Netscape Communicator option, click the Continue button to start the installation, and follow the prompts that appear on your screen to complete the installation.

To run Netscape Communicator, double-click the program's icon on your Windows 98 desktop. Alternatively, click the Start button in the lower-left corner of your screen and choose Programs⇨Netscape Communicator⇨ Netscape Navigator from the menus that appear.

For more information about browsing the Web, see Units 1, 2, 3, and 4. To learn more about Netscape Communicator, choose Help⇨Help Contents from the program's menu bar, or press F1; and visit the program's Web site at `home.netscape.com`.

Outlook Express

Outlook Express 4.7 from Microsoft Corporation is a free electronic mail program that's typically bundled in with Internet Explorer. If you don't already have Outlook Express, you can install it by first following Steps 1 through 8 of this appendix's "Installing the Programs" section. When you see the software categories menu, click the Cruising the Web category, click the Internet Explorer option, click the Continue button to start the installation, and follow the prompts that appear on your screen. When you're asked whether you want to perform a Minimal, Standard, or Full installation, be sure to select Full, since this is the only option that installs Outlook Express along with Internet Explorer. Finally, continue following the prompts to complete the installation.

To run Outlook Express, click the Start button in the lower-left corner of your screen and choose Programs⇨Internet Explorer⇨Outlook Express from the menus that appear.

For extensive information about using Outlook Express, see Units 5 and 6. You can also learn more by visiting the Internet Explorer Web site at `www.microsoft.com/ie`.

Paint Shop Pro

Paint Shop Pro 4.14 from JASC, Inc. is a superb shareware graphics program. Paint Shop Pro lets you view images in virtually any graphics format you're likely to encounter on the Internet. In addition, it lets you edit and crop images, convert images from one file format to another, and even create pictures from scratch, which are all useful features for creating your own World Wide Web pages.

To install Paint Shop Pro, follow Steps 1 through 8 of this appendix's "Installing the Programs" section. When you see the software categories menu, click the Working Offline category, click the Paint Shop Pro option, click the Continue button to start the installation, and follow the prompts that appear on your screen to complete the installation.

To run Paint Shop Pro, click the Start button in the lower-left corner of your screen and choose Programs⇨Paint Shop Pro⇨Paint Shop Pro 4 from the menus that appear.

To learn about how Paint Shop Pro can help you create Web pages, see Unit WP (which is stored on the CD in document file WebPage.pdf). For information on how to use Paint Shop Pro, click the floating question mark icon on the program's toolbar, or choose Help⇨Help Topics from the program's menu bar. Also, visit the program's Web site at `www.jasc.com/psp.html`.

ThunderBYTE Anti-Virus

ThunderBYTE Anti-Virus version 8.05 is a shareware utility from Authentex/NovaStor that detects a nasty type of program known as a *virus*. Defined broadly, a *virus* is a program — typically hidden inside another, benign program — that's created to deliberately wreak havoc with computers by destroying their data.

The odds of encountering a virus are low, but it's a good idea to play it safe by scanning any program you're about to run for the first time using a tool such as ThunderBYTE. We also recommend that you at least occasionally scan your entire hard disk for viruses. If you detect a virus, you can also use ThunderBYTE to eliminate it.

To install ThunderBYTE Anti-Virus, follow Steps 1 through 8 of this appendix's "Installing the Programs" section. When you see the software categories menu, click the Working Offline category, click the ThunderBYTE Anti-Virus option, click the Continue button to start the installation, and follow the prompts that appear on your screen to complete the installation.

To run ThunderBYTE Anti-Virus, click the Start button in the lower-left corner of your screen and choose Programs⇨TBAV for Windows 95⇨TBAV for Windows 95 from the menus that appear.

For additional information on viruses, see Lesson 3-2. To learn more about using ThunderBYTE Anti-Virus, choose Help⇨Help Index from the program's menu bar, and visit the program's Web site at `www.thunderbyte.com`.

WinZip

WinZip 6.3 from Nico Mak Computing is an invaluable file compression/decompression shareware utility. Many files you'll find on the Internet are *compressed* — that is, shrunken in size via special programming tricks — both to save disk storage space and to cut down on the amount of time they require to be downloaded. In addition, WinZip allows a collection of different files to be packed together into a single zip file, allowing you to download an entire software package (complete with installation files, program files, and document files) in one step. Even if you aren't interested in downloading files from the Web, you may occasionally receive compressed files as e-mail attachments. After you have a compressed file on your hard disk, you can use WinZip to decompress it and make it useable again.

Notes:

To install WinZip, follow Steps 1 through 8 of this appendix's "Installing the Programs" section. When you see the software categories menu, click the Working Offline category, click the WinZip option, click the Continue button to start the installation, and follow the prompts that appear on your screen to complete the installation. (***Tip:*** When you're asked whether you want the program to operate in WinZip Wizard or WinZip Classic mode, we recommend you choose WinZip Classic, which we consider easier to use.)

To run WinZip, simply double-click a file you want to work with that's been zipped (that is, that's been compressed and has a name ending with the letters *zip*). WinZip automatically launches itself and then displays the contents of the file.

Alternatively, run WinZip by clicking the Start button in the lower-left corner of your screen and choosing Programs⇨WinZip⇨WinZip 6.3 32-bit from the menus that appear. You can then load a zipped file by clicking the WinZip window's Open button (or by choosing File⇨Open Archive), selecting the file you want via the dialog box that appears, and clicking the box's Open button.

After you've loaded a zipped file, its contents are displayed in the WinZip window. These contents may consist of dozens of different files. To decompress them, follow these steps:

1. **Click the Extract button near the top of the WinZip window.**

   An Extract dialog box appears. If you want to decompress the entire contents of your zip file (as opposed to only selected files), make sure that a bullet appears to the left of the All files option.

2. **Use the Folders/Drives box to select a folder for storing the decompressed file(s).**

   If your zip file contains the installation files of a program, choose an empty folder for storing these temporary files. If you don't already have such a folder, you can create one now by opening a Windows Explorer window, choosing File⇨New⇨Folder, and naming the folder something like Temp.

3. **Click the dialog box's Extract button.**

   The contents of your zip file are decompressed and copied to the folder that you selected.

4. **Switch to the folder you selected to work with the decompressed file(s).**

   If the contents of your zip file were data files or complete program files, then you can now simply go ahead and use them.

   If the contents were installation files, however, you must take the extra step of running an installation program before you can use the software that you've downloaded. In this case, look for a file named Setup.exe or Install.exe; double-click the file; and follow the prompts that appear on your screen to complete the installation.

   Alternatively, if you aren't sure what to do, or if you run into trouble, double-click a text file named something like Readme.txt or Read1st.txt to read notes about the program's installation requirements, and then follow the instructions to perform the installation.

Finally, if you've managed to install and run the program but are still confused, try pressing F1 or clicking a Help menu option, and then look up your question using the online help system that appears.

5. **Optionally delete your original zip file to free up disk space. If you unzipped temporary installation files, delete them as well after you've completed the installation.**

   You're all set!

For additional information on WinZip, see Lesson 3-2. To find out more about how to use the program, choose Help⇨Contents from the program's menu bar, or press F1; and visit the program's Web site at www.winzip.com.

WS_FTP LE

WS_FTP LE 4.6 from Ipswitch, Inc. is a free (for noncommercial use) Windows File Transfer Protocol, or *FTP*, program that you can employ to find files on the Net, and to copy files between your PC and a computer on the Net. FTP programs were more useful before the World Wide Web took hold and made finding and downloading files a snap. However, FTP programs are still handy for more complex activities, such as uploading files to be used by your own Web pages.

To install WS_FTP LE, follow Steps 1 through 8 of this appendix's "Installing the Programs" section. When you see the software categories menu, click the Cruising the Web category, click the WS_FTP LE option, click the Continue button to start the installation, and follow the prompts that appear on your screen to complete the installation.

To run WS_FTP LE, click the Start button in the lower-left corner of your screen and choose Programs⇨WS_FTP⇨WS_FTP95 LE from the menus that appear.

For more information about downloading and uploading files, see Lesson 3-2; and for more information about publishing Web pages, see Unit WP (which is stored on the CD in document file WebPage.pdf). To get details about using WS_FTP LE, click the Help button from the Session Properties dialog box or the program's main window. You can also visit WS_FTP LE's Web site at www.ipswitch.com. (Portions of this software Copyright 1991-97, Ipswitch, Inc.)

Removing Programs

Just because you install a program doesn't mean that you want to keep it forever. For example, you may decide that a program you've installed isn't very useful — or just isn't as good as another program you recently discovered that does the same thing. Even if you have no problems with the program, you may eventually want to remove, or *uninstall,* it so that you can install a new and improved version of it.

Notes:

Many programs include some sort of uninstall feature. Therefore, first try one of the following approaches:

- Click the Start button in the lower-left corner of your screen and click Programs to display a list of software. Click the name of the software you want to remove, and then look for a program named something like Uninstall or Remove. If you see such a program, click it to run it and then follow the on-screen prompts to remove the software.
- Open a Windows Explorer window, locate and double-click the folder of the software you want to remove, and look for a program in the folder named something like Uninstall or Remove. If you see such a program, double-click it to run it and then follow the on-screen prompts to remove the software.
- Click the Start button in the lower-left corner of your screen, click Settings from the menu that appears, and click Control Panel from the second menu that appears to open a Control Panel folder. Double-click an icon in this folder named Add/Remove Programs to display a list of software you can uninstall, and then scroll through the alphabetical list. If you see the name of the program you want to delete, click it to select it, click the Add/Remove button, and then follow the on-screen prompts to remove the software.

If none of those suggestions work, and if you're certain the program's files don't affect anything on your PC other than the program itself, simply locate and manually delete the program's folder. For example, open a Windows Explorer window to locate the folder, right-click the folder (that is, click it with your *right* mouse button), click the Delete option from the menu that appears, and (if necessary) click a Yes button to confirm the deletion.

Note: Always think twice before deleting to ensure that you don't mistakenly erase an item you want to keep. Also, never delete a file or folder unless you know exactly what you're doing. If you have any doubts, create a temporary folder named Trash or Junk, and *move* the items you want to eliminate into this folder; if no problems occur over the next month as a result of the move, delete the folder's contents.

If You've Got Problems (Of the CD Kind)

If a program you've installed from the CD doesn't work, the two likeliest reasons are that your PC doesn't have enough memory (RAM) for that particular program, or you have other programs running that are affecting the installation or running of the program. If you see error messages such as `Not enough memory` or `Setup cannot continue`, try one or more of these suggestions, and then try installing or launching the program again:

- **Turn off any anti-virus software you have running.** Installers sometimes mimic virus activity and may make your PC incorrectly believe that it is being infected by a virus.

- **Close all other programs you have running.** The more programs you're running, the less memory is available to other programs. Other programs may also confuse the installation program.
- **Add more RAM to your computer.** You can have this done by your local computer store. More memory can both significantly boost the speed of your PC and allow you to run more programs at the same time.

If you still have trouble with installing the items from the CD, please call the IDG Books Worldwide Customer Service phone number: 800-762-2974 (outside the U.S.: 317-596-5430).

A Final Reminder about Shareware

Some programs on the *Dummies 101* CD are free, but most of them are shareware. As we mentioned near the beginning of this appendix, shareware programs are available to you for an evaluation period, after which you're expected to either stop using them or pay for them. Sending a registration fee to a shareware publisher typically entitles you to technical support and notifications about new versions . . . and it also makes you feel good. Most shareware operates on an honor system, but it's just plain sensible to support the shareware concept and encourage the continued production of quality low-cost software by sending in your payment for the programs you use. You can typically get information about where to send your payment for a shareware program by checking its online help and/or by visiting its Web site. When you do, tell them that Hy and Margy sent you!

Index

Symbol

A

B

C

D

E

(continued)

F

G

H

I

K

L

M

(continued)

P

Q

R

S

IDG Books Worldwide, Inc., End-User License Agreement

READ THIS. You should carefully read these terms and conditions before opening the software packet(s) included with this book ("Book"). This is a license agreement ("Agreement") between you and IDG Books Worldwide, Inc. ("IDGB"). By opening the accompanying software packet(s), you acknowledge that you have read and accept the following terms and conditions. If you do not agree and do not want to be bound by such terms and conditions, promptly return the Book and the unopened software packet(s) to the place you obtained them for a full refund.

1. **License Grant.** IDGB grants to you (either an individual or entity) a nonexclusive license to use one copy of the enclosed software program(s) (collectively, the "Software") solely for your own personal or business purposes on a single computer (whether a standard computer or a workstation component of a multiuser network). The Software is in use on a computer when it is loaded into temporary memory (RAM) or installed into permanent memory (hard disk, CD-ROM, or other storage device). IDGB reserves all rights not expressly granted herein.

2. **Ownership.** IDGB is the owner of all right, title, and interest, including copyright, in and to the compilation of the Software recorded on the disk(s) or CD-ROM ("Software Media"). Copyright to the individual programs recorded on the Software Media is owned by the author or other authorized copyright owner of each program. Ownership of the Software and all proprietary rights relating thereto remain with IDGB and its licensers.

3. **Restrictions on Use and Transfer.**

   (a) You may only (i) make one copy of the Software for backup or archival purposes, or (ii) transfer the Software to a single hard disk, provided that you keep the original for backup or archival purposes. You may not (i) rent or lease the Software, (ii) copy or reproduce the Software through a LAN or other network system or through any computer subscriber system or bulletin-board system, or (iii) modify, adapt, or create derivative works based on the Software.

   (b) You may not reverse engineer, decompile, or disassemble the Software. You may transfer the Software and user documentation on a permanent basis, provided that the transferee agrees to accept the terms and conditions of this Agreement and you retain no copies. If the Software is an update or has been updated, any transfer must include the most recent update and all prior versions.

4. **Restrictions on Use of Individual Programs.** You must follow the individual requirements and restrictions detailed for each individual program in Appendix B of this Book. These limitations are also contained in the individual license agreements recorded on the Software Media. These limitations may include a requirement that after using the program for a specified period of time, the user must pay a registration fee or discontinue use. By opening the Software packet(s), you will be agreeing to abide by the licenses and restrictions for these individual programs that are detailed in Appendix B and on the Software Media. None of the material on this Software Media or listed in this Book may ever be redistributed, in original or modified form, for commercial purposes.

5. **Limited Warranty.**

   (a) IDGB warrants that the Software and Software Media are free from defects in materials and workmanship under normal use for a period of sixty (60) days from the date of purchase of this Book. If IDGB receives notification within the warranty period of defects in materials or workmanship, IDGB will replace the defective Software Media.

   (b) IDGB AND THE AUTHOR OF THE BOOK DISCLAIM ALL OTHER WARRANTIES, EXPRESS OR IMPLIED, INCLUDING WITHOUT LIMITATION IMPLIED WARRANTIES OF MERCHANTABILITY AND FITNESS FOR A PARTICULAR PURPOSE, WITH RESPECT TO THE SOFTWARE, THE PROGRAMS, THE SOURCE CODE CONTAINED THEREIN, AND/OR THE TECHNIQUES DESCRIBED IN THIS BOOK. IDGB DOES NOT WARRANT THAT THE FUNCTIONS CONTAINED IN THE SOFTWARE WILL MEET YOUR REQUIREMENTS OR THAT THE OPERATION OF THE SOFTWARE WILL BE ERROR FREE.

   (c) This limited warranty gives you specific legal rights, and you may have other rights that vary from jurisdiction to jurisdiction.

6. **Remedies.**

   (a) IDGB's entire liability and your exclusive remedy for defects in materials and workmanship shall be limited to replacement of the Software Media, which may be returned to IDGB with a copy of your receipt at the following address: Software Media Fulfillment Department, Attn.: *Dummies 101: The Internet For Windows 98,* IDG Books Worldwide, Inc., 7260 Shadeland Station, Ste. 100, Indianapolis, IN 46256, or call 800-762-2974. Please allow three to four weeks for delivery. This Limited Warranty is void if failure of the Software Media has resulted from accident, abuse, or misapplication. Any replacement Software Media will be warranted for the remainder of the original warranty period or thirty (30) days, whichever is longer.

   (b) In no event shall IDGB or the author be liable for any damages whatsoever (including without limitation damages for loss of business profits, business interruption, loss of business information, or any other pecuniary loss) arising from the use of or inability to use the Book or the Software, even if IDGB has been advised of the possibility of such damages.

   (c) Because some jurisdictions do not allow the exclusion or limitation of liability for consequential or incidental damages, the above limitation or exclusion may not apply to you.

7. **U.S. Government Restricted Rights.** Use, duplication, or disclosure of the Software by the U.S. Government is subject to restrictions stated in paragraph (c)(1)(ii) of the Rights in Technical Data and Computer Software clause of DFARS 252.227-7013, and in subparagraphs (a) through (d) of the Commercial Computer–Restricted Rights clause at FAR 52.227-19, and in similar clauses in the NASA FAR supplement, when applicable.

8. **General.** This Agreement constitutes the entire understanding of the parties and revokes and supersedes all prior agreements, oral or written, between them and may not be modified or amended except in a writing signed by both parties hereto that specifically refers to this Agreement. This Agreement shall take precedence over any other documents that may be in conflict herewith. If any one or more provisions contained in this Agreement are held by any court or tribunal to be invalid, illegal, or otherwise unenforceable, each and every other provision shall remain in full force and effect.

Dummies 101 CD Installation Instructions

Before you can use the programs on your *Dummies 101* CD, you need to install them on your hard disk. Follow these steps to run and use the CD's Installer program:

1. **Insert the *Dummies 101* CD into your computer's CD-ROM drive.**

   Be careful to touch only the edges of the CD and to insert the disc with its label side up.

2. **Click the Windows 98 Start button (located in the lower-left corner of your screen) and locate the Run option.**

   If you don't immediately see the Run option (which is near the bottom of the Start menu), place your mouse pointer on the small black arrow located near the bottom edge of the menu until the menu scrolls up sufficiently to display the Run command.

3. **Click the Run option.**

   A Run dialog box appears that lets you type the name of a program you want to run. If a program name already appears highlighted in the box, ignore it; the text will be replaced as soon as you begin typing.

4. **Type** d:\setup **— that is, the letter d, a colon (:), a backslash (\), and the program name** setup.

   If your CD-ROM player isn't at D:, type the letter appropriate for your drive. (If you're not sure what letter to type, see the "If you don't know the letter of your computer's CD-ROM drive" paragraph that appears at the end of this exercise.)

5. **Press Enter or click OK.**

   The Run dialog box closes, and the CD's Installer program launches.

   If this is the first time you're running the Installer, an IDG Books Worldwide, Inc., license agreement is displayed. This is the only time you'll see this document.

6. **Read (or at least skim) the license agreement to make sure that you're comfortable with its terms. When you're ready, click the Accept button.**

   If you don't click Accept, you can't use the Installer program. After you click, a message box appears. The message box just lets you know that it might take a moment for the Installer to appear.

7. **Click OK.**

   After you click, an opening screen appears.

8. **Click choose Software, and a menu with software categories appears.**

   The menu displays four software categories: Getting Connected (for programs that connect you to the Net or improve your connection); Cruising the Web (for programs that let you interact with the Web); Sending Messages (for programs that help you interact with others on the Net); and Working Offline (for programs you can use with files you've downloaded from the Net). This is the Installer's *main menu,* which is so named because all your other selections stem from this initial menu.

9. **Click a category you're interested in.**

   A submenu displays the particular programs grouped under the category you selected.

10 Click a program you're interested in.

A description of the program appears. Read the description carefully, because it may include steps you need to follow to install and run the program properly.

11 Click the Continue button near the bottom of the screen if you want the program to be installed on your hard disk.

Alternatively, click the Cancel button in the lower-right corner to return to the previous screen, and then skip to Step 12.

After you click the Continue button, installation for the program you selected begins.

12 Follow the prompts that appear on your screen to complete the installation of the program.

When the installation is finished, you return to the submenu of programs in the last category you selected.

13 Return to Step 9 to explore another program on the submenu, or click the Go Back button repeatedly to return to previous menus (until you reach the main menu, which is as far back as you can go).

Continue clicking program names until you're done exploring and installing all the programs in which you're currently interested.

14 When you're finished installing all the programs you currently want, click the Exit button in the lower-right corner of the Installer window and then click the Yes button to confirm you're done.

The Installer program closes. You can now start using the new software you've installed on your hard disk!

If you don't know the letter of your computer's CD-ROM drive: Most PCs assign the letter D to a CD-ROM drive. To find out which letter your CD-ROM drive uses, double-click the My Computer icon on your Windows 98 desktop. A window appears that lists all your drives, including your CD-ROM drive (which is usually represented by a shiny disc icon), and shows you the letter of each drive. When you're done examining the My Computer display, exit by clicking the window's Close button in its upper-right corner.

To examine the *Dummies 101* CD's contents: You can use the *Dummies 101* Installer program to install all the software on your CD. However, if you're simply curious about the CD, you can examine its contents after you exit the Installer by opening a Windows Explorer window and double-clicking the CD's icon.

If you have problems with the installation process, you can call the IDG Books Worldwide, Inc., Customer Support number: 800-762-2974 (outside the U.S.: 317-596-5430).

Discover Dummies Online!

The Dummies Web Site is your fun and friendly online resource for the latest information about *...For Dummies®* books and your favorite topics. The Web site is the place to communicate with us, exchange ideas with other *...For Dummies* readers, chat with authors, and have fun!

Ten Fun and Useful Things You Can Do at www.dummies.com

1. Win free *...For Dummies* books and more!
2. Register your book and be entered in a prize drawing.
3. Meet your favorite authors through the IDG Books Author Chat Series.
4. Exchange helpful information with other *...For Dummies* readers.
5. Discover other great *...For Dummies* books you must have!
6. Purchase Dummieswear™ exclusively from our Web site.
7. Buy *...For Dummies* books online.
8. Talk to us. Make comments, ask questions, get answers!
9. Download free software.
10. Find additional useful resources from authors.

Link directly to these ten fun and useful things at **http://www.dummies.com/10useful**

For other technology titles from IDG Books Worldwide, go to **www.idgbooks.com**

Not on the Web yet? It's easy to get started with *Dummies 101®: The Internet For Windows® 95* or *The Internet For Dummies®*, 5th Edition, at local retailers everywhere.

Find other *...For Dummies* books on these topics:
Business • Career • Databases • Food & Beverage • Games • Gardening • Graphics
Hardware • Health & Fitness • Internet and the World Wide Web • Networking • Office Suites
Operating Systems • Personal Finance • Pets • Programming • Recreation • Sports
Spreadsheets • Teacher Resources • Test Prep • Word Processing

IDG BOOKS WORLDWIDE BOOK REGISTRATION

Register This Book and Win!

We want to hear from you!

Visit **http://my2cents.dummies.com** to register this book and tell us how you liked it!

- Get entered in our monthly prize giveaway.
- Give us feedback about this book — tell us what you like best, what you like least, or maybe what you'd like to ask the author and us to change!
- Let us know any other *...For Dummies*® topics that interest you.

Your feedback helps us determine what books to publish, tells us what coverage to add as we revise our books, and lets us know whether we're meeting your needs as a *...For Dummies* reader. You're our most valuable resource, and what you have to say is important to us!

Not on the Web yet? It's easy to get started with *Dummies 101*®*: The Internet For Windows*® *95* or *The Internet For Dummies*®, 5th Edition, at local retailers everywhere.

Or let us know what you think by sending us a letter at the following address:

...For Dummies Book Registration
Dummies Press
7260 Shadeland Station, Suite 100
Indianapolis, IN 46256-3945
Fax 317-596-5498